FEMINISM AND POLITICAL ECONOMY

FEMINISM AND POLITICAL ECONOMY
Women's Work, Women's Struggles

Edited by
HEATHER JON MARONEY
and
MEG LUXTON

METHUEN

Toronto New York London Sydney Auckland

Canadian Cataloguing in Publication Data
Main entry under title:

Feminism and political economy : women's work, women's struggles

Bibliography: p.
Includes index.
ISBN 0-458-80610-2

1. Feminism. 2. Women — Social conditions.
3. Women — Employment. 4. Women's rights.
I. Maroney, Heather Jon. II. Luxton, Meg.

HQ1154.F45 1987 305.4'2 C86-094213-9

Grateful acknowledgment is made to the *New Left Review* for permission to reprint "Feminism at Work" by Heather Jon Maroney.

Cover photograph (International Women's Day March in Toronto, March 1984): Canapress Photo Service

Cover design: Word & Image Design Studio/Sandi Meland

Printed and bound in Canada
1 2 3 4 87 91 90 89 88

To our sisters

Contents

Acknowledgments

Many books begin as conference presentations; this one began as a critique of two conferences. Most papers at the "Left in the 1980s" conference in Vancouver 1980 failed to mention gender relations or women. When one of us protested this all too familiar absence, a (male) member of the Studies in Political Economy in Canada committee offered to support a book on feminist political economy. A year later only three men and over one hundred women attended a special session on feminism and politics at the 1981 Learned Societies meetings in Halifax. The gender balance was almost inverse at a conflicting Political Economy Network session. The choices that men made confirmed the conviction of many feminists that there is no point in even trying to talk to "the boys" as they just won't listen and that one more failure of political economy to address "women's issues" confirmed its incapacity ever to do so. When some of us protested that the division between political economy and feminism was conjunctural and not fundamental, we were told to "put your pen where your mouth is."

Reflecting these origins, one aim of this book is to speak simultaneously to two audiences. To feminists we argue that a political economy framework, particularly marxism, offers an important way to understand the situation of women. To those working within political economy we insist that without an analysis of sex/gender systems their analysis is flawed and incomplete.

Another aim is to present to a general audience the results of new feminist research on women's work and women's struggles. As we reviewed the literature, we were struck by how little work on women was actually available. For the most part, research on the political economy of women was begun in the 1970s, often for graduate degrees. Because there was neither an established body of empirical work nor clearly delineated conceptual frameworks, each person had in a sense to start anew. The combination of sexist hiring practices and the underfunding of universities and research has meant that most of these researchers were at best tenuously employed in academia. And so the articles in this book were produced during time snatched away from a triple day of paid work, domestic labour, and feminist politics. For most there was never a time for uninterrupted concentration; there were none of the resources which make intellectual work so much easier—the security of tenure, secretarial help, free xeroxing, research assistants, access to a computer.

Over the years many people have helped us with this book. We want to thank Studies in Political Economy of Canada for seed money and its representatives, Mel Watkins, Wally Clement, and Daniel Drache, for their support. In particular we thank Daniel Drache for encouraging us to believe that the project was possible and for his careful reading of the final manuscript. The following people shared their expertise and support: Pradeep Bandyopadhyay, Naomi Black, Paul Campbell, Jan Campbell-Luxton, Michelle Campbell-Luxton, Bruce Curtis, Barbara Everison, Bonnie Fox, Roberta Hamilton, Debra Harrison, Linda Kealey, Bruce Kidd, David Livingstone, Maxine Molyneux, Margaret Pearce, Ester Reiter, Wally Seccombe, Madge Tennant, Mariana Valverde, Andrew Wernick.

Notes on Contributors

Karen Anderson teaches sociology at King's College, University of Western Ontario. She has published a number of articles on gender relations among the seventeenth-century Hurons.

Hugh Armstrong received his Ph.D. in sociology from the Université de Montréal and teaches at Vanier College. A manuscript editor for *Studies in Political Economy*, he has, with Pat Armstrong, co-authored *The Double Ghetto, A Working Majority*, and several articles. They have two daughters.

Pat Armstrong has been teaching sociology and women's studies at Vanier College in Montreal but will, in 1987, join the faculty at York University in Toronto. A co-author, with Hugh Armstrong, of *The Double Ghetto* and *A Working Majority*, she has also written *Labour Pains: Women's Work in Crisis* as well as numerous articles on unemployment and on Canadian families.

Carolyn Egan is a socialist feminist who has been active in the Toronto women's movement for many years. A co-founder and member of the community board of the Immigrant Women's Centre, she is also involved in the International Women's Day Committee, the labour committee of Women Working with Immigrant Women, and the Ontario Coalition for Abortion Clinics.

Sue Findlay has been a part of the struggle for women's liberation in Canada since the early 1960s. Active in women's groups in Ottawa and more recently in Toronto, she also worked in the federal state bureaucracy between 1972 and 1980 as Director of the Women's Program, Department of the Secretary of State, and as Ottawa vice-president of the Canadian Advisory Council on the Status of Women. She is currently working on her Ph.D. thesis on women and the state.

Charlene Gannagé has been active in the Toronto women's movement since the 1970s. The author of *Double Day, Double Burden: Women in the Garment Industry*, she currently holds a postdoctoral fellowship at York University, teaches sociology at the University of Toronto, and coordinates a union research project on technological change.

Shelley Gavigan is a former Saskatchewan legal aid lawyer and was active in the women's movement in Saskatchewan throughout the 1970s. She has written on reproductive issues, sociology of law, and feminist critiques of law and holds graduate degrees in law and criminology. She is currently Assistant Professor, Osgoode Hall Law School.

Alena Heitlinger chairs the sociology department of Trent University. Born in Czechoslovakia, she has published several articles on the position of women in Eastern Europe as well as *Women and State Socialism* and *Reproduction, Medicine and the Socialist State*. She has two children.

Diane Lamoureux teaches political science at Université Laval. Involved in the feminist movement in Montréal since the late 1970s, she is currently a member of the editorial board of *RFR/DRF* in Toronto and *Les Cahiers du GRIF* in Paris. She has published a book on feminism in Québec, *Fragments et collages*.

Meg Luxton teaches social science and women's studies at York University. The author of *More Than a Labour of Love: Three Generations of Women's Work in the Home*, she is currently researching the division of labour in family households and in the paid labour force.

Patricia Marchak is Professor of sociology at the University of British Columbia, author of *Ideological Perspectives on Canada*, *In Whose Interests*, and *Green Gold: The Forest Industry in British Columbia*, and editor of *The Working Sexes: Symposium Papers on the Effects of Sex on Women at Work*. She is a past president of the Canadian Sociology and Anthropology Association and serves on the editorial boards of *Studies in Political Economy* and *Current Sociology*.

Heather Jon Maroney has taught women's studies and sociology at Trent University. A longtime activist in the women's movement, she has just finished a study of contemporary women's movements in Quebec.

Harriet Rosenberg teaches social science at York University. Her research on cross-cultural patterns of social reproduction and caregiving has been carried out in North America, France, and Africa.

Susan Russell has done postgraduate work on women and education. A member of the Sociology Department of Concordia University in Montreal for the past eight years, her main teaching area has been a course for graduate and undergraduate students on sex roles.

Lorna Weir has been active in feminist, gay, and Third World support politics. She currently works with the Canadian Women's Movement Archives and holds a postdoctoral research fellowship from the Social Sciences and Humanities Research Council of Canada at Oxford University and the Ontario Institute for Studies in Education for research on population regulation and state formation in late seventeenth-century England.

FEMINISM AND POLITICAL ECONOMY

Editors' Introduction

Feminism is an emancipatory project. It aims to examine women's oppression, expose the dynamics of male domination and female subordination, and, guided by that analysis, fight for women's liberation. Stated in this form the project is political and ideological, but it also has important theoretical implications for work in the human sciences. First, it has constituted a new object for investigation: "the sex/gender system" (Rubin 1975). Second, the sex/gender system itself has only become visible from the distinct standpoint of women (Smith 1974, 1979; Hartsock 1983). Reflections on this new standpoint have in turn provoked debate about the status of all knowledge in the human sciences, thus raising more general epistemological questions (see especially Harding and Hintikka 1983; Fee 1981; Daly 1978). The effort to develop feminist theory is, as a result, extraordinarily complex, requiring both a reinterpretation of human history and a rethinking of existing theoretical and political traditions.

For the most part, feminists have argued that no single dimension, whether biological, sexual, economic, psychological, political, or historicist, is adequate to explain the origins and persistence of gender hierarchies. Rather they have sought to understand women's situation as a multidimensional complex of material and ideological forces, fundamentally structured by power relations. This perspective has inspired much research and theorizing, animating work in new fields such as cultural studies (Garner, Kahane, and Sprengnether 1985) as well as reappropriating older traditions, so that we can now speak of a body of feminist theory (Jaggar 1983; Burton 1985; Donovan 1985; Jameson 1983).

The new body of theory is, however, far from coherent or evenly developed. Attempts to reconstruct an integrated feminist theory have had to rely on work already shaped by the objects of study, methods, and theories of existing disciplines. Even where commitments to multidimensional analysis mean that some disciplines are in principle open to one another, it is often difficult to integrate the insights of work developed from such specialized perspectives as psychoanalysis, semiotics, or marxism. In the simplest cases, such failures can be ascribed to the partial results of specialized work. There is simply not enough work to make integration possible. More serious problems arise, however, from the tendency of such perspectives to see their theoretical approaches as already globally complete rather than to adopt an authentically multidimensional or interdisciplinary framework.

Feminist theory has worked toward four aims: first, recovery—discovering the women "hidden from history" (Rowbotham 1973); second, a deconstruction of existing non-feminist theories to reveal their androcentric assumptions (Millman and Kanter 1975; Kelly-Gagol 1977; Weisstein 1971; Clark and Lange 1979; Tanner and Zihlman 1981; Vickers 1984); third, the reconstruction of theory based on revalorizing the feminine and what women do (Reiter 1975; Gilligan 1982; Amsden 1980); and fourth, metatheoretical critique—a feminist reflection on theory construction (O'Brien 1981; Harding and Hintikka 1983). In so far as dominant disciplinary tendencies, in history for example, have remained resolutely atheoretical, they have fostered simple recovery. Other disciplines, like sociology, that pretend to greater theoretical sophistication encouraged an early focus on deconstruction, attacking, for example, the sexist bias in structural-functionalism. As might be expected, philosophers have contributed to raising metatheoretical consciousness. Thus the refraction of feminist theory in different academic disciplines has complicated the logic of its development.

Because feminism is both an intellectual project and a political movement, theoretical and methodological debates are also political and strategic, and differences at the level of the former both reflect and inform divisions in political practice. The various political tendencies of the contemporary women's movement have generated their own approaches to feminist theory. For example, liberal pluralism adds women on (Jaggar 1983: 173–206); radical feminism seeks to establish a new synthetic theory (Firestone 1970; Bunch 1981; MacKinnon 1982, 1983a; Delphy 1984) and socialist feminism is engaged in understanding the relationship between sex/gender and class (Eisenstein 1979; Smith 1977; Barrett 1980; Sargent 1981; Cockburn 1983; Vogel 1983). Each is pulled in opposing directions.

Feminists have been drawn together by their intellectual commitment to criticize "malestream thought" (O'Brien 1981: 6) and to oppose the oppression of women. Their solidarity is strengthened by the excitement of developing shared knowledge for women or working together to establish women's studies programs or fight for equal pay. On the other hand, in so far as they are convinced that the flaws of a particular global paradigm like liberalism, marxism, or psychoanalysis can be corrected by the integration of women and gender relations, they are drawn to that parent paradigm. Much debate concerns the parent paradigm's capacity to integrate or expand feminist theory.

While studying "women" has permitted this flowering of feminist scholarship, the category is not natural, but ideologically constructed. This global concept—"women"—and a politics of sisterhood can obscure very important differences among women, especially those of class, race, political geography, ethnicity, age, and sexual orientation. Analyses of sex/gender systems and sexism have all too often assumed that the experiences and perspectives of white, heterosexual, Western European and North American middle-class women can be generalized for all women. The validation of difference is essential to feminism's central intellectual and political task. Feminists and the women's movement cannot speak for all women. Instead, our task is to empower all women so that they can speak for themselves. The recognition of difference is also vital to the effort to build general theories which genuinely account for women's oppression.

Feminist theory cannot escape problems of differences arising when the abstract and general are made concrete and particular. General theory must be modified if it is to grasp specific determinations in actual societies. What holds for Britain may not hold for Canada, and what applies in Nova Scotia may not explain Quebec. Such cultural, national, and historical differences are not merely obstacles to theoretical cohesion but reflections of the rich variation of social life. Although in a real sense international, feminist theory is also influenced by national intellectual traditions and social contexts. This theoretical fragmentation cannot be overcome by sweeping generalizations which gloss over real differences, or amiable but sloppy eclecticism which attempts to patch together traditions based on divergent paradigms.

Still, if we are to move beyond the current theoretical fragmentation, a start must be made somewhere. With that caution, this collection offers the view that despite its well-known limitations—for example, the persistent failure to theorize sexuality — the adoption of a political economy perspective provides, among the various present options, a promising point of departure for the development of a truly synthetic feminist theory.

1 From Feminism and Political Economy to Feminist Political Economy

HEATHER JON MARONEY and MEG LUXTON

Tasks for a Political Economy of Women in Canada

Feminists attempting to develop a political economy of women in Canada face a complicated set of tasks. First, at the level of theory, they confront several distinct prefeminist political economy traditions: liberal political economy, marxism, and an amalgam of these which has come to be known as the Canadian political economy tradition (see Drache and Clement 1985). Feminist theory itself is not homogeneous but is divided both by liberal, radical, and socialist orientations and by the diverse intellectual traditions of the social sciences and humanities (Jaggar and Rothenberg 1984). Indeed, proponents of the three main politico-theoretical feminist variants have appropriated political economy categories and approaches in different ways. Liberal feminism draws on liberal political economy, while both radical and socialist feminists find their sources in marxism (Jaggar 1983). As a result, the traditional political economy approaches have been revised differently by diverse feminist tendencies.

Second, while political economy has had a powerful influence on the overall development of feminist theory, the political economy revival (*Studies in Political Economy* 1981(6): 3) has itself been slow to respond to the challenge of feminism. Too often, theories of class and the state, of race and nationalism, and of the relationship between the household and the labour force have not been revised; women have simply been added on. Feminist theory offers political economy not merely a way to correct the lacunae which result from its sex-blindness and androcentrism, but the possibility of realizing its promise and claim to be a holistic theory (*Studies in Political Economy* 1979(1): v–vi). We take for granted the importance of feminism, but here we want to argue (more contentiously) for the importance of political economy to feminism and for the potential congruence of these two perspectives. Like feminism, both liberal and marxist political economy have assumed as their task

> a study of society as an integrated whole, based on contributions from social scientists from all disciplines . . . [which can] identify and analyse social relations as they relate to the economic system of production. (Drache 1978: 4–5)

Thus political economy can be contrasted with neoclassical and institutional economics which envision a neutral market driven by blind economic forces, where an economically rational "man" pursues "tastes" and "preferences" which are derived exogenously from a separately determined culture or psychology. It is also distinguished from liberal political theory, which assumes the exercise by individuals of citizenship rights independent of economic power.

Political economy, like feminism, sees social relations as conditioned by economic structures and processes. It also understands economic arrangements in turn as determined by power relations that are maintained and reproduced through mechanisms of ideological control. There is then a certain preliminary congruence between feminist theory and political economy (whether liberal or marxist). Both try to understand society in a multidimensional and holistic way. Both understand power as a fundamental category. In principle the two could be synthesized to the advantage of both.

What political economy offers feminism is powerful conceptual categories, a (usually sex-blind) macrostructural theory of economic, political, and social structures and a body of historical research. Malestream political economy has analyzed how the form and level of economic development, including technology, shape the organization of work, class structure, and the state. These relations provide an indispensable context (necessary but insufficient) for feminists trying to understand, for example, how gender inequalities operate in the labour force; how the state structures and maintains gender hierarchies and how those hierarchies relate to other structures of domination and exploitation such as race, class, and imperialism.

Because malestream political economy is seriously flawed by a sexism that ignores the sex/gender dimension and marginalizes women, it has been unable to live up to its claim to "study . . . society as an integrated whole." Feminism challenges political economists to take gender and sexual dimensions seriously so as to correct and expand their analysis of society as a whole. This is not to claim that even a feminist political economy approach can analyze all social phenomena. Some dimensions of interpersonal interaction, representation, ideology, psychic structures, and sexuality are beyond the limits of competent political economy. Rather it is to insist that the research agendas of such discourses as psychoanalysis or cultural theory must take account of the impinging dimensions of reality that political economy reveals. It may be, for example, that the psychic hooks of gender identity differ for women of different classes or races

(Lorber 1981). It is, at the same time, to warn political economy to avoid any tendencies to intellectual imperialism and to caution it to engage seriously with the dimensions of social life captured by other forms of theory.

Finally, a feminist political economy must develop a reflexive understanding of how specific enduring features of the socio-political environment shape its own theoretical development. In Canada, for example, these include a history of dependence on first Britain and later the United States, the subordination of indigenous native societies, and the unresolved political and national status of Quebec. As a result, from 1960 to 1980, during the period when feminist theory and politics were being developed, other social movements supporting Canada's independence from the United States and the national liberation of Quebec gave priority to nationalist issues (Monière 1977; Coleman 1984). As a consequence, theories influenced by feminism and nationalism took divergent paths in English Canada, though they shared common ground at least initially in Quebec. As a result, feminists working in Quebec and in English Canada have been isolated from one another. Nationalism — both Canadian and Québécois — and feminism have served to compartmentalize intellectual developments already suffering from major political-intellectual and disciplinary divisions.

In Quebec, a rising wave of nationalism influenced the development of a women's liberation movement by restricting and isolating the organizing cadre (O'Leary and Toupin 1981; Brodeur et al. 1981; Maroney 1978). In the late 1960s, women activists often held a stage theory in which women's liberation was to follow that of the nation or at least occur at the same time as national liberation. Their political economic theory, exemplified in the approach of the journal *Québécoises deboutte!* was an anticolonialist version of marxism (Lamoureux this volume; Lanctôt 1980). While some francophone feminists read American radical feminist writers, such as Kate Millett (1969), Ti-Grace Atkinson (1974), and Shulamith Firestone (1970), or were influenced by the "Wages for Housework" position represented by Selma James (Dalla Costa and James 1972; *Québécoises deboutte!*), most work in English was inaccessible. Later, as feminist theory developed in France, Quebec feminists increasingly turned to it (O'Leary and Toupin 1981). A division between anglophone and francophone feminists, initially one of language, was reinforced by bitter political disputes over the national question within the first (bilingual) women's liberation group in Montreal (Maroney 1978; Lanctôt 1980). Thus, a nationalist focus in Quebec and English Canadian national chauvinism or linguistic incompetence in French combined to prevent dialogue and ensure autonomous developments in both feminist communities. As a result, English Canadian feminists have not taken into account provocative work from Quebec. For example, English Canadian feminists have not responded to important contributions on the state by Nicole Laurin-Frenette (1979, 1982) or Nadia Fahmy-Eid (Fahmy-Eid and Laurin-Frenette 1980); Yolande Cohen (1981, 1982) is a partial exception.

In English Canada, the embryonic women's liberation movement of the mid-1960s was simultaneously more open to marxism than the American movement and less bound by the conventions of traditional marxism than the British. In Canada, unlike the United States, social democratic political traditions have maintained an openness to socialist politics and theory that partially blunted the force of Cold War ideology. As a result, socialist theory and practice have survived in the Canadian intellectual and political marketplace. On the other hand, because Canadian socialism was largely based in broad popular movements rather than in organized labour movements as in Britain (Lipset 1971; Penner 1977), it has been relatively more receptive to feminist challenges. As a consequence, a distinct socialist-feminist current, sympathetic to if critical of marxism, developed early in the Canadian women's movement and shaped its attitude to political economy (Maroney this volume; Discussion Collective No. 6 1972; FitzGerald, Guberman, and Wolfe 1982; Barrett and Hamilton 1987).

Feminism and "The Canadian Political Economy Tradition"

While it might be expected that the Canadian political economy tradition could assist in analyzing the situation of women in Canada, neither its theoretical apparati nor its substantive historical work has been used as a basis for a distinctly Canadian political economy of women. For francophone feminists, the Canadian political economy tradition is insignificant because its proponents have tended to conceive of Quebec as a province, not a nation. Instead, as Diane Lamoureux, Veronique O'Leary, and others have pointed out, efforts to develop feminist political economy theory have drawn on analyses of underdevelopment and anti-colonialism. While feminists in English Canada have drawn on the same paradigms that inform the Canadian political economy tradition, they have not engaged with that literature directly.

Canadian political economy in both its liberal and marxist traditions focuses on the development of the Canadian social formation as a particular example of what one school terms "industrial society," the other "the capitalist mode of production." Political economy has largely concentrated on:

1. the specific character of economic development in Canada, especially the significance of extractive industries and dependency (Innis 1936, 1954, 1956, 1970; Lower 1938; Mackintosh 1938; Watkins 1977b)
2. the process of state formation and the nature of the Canadian state (Ryerson 1968; Panitch 1977; Mahon 1979)

3. the national question and issues of regionalism (Bourque and Laurin-Frenette 1972; Watkins 1977a; Berger 1977; Brym and Sacouman 1979; Bourque and Légaré 1979; Légaré 1982; Matthews 1983)
4. the composition of the ruling class and the formation and maintenance of elites (Porter 1965; W. Clement 1975, 1983; Fournier 1976; Niosi 1981; Brym 1985)
5. the formation, composition and character of the working class (Horowitz 1968; Tremblay 1970; Cuneo 1979; Pentland and Phillips 1981)
6. the media and cultural production in Canada (Innis 1964, 1980; Salter et al. 1981; Smythe 1981; Leiss, Kline, and Jhally 1986)

The feminist critique of sexism is entirely appropriate to Canadian political economy, both in its classical developmental phase, represented by Lower, Innis, and Mackintosh, and in its more recent revival, represented by the journal *Studies in Political Economy* among others. Both Innis, the patriarch, and Porter, the elder statesman, produced extensive analyses of economic and social organization predicated on unrecognized assumptions of gender. As for the rising sons (and occasionally daughters) of the political economy revival, while they have realized that "women" exist as a social category and political force, and supported in principle work on "women," they have not yet, for the most part, incorporated this understanding into their work. While they increasingly include a discussion of women, they have yet to move beyond the stage of "adding women on" to make a genuine attempt to theorize gender. Subjecting existing Canadian political economy theories to a detailed feminist critique will occur as feminists further their study of the specificity of women in Canada and Quebec and begin to theorize gender relations as part of the developing Canadian social formation. Here we want to suggest briefly how some formative works in Canadian political economy might differ if gender were incorporated.

Gender in the Canadian Political Economy Tradition

Innis's work on the fur trade focuses on technology and commerce, thereby obscuring the relations of production so that technology rather than social relations appears to facilitate the development of trade. The human actors, both whites and Indians, appear as necessary but secondary adjuncts to the furs. Human beings as investors, traders, or hunters disappear from the scene.

When Innis occasionally recognizes human labour, his androcentric orientation is revealed. In *The Fur Trade* ([1930] 1970), he notes that in the early development of the fur trade, European entrepreneurs sent young French men into the bush to learn Indian ways and to encourage increased fur gathering by the Indians. Recent feminist studies have shown that because of gender divisions of labour and sexual ties which cross-cut both Indian and white societies, the work of native women was vital to this enterprise (Van Kirk 1980; Brown 1980; Anderson this volume). White men depended on the knowledge, political skills, and labour of native women to gain access to the resources necessary for both survival in the bush and successful trading. Furthermore, sexual and co-habitation relations resulted in children with a dual cultural heritage who provided the most useful labour force in the fur trade for several generations (Jennifer Brown 1982). Innis may have paid scant attention to men as labourers, but he noticed women not at all. For Innis ([1930] 1970:4), the demographic patterns, reproductive practices, and (reputed) monogamous marital habits of the beaver warranted more attention than any discussion of the same among humans.

In later studies of the mining and timber industries, Innis (1936) considered labour questions somewhat more fully. He noted that the problems faced by timber and mining companies in constructing a stable northern labour force limited economic development. Even so, he failed to consider the role of women, gender divisions of labour and sexual reproduction in creating the conditions necessary for the expansion of production. For most companies, the solution lay in attracting "men with families," i.e., women (Luxton 1980:26–27). These women established and maintained a quality of domestic and community life which meant that male workers were likely to remain on the job. They also bred and socialized future generations of workers and they themselves became a source of cheap labour for service and distributive industries (Marchak this volume). Through his studies of these industries, Innis refined a theory of economic development as a result of staples extraction which has not only remained important but has also been incorporated by the nationalist revival of the Canadian political economy tradition. Both at its level of analysis—the exchange of staples rather than the social relations of labour — and in its androcentrism, its theory has been closed to women and gender.

John Porter approached the question of class through a sociological model of inequality. Because he dealt directly with social relations, the weaknesses of his model are more immediately obvious. In his major study, *The Vertical Mosaic* (1965), he neither described gender as a hierarchy nor theorized it as a structure of inequality related to other structures of inequality. Although he acknowledged that elite groups in Canada were almost entirely male and operated largely through a network of "old boys," he both underplayed the exclusion of women and failed to consider the implications of gender stratification in forming and maintaining class stratification. For elite theory, an awareness of gender divisions raises questions about the influence of shared or conflicting gender identities on and between elites. How does masculine or feminine identity affect capacities to work within these groups? Feminists working in a framework of class analysis have pointed to the mediation of gender by class structures (Barrett 1980). Some, following Heidi Hartmann (1979), have argued that patriarchal solidarity among men of different classes is responsible for the maintenance of women's oppression. Others have begun the task of rethinking class as a gendered structure (Cockburn 1983; Barrett and McIntosh 1982:47). Gender relations also serve to reproduce class in various ways. Marriage and fertility patterns affect the formation and dispersal of capital pools. Conversely, class ideologies and state practices help to determine fertility (Petchesky 1984). An engendered class analysis would also include an investigation of how women's volunteer activities are essential in reproducing class ideologies and practices (Kealey 1979; Noble 1979).

The new generation of thinkers associated with the Canadian political economy revival has followed all too closely in the footsteps of the founding fathers. While work in this area is diverse, the marxist current around the journal *Studies in Political Economy* is arguably its most important representative. Developing during the same period as feminist political economy, it remains, like political economy in general, largely untouched by it. In *Studies in Political Economy*'s first nine issues, only three articles dealt in any way with women, one of them only peripherally (Noble 1979; McFarland 1980; Vaillancourt 1982). Others reproduced serious errors due to masculinist biases. For example, Apple's (1980) discussion of "full employment" in the postwar decade strikingly ignores women's legally enforced structural unemployment. More seriously, the 1981 special issue "Rethinking Canadian Political Economy" rethought in the same old androcentric categories. Not one of the articles attempted to evaluate or integrate feminist critiques. Recently, some feminist theory and several articles on women have found their way into its pages (see no. 10, 1983). This work has not yet made an impact on Canadian political economy in general. But feminists have posed a challenge: political economy must realize that "gender" is not just a fancy word for "women" but a fundamental social structure. It is not surprising that feminists have largely ignored the Canadian political economy tradition on its own demerits, with feminist political economy in Canada developing quite separately, drawing its inspiration from general theoretical traditions of political economy and feminism developed largely in Britain and the United States.

The Feminist Encounter with Political Economy

A liberal political economy perspective, traceable to the work of John Stuart Mill, underlies much feminist work where no theoretical alternative is specified. From Mill's ([1869] 1970) "On the Subjection of Women," it draws an object for analysis, failure of equality of opportunity; an explanation, hidden barriers to attainment; and a strategy, legal and educational reform. Like political theory, a liberal feminist political economy framework does not analyze the nature of class society (although it may castigate the actual operation of the capitalist market for manipulation and sexism) nor does it, in the main, problematize "the family" as an institution.

Although divided on the issue of the universality of patriarchy (Rosaldo and Lamphere 1974; Brownmiller 1975) versus the historicity of matriarchy (Alpert 1975; Diner 1965; Love and Shanklin 1978; Bamberger 1974; Webster 1975), radical feminist theory has taken the structure and dynamic of male domination and female subordination as its object. Those studying this power relation from within the general parameters of political economy have claimed a thoroughly revised historical materialism, often drawing on Frederick Engels for their method (Parker and Leghorn 1981; Weinbaum 1978). An early exponent of radical feminism, Shulamith Firestone (1970), theorized a feminist political economy in which biological sex differences and oppression were the material base for all other forms of inequality. More recently, while some radical feminists have modified biological explanations to stress "male" power (Dworkin 1979; Barry 1979; Echols 1984), others explain women's subordination on the basis of their common activities as housewives in a patriarchal family (Delphy 1984). However, within the range of perspectives encompassed by political economy, the variant which has engaged feminist theory most profoundly has been western marxism.

Feminism and Marxism

Classical marxist theory was attractive to the women's liberation movement of the late 1960s because it explicitly acknowledged women's oppression, arguing for a radical social transformation to liberate women. As participants in civil rights and new left movements, women activists had already turned to marxist theory and socialist history for a critique of class society and guidelines for political practice (Mitchell 1971; Kostash 1980). The relevance of marxism to feminist theory has since been widely discussed and its central concepts and methods scrutinized. Feminists have criticized it for largely ignoring women, for a sex-blindness which disguises sexism, and for failing to theorize gender (Coward 1983; Baxandall et al. 1976; Sargent 1981). As a result of this encounter, the relationship between marxism and feminism has been subject to a rigorous and extensive examination. At issue is the relative weight of class structures and sex/gender systems as fundamental determinants of different modes of production and social formations (Hamilton 1978; Flax 1981; Phelps 1981; Vogel 1983).

Despite its cogency, the feminist critique often fails to appreciate the influence of marxist theory, particularly as articulated by Engels, on the developing feminist problematics. In *The Origin of the Family, Private Property and the State* ([1884] 1972), Engels offered the first systematic theory of the way sex and class structures combine in the economy and the state to determine women's oppression. What has engaged the contemporary feminist theoretical imagination is his provocative, if undeveloped, perception that social life is dually determined by the production of the means of subsistence and the propagation of the species:

> According to the materialist conception, the determining factor in history is, in the final instance, the production and reproduction of immediate life. This, again, is of a two-fold character: on the one side, *the production of the means of existence*, of food, clothing and shelter and the tools necessary for that production; on the other side, *the production of human beings themselves*, the propagation of the species.
> ([1884] 1972: 71; emphasis added)

This emphasis on the two-sided character of social life was picked up by feminists confronting a situation where women with children were entering the paid labour force in unprecedented numbers and where new contraceptive technologies were significantly altering biological reproduction. There are, however, empirical and theoretical problems in Engels's formulation which have been incorporated and even amplified in contemporary feminist theory.

In *The Origin* sexism and economism combined to distort Engels's understanding of the relationship between his two central concepts — "the production of the means of life" and "the production of life itself." First, Engels fragmented his concept of the two-fold character of "the production of immediate life," mapping gender divisions onto it. Naturalizing and projecting the prevailing ideal of the sexual division of labour in nineteenth-century capitalist societies onto all of human history, he erroneously assumed that women were responsible for "looking after the house and the preparation of the food, and clothing" ([1884] 1972: 218) while men were responsible for procuring "the necessities of life" ([1884] 1972: 220); that is, he projected a male provider/female housewife model on all societies. As a result, he conceptualized a division of labour in which the production of the means of subsistence — a process he termed "labour" — was associated with men and the economy, while the production of life itself — or as he put it "family" — was left in a non-economic sphere populated by women. Indeed, Engels's concept of "the production of life itself" fits into a vague residual category, "the natural economy," which Marx used to designate all non-commodity subsistence modes of production. The natural economy is itself a naturalist concept for Marx and Engels, who theorized that through history the production of the means of life developed from the natural to the social while the production of life itself remained natural.

Second, his understanding of social complexity was undermined by a narrow economism regarding family and sexuality. Despite his assertion that:

> The social organization under which the people of a particular historical epoch and a particular country live is determined by both kinds of production: by the stage of development of labour on the one hand and of the family on the other ([1884] 1972: 71–72)

his historical reconstruction incorrectly assumed that changes in family form, sexual practices and norms, and women's status resulted only from changes in the organization of "labour." Changes in "family" could not occur independently; nor could they affect economic organization. Thus, the effect of sexuality, historically specific forms of biological reproduction, and familial activities was reduced if not nullified.

The conceptual error had strategic consequences. He argued that with changes in "labour" came changes in both property forms — the development of private property — and social and political organization — the emergence of classes and state structures. Because he assumed that men "naturally" controlled economic production, he took for granted their ownership and control of the wealth generated by new property forms and their possession of social and political power. The development of class society thus resulted in women's oppression—"the world historic defeat of the female sex" ([1884] 1972: 120). From this analysis, Engels concluded that women's liberation would automatically occur through the elimination of classes, the reduction of women's domestic labour through its socialization, and the integration of women into "labour" ([1884] 1972: 138, 221).

While feminist critics have corrected for sexism, economism, and strategic inadequacies in appropriating the central Engelsian insight, they have not come to grips with a more general problem of theoretical incoherence in Engels. The various sets of concepts, that is, "the production of the means of life" and "the production of life itself," "labour" and "family," and class oppression and the man's domination of the woman are not symmetrical. Furthermore they are not adequately related in a systematic theoretical statement by Engels. We have argued above that instead he incorrectly mapped these three sets of concepts onto one another to equate labour with men and family with women. Particularly in the early stages of the encounter between contemporary feminist theory and marxist political economy, these errors were accepted and unwittingly amplified. In seeking to clarify such concepts, feminists adopted the current marxist convention by which the production of the means of life was simply shortened to "production." The production of life itself, termed "reproduction," was taken to be a parallel concept. This terminological correction only hardened and mystified Engels's dichotomy. Despite a recognition of the importance of female labour market participation, feminist theory often equated production, the economy, and, implicitly, men, on the one hand, and reproduction, family, and women on the other. This led to two theoretical errors. First such formulations made it difficult to grasp the family itself as a set of economic relations; second it embedded a theoretical dualism not easily resolved. It was the fact that Engels's terms were somewhat ambiguous or ill-defined that permitted a more flexible interrelation of the key terms corresponding to his recognition of the unitary character of "the production and reproduction of immediate life."

Prior to the 1960s, Engels's theory of women's oppression and emancipation dominated the program of socialist movements on the "Woman Question" (Bebel [1883] 1971; Zetkin 1984; Thönnessen 1973; Heitlinger 1979). No alternative global theories were developed. Indeed, the only contending theories were conservative and defended women's subordination. For the most part, feminist scholarship linked to the late nineteenth- and early twentieth-century women's movement was limited to recovering women's economic history and analyzing their actual economic participation (Clark [1919] 1982; Pinchbeck [1930] 1981). A partial exception was the work of Charlotte Perkins Gilman ([1898] 1966) which identified women's economic dependence on men as the main barrier to their success. Declaring that most homes were inefficient, unsanitary, and the site of unremitting toil for women, she advocated removing all housework from the home, to provide paid employment for women under more rational conditions (Gilman [1903] 1972). Another, more significant, exception was Simone de Beauvoir's ([1949] 1968) impressive and pathbreaking *The Second Sex*. Adopting uncritically Engels's dualism, she was the first to use production and reproduction as parallel terms. While she asserted that biology is historically determined and identified "one of the most basic problems of women" as "the reconciliation of her reproductive role and her part in productive labour" ([1949] 1968: 108), her existentialist phenomenology ultimately relegated "woman" (as "Other") to a male-defined realm of nature, and she was unable to demonstrate how women's two roles were linked politically and economically. She later criticized this approach herself:

> I should provide a more materialistic, not an idealistic, theoretical foundation for the opposition between the Same and the Other. I should base the rejection and oppression of the Other not on antagonistic awareness but upon the economic explanation of scarcity . . . this would not modify the argument . . . that all male ideologies are directed at justifying the oppression of women, and that women are so conditioned by society that they consent to this oppression. (de Beauvoir 1977: 483–84)

The contemporary breakthrough in feminist theory originated with the 1960s revival, first of liberal feminist interest groups and later of radical political and cultural movements for women's liberation. In *The*

Feminine Mystique Betty Friedan (1963) argued that American women suffered from a lack of identity due to their attempts to find fulfillment as full-time housewives. She castigated both the failure of mass co-education to provide equality of opportunity and the manipulation of women through commercial advertising. In her analysis, the chains which hold women down are ideas, and the economy is merely contingent. Her framework—which acknowledged Mill's liberalism and mirrored de Beauvoir's approach—did not advance beyond description.

Juliet Mitchell's innovative synthesis of classicial marxism, de Beauvoir's feminism, and existentialist psychoanalysis made the first major advance. In "Women: The Longest Revolution," a 1966 paper which she later reworked as the core of *Woman's Estate* (1971), Mitchell reviewed socialist theory on women, criticizing marxists for their economism and de Beauvoir for her ahistorical idealism. If marxism has left the liberation of women as a "normative ideal . . . not structurally integrated into [socialist theory]," then for de Beauvoir socialism "emerges as a curiously contingent solution . . . in a muffled epilogue" (1984: 25). Mitchell's attempt to transcend such limitations led her to complicate the analytic paradigm: women's condition was a complex unity of four (not two) interlocking structures—production, reproduction, socialization, and sexuality. Exploitation and subservience in production made women dependent on men. This oppression was compensated for by women's apparent dominance in the family, an institution which "partakes" of three of these structures—reproduction of children, sexuality, and socialization (1984: 30–43). She rejected essentialist and structural-functionalist views, arguing that the social organization of the family is historical and must be transformed for women's liberation.

For political economy, however, she left several problems unsolved. First, the structures were imperfectly differentiated (socialization from reproduction of children) and socially and conceptually different. Second, she specified no material base or set of economic linkages between production and the family. Instead the family was connected with the material structures of production mainly by ideological means. Finally, given her tendency to collapse sexuality, socialization, and reproduction into "the family," and to analyze in terms of "the family" rather than the structures, the four structures she posited were reduced in practice to Engels's two. Indeed she further formalized that dualism in terms which are still central to feminist theory: mode of production and mode of reproduction (1984: 32). Mitchell's structural analysis also led her to pay scant attention to politics, particularly at the macro level of the state and of class and political organizations. While radical feminists, on the other hand, emphasized power in gender relations, they tended to do so in the intimate interactions of everyday life with no theory of the state. Socialist feminism has been slow to investigate both the state and the women's movements

(Laurin-Frenette 1979; Wilson 1977; Brossard 1981; Yanacopoulo 1981; Findlay this volume).

Although later scholarship has challenged and corrected her theoretical conceptualizations and specific propositions, the importance of Mitchell's work cannot be overestimated. She presented an overview of women's oppression so sweeping that almost all subsequent analytic developments have addressed problems she identified as key. Her work provided the basis for the development of a contemporary political economy of women and suggested the possibility of a future feminist political economy.

A Political Economy of Women in Canada

Mitchell's article, which was reprinted as a pamphlet by the Canadian Union of Students and circulated widely among activists in new left politics in Canada and Quebec, served to catalyze feminism in this current.[1] In 1967, four women presented a paper, "Sisters, brothers, lovers . . . listen . . . ," based on Mitchell's analysis, to a membership conference of the Student Union for Peace Action (SUPA), a leading new left organization in English Canada (Bernstein et al. 1972). This paper, which castigated sexism in capitalist societies in general and in the Canadian left in particular, called for a movement to fight for women's liberation. Because it captured the feelings of many women activists, it became a key document for the Canadian women's liberation movement. Its enthusiastic reception also established Mitchell's analysis as integral to the development of a political economy of women in Canada. As a result, much of the subsequent research and theory building was organized in terms of Mitchell's four structures.

Women's Work

Of the topics explored so far in the political economy of women, the sexual division of labour has received the most systematic attention. Initially, researchers sought to recover the history of women's work and to document the contemporary situation of employed women. In Canada and Quebec since the seventeenth century, women have been cyclically recruited as immigrants in ways that varied by class and economic position in the home country, on the basis of new world demographic imbalances and labour force demands (Johnson 1975; Roberts 1979; Silvera 1983; Arnopoulos 1979; Phillips and Phillips 1983). Women's childbearing capacities and their labour were both essential to the settlement process (Hill 1973; Folché-Delbosc 1977). The origins of contemporary patterns of sex segregation and wage differentials, as well as early patterns of resistance, were established both in rural agriculture and in the cities as women moved into the labour market that developed with industrial production (Cross 1973; Binnie-Clark 1979; Brandt 1981; Bradbury 1984). The effort to document the unrecognized experiences of women continues, particularly for working-class, native, black and immigrant women (Ng and Ramirez 1981; Penney 1983; Talbot 1984; Sand 1985; Green 1985).

Later, analysts began to deconstruct ideologies which naturalize women's domestic activities, fetishize the wage, and exclude the household from the domain of political economy (Seccombe 1974; Armstrong and Armstrong 1984). All variants of political economy now recognize that what goes on in the household has economic significance (Amsden 1980). That recognition allows, and should indeed require, rethinking the various economic paradigms underlying different political economy perspectives (Boyd 1977).

Again we see congruence between feminism and political economy frameworks. While some liberal political economists advocate calculating the value of housework into the gross national product (Hawrylyshyn 1978), the neoclassical paradigm of the "new home economics" assumes liberal individual choice and applies criteria of economic rationality to the household and investigates its relation to the labour market (Becker 1965). Inverting the dual problematic of economism, some radical feminists substituted domestic labour for "production" as the basic economic motor. In the "Wages for Housework" tendency, which developed Selma James's presentation of the work of Mariarosa Dalla Costa, women's oppression was reduced to the unwaged character of domestic labour (Dalla Costa and James 1972). Radical feminists identified housework and other domestic responsibilities as the locus of women's oppression by men. Christine Delphy, for example, described marriage as a "work contract" which establishes the man as head of the family and gives him the right to appropriate all work done in the family, especially his wife's in providing domestic services and raising children. For Delphy, marriage was a relation of slavery (Delphy 1984: 101).

The Canadian women's liberation movement has made important contributions to the marxist feminist analysis of women's work in the home. This is perhaps the only instance where Canadian contributions have been internationally recognized. The earliest initiative was Margaret Benston's "Political Economy of Women's Liberation" (1969). She argued for the application of classical marxism to the study of women, claiming that housework was a distinct and archaic form of precapitalist production of use values in goods and services for direct consumption in the household. Peggy Morton's "Women's Work is Never Done" went further, attempting to expand marxist theory to incorporate the sexual division of labour (1972). She was the first to argue that "the family [is] a unit whose function is the maintenance and reproduction of labour power," a commodity essential to the capitalist production process (1972: 53). Expanding on Morton's argument that women's work in the home contributes to the production of labour power, Wally Seccombe used the conceptualization of the reproduction of labour power to examine the connections between unpaid labour in the household and the dynamics of paid labour (1974, 1975). He also tried to stretch marxist value analysis to include the relationship between unpaid domestic labour and wage labour.

These formulations sparked "the domestic labour debate" (Molyneux 1979). International, multidimensional, and highly contentious, the debate focused on such issues as whether domestic labour is productive or unproductive in the technical marxist sense of producing surplus value, whether domestic labour is integral to the capitalist mode of production or is only indirectly related to it, whether unpaid domestic labour serves to raise or lower the value of the husband's labour power, whether housewives are part of the working class, and whether domestic labour could be replaced by capitalist commoditization (Fox 1980).

For political economy, this debate generated several conceptual breakthroughs, the most significant being the claim that paid and domestic labour are not distinct and separate, but two sides of the same coin, necessary both for capital accumulation and for the reproduction of classes. This sophisticated rethinking of "the two-fold character of production" avoided Engels's compartmentalized formulation. The recognition that the relation between the two was not merely ideological but structural laid the basis for an extensive reconceptualization of many issues, including women's class position, their relation to men, and the place of the family household system in the capitalist mode of production (Luxton 1980; Seccombe 1980a, 1980b, 1983; *Atlantis* Fall 1981).

Canadian marxist feminists have made major contributions to understanding the relationship of women to the process of labour market construction and capital accumulation (Armstrong and Armstrong this volume, 1983; Armstrong 1984; Lowe 1980; Connelly and MacDonald 1983; Fox and Fox 1983). As semi-dependants (real or assumed) women both provide for the cheap reproduction of labour power and act as a reserve army of labour to be employed according to capitalist needs in war and peacetime (Connelly 1978; Pierson 1986). While American scholars have used creatively liberal approaches to the political economy analysis of labour force and household (Berk 1980; Feinstein 1979), few Canadians have used this perspective (Cook 1976; Eichler 1983). Whether marxist or liberal, such theoretical elaborations and empirical investigations require revisions of traditional political economic conceptions of the operation of the labour market and construction of the labour force (Marchak 1977). They also establish the basis of a political economy of family form (Cameron 1983; Wilson 1986) and contemporary gender relations (Smith 1973; Porter 1985; Luxton 1981, 1983; Burstyn, Smith, and Ng 1985; Luxton and Rosenberg 1986; Gannagé this volume; Luxton this volume).

In trying to examine the interaction between unequal jobs and incomes in the labour force which coerce women into marriage, and family responsibilities which prevent "free" competition for women in the labour market, the role of the labour movement in gender politics has come under scrutiny. While it is clear that nineteenth-century Canadian trade unions, like trade unions elsewhere, adopted protectionist policies which excluded women, the contemporary situation is less clear. Marchak (1974a) has argued that labour unions preserve and reproduce salary inequities. Baker and Robeson (1981) have argued that not only do unions not help women, but their policies are sexist. In contrast, authors like Gunderson (1975) and White (1980) have pointed out that salaries, working conditions, and job security are superior for unionized women to those of their non-unionized sisters working in similar jobs (Armstrong and Armstrong 1983). Furthermore, experience has shown that, even where unions are committed to improvements for women workers, employers, including governments with equal pay policies, have proven resistant to implementing gender equality (Gaucher 1981). More important, in a situation where the proportion of women in the labour force and the labour movement has steadily increased and the areas of traditional male trade union support such as heavy industry have declined absolutely, the labour movement has responded flexibly and rapidly to demands from its female members with internal policy changes and public campaigns on women's issues (Genge 1986). There is an increasing amount of research on gender politics in the labour movement (Geoffroy and Sainte-Marie 1971; Bank Book Collective 1979; Briskin and Yanz 1983).

Although a political economy framework was originally constituted through the study of capitalist economic development, its conceptual framework has been used to investigate non-capitalist social formations and modes of production. The study of women in non-capitalist social formations elucidates the complex relations among childbirth and child-rearing practices, women's control over subsistence production, and the gender division of labour in determining the relative statuses of women and men in different modes of production (Blumberg 1978; Sacks 1979). They also show that the distribution of labour between women and men varies, both cross-culturally and through time (Leacock 1978; Lee 1979). Cross-cultural (and cross-national) comparisons allow exploration of the subtle political components which configure gender relations in societies with similar subsistence patterns. In particular, studies of native societies confirm the contention that gender stratification and patriarchal social structures were consolidated as a result of religious and economic imperialism (Bourgeault 1983; Anderson 1985, this volume).

This work lays the basis for a general theory of gender and of the emergence and transformation of gender hierarchies (Nash and Fernandez-Kelly 1983; Etienne and Leacock 1980). Such a general theory of gender (and its transformation) rebounds in turn on theories of modes of production (and their transformations) to reveal that their exclusion of gender renders them incomplete (Seccombe forthcoming; Anderson this volume).

Reproduction: Biology, Sexuality, Socialization

The effect of childbearing and childrearing on women's oppression has been central to feminist theory. Unlike classical marxism, which effectively let slip "the production of life itself" into an untheorized natural sphere, feminist theory beginning with de Beauvoir and Mitchell has argued that "reproduction" is shaped by historical and political economic determinations. This issue is not only central to feminist political economy but also regenerates a long-dormant concern of classical political economy — the production of populations as well as the production of goods. Reproblematizing this issue was a necessary corrective to economist reduction in both liberal and marxist political economic paradigms.

A major theoretical advance was represented by Gayle Rubin's notion of a sex/gender system as:

> the set of arrangements by which a society transforms biological sexuality into products of human activity. (1975: 159)

Rubin's distinction between sex as biological and gender as socially constructed standardized a language for making this critical distinction. She also attempted to synthesize Marx, Lévi-Strauss, and Freud, arguing that the sex/gender system contained three elements: biological reproduction, gender roles, and sexuality (identity, orientation, and practices). These elements were linked to production in two ways. The division of labour directly shaped cultural definitions of gender, while sexual desire was shaped by the institutions of the family and the necessity of biological reproduction.

Making "reproduction" a central category of feminist theory has stimulated some excellent historical and cross-cultural research analyzing how "reproduction" is embedded in a society's political, economic, and social structures and how those structures make possible women's capacities to be autonomous actors or subject women to male control. But there are several problems with this approach. First, reproduction used as a unitary category conflates biological and social processes; despite a recognition that they are analytically distinct, it has tended to recollapse procreation, sexuality, and socialization. Second, a view of parallel structures has led to problems of dualism in theories which have not been able to analyze the relationship between the two posited social structures. Third, the terminology of reproduction entangles feminist theory in other conceptual confusions. As Felicity Edholm, Olivia Harris, and Kate Young have noted:

> The concept of reproduction has been taken up both by Marxists concerned to account for succession and change . . . and by those attempting to theorize the situation of women, in such a way that the particular biological tasks of women are frequently conflated with the overall process of social reproduction. (1977: 103)

They further point out the problematic use of the term "reproduction" in marxism. Employed by those attempting to break with economist formulations of marxism in favour of analyses which were more inclusive of ideology and politics, "reproduction" was used to refer variously and sometimes eclectically either to "simple" versus "expanded" reproduction, to the reproduction of the relations and forces of production, to the conditions of reproduction of the mode of production, or to the reproduction of the social totality. The first two leave unchallenged the narrow sex-blind economism of the traditional usage of "the mode of production"; the last has not successfully differentiated nor related the various processes involved in either a mode of production or a social formation.

Biology

Studies of biological reproduction mostly have emphasized the extent to which "biology" is mediated by social and historical forces. In general, this research has shown that childbirth and childcare are profoundly determined by political and economic conditions. Rates of fertility and rates and age of marriage to which they are linked, ideologies and the practical organization of childcare, the organization and control of childbirth, and population control programs including the availability of contraception and abortion have all changed historically relative to social and economic shifts (Levine 1977; Tilly and Scott 1978; Gordon 1977). These dimensions have all been subject to state regulation and male control at various times and have been issues for political struggle (Petchesky 1984; Gavigan this volume; Heitlinger this volume). Feminists emphasize those factors which increase or decrease women's control over fertility and birth. More recently, this has led to a concern with environmental influences, particularly those related to work on fetal and maternal health (Chavkin 1981; Rosenberg this volume). While most work in this area has been done for Britain and the United States, some recovers Canadian history and exposes contemporary Canadian social dynamics (Tomic-Trumper 1986).

Feminists have been reluctant generally to confront the full implications of biological reproductive difference, partly in reaction against the use of biological determinist arguments to justify women's subordination as a natural outcome of the maternal role. An early exception was Firestone's (1970) argument that reproductive biology is the direct source of women's oppression; she constituted the reproductive triad — female, male, and infant — as a "family" which inevitably generates complementary but asymmetrical psychologies of male power and female dependence. More recently marxist feminists have called for a reconstruction of political economy based on an analysis which includes biology. Johanna Brenner and Maria Ramas (1984) have argued that "the biological facts of reproduction" or "the exigencies of biological reproduction" must be considered in a materialist account of women's oppression. Pat Armstrong and Hugh Armstrong have insisted that in developing "a political economy that is sex conscious as well as class conscious" and "in attempting to provide a material explanation for women's subordination" women's bodies and their childrearing possibilities must be taken into account (Armstrong et al. 1985).

Nancy Folbré (1983) argues that a political economy of fertility decision making exists in "patriarchy" (understood as "the rule of the fathers"), where the economic benefits or disadvantages of children to fathers relates directly to male control over women's procreative capacities. Diana Gittens (1982) argues that as the dependent-wife family household became increasingly nuclear, men gained control over fertility decisions. Quebec feminists have uniquely addressed the question of fertility from within a perspective which seeks to understand the political, ideological, and economic substructures of the high birthrates typified as "la revanche des berceaux"—the revenge of the cradle. While such investigations hold out the promise of a feminist political economy which understands biology, such theorizing has not yet been realized.

A different challenge to political economy is posed by Mary O'Brien (1981). Sharing hegelian and marxist roots with one branch of political economy, her feminist revision criticizes political theory and political economy for failing to theorize birth. Focusing on its consciousness-producing aspects, she expands the category of labour to include women's labour in birth and childcare, an expansion which necessarily introduces gender differences. The male relation to species reproduction is, as O'Brien puts it, one of alienation which commences with the ejaculation of the seed. Male reproductive consciousness is consequently dualistic, divided from nature and preoccupied with

> creating institutional and ideological modes of continuity over time to heal the discontinuous sense of man the uncertain father. (1981: 131)

In contrast, women's reproductive consciousness is historically continuous and integrated with the species and nature. While this theory makes only the vaguest return to the concrete and sets up a dualism of its own in which women's productive contribution disappears, it nevertheless offers an analysis which allows a connection between gender differences in reproduction and the political theories which historically have structured and maintained institutions like the family and the state and which in contemporary (capitalist and postcapitalist) societies support a rapacious productivism. At the most general level she proposes a theory in which gender structures (the "mode of reproduction") and the organization of production are mediated by consciousness which is itself produced through differentiated forms of labour.

Sexuality

Difficult as it has been to expand political economic analyses with biological reproduction, incorporating sexuality into a political economy framework has been even more problematic. In the late 1960s an often confessional literature by radical and marxist feminists alike denounced "the sexual objectification of women" and, influenced by de Beauvoir, insisted that women were capable of becoming fully active sexual subjects. The study of the commodification of sexuality was initially influenced by preexisting syntheses of marxism and psychoanalysis — Wilhelm Reich's ([1931] 1971, [1945] 1969) emphasis on the role of sexual repression in the maintenance of authoritarian ideological and political systems and Herbert Marcuse's (1955) analyses of repressive desublimation (Wernick 1983, 1987).

Combining these with the feminist concern with sexual objectification, one line of research has shown how female sexuality, whether in person or in culturally coded representations, has been exploited in the labour and consumer markets. Female sexuality is used overtly to sell products to men; "attractiveness" (the polite form of sexuality) is demanded of women who must provide "service with a smile" (Reiter 1985; Hochschild 1983) and is sold directly through products that promise to enhance the beauty of women themselves. More recently, the sex industry has been identified as a multimillion-dollar business that directly packages female (and, increasingly, male) sexuality. In contrast with the moralizing repugnance of right-wing critics, feminists have stressed the poverty and economic vulnerability of young women entering sex trades where they can certainly make more money, faster, than anywhere else.

If political economy analyzes objective structures (of oppression), then psychoanalysis can illuminate their internalization, their investment with sexual energy, the way in which they are engendered (Mitchell 1974; Hamilton 1986; Horowitz 1977). In principle, the combination of these two analytic approaches should illuminate the structures of domination (or liberation) of the external social and internal psychic realms. However, the response of political economy to psychoanalysis has often been indifference and that of socialism outright hostility.

By the late 1970s, a new social constructionist approach emerged, influenced in part by Michel Foucault's (1978) attack on sexual essentialism, and largely oriented to a study of homosexuality. John d'Emilio (1983a, 1983b) and Bert Hansen (1982) have recently argued that homosexuality as an identity and a community (rather than as a sexual act) could only emerge with the development of urban industrial societies where market relations could supply domestic requirements and urban social density promised anonymity. While the available evidence leaves in doubt the extent of lesbian sexual activity (Rich 1980) it also seems clear that higher education and the possibility of being self-supporting in a labour market stripped of kin ties was important in the development of lesbian communities (Sahli 1979; Faderman 1981; Vicinius 1982, 1984). As for heterosexuality, movements of sexual reform, whether in Germany in the 1920s (Grossmann 1983) or contemporary North America (Vance 1984) have been recuperated to support a labour-divided, modified patriarchal family. Similarly, heterosexuality, or the institutionalization and privileging of heterosexuality, has shifted with changes in productive modes. In non-industrial societies, the control of female sexuality and of women as marriage partners has also received some attention. For example, Bridget O'Laughlin's (1974) analysis of the development of bride price among the Mbum Kpau clearly shows that a basis for economic stratification lies in the patriarchal control by male elders of young men's work and young women's marriageability and sexuality by male elders and that these relations are culturally coded in difference and taboo.

Overall, four questions have been raised. First, is there a relation between sexuality and class structures? Second, what accounts for foregrounding sexuality as a dimension of identity? Third, how is sexuality shaped by the commodity relations of advanced capitalism, and, fourth, what is the relation of sexual liberation to socialism and feminism? McCaskell 1983; Burstyn 1985; Valverde 1985).

Socialization

The feminist contention that "woman is made, not born" led to an early interest in socialization (Ambert 1976). Although all feminist variants criticized gender codes and the critical absences of women in everything from nursery rhymes, school books, and clothing to "great literature" (Cheda 1971, 1972), different approaches exist among the three variants. Liberal feminists have concentrated on content analyses which demonstrate that women are either underrepresented or portrayed as stereotypes (Royal Commission on the Status of Women 1970; CRTC 1982). Radical feminists have problematized a "politics of pleasure and danger" (Dubois and Gordon 1984) in sexual imagery, stressing sexual exploitation of and violence against children and women (Brownmiller 1984), a theme that has more recently engaged the attention of socialist feminists (Guberman and Wolfe 1985).

Marxist feminists have tended to express this in terms of a concern with ideological structures and their role in forming consciousness and reproducing social formations. Research informed by such concerns has developed in two distinct directions. One effort, pioneered by British feminists, has investigated the institutional structures and practices which maintain and reproduce social relations, particularly state intervention in childcare through social welfare, school, and family policies (Wilson 1977; Dale et al. 1981; Riley 1983) This is an inchoate literature generally, and there is very little Canadian work (Russell this volume; Pierson 1977; Schultz 1979, 1982). Much of what there is has been generated by activists in the daycare movement concerned more with immediate political gains than with theorizing (Ross 1979). Academic work has concentrated on recovering the history of childhood and of schooling (N. Sutherland 1976; Prentice 1977a, 1977b; Synge 1979; Dumont-Johnson 1980; Parr 1982; Fahmy-Eid and Dumont 1983).

The second effort has sought to explore how ideology finds a base in psychic structures. Unlike the analysts of paid work and housework, proponents of this approach tend to locate women's oppression in an ideological sphere. In *Psychoanalysis and Feminism* Mitchell (1974) argues that patriarchy is an autonomous mode with culture and psychic structures ruled by the "Law of the Father." Following in the path suggested by the Frankfurt school, Nancy Chodorow (1978) has argued that identity and personality are shaped by class and gender to produce a desire and capacity for mothering in women across classes while at the same time generating class-differentiated psychic bases for work among men. Chodorow, Dorothy Dinnerstein (1976) and others hold that sexual asymmetries in childrearing create a psychic base for misogynistic ideologies of male superiority.

Semiotics, structuralism, and post-structuralism have influenced a concern with extra-familial socializers, particularly language and image in art, film, music, and literature (Steele 1982; Jacobowitz 1986). Although often informed by political economic categories, this work has neither provoked political economy to take up the challenge posed by psychoanalysis nor has it addressed the theoretical issues of political economy. Indeed, much work on the creation of masculine and feminine subjectivity and the representation of gender difference (and hence also its reproduction) has jettisoned any conception of the material, conceiving instead (especially in discourse theory) a sphere of autonomous ideology (Gallop 1982).

Clearly no hard boundaries exist between procreation, sexuality and socialization. More importantly, understanding reproductive biology as more social than instinctive requires an appreciation of how identity, cultural codes for gender, and sexual desire are part of a concrete dialectical totality. Nevertheless, it is important to keep them analytically distinct; otherwise, their conflation produces an undifferentiated, premature totalization which reinforces the problem of theoretical dualism. An analysis of the structures which determine women's lives must consider both paid work in the labour market and unpaid work in the household, theorizing all dimensions as part of a complex totality. It must also investigate the political dimensions of women's situations. One of the most fruitful developments in this direction has been the integration of the politics of gender relations into a political economy of class (Bacchi 1983), breaking from historical studies of women's movements as isolated phenomena (Cleaverdon 1974). While there has been little published on contemporary Canadian women's movements (Corrective Collective 1972; FitzGerald, Guberman, and Wolfe 1982; Morris 1980; Doerr 1984; Miles 1985; Egan this volume) there have been some initial investigations of their development and of their relation to the state (Kome 1983; Findlay this volume) and to other movements: national (Lavigne, Pinard, and Stoddart 1979; Lamoureux this volume), left-wing (Kealey 1984; Sangster 1985), and sexual (Weir this volume).

Toward a Feminist Political Economy

Still in its formative stages, feminist political economy has attempted to understand the structure of women's oppression and develop a strategy for liberation. Unlike some forms of feminist investigation, theoretical complexity is demanded of feminist political economy by both the theory it inherited and its strategic goals. Both push it beyond recovery and critique to a theoretical reflexivity and holistic analysis. At this point, several analytic and methodological theses, necessary preliminaries to any synthesis, have been established. As well as providing guidelines for the study of women, they must be integrated into political economy for it to fulfill its promise as the "study of society as an integrated whole."

First, as gender differentiation occurs universally and is a necessary precondition for class hierarchy, gender divisions are at least as fundamental and significant as class divisions. They must be seriously analyzed in all cases, and only sidelined if they are proven insignificant.

Second, all classes are gendered, and gender is fundamental to conflict within and between classes. Similarly, state formations and practices of rule are implicated in the maintenance and change of gender structures. In analyzing class formation and struggle, gender must be investigated; similarly, the determination of gender structures by class and state formations must be taken into account.

Third, sex/gender systems are dialectically co-determined with economic structures. The propagation of the species and the reproduction of labour (power) must be integrated into accounts of economic development; conversely, gender structures must be understood as having economic foundations.

Fourth, biological reproduction is neither natural nor instinctive. The naturalism which assumes that the reproduction of human beings can be left to instinct must be rejected and an analysis of its relation to economic and gender structures be put in its place.

Fifth, gender is among the deep structures of culture; cultural codes organize and express gender. In the study of culture as in the study of class, the operations of gender must be explicated.

Sixth, sexuality is harnessed and shaped in relation to gender, class, race, and economic structures. The implications of sexual dynamics should be explored when trying to understand these forms of stratification.

Seventh, the identity of individuals, including sexual identity, is formed in relation to location in gender and economic divisions. Individual and sexual identity must be analyzed not in terms of an abstracted psychology but in relation to this location.

The acquisition of these theses has been a major gain both for feminism and for political economy. The task now is to explore their implications and begin the systematic development of a feminist political economy.

Note

1. While we draw attention to some of the contributions of francophone feminists in the final section of this paper, the focus of this review is primarily on work written in English. Furthermore, our aim in this paper is to indicate the trends and intellectual developments rather than to provide a comprehensive review of all materials published in English on Canadian women. There are many extensive bibliographies available, and a number of excellent journals regularly review the state of the art. For general sources on women in Canada see: *Atlantis*; *Canadian Women's Studies/Cahiers des femmes*; *Resources for Feminist Research/Documentation sur la recherche féministe*; *Fireweed*; Eichler 1975, 1985; Latham and Kess 1980; Zaremba 1974; Stephenson 1973; Cook 1976; Matheson 1976, Trofimenkoff and Prentice 1977.

I The Politics of the Women's Movement

2 Facing the State: The Politics of the Women's Movement Reconsidered[1]

SUE FINDLAY

Between 1966 and 1979, the Canadian state was engaged in organizing its formal response to women's demands for equality. Although some concrete legislative and policy initiatives were introduced in this period, the response of the state focused largely on integrating the representation of women's interests into the policy-making process. This was done both by establishing a network of programs and advisors to represent women's issues in the policy-making process in the state bureaucracy, and by appointing a Minister Responsible for the Status of Women to represent women's interests at the executive level of the state. Throughout this process the state demonstrated a commitment to consult with the women of Canada, and in so doing not only validated the faith of liberal feminists in the strategy of reform by the state, but constructed a relationship with them that established liberal feminism as the "public face" of the women's movement.[2]

By 1980, however, it was becoming increasingly obvious that this response on the part of the state and the political strategies of liberal feminism had failed to produce substantive changes in the everyday lives of women or in the relations of power between women and men at the societal level. New legislation had confirmed women's right to equal treatment and opportunities, but economic exploitation and the various forms of sexual violence against women continued to limit women's ability to exercise these rights.[3] The resistance of the state — including both federal and provincial governments — to consultations with feminists about ways to guarantee women's rights in the new Constitution was a stunning display of the limits of state commitment to actively promote women's equality. Feminists organized a massive campaign against this resistance and, according to some feminists, "won an overriding statement of equality, entrenched in the Constitution" (Kome 1983: 113), but the incident reinforced the growing scepticism within the women's movement about the willingness of the state to defend women's equality in the face of the more powerful interests in society such as those that were vocal in the constitutional debates.

Since then, the political differences within the women's movement have begun to surface a little more clearly as feminists struggle to understand how the movement can more effectively pressure the state for reform. Liberal feminists are arguing more emphatically that success rests on increasing the numerical representation of women in the mainstream of the political system and on strengthening the public credibility of the movement.[4] It was this perspective that prompted the National Action Committee on the Status of Women (NAC) to organize a nationally televised debate on women's issues with the leaders of the major parties in the 1984 federal election.[5] However, although the politicians' willingness to integrate women's issues into their election platforms convinced the public that the women's movement was becoming one of the most powerful lobbying groups in Canada, the follow-up has been disappointing.

Socialist feminists reject the notion that women's equality can be achieved within the existing system, and argue that the interests of capitalism and patriarchy shape the politics of the state in a way that is antithetical to women's interests. Emphasizing the hegemony of these interests in society, their analysis has to a large extent led to a functionalist or instrumentalist definition of the state.[6]

A more convincing definition of the state that reflects the struggles that characterize the policy-making process describes the state as the organizer of hegemony rather than the object of it. While the interests of capitalism and patriarchy might dominate at the societal level, the internal conflicts and competition within and among these forces makes it impossible for them to impose a unified position on the state, or to defend their interests against opposing interests in the political sphere. The role of the state, then, is to organize a unity of interests among the dominant groups and disorganize potential challenges to this unity. Struggles between and among these groups are thus reflected (not directly represented) in the policy-making process, where policies are negotiated in what has been called an "unequal structure of representation" (Mahon 1977: 165–98) to maintain the interests of the dominant groups. It is through this process that the hegemony of the dominant groups is organized and reorganized to control and incorporate the challenges of subordinate groups such as women.[7]

But while both of these perspectives offer valuable insights into the relation between the state and the dominant interests and the maintenance of women's oppression, their implicit determinism leaves little incentive to explore the relationship between the state, the women's movement, and the latter's potential to struggle effectively at the political level to transform the relations of power. The clue may well lie in analyzing our experience of the state in the past two decades, both as activists in the women's movement and as feminists working within the state. By analyzing the way the state has organized its response to women's demands for equality, we can see that this response is not so much a product of the negotiations between the interests of women and those of the dominant groups within the unequal structure of representation, but of struggles between the *state* and feminists as to *how* the state would define women's interests and integrate them into the unequal structure of representation. Although faith in the institutions and practices of liberal democracy made it difficult to resist the proposals of the state to promote women's equality, our experience demonstrates the state's vulnerability in this period and the opportunities that we had to challenge its proposals.

Important questions are posed for the women's movement. Is this state of vulnerability (and hence our potential to use the state for our revolutionary purposes) unique to this period when the issue of equality had no place in the unequal structure of representation of the Canadian state, or does the opportunity continue to present itself in our struggles to define our demands for reform by the state on the particular issues that shape our inequality?

Constructing the Process

Organizing the representation of women's interests within the state was not simple. The process was marked by the resistance of a state dominated by men and their patriarchal perceptions of the relevance of women's issues to the political process, men who were committed to national policies reflecting dominant political interests. It was also marked by a recognition that the state should and must be seen as representative of the people as opposed to particular groups. While the need for legitimation motivated a public state response to demands for equality, the resistance established limits to the reforms the state was prepared to initiate.

The process of organization evolved in a contradictory way, alternating between resistance and response as the state mediated between and among various political interests. But resistance mostly dominated the process, particularly as it became more decisively located in and subjected to the rules and regulations of the state bureaucracy in the latter stages of the period studied. Responsiveness was limited to brief periods and was almost entirely due to converging political forces at a particular moment rather than reflecting any rational commitment to women's equality.

Overall, although an analysis of this process demonstrates the success of the women's movement in pressuring the state to represent women's interests in the policy-making process, it also demonstrates the success of the state in constructing this representation in a way that controlled women's demands and limited reforms.[8]

1966–1972: Defining Equality

In September 1966, several hundred of Canada's well-educated and publicly minded women gathered in the Railway Room in the Houses of Parliament to demand government action to improve the status of women. The meeting was a landmark in this second phase of women's struggle for equality, initiating a relationship (which still exists) between organized spokespersons for women and the state. In this case, the attending Cabinet ministers were appropriately receptive to the issues raised; not much later the Royal Commission on the Status of Women was appointed by Prime Minister Lester B. Pearson.

Accounts of this meeting stress the organizers' militancy, noting the daring ultimatum that Laura Sabia, then president of the Canadian Federation of University Women, issued to the government following the meeting: should the government not respond to demands, she threatened, two million women would storm Ottawa (Morris 1980). Despite the sexism that pervaded the state and other male-dominated institutions, the centrality of issues of inequality and discrimination in the 1960s made it virtually impossible to ignore women's demands for equality.

This centrality sprang from the obvious contradictions of abundance and affluence on the one hand and persistent poverty and powerlessness on the other. The Western world had still not freed itself from the spectre of communism that emerged following World War II. With the rise of Quebec nationalism and the civil rights movement, the state was particularly vulnerable to attacks by national liberation, civil rights, and anti-poverty movements that exposed its limited capacity to protect individual rights to equality and justice, defining these limits as collective conflicts of class, race, and sex, not individual problems. The search was on for solutions that would demonstrate the commitment of liberal democracies to equality without compromising their reliance on capitalism.

A framework of equal opportunity dominated the Western state's responses to these issues. Diverting attention from explanations focusing on class, race, and sex, the problems were defined as a lack of access to the system due to individual or group discrimination and a lack of education preventing people from exercising their rights and responsibilities. The solution was a series of programs designed to remove discriminatory barriers and promote the education of the "disadvantaged."[9] It was a persuasive argument, one that even tempted radicals into various forms of cooperative relationships with the state in order to use its resources for their own political agenda.[10]

Canada was no exception to this general trend: as well as the inequalities between the two founding nations, youth, the elderly, natives, and "multicultural" groups, the question of women began to surface. In 1964, Canada had already ratified the International Labour Organization's Convention that committed Canada to pursue a "national policy designed to promote . . . equality of opportunity and treatment in respect of employment and occupation with a view to eliminating any discrimination in respect thereof," and turned its attention to women's plight in a Public Service still operating under a policy that denied married women permanent status (Archibald 1970: 17). By 1967, sex discrimination in the Public Service was considered sufficiently serious to warrant inclusion in the new Public Service Employment Act. At the same time, a pilot program was initiated to encourage married women with children — and degrees in subjects related to areas suffering from "man" power shortages — to enter the Public Service on a part-time basis (Archibald 1970: 111).

By 1966, the Canadian government, visibly committed to promoting equality and justice for the "disadvantaged," had taken some steps toward recognizing women's inequality. Following the 1966 Railway Room meeting, there was little struggle over the appointment of a Royal Commission. Such a request was completely compatible with the equal-opportunity framework which shaped state responses to other social issues in the 1960s, and the government was undoubtedly aware of its successful use by other governments in winning favour with the women's movement. In fact, the request provided the state with the opportunity to publicly announce its commitment to women's concerns about equality and to claim credit for attempts to promote equal employment opportunities. The process of legitimation was underway. The Royal Commission on the Status of Women was appointed in 1967 with a strong representation of human rights activists and with journalist Ann Francis (Florence Bird) as "Chairman." Its terms of reference clearly limited the inquiry to matters of equal opportunity. The Commission was directed to "recommend what steps might be taken by the Federal Government to ensure for women equal opportunities with men in all aspects of Canadian society." (Royal Commission on the Status of Women 1970: vii). However, its appointment was considered a victory by the growing number of middle-class and professional women who believed that government action might lead to opportunities for them. Young marxists were more sceptical (Kowaluk 1972; Discussion Collective No. 6 1972; 40–42). Regardless of political orientation, many women participated in preparing briefs for the Commission. This involvement of thousands of women from communities across Canada in advising the government on reforms led them to identify with the Commission and its Report.

Because of this involvement in the Commission's process, its real significance went far beyond the report tabled in Parliament in 1970. First, the political agenda established by the report lasted well into the 1970s. Although new issues inevitably emerged as the movement grew, this agenda defined the major issues and a strategy for change. In spite of a limited equal-opportunity framework, the Report contained a well-articulated, comprehensive set of recommendations that echoed the concerns of most Canadian women who participated in the hearings and helped to shape a newly developing feminist consciousness. It therefore legitimately claimed to define the issue of equality, and indeed Canadian feminists were prepared both to take the recommendations of the Commission to the public for further study and to pressure the government for their implementation.

Equally significantly, the Commission catalyzed the organization of an important sector of the women's movement. Status of women groups such as the Vancouver Status of Women Council, the Ontario Committee on the Status of Women, and the Newfoundland Status of Women Council emerged in the early 1970s to examine and promote the Commission's recommendations. It was not long before groups also saw the need to organize around single issues, with new groups created to address issues like sex stereotyping in the media, property laws, daycare, rape, and equal pay for work of equal value. At the same time, as state legitimation of the status of women issue made women's immediate problems and crises visible, a network of alternative feminist services developed at the community level. Overall, the investigation, the Report, and women's self-organizing was positive.

However, politicians did not rush to respond to the Commission's recommendations. Instead, the report was subjected to a cumbersome bureaucratic review by an interdepartmental committee organized by the Privy Council Office. Given the lack of expertise on women's issues within the bureaucracy, the need to educate many participating officials, and the scope of the issues, this complex process took more than two years to complete. But despite the detailed advice from the interdepartmental committee, and the 1971 appointment of a minister to represent women's issues in the Cabinet, the Commission's report still fell on barren ground when it finally was placed on the Cabinet agenda. In February 1972, Cabinet approved the Report *in principle only*, with the result that ministers were given complete discretion concerning implementation of recommendations in their own departments. No particular directives were issued, as they would normally be when an issue had priority; no priorities were established among the recommendations; no resources were earmarked. The enthusiasm for justice and equality characterizing the 1960s and the early years of the Trudeau administration was on the wane; the motivation to address women's equality was lost. By 1972, the government had only managed to take two initiatives, both relating more to the bureaucracy's capacity to organize its response to demands than to developing policies or programs for substantive changes in women's lives. In 1971, the Office of Equal Opportunity was established in the Public Service Commission; in 1972, a Co-ordinator of the Status of Women was appointed in the Privy Council Office. Neither initiative was considered noteworthy by a women's movement anxious for the implementation of specific policies.

By May 1972, government inaction provoked liberal feminists to more collective action. Many of the women at the 1966 meeting formed NAC and called for the first national conference on the status of women, the Strategy for Change Conference. Inspired by the excitement and energy of hundreds of women discovering a reality that promised to change their lives, the conference gave great impetus to the developing movement. The reliance on government persisted, but it was coupled with a belief that building an autonomous movement was necessary to overcome government resistance. Thus anger at the government for failing to implement the recommendations was authentic, reflecting frustrations with the male-dominated state, but it did not reflect a decision to abandon the strategy of reform by the state.

1972–1975: Struggles within the State

If the period between 1966 and 1972 defined the issues and activated the women's movement, the next three years saw feminists in the movement and within the state bureaucracy struggling to have women's interests represented by the state at the Cabinet level and in program and policy development. Its parameters were formally established by the Cabinet decision to adopt the Report in principle only. The implicit lack of political leadership left the status of women issue dangling between the feminist perspective and a more hierarchical perspective dominating the state bureaucracy. It was also vulnerable to attempts by senior management to subordinate women's issues or incorporate them into an agenda of priorities increasingly focused on national unity. Although the political imperatives of a decision to participate in International Women's Year (IWY) in 1975 partially checked this bureaucratic impulse, the struggle continued, even jeopardizing Cabinet's intent to use its support of IWY as a public confirmation of its commitment to women's equality.

The reaction to Cabinet's "decision" on the Report of the Royal Commission by a bureaucracy already overburdened with making sense of the multitude of issues foisted on it by the reform-oriented 1960s was predictable. Not only was caution invited, but resistance appeared to be condoned. Far from heralding a beginning of the end of women's inequality, the Cabinet decision established limits to the state's response to feminist pressure — limits to be exercised largely by the bureaucracy.

However, it was still necessary for the bureaucracy to give visibility to Cabinet's approval in principle, in a way that would placate a watchful women's movement. Both the underrepresentation of women in the bureaucratic decision-making process and lack of expertise on women's issues made it difficult to argue that the state could act in the interest of women's equality. The bureaucracy's task was to correct this situation, both by increasing its own expertise and by appointing women to decision-making positions who would be seen to understand and represent the issue. The bureaucracy had to be seen as capable of implementing the commitment of Cabinet.

As a result, advisors were appointed in departments with mandates so clearly related to women's issues that failure to focus on women's status would have been politically embarrassing. These departments were:

- Justice. A natural, since the removal of discriminatory legislation was an unavoidable priority.
- Health and Welfare. Daycare and abortion and family planning were the priorities of the movement.
- Secretary of State. The recognition and support of women's organizations recommended by the Commission was the obvious responsibility of the Citizenship Branch of this department.
- Employment and Immigration. Women's experience with the sexism of the Canada Employment Centres raised some of the most vehement reactions to government programs in the early 1970s.

Completing this heterogeneous network of women's advisors scattered in tiny offices were the already established Women's Bureau in the Department of Labour, the Office of Equal Opportunity in the Public Service Commission, and the Office of the Co-ordinator of the Status of Women in the Privy Council Office.

For the most part, these advisors were selected from among the few available senior women already in the Public Service. Although most had some experience with women's issues, as temporary staff of the Royal Commission, as members of the interdepartmental committee that reviewed the Commission's Report, or in developing policies linked to women's issues like daycare and family planning, they were not feminist activists. They were public servants, generally unprepared to challenge existing procedures and priorities, particularly from a feminist perspective. They needed access to this perspective to guide them on issues their ministers and departments might confront. But because they were not personally rooted in the women's movement and did not establish any systematic liaison with it, they relied on sporadic connections with women's organizations through conferences or newsletters. In addition to those offices and advisors established within the bureaucracy, the semi-autonomous Canadian Advisory Council on the Status of Women (CACSW) was established in 1973. Although the knowledge and contacts of Dr. Katie Cooke, the former bureaucrat appointed as its first chair, provided access to the policy-making processes, the CACSW was essentially a political body prone to all the abuses of patronage. It has frequently been the site of conflict between the few feminists who met the political criteria for appointment by the Cabinet and those members appointed as a reward for their commitment to the priorities of the party in power. More importantly, its actual mandate and location in the state structure meant that it was unable to represent women's issues as the Commission and liberal feminists had expected.

Thus an organizational framework was established through which women's issues were represented in the decision-making processes within the state bureaucracy. This framework guaranteed real limits for policies proposed to Cabinet and resources directly available to feminist projects. Regardless of the extent to which a feminist perspective was reflected in the work of the women within that framework, advisors faced resistance from the male-dominated bureaucracy, on the part of both management and their male colleagues. Although feminist proposals rarely found their way onto senior management agendas, when they did they were met with impatience and what might be called "willful misunderstanding." Advisors were frequently subjected to "friendly" ridicule or dismissed more aggressively as "women's libbers" or "lesbians." Today, many of these "innocent" exchanges would be labelled and, one would hope, punished as sexual harassment, but at that point such behaviour was considered "natural."

An exception to this pattern was the development of the Women's Program in the Department of the Secretary of State. Organized by feminists who had decided that the resources of the state could be used to support the development of the women's movement and located in a department that had a history of creating programs for the "disadvantaged," the Women's Program was for a time able to present a feminist challenge to bureaucratic attempts to subordinate and incorporate demands for equality.

In 1972, a feminist was hired on a short-term contract to document women's funding needs for the Citizen Participation Program in the Citizenship Branch of the Department of the Secretary of State. She used this position to consult with women's groups across Canada about possible criteria and priorities for funding groups active in changing the status of women. In 1973, she was hired as a permanent advisor on grants to women's organizations and, with a list of useful projects and activists willing to work for the state if it would help to build the women's movement, soon established a group of almost fifteen feminists to work on various short-term projects. Without Cabinet mandate or official Department approval, the de facto program developed a departmental equal employment opportunity program, initiated a research project to review sex stereotyping in the media, supported the release of the first Canadian feminist record, and financed the production of a film documenting the Strategy for Change Conference. Although the budget for grants ($200,000) was extremely small, close consultation with provincial groups allowed strategic placing of funds to maximize growth and provide opportunities for building a national perspective on specific issues such as "women and politics."[11]

Unlike most women who were appointed as advisors in other departments, those in what officially became the Women's Program in 1974 held themselves accountable to the women's movement rather than to government priorities. All were defined as feminists and were largely drawn from feminist groups. Liaison with the women's movement was built into every aspect of the Program's work. A feminist perspective clearly determined the Program's development, and was reflected in project definition, staff recruitment, and the Program's organization and management. All of this was possible of course, not because of bureaucratic commitment to feminization of structures and practices nor because of a devious plot to co-opt the women's movement, but because of the relative invisibility of these activities due to the ad hoc (some might say "subversive") nature of the Program. Without this invisibility, government insistence on adherence to its own priorities and procedures might have made the Program's relationship with the women's movement impossible.

The federal government's credibility with the women's movement in this period came from the Program's ability to deliver resources to the projects defined as priorities by the movement, and to minimize the dangers of co-optation by establishing procedures to hold the Program accountable to the movement—to the extent that this was possible for a program located within a state bureaucracy.

Thus a feminist perspective influenced the state's response to the status of women issue and was concretized in the Women's Program. Over the next few years, this program became the internal basis for challenging the state, a challenge manifested in struggles both between the movement and the state and within the state between the Women's Program and the managers of the bureaucracy.[12]

Until the political imperative of IWY surfaced, the status of women issue, forced to rely on pressure from a relatively weak women's movement for political attention, floundered within the bureaucracy.

IWY was a temporary reprieve from this pattern. In the fall of 1973, Cabinet endorsed Canada's participation in the special year established by the United Nations to promote women's equality among its member countries. The Office of the Co-ordinator of the Status of Women was instructed to encourage as many departments as possible to submit program proposals related to their mandates, co-ordinating these plans into a comprehensive display of government activity to improve the status of women.

Given the green light for the first time, the advisors on women's issues, led by the Co-ordinator of the Status of Women, met to develop guidelines for the overall program and establish criteria for additional funding for the departments for the year. However, much to the dismay of feminist advisors, the guidelines and criteria were couched in terms that supported and displayed the government's commitment to women's equality rather than endorsing new policies and programs. The Women's Program proposal to direct funds to women's groups to develop their own projects was soundly defeated in the first round of meetings. It seemed at one point that there was no way to use the political opening provided by IWY for effective progress on women's issues, reducing the opportunity for reform to a public relations exercise before it reached the stage of Cabinet approval. The struggle between government priorities and feminist priorities, as well as the struggle among the advisors for scarce resources and the status accompanying the allocation of resources, provided a depressing example of how difficult it was to represent women's interests inside the state bureaucracy.

However, the bureaucracy — both the advisors and management — underestimated the determination of feminists to take advantage of any situation to advance their cause. Alerted to the rejection of the Women's Program proposal, several members of the CACSW successfully petitioned the Minister Responsible for the Status of Women to have it reinstated and to encourage other departments to allocate funds to women's groups. Later, feminists were able to force a change in the proposals made by the bureaucracy. This time the target of their complaints was a series of large-scale, expensive regional conferences to discuss issues that they maintained were already well documented by the Royal Commission and subsequent studies. Again, the feminists went to the political level with their protest, but this time they also made their views known to the press. And again, the Minister Responsible for the Status of Women instructed his staff to develop more appropriate plans to gain the approval of the women's movement. He did not however, yield to the protests against the "Why Not?" campaign, a nation-wide publicity campaign aimed at encouraging private sector participation in promoting equality of opportunity for women. In spite of persuasive arguments by feminists about costs, the ambivalent nature of the message, and its development by an all-male advertising firm, the government insisted on maintaining at least one program that would display its commitment to women's equality to the public at large.

Faced with these protests and with departmental inability to develop specific proposals due to lack of expertise on women's issues or contact with the women's movement, senior officials in the bureaucracy reluctantly turned to those rather suspect feminists in the Women's Program to rescue the credibility of the government's IWY program. In the end, the Women's Program was allocated approximately half of the $5 million approved by Cabinet for IWY for an extensive program of grants, cultural projects, and seminars for feminist discussion of reform with responsible "decision makers." The Office of the Co-ordinator of the Status of Women, still responsible for the overall co-ordination of the IWY program, received the other half of the budget. About two-thirds of the total budget for IWY was allocated to activities for women, either to groups to support their own projects, or to individual women to support program participation organized through these two government offices.

Feminists won this round. Or so it seemed at the time.

1976–1979: Establishing the Limits of State Reform

Although IWY made possible important funding to feminist projects, the focus on women's equality was otherwise largely symbolic. IWY did little to encourage the government to adopt permanent programs and policies in response to feminist demands. In fact, if anything, confrontations with the women's movement and feminists inside the state bureaucracy during the planning of IWY increased the resistance of senior officials in the bureaucracy to the integration of women's issues and encouraged politicians to reassess their view that there was a political advantage to be had by promoting women's equality. In the period following IWY, the state appeared to be determined to assert its control over the definition of the federal response to women's demands and to turn its attention to the *real* issue of the day — national unity.

The first step was to control the influence of the feminist perspective within the bureaucracy, represented mainly by the Women's Program, and to develop a system of representing women's issues that would be more accountable to government priorities. As soon as the pressure of IWY ended, persistent rumours emerged about the imminent demise of the Program or drastic cuts in budget and staff. And, in fact, the Program was constantly requested to defend the usefulness of such a small program in affecting such a large issue. Rather than eliminate the Program, and risk rousing the ire of the ever-watchful women's movement, management chose a much more subtle form of control. The battle between the Women's Program and senior management concerned not the content and direction of the Program, but organizational issues — the primacy of bureaucratic rules, regulations, and procedures. There were periodic outbursts against particular funding policies, for example the threat to support for women's centres occasioned by then Justice Minister Otto Lang's attack on the Saskatoon Women's Centre for allegedly performing and procuring abortions, but for the most part the battle centred on organization charts, job classifications and descriptions, criteria for recruiting and hiring staff, budget forecasts and accountability procedures, contract regulations, and the relative responsibilities of regional and national program staff.

The Program largely managed to defend its feminist orientation, but the battles absorbed the time and energy of the staff and turned them inward. As a consequence their relationship with the women's movement began to suffer. The problem was further exacerbated by a new decentralizing of federal programs, which in the case of the Women's Program meant the control of resources by regional staff dominated by men who were largely insensitive — if not overtly hostile — to the activities of both the women's movement and the Women's Program. With regional directors resenting apparent interference in their territory and client groups, one can imagine difficulties in maintaining the ongoing liaison with women's groups that had been central to the usefulness of the Program to the women's movement. Given the imposition of the rules and regulations and the commitment to the relative autonomy of the regional staff, the Program was in danger of being reduced to a granting agency with staff increasingly unable to bend the bureaucratic rules to fit the specific and changing needs of women's groups. The inevitable weakening of the Program's credibility with the movement in turn weakened the Program's power within the government as an advocate for women's issues. In the next few years, many feminist activists concluded they could be more useful outside the government and left the Program. The feminist perspective within the bureaucracy was losing its material base.

To bring the representation of women's interests more firmly under the control of the government, the Minister Responsible for the Status of Women decided that he must increase his own capacity to organize the official response to women's demands. This he proposed to do in two ways. One was to establish his own "ministry" to advise him on policies related to women's issues and to be the liaison between the government and the women's movement; the other was to establish a mechanism to integrate women's issues into the policy-making processes of all government departments as a basis for a comprehensive response to the status of women issue in Canada.

In 1976, the Office of the Co-ordinator of the Status of Women was removed from its original home in the Privy Council Office and established as an independent responsibility centre within the bureaucracy reporting directly to the Minister Responsible for the Status of Women. In addition to its role as advisor to the Minister, the Office was to take on the task of informing the public about government initiatives to promote women's equality. Still sensitive to feminist criticisms of his efforts during IWY, the Minister wanted to project a more positive image of government initiatives than the one he assumed emerged from feminists working in the bureaucracy.

The reaction of the women's movement was confusion. Accustomed as feminists were to relating either to the CACSW or to the Women's Program, yet another program with a public orientation seemed to confirm their view of the government as disorganized and lacking commitment to develop a co-ordinated and coherent plan for improving the status of women. Thus the public face of the Office of the Co-ordinator did little to inspire the movement's confidence, and the distribution of the Minister's speeches and glossy newsletters recounting departmental activities did little to win the support of women's groups desperate for resources for their own projects.

Internally, the effectiveness of the Office as an advisor to the Minister was limited by the low priority given to women's issues throughout the government and the difficulty of playing a co-ordinating role in a bureaucracy that still resisted central planning. But although many feminists argued that a ministry of women that could undertake the development of a comprehensive policy to promote women's equality on its own was the only answer to the difficulties experienced by the Office, the Minister advocated an integration model. In 1976, he launched his "integration" campaign with an aggressive appeal to his Cabinet colleagues and their deputy ministers. The Office of the Co-ordinator was to be responsible for the monitoring of departmental progress, backed up by a rather obscurely worded Cabinet directive.

Attempts to implement the "integration" directive was to become the source of immense frustration for countless public servants, as they first tried to interpret the directive and give it some substance and then fought to contain its enormous implications in the framework of departmental responsibilities that they regarded as already too complex. The directive was easy to resist, given the lack of formal authority or informal power of the Office of the Co-ordinator and the apparent unwillingness of the Minister to enforce it.

In spite of these initiatives, by 1978 no comprehensive policies had been developed in response to women's demands or to the recommendations of the Royal Commission. The status of women issue had achieved some formal bureaucratic recognition due to the integration directive and elevation of the Office of the Co-ordinator to departmental status, but little substantive progress had been made since the initial flurry of legislative changes of overtly discriminatory practices. The exception was legislation on equal pay for work of equal value, though its effectiveness was yet to be proven. Government capacity to represent women's interests seemed to be at a standstill.

Unfortunately, neither the women's movement nor the CACSW, its formal representative to the government, took advantage of the moment to press the government for reforms. The CACSW wielded almost no influence in this period, with government contacts reduced to token Ministerial appearances at quarterly meetings. A new president, Yvette Rousseau, had been appointed from the Quebec labour movement in 1976. Although well connected with the Liberal party establishment, she did not have her predecessor's knowledge of how to operate in the nation's capital. It was much easier for the Minister to turn to the Office of the Co-ordinator for this knowledge. At this time the CACSW was neither a challenge to the government nor a particular support to the women's movement, apart from several useful but poorly distributed research reports.

As for the women's movement, a new perspective on political strategies minimized the value of challenges to the state. The women's movement as a whole emerged from IWY with a stronger, broader base of support and more clearly defined issues. It also had a greater investment in a wide range of ongoing projects requiring funds and woman power. At the same time, feminists' experience with "decision makers" during IWY seminars and conferences gave them new insights into the depth and complexity of resistance to women's equality in both the public and private spheres. This resistance withstood the moral and political challenges of the most seasoned feminists.[13] Strategies of individual confrontation and mass demonstrations seemed ineffective for getting specific changes made in policies and programs.

As a result, different sectors of the women's movement began to marshal their knowledge of specific issues and growing experience with politicians and bureaucrats to develop a new and more "professional" relationship with government. In 1976, armed with research and with a membership reflecting the experience of lawyers, accountants, economists, and sociologists, liberal feminists began to emphasize a strategy of consultation and negotiation with government. It was the leadership of NAC that launched this strategy, although some members thought it conflicted with NAC's responsibilities to regional and community-based groups.

This more moderate and manageable strategy appealed to a government tired of the "militant feminists" of the early 1970s. It also provided a recalcitrant bureaucracy with a feminist perspective to be kept at arm's length. The development of policies for changes in the rape laws and equal pay for work of equal value impressed some sectors of the women's movement with the government's efforts on the one hand, and rescued the bureaucracy from its reliance on feminist advisors on the other hand. However comfortable this relationship might be in the short run, a sustained reliance on the movement's experts would weaken state autonomy required to mediate interests and keep women's equality within the limits of bourgeois domination. Politicians and bureaucrats still had to develop independent strategies and expertise to convincingly represent and control women's issues.

Although one would not want to exaggerate its concern in 1978 about the need for visible progress on the status of women issue, it is true that the government, like the public at large, was becoming more aware of the inequities and violence in the everyday lives of women. The status of women in Canada was finally becoming a public issue and, as such, one that required more systematic government intervention.

However, the impetus to challenge bureaucratic resistance and to direct departments more forcefully to integrate the issue into their responsibilities appeared to come from the United Nations' request for a Plan of Action from its member countries as a part of the program of the Decade of Action on women's equality declared at the UN Conference in Mexico City during IWY.

The Office of the Co-ordinator gladly abandoned its previous and hopeless attempt at "integration" by persuasion in order to co-ordinate the first comprehensive federal plan of action to improve the status of women. The committee process established was slow, and departments resisted requests to send their senior officials to meetings, thus complicating and extending the approval process for departmental proposals to be included in the Plan. However, by 1978–79, a growing number of women and men in the bureaucracy's middle ranks, who either through personal or work experience had had their consciousness raised, struggled to make the Plan a meaningful document. Its reliance on research, pilot projects, impact studies, and information co-ordination, however, was quickly dismissed by the women's movement as unnecessary repetition and delay. *Towards Equality for Women*, released to the public in 1979, was never a best-seller (Status of Women Canada 1983).

However, both the policy-making process and the final Plan itself demonstrate the limits of the state's response to women's equality and therefore deserve further analysis. By limiting the direct participation of feminists in the policy-making process that had characterized the development of state policies in the early years, the state was making an implicit statement about its relation with the women's movement. In the details of the Plan, the limits of government principles, issues, and strategies were publicly declared for the first time.

For the most part, the Plan looked familiar. The liberal commitment to equality was confirmed and extended by a seemingly radical concern with economic independence. The analysis reflected a typically liberal formulation of the problem: discrimination, lack of access, public attitudes, lack of education and information. Noticeably absent were issues which were the major focus of organized feminist demands: abortion, daycare, and mandatory affirmative action. These omissions cannot be dismissed as oversights, for the Plan went through various stages of approval, from committees, departmental officials, deputy ministers, ministers, and finally to Cabinet. Any omissions would have been caught by this process. Although there were undoubtedly struggles at many stages concerning what to include, the final Plan is correctly seen as a political decision to limit reform policies. While feminist struggles for reform on those issues omitted might continue, the government had defined the issues on which it was prepared to act. For feminists working within the state, the struggle had been narrowed to those issues selected at the political level. It was a step backward from the Report of the Royal Commission on the Status of Women.

It was also a step backward from the cozy relationship between the government and feminist experts from the women's movement. Neither the CACSW nor these experts were invited to contribute to the planning process. Deliberations and preliminary policy recommendations were considered officially secret. Even if consultations had been arranged, the discussion of issues had moved too far into the bureaucratic maze of considerations shaping policy for outside experts to defend a feminist perspective that reflected women's realities. The relationship between the women's movement and the state had shifted once again. The strategies of consultation and negotiation so finely honed since IWY were no longer sufficient to affect government response. The struggle was almost entirely in the hands of those feminists within the state with access to, and knowledge of, the decision-making processes. Access for representatives of the women's movement was limited to token consultation after the Plan was printed.

By the time the Plan was completed in 1979, it was clear that it would be primarily those feminists in Status of Women Canada, as the Office of the Co-ordinator was then called, who must defend the feminist perspective in the government's response. The bureaucracy had demonstrated once again its resistance to integrating women's issues. Feminists had little hope of influencing policy within their individual departments and were discouraged from co-operating with feminists in other departments to address issues that cut across departmental lines. It would be up to Status of Women Canada to steer a path through interdepartmental rivalries, to monitor the progress of individual departments in meeting their commitments to the Plan, and to obtain political approval to initiate independent action where both measures failed to produce results.

Implications for the Women's Movement

By 1980, the representation of women's interests was well established in the structure of the federal state. The Minister Responsible for the Status of Women provided leadership and co-ordination at the Cabinet level, and the Plan of Action specified individual ministerial responsibilities. At the bureaucratic level, although attempts to integrate status of women concerns into federal departmental activities failed to compete successfully with other priorities of a male-dominated system, Status of Women Canada emerged from the Plan of Action exercise with a stronger, better-defined mandate, including a Cabinet directive to co-ordinate federal policies on sexual violence. By including the Co-ordinator of Status of Women Canada in the deputy ministers' committee of the newly created Ministry of State for Social Development, that office emerged from the isolation associated with the low priority of its mandate, with a chance in theory to present a feminist perspective in the decision-making process. Cabinet's requirement that all documents include a section on new policy implications for the status of women gave the office added authority. The loose network of advisors and programs in those departments with special responsibilities for women completed the picture. In addition to these measures, the government, conscious of the effect of women's underrepresentation in senior management on the mind of the public (i.e., women), took a first step toward affirmative action for women in the Public Service.

Looking at this period from the feminist perspective, it can also be seen that, in the process of integrating the status of women issue into the policy-making process, the state had significantly modified the radical implications of women's demands for equality by incorporating them into an equal opportunity framework and by limiting the participation of representatives from the women's movement to token consultations. The contribution of feminists to the policy-making process was limited to those who, following IWY, successfully made the transition from feminist advocates to career public servants representing a feminist perspective. The actions of the liberal feminist wing of the movement were limited to relatively restrained periodic ministerial and bureaucratic lobbying rather than the embarrassing confrontations that had characterized IWY. By 1980, the Plan of Action had established the limits to state reforms, and relations with the women's movement were largely ritualized. An "unstable equilibrium of compromise" seemed to have been struck between the state and most of the movement (Poulantzas 1978: 192). The heavy-handedness of the Minister Responsible for the Status of Women, Lloyd Axworthy, in his interference in the CACSW's plans to consult women about the Constitution briefly shattered this compromise, when feminist protest once again threatened the legitimacy of the state's claim to represent women's interests, but in the end as protest failed to move beyond attacks on individual politicians and their representatives in the CACSW, equilibrium was reestablished.

At times when the state is more vulnerable to women's demands, feminists can play a more active role in the development of state proposals to promote women's equality. Taking advantage of the state's need for legitimation, they can establish feminist alternatives to the bureaucratic mode of operating that reinforces patterns of inequality, or advocate policies that challenge the ideology of capitalism and patriarchy. The reforms that emerge from these periods are not necessarily permanent, but their value should not be underestimated as a response to the immediate needs of women and as a way of weakening the hegemony of the dominant groups that oppose women's equality.

It should be emphasized, however, that the potential for successful challenges depends on the extent to which feminists inside the state have been able to maintain their relations with the women's movement and to use their position to advocate reforms that will affect women's lives rather than reforms that have only symbolic value. If these positions are abandoned to career public servants, the representation of women's interests within the state bureaucracy must be considered as potentially damaging to women's struggle for equality.

As we move through the 1980s and into our third decade of struggle to end women's oppression, we do so with a clearer understanding of how our reliance on the state to represent our interests in the policy-making process contributes to the limits of reforms on this issue. We have also come to understand the opportunities that the state presents to us to transcend these limits in periods when it struggles for legitimation or for an "unstable equilibrium of compromise" to satisfy conflicting interests. The state has attempted to contain our demands for equality by reasserting its capacity to represent our interests and by validating liberal feminism as the "public face" of the women's movement. But it cannot deny the accumulation of almost two decades of contradictions between political commitments and the persistence of women's inequality.

It is time for those of us in the women's movement to face our experience with the state and to reconsider our political strategies on the basis of the understandings that this experience has given us about how women's inequality is maintained by the state and how we might challenge this maintenance.

Notes

1. I would like to thank the editors of this book for their encouragement to write about my experiences in and of the state. I would also like to thank in particular Rianne Mahon and Leo Panitch for sharing with me their thoughts on the Canadian state, their understanding of my project, and their detailed comments on this particular article. Many others have read and contributed comments on this article, including Hugh Armstrong, Jan Barnsley, Naomi Black, Meyer Brownstone, Varda Burstyn, Barbara Cameron, Peter Findlay, Geraldine Finn, David McGregor, Melanie Randall, and Gillian Walker. The editorial advice of Phil Masters made it possible to complete the article at last.
2. The Royal Commission on the Status of Women (1970) recommended the appointment of an advisory council (166), a Women's Program Secretariat in the Privy Council (61), and a women's division in a human rights commission (165). Women's groups were consulted extensively about the development of the Women's Program, and most groups considered the appointment of advisors within the federal bureaucracy a positive step that would increase their access to resources and the policy-making process.
3. See, for example, *10 Years Later (1979)*, the Canadian Advisory Council on the Status of Women's assessment of the state's progress in implementing the recommendations of the Royal Commission. *As Things Stand* (1983) reiterated Council concerns about the lack of progress.
4. This position was advocated by Chaviva Hosek, president of the National Action Committee on the Status of Women, in a public lecture sponsored by the Women's Studies Program of the University of Toronto in March 1986.
5. In previous elections, NAC had sponsored public forums on women's issues with each of the federal leaders. Prime Minister Trudeau refused to participate in these forums. However, he did grant a private consultation with the executive of NAC in 1979 (Ritchie and Cohen 1981).
6. For an understanding of the debates on the role of the state in maintaining women's oppression, see Barrett (1980), Burstyn (1983), Eisenstein (1981),

McIntosh (1978), Laurin-Frenette (1982), Riley (1983), Schirmer (1982), and Wilson (1977).

7. This perspective on the state is best expressed in the work of Nicos Poulantzas (1978).
8. The following description of the development of the representation of women's issues in the state relies almost entirely on my experience in the state bureaucracy between 1972 and 1981, as Program Advisor in the Citizen Participation Program and Director of the Women's Program in the Department of the Secretary of State, Ottawa vice-president of the Canadian Advisory Council on the Status of Women, and policy analyst in the Ministry of State for Social Development.
9. This was the perspective on which the U.S. "War on Poverty" was based. In Canada, a less comprehensive campaign was initiated by the federal government in 1964 with the creation of the Special Planning Secretariat in the Privy Council Office.
10. In the mid- to late 1960s, former student radicals and community activists were hired by the state to integrate the new concept of participatory democracy into federal policies and programs. By 1971, however, these radicals had been defined as subversives by then Solicitor-General Jean-Paul Goyer, who labelled their activities as "extra-parliamentary opposition" and placed them on a blacklist. Both the Director of the Women's Program and the Co-ordinator of Status of Women Canada in the period described were included in this list as a result of previous involvement with the state's participation programs.
11. The first national Women and Politics Conference was held in Toronto, in May 1973.
12. One example of this problem was the attempt made in 1974 to remove me from my position as Director of the Women's Program with the accusation that I was "a crusader for women's rights" and "antagonistic to management."
13. The resistance that women politicians met from the Minister Responsible for the Status of Women in response to their request at the IWY seminar on "Women and Politics" for an official accounting of government progress in implementing the Royal Commission recommendations provided them with stunning proof of the barriers that women still faced in attempting to persuade the state to undertake reforms.

3 Nationalism and Feminism in Quebec: An Impossible Attraction

DIANE LAMOUREUX

The political situation in Quebec after 1980 is often described in left-wing intellectual circles as one of postnationalism.[1] This new conceptualization marks a departure from political analyses of the 1960s and 1970s, when the influence of the national question on all social movements was stressed. The emphasis on nationalism is not meant to suggest that it was the only movement to grow in a spectacular way over the last two decades, but rather to acknowledge its central role in Quebec politics and its influence, direct or indirect, on the ensemble of social movements.

The women's movement which developed at the end of the 1960s could scarcely remain untouched by ongoing struggles for national rights, but it responded in seemingly contradictory ways. The slogans and actions of the Front de libération des femmes (FLF), Quebec's first contemporary feminist group, seem to suggest that they succumbed to the nationalist fervour more easily than any other social movement. And yet, the fact that it was also women who, banded together as "Yvettes,"[2] formed the major popular opposition to the Parti Québécois (PQ) project of sovereignty-association may well lead to the opposite conclusion: nationalism had not struck the same chord in women as it had in men.

Neither of these superficial interpretations, i.e., that women are either "nationalist" or "anti-nationalist," can adequately elucidate the contradictory relationship that has prevailed between the women's movement and nationalism over the last twenty years in Quebec. On the one hand, nationalism provided women with a political vocabulary with which they could analyze their oppression. On the other hand, nationalism has always held a misogynous view of women. There is thus a constant tension at the root of the relationship between the two movements and their corresponding ideologies. In this paper, I analyze this tension and examine some of the possible directions the feminist movement could take in a postnationalist era.

Nationalist Language and the Theoretical Definition of Oppression

In order to understand the language employed by the feminist movement, it is necessary to look at the political traditions it grew out of. Internationally, the two determinant influences were marxism, which analyzed economic oppression, and decolonization/national liberation movements, which were more concerned with extraeconomic forms of domination. For various reasons,[3] nationalism has had a more lasting influence on feminism in Quebec. The definition of oppression found in anti-colonial writings, particularly those of Albert Memmi ([1960] 1972) and Franz Fanon (1961), the most important theoreticians of national liberation movements, was integrally adopted by feminists and applied to the situation of women.

The parallel between national liberation and women's liberation, first drawn by Simone de Beauvoir, has served as a springboard for both French and American radical feminist theory. In *Le deuxième sexe* (translated as *The Second Sex*) de Beauvoir wrote:

> . . . il y a de profondes analogies entre la situation des femmes et celle des Noirs: les unes et les autres s'émancipent aujourd'hui d'un même paternalisme et la caste naguère maîtresse veut les maintenir à "leur place", c'est-à-dire à la place qu'ils ont choisie pour eux: dans les deux cas elle se répand en éloge plus ou moins sincère sur les vertus du "bon Noir" à l'âme inconsciente, enfantine, rieuse, du Noir résigné et de la femme "vraiment femme" c'est-à-dire frivole, puérile, irresponsable, la femme soumise à l'homme. (1968: 27)[4]

This analogy was further developed by Christine Delphy, one of the most important theoreticians of French radical feminism. Her defence of organizational autonomy for the women's movement and her analysis of the process of consciousness raising is based entirely upon an analogy with the self-organization of American blacks. Delphy (1977: 29) argues that oppression is never immediately visible to the oppressed and points out that the first step toward liberation involves shedding the negative self-image, acquired from seeing oneself through the eyes of the oppressor.

> Ce n'est pas un hasard si l'exclusion des Blancs a coincidé et avec la mode afro . . . et avec l'apparition du slogan "Black is beautiful". La non-mixité était la conclusion logique et historique de la lutte contre la haine de soi. Les faits concrets — l'histoire concrète de la lutte, et des noirs et des femmes — comme les implications logiques de la proposition que la libération des opprimés est d'abord, sinon seulement, l'oeuvre des opprimés, amènent à la même conclusion: les oppresseurs ne sauraient jouer le même role dans les luttes de libération que les opprimés![5]

According to Delphy, only by taking the struggle against their own self-hatred as a starting point can women become conscious of their oppression, at first individually, and later on a social scale. In this view, the search for identity is fundamental for any movement seeking to define political goals.

The similarity between Delphy's reasoning and that of Memmi and Fanon is obvious. More recently, Suzanne Blaise (1981), acknowledging their theoretical paternity, defines women as the "Third World" of patriarchy, traces the contemporary feminist awakening to anti-colonial struggles, and rather mechanically selects examples from the recent history of French feminism to illustrate quotes from Fanon and Memmi.

Radical Nationalism and Feminism in Quebec

In Quebec, *Parti Pris*, a left-wing nationalist journal of the sixties, developed and popularized a language of anti-colonialist struggle. The analyses published by *Parti Pris* generally agreed that Quebec's history of colonial oppression had left it in the position of a Third World nation. From this perspective, the strategic objectives of the revolutionary movement were defined as

> . . . le remplacement du pouvoir colonialiste et impérialiste, et du pouvoir de la néo-bourgeoisie par le pouvoir des classes travailleuses. Nous croyons que le chemin qui nous conduira là, c'est celui de la révolution nationale démocratique accomplie sous l'impulsion des classes travailleuses. D'abord, elle passe par la décolonisation, l'un des aspects essentiel, elle est une lutte de libération nationale. (1967: 249)[6]

Just as national liberation struggles in the Third World inspired the radical nationalist movement in Quebec, the FLF was in many ways an outgrowth of radical nationalism. Not only was the vocabulary of decolonization the most readily available, it also appeared to be a foolproof guarantee that the feminist movement was "authentically revolutionary."

One of the most important slogans of the feminist movement in the late 1960s was "Pas de libération des femmes sans Québec libre, pas de Québec libre sans libération des femmes."[7] This slogan not only indicates the importance of the national question in the political radicalization of women, it also shows that feminists saw their struggle, first and foremost, as part of a wider struggle for national liberation.

The *Manifeste des femmes québécoises*, intended as a feminist response to the manifesto of the Front de libération du Québec, also bears witness to the importance of this analytical schema for the feminist movement.

> On doit savoir que nous lutterons pour la libération des femmes à l'intérieur du mouvement révolutionnaire et que nous ne tolérons plus d'être discriminées à l'intérieur même de ce mouvement. Donc, huit mois après le manifeste du Front de libération du Québec, voici le manifeste des femmes. (Collectif 1971: 13)[8]

This document made constant reference to colonialism to explain both relations between women and men and most women's failure to revolt openly against their own oppression. Memmi's typology of the self-destructing colonial, who transforms the impossible revolt against the colonizer into self-hatred, was applied to women. Indeed, the reference to colonialism was so pervasive and automatic that the FLF's daycare cell actually referred to the "struggle for women's national liberation." Narrow nationalism was not, however, a consistent feature of FLF politics.

While the primary goal was "organiser radicalement la prise de conscience féministe," a wider context for women's liberation was emphasized.

> Il devient clair pour nous les femmes qui'il faut faire la révolution si nous voulons que ça change. Ce qui est en jeu, ce n'est pas seulement notre libération mais aussi la libération de notre peuple et de tous les peuples de la terre. (Collectif 1971: 51)[9]

For the most part, the FLF worked simultaneously on three fronts: against national, sexual, and social inequality.

However, nationalist consciousness frequently got the upper hand and eroded the solidarity that was so necessary among the few francophone and anglophone activists who shared the same set of feminist political ideals.

> Parfois, certaines positions ont une teinte nationaliste et déplacent les problèmes en insistant sur les aspects ethniques et culturels de la domination des Québécois: on refuse de travailler avec des femmes anglophones même si elles parlent français et s'orientent dans la même perspective, parce qu'elles sont dans une position dominante par rapport à nous. (Houle 1972: 11)[10]

In spite of a good deal of questioning on the part of its activists whether their primary identity was national or sexual, the FLF proved to be unable to articulate both feminist and nationalist themes in practice. Because most activists saw the feminist struggle as part of a broader struggle for national liberation, their main political goal was to strengthen a radical current within the national movement which would not discriminate against women. The radical nationalist current with which the FLF was ideologically affiliated gradually became less preoccupied with the national question and adopted a more socialist, and ultimately marxist, orientation.

Despite the turn to socialism by sections of the nationalist and feminist movements, the extension of the anti-colonialist metaphor to women proved to be still powerful. With the emergence of a radical feminist current in Quebec in the seventies, the credibility of the parallel between nation and sex was renewed. In an analysis of the common characteristics of the two oppressions, Michèle Jean (1977: 81) compared "féminitude" and "Québécitude":

> La vérité qui est pour le Québec que les Québécois ont vécu dans la Confédération une oppression essentielle et que les femmes ont vécu et vivent dans un monde fait et pensé par les hommes, une oppression essentielle."[11]

In general, however, debates over the relationship between nationalism and feminism were put on the back burner, to become reheated only as the referendum approached. It may seem paradoxical that, during the 1970s, just as the national question became the dominant issue in Quebec politics, it waned in importance for the feminist movement. In order to understand why this is so, it is necessary to examine the evolution of nationalist thought concerning women.

Nationalism and Misogyny

In this section I draw extensively on what Marcel Rioux (1968) called the "idéologie de la survivance" — ideology of survival — to show how traditional thought subordinates women to the goal of national consolidation through the institution of the family. The ideology of survival, partially inspired by the thought of Lionel Groulx (1919) accorded a double importance to the family as the institution responsible for the physiological and cultural reproduction of the nation. At the risk of caricature, let us quickly sketch Groulx's vision of the role of women and the family in the fate of the French Canadian nation.

The cornerstone of the ideology of survival is the myth of national origin. New France was seen as an era of French cultural expansion wiped out by the hideous misfortune of the British conquest, which temporarily coerced the French Canadian people into a state of submission. The darkness of the present was forgotten as traditional nationalism rewrote the past in glorious terms, offering it as a guarantee of a resplendent future. A direct link was posited between the past and the future: the present was obliterated, and along with it the political dimension of the national question was reduced to a mere cultural matter.

A bright future depended on two conditions: first, the maintenance of the specificity of the Québécois nation (which implied a group large enough to resist the pressures of external encroachment), and second, a system to pass culture and tradition from one generation to the next so that this specificity could withstand the test of time. Traditional nationalism identified the family as the institution that could best fulfill these two roles:

> Toutefois, la famille canadienne-française revendique un apanage encore plus glorieux, résultat, lui aussi, de son esprit de foi, de la chasteté de nos moeurs, la famille canadienne-française enfante de l'avenir. (Groulx 1919: 295)[12]

Once the central role of the family had been established, with its implications of a precise role for women, the stage was set for the entire discourse of "la revanche des berceaux" — revenge of the cradle. The French Canadian elite, faced with the dilemma of being a minority in a country that it did not control, chose to adopt a pronatalist policy rather than to formulate a political strategy that would allow it to resolve the national question. The phenomenon of high fertility, "la revanche des berceaux," cannot be interpreted in solely economic or demographic terms, although these factors were influential.

After 1763, when local elites deserted the cities and returned to France, Quebec became a patchwork of isolated rural communities, a process that became even more pronounced with the defeat of 1837–38. Agriculture developed on a small scale and in an autarchical manner outside the networks of commercial exchange. This form of agricultural production required a large labour force; the availability of greater numbers of people would seem to lead to higher productivity and thus decrease the likelihood of entering into relations of external dependence. This observation has led some writers to emphasize the economic importance of the family:

> On constate sans peine que le discours d'ordre politique et religieux, qui encourage la natalité pour des raisons morales et idéologiques . . . ne vient que conférer un sens au second degré, à un procès de reproduction dont la logique première s'inscrit dans ce mode de peuplement et de production agricole. (Laurin-Frenette 1979: 85)[13]

But this kind of economic interpretation neglects the fact that Quebec land was not as fertile as Quebec mothers. A high birthrate combined with poor agricultural output and shortages of arable land led first to emigration and ultimately to assimilation for francophones who left their rural communities for the Canadian west and the U.S.A.

Rather, the ideological role of the family was of greater importance than its economic role in sustaining high birthrates. It was seen as the only institution that was under the nation's complete control, that refused all compromise with foreign domination; it was the key to the future. The revenge of the cradle was both a defensive response to the large influx of immigrants and an assertive policy designed to regenerate the national group. In this context, no societal project was complete without a coherent family policy.

In *Notre maître le passé* (1924: 104–5), Lionel Groulx emphasized that the vocation of "old maid" was outlawed in New France in 1669. A refusal to marry or to procreate was met with fines, while those who complied were financially rewarded. A good French Canadian family was a large one, incomplete without the constant chatter of children. These legal and ideological constraints help explain why New France sustained the highest birthrate of any country of European origin right up to the 1960s.

> Dans un pays où il paraissait nécessaire à la survie d'accroître à un rythme effréné le nombre des enfants, il fut "enjoint" aux femmes de produire des enfants catholiques et français et de les mener elles-mêmes à l'âge adulte ou, si la chose ne leur sourirait pas, de se consacrer au service de Dieu et au soins des malades, des orphelins, des écoliers et des démunis, le célibat laïque étant taxé d'égoisme et d'individualisme. (Jean 1977: 14)[14]

Indeed, the revenge of the cradle proved to be so durable that in the 1960s demographers were still calculating the number of children each francophone family should have to maintain or increase their weight within Quebec and Canada (Henripin et al. 1981). Many members of the Parti Québécois also saw a high birthrate in a positive light. Jacques Grand'Maison (1970: 53) was quite explicit: "Cette expansion démographique tant décriée a joué un rôle des plus positifs dans notre avenir collectif."[15]

Nationalists saw the family not only as the basic unit of society; it was also the microcosm of the nation. Although the nation was oppressed in all other domains, within the structure of the family it could flourish. The maintenance of the family thus became the sine qua non of national survival. This connection serves to explain, in part, why nationalists frequently adopted very reactionary positions on issues affecting women, including, for example, the right to vote and the right to gainful employment. It also explains the nationalist outcry against the federal government's 1925 law legalizing divorce. Even the Fédération Nationale St.-Jean Baptiste (the women's branch of the Société St.-Jean Baptiste), pioneers of the suffrage movement, abandoned their struggle when pressured by religious and nationalist elites (Lavigne, Pinard, and Stoddart 1979). After the Second World War, these same elites campaigned to get women out of the workforce and back to their kitchens, relegating them to the role of full-time housewives.

The overwhelming importance of the family's socializing role went hand in hand with the weakness of Quebec's educational system. As Yolande Pinard (1977: 65) has pointed out, "l'idéologie cléricalo-nationaliste assigne une fonction supplémentaire aux femmes: celle de gardienne de la foi chrétienne, de la langue et des traditions."[16] Language, culture, and tradition, the seeds from which nationalist ideology was cultivated, are all learned first in the family. The ideological importance accorded to women's role as educators, and the periodic absence of husbands who left the homestead to find work, has led some observers to speak of a matriarchy in Quebec.

The idea of a matriarchy is a myth at several levels. Since their prestige was directly proportional to the number of children they produced, women had no value in their own right, but only as mothers. Even as mothers, however, their labour had no intrinsic value, but was seen as instrumental in achieving the greater goal, national survival. The contemporary heritage of this prescription was vividly sketched in Denise Boucher's (1979) portrait of the alienation of a woman who, having undergone repeated pregnancies, could only feel emptiness once deprived of her children.

In a context where the family is perceived as the microcosm of the nation, the mother's role of bearing and rearing children takes on special significance:

> En outre, dans les nations opprimées comme le Québec, l'Irlande et l'Euskadi, et venant renforcer l'idéologie véhiculée par l'Eglise catholique, des arguments nationalistes sont avancés par des représentants de la classe dominante afin de maintenir les femmes "à leur place". Le mythe de la femme/mère comme seul pôle de stabilisation sociale, affective ou politique s'ajoute au puritanisme religieux. (League ouvrière révolutionnaire 1978: 16)[17]

To be "in the family way"—preferably year after year—was the patriotic duty of Québécois womanhood. The Société St.-Jean Baptiste had constant praise for this kind of patriotism from mothers:

> La mère canadienne-française n'est inférieure à aucune autre en héroisme et . . . elle est même supérieure au plus grand nombre. . . . Fortement attachée à la foi catholique, elle donne à l'Eglise et à la Patrie autant de fils vaillants et de filles vigoureuses qu'il plait à la Providence de lui réclamer pour le salut des causes le plus sacrées. (Frechette 1943: 132)[18]

But such acts of faith in the procreative will of the French Canadian mother and her seemingly important role in the family should not lead to the conclusion that there was a matriarchy in Quebec. On the contrary, she was deprived of her most basic rights:

> L'immobilisme où se trouvait alors la société canadienne-français depuis trois générations n'allait certes pas inciter les législateurs à innover dans les structures familiales et matrimoniales. Le double principe de la puissance maritale et paternelle fut établi dont la principale conséquence fut l'incapacité juridique de la femme mariée. (Dumont-Johnson 1968: 15)[19]

As for the maternal role in the transmission of national values, it was a profoundly dominated one. The words of women were of importance only when they echoed the discourse of the church and the educational system which were, and still are, for all intents and purposes, the same. Women did indeed play a vital role in the transmission of ideology, but they had no input into what they taught. They merely repeated and amplified in the home a discourse defined by clerical nationalists. Just as she "kept" her husband's house, she "kept" an ideology that was not her own:

> Il nous semble cependant que l'autorité spécifique de la femme, dans la famille, vient surtout du fait que c'est à partir de cette place qu'est assurée l'articulation structurelle de l'unité familiale à l'Eglise comme appareil général de contrôle et de reproduction. Le discours de la mère est celui du curé et c'est à ce titre qu'il s'impose à la famille, y compris au père. C'est d'ailleurs à ce titre que la femme a accès à la lecture et à l'écriture. (Laurin-Frenette 1979: 86)[20]

The notion of a Quebec matriarchy is also inadequate precisely because its limited perspective on women in the family failed to consider either their situation outside the family or the place of the domestic sphere in the hierarchy of social values. Nationalist ideology was founded upon a strict separation of powers which originated with the distinction between the Kingdom of Caesar and the Kingdom of God in the Catholic interpretation of the New Testament. Women's domain is the household and the family, while men are charged with the matters of the public world. Nationally, this division translated into reserving agriculture and the liberal professions for francophones, while allowing industry and commerce to remain in anglophone hands.

This strict separation of spheres of activity found its most systematic expression in Henri Bourassa's ideological definition of difference. In his view, even if the two spheres were complementary, one must in any case provide leadership for the other. Just as the Kingdom of God is ultimately paramount to that of Caesar, the world of men dominates the world of women. Thus, even when the father is absent, he remains head of the household:

> A vrai dire, la seule fonction réservée au père dans la famille, c'est l'autorité. Il ne s'occupe de rien autre si ce n'est d'être le pourvoyeur attitré, et l'éducation des enfants n'est pas fondamentalement de son ressort, mais il dirige tout de même. (Gagnon 1974a: 24)[21]

The PQ or the Attempt to Modernize Tradition

The Parti Québécois, as both the hegemonic leader of the modern nationalist movement and the governing party, combined traditional nationalism with a specific political conception of modernization. Although the PQ was able to propose a political alternative to the national question that went beyond folklore and culture, its development was very uneven, and disparate elements continued to exist within péquiste ideology. Traditionalism weighed heavily, particularly with reference to women and to the education system.

Although it has evolved over the years, the PQ's program has consistently expounded a conception of women's social role that has little in common with feminism. The 1970 version particularly marginalized women, who were only discussed in the chapter on "The Family and Childhood." There, the old themes of traditional nationalism were rehashed:

> Cellule de base de toute société, la famille subit présentement, chez nous comme ailleurs, non seulement les secousses et les mutations d'une époque proprement révolutionnaire, mais également toute l'insécurité qui découle de l'absence d'une politique familiale digne de ce nom. L'une de nos grandes priorités sera donc, après l'avoir défini en association avec les principaux groupements familiaux, d'instaurer et d'appliquer une telle politique dont plusieurs des préoccupations essentielles sont d'ailleurs d'une évidence aveuglante et d'une urgence fort douleureuse. (PQ 1970: 75)[22]

Once again, women were recognized solely for their roles as mothers and as wives, within the classical nuclear family structure, and not as individuals in their own right. Within this view, all discrimination against women was expected to magically disappear with the revision of family law, the extension of government grants to family planning associations, the establishment of a network of daycare centres and mothers' help, and welfare allowances for single mothers.

By 1979, the overall tone of the PQ's program had changed to accommodate the modernization of women into a dual role of worker and housewife-mother. The Conseil du Statut de La Femme (CSF), an advisory body established in 1973, was central to this development. Although created before the Parti Québécois came to power, it was only with their election in 1976 that it took on real importance, marked by a budget increase from $225,400 in 1974–75 to $1,500,000 in 1979–80. In the wake of the CSF's 1978 report *Egalité et indépendance*,[23] women were recognized as a disadvantaged social group, and several new recommendations were adopted by the party. But its "women's rights" perspective remained inextricably tied to the family and was primarily designed to ease women's maternal and familial roles, which the contradictory imperatives of paid employment and motherhood in modern society have made more difficult to fulfill.

But this relatively recent emphasis on modernization did not mean that the PQ had made a definitive break with traditional nationalism. When a political party is in power, it is more reasonable to judge it on the basis of its concrete policies rather than its programmatic intentions. The ideological ambiguity of the PQ was manifested in government policy. Although its political weight has declined, the presence of the CSF appeases the more modern factions of the party, while increased measures to keep the birthrate up — parental leave, housing assistance, tax credits — satisfy the traditionalists.

But even in its modernizing aspect, the PQ's role cannot be interpreted in an entirely positive light; its intentions are hardly innocent. It has used governmental and paragovernmental institutions — most importantly the CSF — to promote a view of women's liberation which presupposes that the solution to sexual inequality lies in appropriate legislation. This view was held by Quebec's former minister responsible for the status of women, among others:

> Il y avait longtemps, en 1976, que j'avais constaté qu'en dehors de la crise profonde des mentalités, la solution à nombre de problèmes identifiés par les femmes quant à leur statut inférieur se trouvait dans les parlements. Egalité juridique, égalité des chances au travail comme dans l'éducation, contrôle de la santé et accès aux services qui favorisent l'autonomie des femmes comme les garderies et les congés de maternité, les solutions était souvent à Québec. (Payette 1982: 60)[24]

Apart from legislative gains, the major function of the CSF has proved to be the co-optation of women's demands. This has been accomplished through the intermediary of one of its services, "Consult-Action," which distributes information and provides technical assistance to autonomous women's groups. The CSF is well aware that it only has power to the extent that its demands are backed up by an organized women's movement and that its major strength lies in translating grassroots demands into government policy. Even though its co-optative role has had a negative impact, it is important to remember that women themselves fought for the establishment of institutions like the CSF. The pivotal role played by the state during the Quiet Revolution has meant that most, if not all, social movements active in the subsequent period have continued to address their demands to the provincial government. A glance at the demands of the feminist movement over the last decade is illustrative of this practice. The state has been asked to take over the establishment of daycare services, to legislate maternity leave and equal pay for work of equal value, to legalize abortion, and so on.

When at long last the state answered these demands, it did so on its own terms, leading some observers to refer to state feminism, positing a fundamental agreement between the National Assembly and women's groups:

> Si le fait féministe est, chez nous, partiellement nié et partiellement récupéré (un ministre, oui; des femmes, non), il jouit, au Québec,

> d'un statut officiel: il ne s'exprime pas seulement dans la prise de conscience et les luttes des femmes; il est aussi pris en charge par l'Etat. Un consensus minimum paraît exister entre le mouvement des femmes et le pouvoir politique sur la nécessité d'en finir avec le sexisme, de promouvoir les droits des femmes et de permettre à chacune d'accéder à son plein épanouissement. (Dhavernas 1981: 1902)[25]

A Fatal Attraction

At first glance, it seems difficult to understand why the feminist movement tried so hard to define itself with respect to nationalism, particularly considering the misogynous aspects of the latter. This effort seems even more surprising in light of the totalizing forms nationalism took in Quebec, negating the very existence of separate interests based on one's sex or class.

As I have tried to show, contemporary nationalism lies at the crossroads of the traditionalism challenged by the Quiet Revolution and the modernity that was its result. Thus, as far as women are concerned, modern nationalist ideology valorizes the institution of motherhood at the same time as, in line with its modernizing role, it supports women's rights to gainful employment and free choice on abortion. This ideological ambiguity was brought out in all its colours in the campaign preceding the referendum. Sporadic convergences between the two movements must then be seen within this context of modernization; first, through the left-wing vision of the radical nationalist movement in the 1960s, and later, through the PQ's project of a nation-state. But whatever hopes the feminist movement had concerning modernization were crushed when the referendum was lost.

Publicly, the PQ showed its commitment to an image of "the liberated woman"—that is, the one who has a job and the identity of an individual that goes along with it—by its choice of Lise Payette as Minister Responsible for the Status of Women. But as we have seen, in its program and in its reticence to enact some of its recommendations, the conservative influence of traditional nationalism can still be felt. This ambiguity became explicit in the PQ's respone to the Yvettes' movement.

> Je me suis longtemps demandé pourquoi ce n'est pas le PQ qui a pris à son compte Travail-Patrie-Famille. Du moins en toute logique ç'aurait été plus "normal", plus cohérent puisqu'il est sensé représenter le nationalisme le plus fort. Mais je sais maintenant que la réponse est simple: les femmes du Parti québécois ne les ont pas lâchés d'un pouce. (Lacelle 1980: 15)[26]

The resistance of the Yvettes should be seen in the light of these ambiguities and not simply as an anti-feminist backlash, as Lise Bissonnette (1980)[27] would have it. It seems more accurate to me to interpret the movement as a refusal of any one single model of "the liberated woman," that is, the woman who takes on the double load, who earns her living "like a man," without, however, in any way compromising her femininity. But more importantly, the movement represented a refusal to accept the contempt of politicians, a contempt that was justified in the name of modernization.

What was surprising about the Yvettes was not their rapid constitution as a movement, but rather the way the Liberal Party was able to exploit them for its own ends while the PQ stood helplessly by. Nor is there anything particularly astounding about the Liberal Party's opportunist exploitation of the rejection of modernist ideologies by a significant layer of women, for this is entirely in conformity with the rules of the political game. But the PQ has rarely been caught unarmed for a counterattack, and this is what requires explanation. In this regard, its actions in the postreferendum period are enlightening.

First, the PQ politely thanked Lise Payette, who did not run in the next election, for her services, since she was too closely identified with modernizing the status of women. Second, it blatantly set out on the road to promoting the family and maternal productivity. If the PQ did not strike out any harder at the Yvettes, it is not because they were unarmed, but because they were preparing a subsequent policy turnabout. In this sense, Payette's blunder, and the popular reaction to it, actually reinforced the position of the traditionalists within the party.

The final consequence of the defeat of sovereignty-association was to splinter the political forces which had been united for so many years around a single goal, the construction of a national state. With the shattering of this goal, and the development of serious divisions within its socio-political basis of support, many of the PQ's more modern policies were considerably watered down. And this also constitutes the basis of the 1985 split from the Parti Québécois and its subsequent defeat at the 1985 provincial elections.

Contemporary feminism suffers from a similar ideological balance in many respects. Here, however, the tension does not lie between traditionalism and modernization, but between modernization and autonomy. Although some struggles have been fought in the name of equality with men in a collective process of modernization, others have aimed, in the name of autonomy, to articulate the specificity of women, within both socio-political and private worlds in order to ultimately transcend the limits between those worlds.

The fragmentation of the Quebec political scene since the referendum has made it necessary for feminism, as for other social movements, to develop its theoretical foundations away from the scope of nationalism. But the demarcation is harder to achieve for feminism since it was the only social movement to share so pervasively not only a language but a whole problematic with nationalism.

It is thus time to break away from the political tradition of decolonization, and begin to question the very notion of "women's oppression." That does not mean that women are not oppressed, but it seems increasingly reductionist to claim that all women suffer the same oppression. We must speak, instead, of several oppressions, not in terms of different epiphenomenal manifestations or "classical" class differences, but rather by recognizing that there is a complex system in which different forms of domination overlap. No longer sharing a political vocabulary with our oppressors will at least give us the possibility of going beyond the simplistic and trite, to asking whether the terms we use allow us to advance theoretically and practically.

We must also break from the nationalism/feminism analogy, which has contributed to what Ti-Grace Atkinson (1984) has called feminine nationalism. The use of this analytical parallel has brought some tendencies within the feminist movement to search for a single feminine identity, rather than looking at the plural, multifarious nature of women's existence.

This search for identity, as opposed to a political affirmation of women's experiences, is nationalist in the sense that it develops a merely essentialist vision of women's nature as a new way to explain some political positions taken by women. For example, women are "by virtue of nature" expected to be pacifist, sensitive to ecological issues, critical of the industrial work ethic, etc. . . .

For the last years, Quebec feminism has been undergoing profound change: many questions are being asked, but answers are less numerous. There are some promising signs that feminist problematic is being renewed in various directions. The existence of a radical lesbian tendency, for example, which has broken with the search for a universal feminine identity in order to concentrate its efforts on "sex/class" confrontation, provides a counterweight to essentialist views.

Now that nationalism no longer monopolizes the political stage, the possibility exists for other social movements to take their place. Feminism, although it does not represent a universal solution to all forms of domination, is more than a movement representing the interests of a specific social group. A real break with nationalism and a critique of its conceptual categories increases the likelihood that feminism will contribute in a significant way to radical social change.

Notes

1. Postnationalism refers to a fragmented political situation in which nationalism no longer plays a unifying role; see Serge Proulx and Pierre Vallières (1983).
2. A little background is in order for readers not familiar with these events. During the campaign preceding the 1980 referendum, Lise Payette, then minister responsible for the status of women, made a speech in which she pointed out that children learn sexist stereotypes from school textbooks and

read an excerpt in which traditional masculine and feminine roles were played out by the characters "Guy" and "Yvette."

She then accused the Liberal Party of wanting all women to be Yvettes (good little housewives) and disparagingly applied the label to Madeline Ryan (the wife of Claude Ryan, then leader of the Quebec Liberal Party), a statement retracted shortly afterwards in the National Assembly.

The Liberals exploited news coverage of her blunder to mobilize women under the federalist banner. After a hundred well-known women proclaimed themselves "Yvettes," the "No" forces organized a huge public rally in Montreal attended by some 14,000 women.

3. Most women saw the feminist movement as part of the left until 1975–76. At the time of the FLF (1969–72), the Quebec left was mostly radical nationalist, strongly influenced by decolonization struggles (Cuba, Algeria). Feminists defined themselves in relation to radical nationalism, theorizing their own political struggle in anticolonial terms. After 1972, when the left distanced itself from the PQ, the Centre des femmes was strongly influenced by marxism. But as the subsequently stalinized left denounced feminism as a petty bourgeois deviation, as the influence of radical feminism grew and feminist practice changed, marxism's influence declined. There was then a tendency to return to political, as opposed to economic, concepts to analyze the oppression of women.
4. Translation:

   > . . . there are deep similarities between the situation of women and that of blacks: both are emancipating themselves today from a like paternalism and the former master class wishes to keep them in "their place" — that is, the place chosen for them. In both cases, the former masters lavish more or less sincere eulogies, either on the virtues of "the good Negro" with his unconscious, childish, merry soul — the resigned, submissive Negro — and on the merits of the "truly feminine" woman — that is, frivolous, infantile, irresponsible — the submissive woman. (cf. de Beauvoir [1949] 1968: xxvii)

5. Translation:

   > It is not mere chance that the exclusion of whites coincides with the popularity of the afro and the slogan "Black is beautiful." Unmixed organization was the logical historical conclusion of the struggle against self-hatred. The concrete facts — the concrete struggle of both Blacks and women — and the logical implications of the proposition that the liberation of the oppressed is, first if not uniquely, the work of the oppressed themselves, lead to the same conclusion: the oppressors would not know how to play the same role as the oppressed in their struggle for liberation.

6. Translation:

   > . . . the replacement of the colonialist, imperialist, and neo-bourgeois power by the power of the working classes. We believe that the

way to achieve this goal is through a democratic national revolution, accomplished under the impetus of the working classes. The first step of this revolution is decolonization, an essential aspect of the struggle for national liberation.

7. Translation:

   No women's liberation without a free Quebec; no free Quebec without the liberation of women.

8. Translation:

   We must know that we are fighting for the liberation of women within the revolutionary movement, and we will no longer tolerate discrimination against us within this movement. Therefore, eight months after the manifesto of the FLQ, here is the manifesto of women.

9. Translation:

   It has become clear for us women that we must make a revolution if we want things to change. It is not only the liberation of women that is at stake, but the liberation of our people and all the peoples of the world.

10. Translation:

    Occasionally, some positions have a nationalist tinge, and displace the problem by insisting on the ethnic or cultural aspects of the domination of the Quebecois: we have refused to work with anglophone women, even when they speak French and share our political perspective, because they are in a position of domination over us.

11. Translation:

    The truth is that the Quebecois have lived an essential oppression within confederation, and women have lived and still live an essential oppression in a world made and thought out by men.

12. Translation:

    All the same, the French Canadian family assumes an even more glorious apanage, the result of its faithful spirit, the chastity of our morals: the French Canadian family begets the future.

13. Translation:

    One can see without difficulty that the pronatalist political and religious discourse which encourages a high birthrate for moral and ideological reasons . . . only further rationalizes a process of reproduction whose primary logic lies in population policies compatible with the organization of agriculture.

14. Translation:

    In a country whose very survival seemed to depend upon keeping up a frantic birthrate, women were "called upon" to produce French Catholic children, and to bring them up to adulthood, where, if they were not happy with the system, they could consecrate themselves to the service of God, caring for the sick, orphans, school children, and the poor, secular celibacy being taxed with egoism and individualism.

15. Translation:

    This much-decried demographic expansion has played a most positive role in our collective future.

16. Translation:

    The clerico-nationalist ideology assigns women a supplementary function: they are the guardians of the Christian faith, language, and tradition.

17. Translation:

    In oppressed nations such as Quebec, Ireland, and Euskadi, nationalist arguments are used by the dominant classes to keep women "in their place," thereby strengthening Catholic ideology. Religious puritanism is thus appended by the myth of the woman/mother, as the only source of social, emotional, and political stability.

18. Translation:

    The heroism of the French Canadian mother is no less than any other and . . . she herself is superior to most. Strong in her Catholic faith, she has provided the Church and the Fatherland with as many valiant sons and vigorous daughters that Providence has seen fit to ask of her in gratitude of the most sacred causes.

19. Translation:

    The immobility of French Canadian society for three generations was certainly not going to provoke legislators into reforming the legal structures of the family or marriage. The double principle of matrimonial and paternal power was well established, and its main result was the total legal incapacity of the married woman.

20. Translation:

    It seems to us, however, that the specific authority of women in the family comes from the fact that her position there assures the structural articulation of the family to the Church as the general apparatus of control and reproduction. The discourse of the mother is really that of the priest, which explains how this discourse is imposed on the family, including the father. This link between the family and the Church is, incidentally, all that allowed women to read and write.

21. Translation:

    Should the truth be known, the only real function of the father is authority. He does nothing other than act as the official breadwinner, and, although the education of the children is out of his hands, he directs it all the same.

22. Translation:

    The family, the basic cell of all societies, in Quebec as elsewhere is being shaken and transformed by a revolutionary era. It is also knowing all the insecurity that follows from the absence of a

> family policy worthy of the name. One of the greatest priorities therefore will be, in association with the major family groups, to formulate and apply such a policy, the preoccupations of which are blindly evident and painfully urgent.

23. *Egalité et indépendance* was the CSF's report on the status of women submitted to the PQ government in 1978. The title signifies the double perspective of modernization (equality) and women's autonomy (independence). It is also a play on words, for Daniel Johnson, when premier of Quebec, had used the phrase "equality *or* independence" in negotiations with the federal government.

24. Translation:

> I had already known for a long time, in 1976, that apart from the deep crisis of mentalities, the solution to a good number of problems women had identified as stemming from their inferior status was to be found in government. Legal equality, equality of access to the workplace and to education, control of our health and access to services which help women become more autonomous such as daycare and maternity leave: the solutions to these problems were often in Quebec City.

25. Translation:

> If feminism is partially denied and partially co-opted in Quebec (a minister, yes; women, no) it does enjoy official status: it is not only expressed in the consciousness and struggles of women, it is also, to a certain extent, taken into hand by the state. There seems to be a minimal consensus between the women's movement and the political power about the necessity to put an end to sexism, to promote the rights of women, allowing each woman to fully reach her potential.

26. Translation:

> I had wondered for a long time why the PQ never made use of the Work-Family-Fatherland trinity. For logically at least, this would have been the most "normal" and coherent choice, representing, as it does, the strongest nationalism. But I now know the answer is simple: the women in the PQ would never have let them get away with it.

27. Bissonnette's scathing editorial in *Le Devoir*, Montreal's most respected daily newspaper, castigating Payette for her blunder helped to instigate the Yvettes movement.

4 Socialist Feminism and the Politics of Sexuality[1]

LORNA WEIR

Introduction

The positioning of sexual politics within the theory and group practice of socialist feminism has a complex history. During the late 1970s and early 1980s, socialist feminists in Canada for the most part regarded sexual politics, that is, organized resistance to dominant social forms of sexual regulation, as outside the terrain of socialist feminism, or at best as an afterthought. Since about 1982, the relation of sexual politics to socialist feminism has changed, for many Canadian socialist feminists have participated in the "sex debates" which to date have been principally concerned with the regulation of "pornography," the sex trade, and sexual pleasure. However, we have not, for a variety of reasons, engaged in these controversies as socialist feminists, and thus the lasting significance of the "sex debates" for socialist feminist politics remains unclear.

I wish to argue that sexual politics be permanently integrated into socialist feminist theory and practice, an aim motivated by my own situation as a lesbian who has been active in lesbian, gay, and socialist feminist groups. The place of sexual politics in relation to socialist feminism is connected with some of the fundamental problems of developing a holistic socialist feminist politic. Because sexuality and sexual regulation are not directly managed and controlled by capital, they cannot be interpreted *solely* on the basis of class-theoretical or capital-theoretical analysis. Thus, to claim sexual politics for socialist feminism is inevitably to address a tension in socialist feminism between its class and non-class "popular democratic" aspects. "Popular" or "popular democratic" politics refers to cross-class movements which organize against forms of social oppression; such forms of oppression are not exclusively determined by exploitation arising from production relations. Here I will maintain that rather subtle variants of class reductionism, a political practice based on the proposition that all inegalitarian social relations and social forms derive from and are reducible to class relations, have handicapped socialist feminist understanding of popular democratic politics — of which sexual politics is but one example.

Introducing the concept of popular democratic politics into the vocabulary of socialist feminism is crucial to its growth. If we are to become the majority current within the women's movement we need to address all aspects of gender subordination, rather than simply those which are neglected by other feminist approaches. This is not to say that we should not bring a class analysis to all issues — we do, or at least we have the potential to do so. But developing a non-reductionist class analysis of sexual politics requires some restructuring of our conceptual framework; to elucidate this necessary restructuring is the aim of this essay.

My standpoint throughout is based on the principle that there are *multiple* ethical sexual practices and ethical sexual preferences. Lesbian/gay sex and heterosexuality are thus understood as equally legitimate types of sexual desire. I nowhere undertake a "lesbian educational" to justify lesbianism for heterosexual readers. Should some readers need a fuller discussion of why sexual pluralism is ethically and politically principled, they might refer to Mariana Valverde's recent, thorough discussion in *Sex, Power and Pleasure* (Valverde 1985), Chapter 3, "Lesbianism: A Country that Has No Language" (75–108), and Chapter 7, "Pleasure and Ethics" (177–206), together with an article jointly written by Leo Casey and myself, "Subverting Power in Sexuality" (Weir and Casey 1984).

The Positioning of Sexual Politics in Socialist Feminism

In the last ten years, two broad phases can be distinguished in the positioning of sexual politics with respect to socialist feminism. The first phase, which occurred after the "sexual revolution" of the late 1960s and early 1970s (see Maroney and Luxton this volume), lasted in Canada from the mid-1970s to about 1982. During this period sexual politics was seen as a lesbian interest marginal to socialist feminism. This marginalization affected both poles of sexual politics, namely issues arising from sexual danger (rape, sexual assault and harassment, incest, violence against women) and issues involved in exploring the politics of sexual pleasure and female desire (Vance 1984).

The politics of sexual pleasure were peripheral to feminism as a whole in this period, with the exception of lesbian feminism. However, sexual violence was analyzed extensively and adopted as an issue by radical feminists and many liberal feminists. The founders of rape crisis centres and anti-pornography groups generally belonged to the radical feminist current of the women's movement, while theorists such as Ti-Grace Atkinson (1974), Susan Brownmiller (1975), Andrea Dworkin (1979), and later Catherine MacKinnon (1982, 1983a) analyzed masculine violence as the major shaper of sexual and gender oppression. Socialist feminists often argued that these theories were misguided in their singling out of masculinity (or even biological maleness) as *the* cause of women's oppression. Many socialist feminists also thought that theorizing heterosexuality as an unambiguous site of women's oppression did not deal adequately with the complexities of many women's desire and experience. Yet socialist feminists did not offer any alternative analyses of rape, violence against women, sexual harassment, or sexist cultural forms in this period. There was, I recall, much grumbling but little overt challenging of radical feminism on these topics.

During the mid- to late 1970s radical feminists tended to be in the forefront of feminist work on sexual violence, and lesbian feminists dominated discussion of the politics of sexual pleasure, frequently presenting lesbianism as the only valid sexual preference for women on the grounds that it furthered women's autonomy and prevented the submergence of feminist critique through personal "identification" with men. This attack on heterosexuality appears overstated in hindsight, but it should be remembered that many women, especially young women, initially experience feminism as jeopardizing their caring and sexual desire for men and do not understand that they can combine a critical analysis of gender with heterosexual preference. Older women understand far more readily than young women that desire need not be blind.

Many lesbian feminists subscribed to radical feminism, as for instance the "Radicalesbians," who produced the 1970 manifesto "The Woman-Identified Woman" (Radicalesbians 1973). In contrast, socialist feminists, whatever their sexual orientation, could not subscribe to the politics of woman-identification or lesbian separatism, which presented male domination as the only social oppression to be resisted, and which ruled out working with men under any conditions, frequently in favour of developing a distinct "women's culture." For socialist feminists, cross-gender alliances are essential to the liberation of women because only in alliance with socialists and other progressive groups such as the peace and anti-racist movements will women be able to end class domination. Indeed, all social movements other than the women's movement require cross-gender alliances internally; a feminism which does not understand this will always lack allies and be politically marginal and *de facto* elitist.

While some lesbian feminists were constructing a lesbian sexual politic which, while not always separatist, did not leave much room for work in conjunction with oppressed groups composed of both men and women, socialist feminists reacted rather defensively to the possibility of developing any lesbian sexual politic. They often perceived politically active lesbians to be in constant danger of sinking into the pit of separatism. This meant that socialist feminist lesbians experienced a sharp conflict. Some chose to work primarily in lesbian or gay organizations, where they often felt uneasy with strategies based on a lack of class analysis and the prevalence of the necessary but insufficient concepts of "lesbian pride" or "gay pride" (on the limitations of gay/lesbian pride, see Valverde 1983a). Others continued to work in socialist feminist organizations but felt pressured to prove themselves as "good," that is, socialist and non-separatist, lesbians. Some heterosexual socialist feminists added to this strain with comments which implicitly construed socialist feminism as a politic for *heterosexual* women.

In a 1981 interview with the *University of Toronto Women's Newsmagazine* Sheila Rowbotham, a prominent early socialist feminist, was asked, "how do lesbian rights fit into the theory and practice of socialist feminism?" Her answer was interesting in that it avoided the question altogether:

> Lesbian women have always been involved in socialist feminism and they've argued that while they're fighting for lesbian women, that lesbianism *isn't* an answer to everybody's situation, and also lesbian love and desire *isn't* something that exists *without* being affected by some of capitalist relationships and sexism. They've been intent on *not asserting* lesbianism as an alternative for everybody. (Raymer and Beyerie 1981: 3; emphasis added)

After so many negations, one might wonder if socialist feminist lesbians had to spend all their time apologizing and making heterosexual women comfortable, and why.

Rowbotham's was not an idiosyncratic statement; compare Varda Burstyn's very similar comments in *Fuse* magazine:

> Women *do* experience oppression at the hands of men (although not equally from all men). . . . But . . . I've come to see how much men pay in emotional, spiritual and sexual terms for these particular "privileges". I think that heterosexual women can speak about this now and they should. There are also many lesbian women who recognize the humanity of men — Barbara Hammer is one, but there are many others. And there are many lesbians who have become socialist feminists for this very reason. (Steele 1982; emphasis in original)

To say that "many lesbians recognize the humanity of men" implies that there are many others who do not, a blatantly anti-lesbian statement compounded by Burstyn's obvious difficulty in naming more than one such "good" lesbian. (Hammer is an experimental filmmaker from the U.S.) Moreover, lesbians who become socialists do so not because they happen to like men but because, in congruity with heterosexual women, their analysis leads them to the considered opinion that women's liberation requires the abolition of capital.

Such statements create a category of "good" lesbians, assimilate those lesbians who are socialist feminists (because they don't mind men?) into it, and implicitly distinguish the "good" from the "bad" lesbians who are found elsewhere — lesbian bars, perhaps. Both of the above remarks evaded the central issue: how to theorize the oppression of a particular social group and to assist its defence. This avoidance was symptomatic of a general poverty in socialist feminist sex-political discourse and practice in the late 1970s and early 1980s. The focus of socialist feminism continued to be the relations between gender and class, with emphasis on wage and domestic labour.

Class Reductionism

Within the prevailing dualistic framework of socialist feminism, sexual politics and class politics have been posed as being at opposite poles. At the level of political action, there have been tensions and confrontations between trade union demands and the taking up of issues such as discrimination against lesbians or sexual violence; at the theoretical level, the contest is a predictable struggle between economism (a view that the working class alone will lead anti-capitalist struggle, and that this class is politicized only on the basis of workers' direct experience of exploitation at the site of production) and cultural deviationism (the view that cultural struggles external to class organizing provide the cutting edge of emancipatory politics). An extreme example of these tensions occurred during the 1982 Toronto preparations for International Women's Day, when members of the Community Party of Canada incorrectly told immigrant women's groups that the organizing committee for the Day was dominated by lesbians whose only concern was sexuality, as opposed to the CPC's own true-blue class politics. Socialist feminists are rarely this crude (or this manipulative) but we do tend to plug the vast gap between the marxist theory of the laws of motion of capital and the theory of a capitalist *society* with the handy plug of class reductionism. Let me make a few remarks on class reductionism within socialism before turning to its place in socialist feminism.

Class reductionism envisages all forms of domination as caused and explained by class exploitation. One of its assumptions is that all oppressed groups will be liberated through the abolition of class domination. A danger of class reductionism is its cheerful presumption that the socialist revolution will necessarily lead to reproductive rights for women or freedom of sexual orientation, presumptions we know to be false, not the least evidence coming from the Soviet and Chinese cases. The liberation of the working class may provide the best political opportunity for other types of liberation, but the link between the two is not automatic.

Class reductionism constructs ideology or discourse as an expression of class relations. Class is the "truth" behind appearances. As Chantal Mouffe put it, this kind of politic assumes that "all subjects are class subjects; that each class has a paradigmatic ideology; and that each ideological element has a necessary class belonging" (Laclau and Mouffe 1982: 94). Thus it treats nationalism, for example, as invariably representing the interest of the bourgeoisie, or birth control as a plot against the working class. Yet the ideological meaning of a demand for birth control shifts dramatically depending on the way it is articulated to a class politic: birth control has no fixed class location. Socialists in nineteenth-century England and France understood "family limitation" as a Malthusian trick to decrease their numbers and accommodate the working class to capital; for contemporary working-class women in Canada birth control often means the ability to plan childbearing and work, and to provide a material basis for heterosexual pleasure (for more on the differing class meanings of birth control, see Petchesky 1984). A class reductionist view of ideology cannot explain how the class meanings of a particular ideological element can and do vary because it "explains" the relation between class and other social forms (such as gender) by assuming that class is always and everywhere more fundamental. Class reductionism subordinates all struggles to the contradiction between labour and capital. The most common outcome of this perspective is to take up a particular struggle in order to demonstrate that its ultimate basis lies in class relations and to persuade members of social movements, whether women, ethnic minorities, or ecologists, that they *ought* to be setting out to "smash capital" instead.

In the Leninist tradition the link between class and popular democratic struggles is made as follows: oppression divides the working class, for instance by pitting men against women or whites against blacks, and in order to build a united working class these internal contradictions must be overcome. A deft move: non-class contradictions are recognized and then immediately subordinated to class politics. Lenin himself was deeply ambivalent about popular democratic politics, and could never quite free himself from the misconception that they were a species of bourgeois mystification. His writings on popular democratic politics theorize their significance only in terms of their utility to class struggle.

From the standpoint of feminism, class appears as a particular social form contributing to the social organization of women's gender inequality. Similarly, from the standpoint of class analysis, gender is a particular social form determinant of class organization. Both socialist and women's movements have tended historically to deny their own internal contradictions. Within socialism, suppression of the gender contradiction perpetuates masculine domination inside its organizations and within the working class; suppression of class contradictions tends to exclude working-class women and their interests from the women's movement. These parallels are obvious; more difficult is the question whether a socialist feminism which considers women's demands solely in terms of working-class women can ever be adequate for women's liberation. Such a viewpoint effectively understands women's oppression as a qualification/specification of class, without asking how women's oppression in general is organized. Reducing specific oppressions to qualifications of class eliminates the collective standpoints of these groups and hence the collective experiences that these standpoints articulate.

It would be simplistic to attribute all socialist errors in dealing with popular movements to this type of class reductionism. There are important distortions of the experience of oppressed groups other than those caused by the elusive search for the class truth about popular movements. For feminists, one important distortion concerns the marxist theory of the family, as elaborated in Engels's influential work *The Origin of the Family, Private Property and the State*. Rosalind Coward has pointed out that in this much-read work

> the family is theorized as an economic structure which unites the sexes. . . . The analytical priority of the family subsumed any separate consideration of the division between the sexes as an antagonistic division. . . . Engels made the position of women synonymous with the family. It was this which gave the women's question such a ready place within marxism but which blocked any real theorisation of women or any real acceptance of the centrality of transforming sexual relations. (Coward 1983: 155, 186)

The hypothesized homogeneity of economic interests within "the family" enabled Engels to make families the bearers of a single interest — a class interest. Gender struggle thus magically vanished, while working-class women were told that their liberation would follow on the heels of the abolition of private property.

Thus, a socialist feminist politic must criticize not only class reductionism and economism as distinct tendencies within the socialist tradition, but, perhaps more radically, it must pry apart the syntactical rules governing the conceptual linkages in the grammar of classical marxism. Class reductionism is not a single idea which can be conveniently excised from socialist theory; rather, it is a complex tendency resulting from quasi-axiomatic alignments in its discursive structure. Thus, my critique of class reductionism seeks neither to destroy socialism nor to scrutinize it for those bits that are rotten and must be thrown out; rather, the goal is to rectify the distortions caused by major absences and to help to produce a class and gender politic which will better inform the practice of all socialists.

Socialist Feminism and Class Reductionism

Within socialist feminism, class reductionism (understood in the broad sense sketched above) has taken more benign forms than in the wider left. Its main effect has been to create an internal hierarchy of issues, with those issues having the most apparent class content at the top and those with the least at the bottom. One gets many points for helping to organize a support picket for striking women workers, but few for putting together a lesbian conference.

This ranking scheme is partly inherited by socialist feminists from socialism, but it is also a result of an effective division of labour in the Canadian women's movement as a whole. Socialist feminists work on class-related issues (like equal pay) and coalition politics with other social movements (like trade unions and Third World support groups). Radical feminists are supposed to be active around violence against women, women's culture, and feminist group "process." The hierarchy of issues in these two currents of the women's movement are thus inverted images of one another. (Meanwhile, of course, liberal feminists are thought to be too busy lobbying and promoting their career interests to worry much about any of the political issues listed above.) Although this sketch reflects stereotypes about the various currents of feminism, there is a real historical basis for the stereotypes, as we have seen in the kinds of activities they have actually undertaken and the theory they have produced.

Through the marginalization of sexual politics, the position of lesbians in socialist feminism has been negatively affected. Without claiming that the politics of heterosexism and homophobia are of equal significance to the women's movement/socialist feminism as the politics of women's labour, waged and unwaged, one can still conclude that the *impossibility* of understanding the social organization of lesbian oppression and developing a politic supportive of lesbian needs from a socialist feminist perspective is symptomatic of a very serious flaw in socialist feminism, a flaw affecting lesbians and all women *qua* sexual beings and sexually regulated subjects.

It might be objected that the positioning of sexual politics with respect to socialist feminism has changed as a result of our participation in the second phase "sex debates" since about 1982 in Canada and a year or so earlier in the United States and England. In these debates regarding the politics of sexual pleasure, sexual variation, sexual representation, prostitution, and pornography, many socialist feminists are located in what are called the pro-sex or anti-censorship camps. We have been active in the anti-censorship struggle, where we have argued that increased state surveillance of sexual representation is not the remedy for the sexism of heterosexual pornography (Burstyn 1985; Valverde 1985). In the United States, socialist feminists have published important anthologies (Snitow, Stansell, and Thompson 1983; Vance 1984) which have advanced our understanding of sexuality. American feminist opposition to radical and liberal feminist demands for anti-pornography legislation has been led by socialist feminists.

This increased presence has helped to alter perceptions of sexual politics among socialist feminists in general so that it is no longer construed as a matter for lesbians only. Nor is sexual politics viewed as insignificant; on the contrary it is increasingly seen as a site for both internal debates about strategy for the women's movement and for struggles against state control of sexuality and sexual representation. Even taking all this into account, I believe that the relation of the new sexual politics to socialist feminism is still problematic. It is not at all clear that sexual politics is being centrally integrated into socialist feminism in order to deepen its analysis or to resolve its theoretical difficulties with regard to class and popular democratic struggles.

While socialist feminists are located in what are called the "anti-censorship" or "pro-sex" camps in the sex debates, we do not tend to speak as *socialist* feminists in these discussions. Partly because we have sought to make alliances with liberals and civil libertarians in opposing state regulation of the sexual, we have often spoken as generic feminists, omitting mention of our socialism in order to remain within liberal political discourse and to avoid being dismissed on anti-socialist grounds. This is especially problematic in the United States, where many socialist feminists have developed a sexual politic not just in alliance with liberals but in explicitly liberal or libertarian terms (Vance 1984). The deletion of our socialism may be *tactically* wise, yet we are not self-conscious that this tactic forms part of a larger strategy. Although active in sexual politics, socialist feminists have not claimed their work for socialist feminism. Our alliances with liberals and our political tactics of putting pressure on state structures have disorganized the self-recognition of our political practices.

In addition, current socialist feminist sex-political work has had a limited scope. Although mid-1980s sexual politics does correct the tendency to pose women's sexuality solely in terms of victimization, a politic developed to distinguish ourselves from radical feminists and conservative religious movements and to counter proposals for new types of state regulation of sexual activity is inevitably reactive; its ground is chosen in advance by the opposition. A long-term integration of sexual politics into socialist feminism will require a practice which addresses *both* sexual pleasure and sexual danger.

These above remarks on the bifurcation of socialist feminist practice and socialist feminist theory/self-recognition in sexual politics can be extended to other regions of our socialist feminist practice as well. At the present time in Ontario, socialist feminists provide leadership in the campaigns for abortion clinics and daycare. Those active in these campaigns are struggling to develop clinics and centres which will address the needs of working-class women together with women of other classes. Important alliances have been made with trade unions in each of these areas. What we see, then, in sexual politics, the struggle for abortion access, and the daycare movement are terrains of socialist feminist activism which extend far beyond an abstract notion of a minority of socialist feminists' launching "class intervention" in a preexisting women's movement. In Canada today, socialist feminists are not simply "intervening" but actually helping to define and create significant sectors of the women's movement. I see little sense in thinking that the highest and only authentic form of socialist feminism consists of writing articles for academic journals: surely the political practice of socialist feminists within the women's movement can at least under some circumstances be accurately described as specifically *socialist* feminist, and not simply as "feminist," without connection with our socialism. We are faced with a situation in which our practice far exceeds our theory; in fact, our undeveloped theorization of socialist feminist practice has at times led to an incapacity to claim or recognize the complexity of our organizing.

Given the "crisis intervention" character of mid-1980s socialist feminist sexual politics and the lack of our explicit presence as socialists in the debates, our sex-political work will run the danger of being understood as a fad once the political battles have been resolved. Without discussion of the positioning of sexual politics within socialist feminism, we will, as soon as the currently burning issues of pornography and prostitution have declined in immediate political importance, revert back to a politic focused exclusively on the relations of gender, class, and work. In the next section I will argue that in order to lay a solid foundation for the integration of sexual politics we need to rethink the relation between the class and non-class or popular democratic aspects of our politics.

Class and Popular Democratic Aspects of Socialist Feminism

Socialist feminism is often described as having two constitutive concepts: capitalism and patriarchy, the latter alternately attacked and defended (Young 1980). Critics argue that "patriarchy" incorrectly constructs a homogeneous, essentialist, transhistorical subject, "women," oppressed in a uniform manner across all modes of production (Barrett 1980; Vogel 1983). Others believe that, by enabling us to theorize the specific forms of cross-class gender oppression, the concept of patriarchy helps avoid class reductionism. Patriarchy and capital have acted in our debates as condensed symbols for the social and theoretical relations between gender and class.

The controversies regarding the relative responsibility of capital and patriarchy for women's oppression have posed the tensions between class analysis and gender analysis at a purely theoretical level, at the expense of more strategic explorations of socialist feminist political *practice*. Viewed from a strategic perspective, socialist feminism appears as a duality between class and popular democratic politics. Posing the duality in this way allows rethinking the joining of class and gender politics at a political rather than a purely theoretical level by opening up the question of the significance of popular politics to socialist feminist *organizing*. Here, I want to explore the importance of popular democratic political struggles, and sexual politics in particular, for socialist feminism. Without a better understanding of the positioning of popular democratic politics in our work, class politics will be overvalued and popular politics abandoned as peripheral or even as outside the terrain of socialist feminism. Recognizing the importance of popular democratic politics will help fashion a discursive place for a socialist feminist politic capable of addressing all forms of gender domination.

The class axis of socialist feminism originates in the capital–labour antagonism; its popular democratic axis stems from the power bloc–people (specifically power bloc–women) antagonism. What Gramsci called the "integral state," a synthesis of both coercion and consent which acts as a regulator of both economy and society, is the chief organizer of the power bloc. The state acts to disorganize the people, partly through producing and administering a wealth of politicized social relations which fragment the people into distinct and mutually exclusive groups, such as "homosexuals," "welfare mothers," "juvenile delinquents," "the unemployed," "citizens," and "taxpayers." The political strategy of the power bloc thus not only addresses and manages class subjects: it rules by articulating a heterogeneous assortment of non-class subjects to itself, although these may have an internal class structuring. To create an oppositional bloc, the needs of non-class political subjects need to be addressed and those constituencies mobilized; as Bob Jessop has observed, "popular democratic struggle is first of all a struggle to form the 'people' before it is a struggle between a people and officialdom . . . the mobilization of different categories to produce a unified people is the supreme focus of "popular democratic struggle" (Jessop 1980: 65–66). In the case of rape, for instance, anti-rape work helps form an opposition between the Canadian power bloc (in this instance the courts, the police, and aspects of the mass media) and women, thus contributing to the construction of women as a political subject. For socialist feminism, the popular democratic project of "people formation" takes the form of an attempt to unify women against the power bloc reproduction of masculine domination through the activities of state, capital, and extra-state regulatory institutions.

The building of a politic which combines the popular democratic struggle of social movements and class struggle is one of the most compelling problems of socialism today. Those of us who are socialist feminists therefore need to maintain the popular democratic elements of our politic not only for the sake of feminism but also for socialism, since, as was argued earlier, building socialist feminism goes hand in hand with building a non–class reductionist socialism. The inclusion of the standpoint and experiences of oppressed groups within socialism is critical for the creation of socialist pluralism and more democratic forms of socialist practice — a party of the working class and of those subordinated within the present historical bloc.

Socialists have frequently been hostile to popular democratic movements on the reductionist grounds that by dividing the working class they demobilize class organizing. But, because the working class has been in fact divided on multiple lines, notably gender and race, refusals to address gender issues perpetuate working-class divisions. Building working-class solidarity involves transforming social relations both inside and outside production. Daycare, reproductive rights, and sexual harassment are popular democratic, gender struggles which are anti-state, cross-class issues for the women's movement. Rather than disorganizing the working class, they are crucial to the political formation of the working class at the present time.

In contrast, liberal and radical feminists have taken the opposite view, seeing class politics as undermining the sisterly unity of the women's movement. However, while popular movements have no necessary class character fixed in advance, they are structured by class and organize class relations whether their members know it or not. Decisions about how to explain and pose issues, who to recruit, how and whom to hire, and where to publicize events all involve class-related politics. Refusing to make these implicit class politics explicit contributes to the reproduction of class domination as surely as refusing to challenge gender hierarchy reproduces masculine domination. In general, then, when class and popular politics are seen as outside each other and mutually exclusive, whether by Leninists or non-Leninists, the linking of one to the other comes to be interpreted as undercutting the fictive unity of each.

The analysis adopted here breaks with Leninism, Trotskyism, and Maoism, which, together with more recent theories of "radical pluralism," have collectively understood class politics as the exclusive prerogative of the party of the working class, and thus *outside* popular organizing. I am trying to develop an analysis of class politics as *internal* to the organization of popular movements, and to theorize appropriate ways of organizing in light of this recognition, while simultaneously maintaining the cross-class basis of these movements.

Since class domination is a pervasive feature of the present power bloc in Canadian and other capitalist societies, radical politics has the option of either challenging or failing to challenge its class composition. I want to emphasize the practical importance of class politics to women's and popular organizing because much contemporary theorizing on popular democratic politics has been developed in opposition to class politics and in attempted alliance with "new" social movements, resulting in a potentially disastrous erasure of class considerations to both projects. The process of forming a radical, popular bloc and the process of theoretically understanding this process cannot take place without reference to the class articulation of the power bloc; without this attention an oppositional bloc might well reach an easy accommodation with capital and state structures, and it would certainly risk fracturing along class lines during a period of political crisis. Whether a powerful and united popular bloc could arise solely from what people ignorant of history call "new social movements" (as though the women's movement and the peace movement had been born yesterday) is also questionable. The internal organization of contemporary North American popular movements impedes their capacity for co-ordinated action, especially in relation to other movements. Given these organizational limitations it is difficult to see how the kind of political co-ordination necessary to a united popular bloc could arise *directly* from these movements.

A better sense of the overall strategic purposes of socialist feminism might help us better envision the relation between class and popular democratic elements in our politics. To further the discussion I suggest three major goals for our work. First, as socialist feminists our aim is to help build the working class by overcoming its gender division. This is a project of class formation. Our second goal is to help construct a radical movement in which the liberation of women is integral, and without which the liberation of women cannot be accomplished. In the construction of the new bloc, the popular democratic politics of socialist feminism will make a crucial contribution by fashioning cross-class alliances of women which address gendered subjectivity and the specificity of gender oppression. Third, our intent is not to simply "intervene" in the women's movement, but to become its majority current. This last goal potentially leads socialist feminists into all areas of women's oppression.

Although there is no necessary correlation between popular politics and class disorganization, a miraculous synthesis of the two does not lie within our present socialist feminist grasp. The disequilibrium between popular democratic and class politics within socialist feminism may not be resolvable theoretically or practically by ourselves alone. The two aspects probably cannot be united simply within the bounds of the women's movement; their integration can only be attained, whether in terms of a program or in terms of alliances, on the terrain of a broader socialist party integrating class politics with popular democratic struggles. Given the historic socialist failures in popular democratic struggle, the organizational autonomy of these movements must be guaranteed in future socialist politics. This transformed socialism would probably contain tradeoffs and compromises among the social movements and between the movements and working-class organizations.

I have above implicitly disagreed with a tendency in socialist feminist theory to construe socialist feminism as the total politic—the new, reconstituted socialism. I can see no a priori reason why the oppression of women should be politically privileged over racial oppression, a claim which underlies suggestions that socialist feminism would form the basis of a transformed socialism. Socialist feminists, moreover, need to recognize that socialists of colour have had problems within socialist movements just as women have had, with racism, like gender oppression, being understood as wholly determined by class, and autonomous anti-racist political movements being undermined. This does not mean that anti-racist work falls outside socialist feminism, but only that feminism is based on gender oppression, where racial oppression acts as a social form constitutive of women's subordination, the inverse being true of liberation movements led by and for people of colour. Socialist feminism does not speak for all social movements and hence cannot be a comprehensive politic.

The incorporation of popular democratic struggles within socialist feminism increases our political effectiveness and strengthens our socialism. By appreciating the importance of these struggles we will be less prone to pit cross-class gender oppression against class politics in our work. At a practical level, which of the two goals of socialist feminism receives priority will be decided by factors such as the judgments about the specific context as well as the time, energy, and interests of activists. This is a matter of praxis, not of inflexible theoretical reason. A clearer understanding of popular democratic struggle would help us refrain from class reductionist ways of posing issues and encourage us to act on political terrains which we have often abandoned to liberal and radical feminists.

Conclusion: Toward a Socialist Feminist Politics of Sexuality

A popular democratic terrain of special significance to the women's movement is the politics of sexuality, an area including sexual representation (sexual art, women's romances and soap operas, pornography) sexual violence against women (rape, incest, sexual harassment, international trafficking in women's bodies), sexual pleasure, service trades (prostitution, porn production, phone sex) and sexual minorities. To constitute socialist feminism as the majority voice of feminism it will not be enough to "intervene" in the women's movement with a class perspective, necessary though that remains, for a class-conscious feminism includes more than class issues. If socialist feminism is to displace liberal feminism and become the dominant current within feminism, our politic will have to address all forms of gender subordination, among them sexual danger and sexual pleasure.

The particular content of a socialist feminist sexual politic requires exploration, and is not determined simply by the results of recognizing the popular democratic elements of socialist feminism. This is a particularly appropriate time to begin a discussion of sexual politics as a permanent terrain of socialist feminism, since there is now a widespread interest and participation in sexual politics by socialist feminists. At this point we can only speculate about exactly what a socialist feminist sexual politic might be, but such speculation might at least help us reflect upon and develop a self-conscious awareness of our practices. Mariana Valverde has recently made an important contribution to sexual ethics in the concluding chapter of her book *Sex, Power and Pleasure* (Valverde 1985). Varda Burstyn has formulated a broad series of feminist "positive strategies" for the improvement of social relations of sex (Burstyn 1985). Neither has done so explicitly as a socialist feminist, and I think it would be very interesting and productive to discuss these texts in relation to socialist feminism and to the composition of a socialist feminist sexual politics.

In general, I believe that socialist feminism is not in a situation to develop a theory of sexuality so much as to develop a theory of sexual *politics*. Our particular contribution to feminist sexual politics will probably be at least in part a macropolitical analysis of sexual regulation and its role in the composition and social relations of the power bloc. This analysis of how sex/sexuality is mobilized by the discourses and practices of ruling will deepen our understanding of why it is important to act as a partisan of sexual minorities in their attempts to construct publicly validated sexual difference. A sexual politic integrated into socialist feminism would certainly be also of help in providing an alternative to an ailing lesbian feminism, and help to guide the women's movement during the social debates regarding state regulation of sex and sexual representation.

The inclusion of a sexual politic within socialist feminism poses many difficult questions for socialist feminist groups and organizational practices. The difficulties we are experiencing in developing a sexual politic are part of broader problems we have in organizing a class-conscious popular democratic base in the women's movement. These questions and difficulties are crucial to the growth of socialist feminism, for women are recruited into the women's movement on the basis of the multiple expressions of gender subordination. Where socialist feminism is absent, women will be mobilized by other currents of the women's movement. Organizational practices with respect to all forms of women's oppression belong in principle within the politic of socialist feminism.

Note

1. I would like to thank Mariana Valverde for her help above and beyond the call of friendship and intellectual collaboration in editing this article. I am grateful as well to Alice de Wolff for her comments and support while I was preparing the final version.

5 Feminism at Work[1]

HEATHER JON MARONEY

The most important political phenomenon of the last two decades and one that will continue to mark the politics of the next has been the development of a new feminist consciousness and a movement for women's liberation.[2] In Canada and Quebec, as elsewhere in the advanced capitalist world, fifteen years of ideological and cultural struggle have resulted in the diffusion of the vital sense that women have rights and will not be bound by convention, prejudice, or male privilege. Women's efforts toward collective self-definition have revalorized attributes and activities culturally coded as feminine. This transformation has begun to produce a positive atmosphere for girls growing to womanhood and women of all ages coming to feminism — a reorientation so profound that I (despite an instinctive feminism learned at my mother's knee as we changed our own flat tires) could not have dreamed of it in the giggly, marriage-doomed fifties or even in the messianic cyclone of the sixties. This new-found self-confidence has been a source of inspiration for women in a wide range of social struggles and, increasingly, a radicalizing force for women as workers at the place of work. But, at the close of the seventies, although widely diffused, the new feminist consciousness remained uneven, politically embryonic, and in many cases reactive. More even than in most countries, in Canada and Quebec, feminist consciousness, like the organized women's movement, is fragmented along regional, sectoral, and class lines.[3] Despite real advances, these divisions have prevented feminists from developing a collective assessment of past actions or a coherent strategy on a binational scale.

The Two Waves of the Women's Movement

In one sense, the fundamental questions of strategy—the state, allies, the relation between sexual and class politics, and program — that confront the women's movement in the eighties have been on the agenda since the sixties.[4] They have, however, been given a particular urgency by the current political conjuncture. The deepening economic crisis and the rightward drift in state policies over the past ten years have provoked increasing trade union militancy. At the same time, in the confused ideological aftermath of the sixties, the restrictive cultural atmosphere engendered by the recession has allowed reactionary anti-labour currents —whose anti-feminist, homophobic, Christian fundamentalism is glossed as "pro-family"—to mobilize social discontent in an attempt to overturn the cultural gains of the last fifteen years, especially those made by women.[5] In the face of this combination of resurgent class conflict and cultural backlash, no component of the broad left (from trade unions and social democracy through radical popular movements to the organized far left) has been able to develop an adequate strategy and program. This lack of consensus complicates the development of strategy for the women's movement: we are compelled to elaborate our strategy with little sense of the direction our potential allies might take.

To this task, feminism brings diverse insights from two waves of radicalization: sixties women's liberation and contemporary working-class feminism. Against patriarchal ideology, women's liberationists claimed that women were *oppressed*. All relations between women and men — including institutionalized heterosexuality and the monogamous couple— were, whether women were conscious of it or not, structured and distorted by male power and privilege. What was particularly new in this analysis of male-female relations was the fact that it placed sexuality, marriage, and the family at the centre, asserted that the long-term transformation of gender relations required sexual autonomy for women, and held that the rootedness of women's oppression in all social institutions required revolutionary transformation. From these insights several strategic principles were derived: the necessity of autonomy for the women's movement; the refusal to postpone women's struggles or to subordinate them to any state, party, class, or male-dominated national movement interests; the defence of lesbian choice. These analytic and strategic acquisitions—much more than the classic demands for equal pay and equal work, reproductive freedom, and childcare — are the legacy of sixties feminism for present practice.

In any contemporary evaluation, however, it must be recognized that the present women's movement differs markedly from that of the sixties. In Canada, two developments are particularly significant. A recent successful campaign to include equal rights for women in the Canadian Constitution has strengthened liberal feminism and its orientation to the state. But since the mid-seventies, a radicalization of working women— most immediately visible in several important public and private sector strikes—has profoundly altered the organizational and ideological balance of forces within the movement as a whole. This radicalization is significant not just in itself or in the opportunity that it provides for broadening the struggle, but because the widening of the class basis of feminism deepens our understanding of the way class and gender oppression condenses a global system of domination and opens up new ways to explore questions of strategy and theory that have long perturbed the women's movement and, indeed, blocked its development.

The rise of working-class feminism has not, however, been an unmixed blessing. The occupation of centre stage by workplace struggles has helped to narrow the ideological focus by concentrating attention on economic issues at the expense of cultural and sexual liberation projects *even inside the women's movement itself* and so reinforced a general tendency in the left to economism (Haber 1980; Campbell 1980). Working-class feminism is also weighed down by the reformism which prevails in the three political spheres — trade unions, social democracy, and important sectors of the women's movement — which have so far conditioned its ideological development. But it is also important to remember that, despite the difficult conditions in which it emerged, working-class feminism grew out of militant struggle in the context of an already radicalized leadership of women who nurtured both its class and feminist consciousness. If its feistiness is maintained and if it is able to join forces with socialist and other feminist tendencies committed to overall social transformation, its radicalizing dynamic can profoundly alter class (as well as feminist) politics: broadening workplace struggles, overcoming antagonistic divisions between women and men in the working class, and introducing an anti-economist, anti-bureaucratic politics of liberation into existing working-class organizations.

Against this background, my aim here will be to trace the rise of working-class feminism, to show its contradictory significance in the women's movement, and to begin to explore its implications for socialist feminist theory and practice.

The Growth of Working-Class Feminism

By the end of the seventies, working-class feminism in Canada had become a distinct current in the women's movement. In contrast to the university-based feminism of the sixties, it was rooted in the workplace and oriented, first of all, to the practical achievement of more concrete and, hence, more limited goals. It had its own outlook on what feminism should be: "Of course jobs are a feminist issue: and equal pay and training. Getting women into non-traditional jobs is important right now, because of what will happen with tech change. Of course, in my union when they think they're getting down to the nitty-gritty real feminist issues, the men always ask 'How's the daycare in your town?' — the whole motherhood thing. They don't want to talk about sexual harassment or anything to do with sex. After all, it's not just cross-class, it's workers harassing workers. But unions give you power, and they educate you. It's the only way to unite the working class, through unions and working together."[6]

Underlying the development of working-class feminism are dramatic increases in labour force participation during the 1950s and 1960s for women over twenty-five with children. Women have risen from 17 percent of membership in trade unions in 1966 to 27 percent in 1976.[7] Although the most important single contribution to this increase in unionization was a top-down legislative conversion of provincial and federal staff associations into unions in a rapidly expanding public sector, women workers' readiness to unionize and their militancy in strikes testify to a consciousness that wage work is no longer an episode before marriage and childrearing but a permanent feature of their lives, a recognition that is a crucial component of proletarian consciousness. In these recently formed Canadian public sector unions of clerical and service workers, the combination of a relatively weak bureaucracy and a majority female membership has facilitated the entry and expression of feminist consciousness. As governments have sought to resolve their fiscal crisis through rationalization, semi-professionals like teachers and nurses have met increasingly proletarianized working conditions, pay restraints, and job insecurity, have moved away from corporatist associations or professional aspirations, and have affiliated to trade unions in great numbers. Despite their conservative and sometimes confessional origins, public sector unions, particularly those in the Quebec Common Front, have proved to be both militant and relatively open to women's demands. In some cases, women teachers and nurses, traditionally ruled by an ethic of service and self-sacrifice, have raised explicitly feminist demands in contract negotiations.[8]

Two other developments have begun to bring more women into the trade union orbit and, this time, into the male-dominated heavy industrial unions. First, the entry of women into "non-traditional" jobs in steel, mining, rail, manufacturing, and forest products has been the focus of widespread propaganda by both government and labour, making a greater political impact than the restricted numbers of women would seem to warrant. For government "affirmative action" promised a trendy, low-cost alternative to the enactment and enforcement of rigorous equal value legislation; selective promotion of a few both promotes individualism and serves the interests of formally qualified professional and managerial women (Gillmeister 1980). Government publicity and human rights provisions notwithstanding, campaigns by coalitions of unions, socialist feminists and jobseekers have been necessary to overcome actual employer barriers against female applicants.[9]

If, in this first instance, women have come into unions, in the second, the large industrial unions (especially United Steelworkers of America and United Auto Workers) have turned to women. With recession-induced instability and shrinking employment in the manufacturing sector, unions, forced to find new ways to secure a membership base, have supported organizing drives in small plants or moved to sign up clerical and service workers (at Blue Cross, Fotomat, in legal aid, and so on). Taken together, these developments imply the numerical feminization of the centres of male working-class power and of the labour movement as a whole. These inroads are, however, fragile as layoffs reduce or eliminate the numbers of women machinists, miners, and smelter-workers.

As an organized expression, working-class feminism is partially structured by the existing labour movement and its ideology is most coherently expressed in groupings of feminists in the trade unions. Diverse in their political origins and experience, these nuclei can be divided into: politically self-conscious "trade union feminists," and women workers whose feminist (and trade union) consciousness has crystallized in the course of specific struggles. Within the first group a further distinction can be drawn between women working in established unions and those attempting to set up independent unions.

Trade Union Recalcitrance

In established unions, trade union feminists, often on staff, have set up or given new political life to official union committees on the status of women, worked for women's caucuses, and animated unofficial cross-union formations — like Organized Working Women (Ontario) — as a base to agitate against sexism. Highly developed caucuses leading to committees first appeared in Quebec, where they had led several campaigns: for equal pay legislation, for maternity and parental leave, against sexism in the schools, for women's liberation reports and resolutions which, in line with the "ideological" character of the Centrale des Syndicats Nationaux and the Centrale des Enseignants du Québec, go far beyond workforce equality to call for abortion rights and the socialization of housework, and to criticize marriage as an oppressive institution.[10] Across Canada, their success has been marked by the establishment of equal rights committees in all the provincial labour federations, by the establishment of the Canadian Labour Congress (CLC) women's conferences, and by rapid and dramatic changes in policy. Although the Quebec federations' concern with the global aspects of "la condition féminine" is exceptional, many unions now have the essential elements of a program for workplace equality through economic and social measures: equal value demands, across-the-board rather than percentage wage increases, affirmative action, daycare, and parental "reproductive" leave for childbirth, adoption, or abortion.

Despite the advance represented by the institutionalization of these committees, the intersecting structures of sexism and bureaucratic power in the labour movement replicate and thus serve to reproduce prevailing gender structures. Even where the membership is predominantly female, women are consistently underrepresented in governing bodies, and feminist forces are weak in relation to an entrenched male leadership. Although their paucity can be partially explained by the difficulties for women of adding a third set of union responsibilities to their double day of paid and domestic labour (Gagnon 1974b), the independent effect of sexism must be taken into account. While the commentators in "Women and Trade Unions"[11] recognize that many men in unions are supportive of, if sometimes confused by, women's attempts to redefine gender boundaries, they nevertheless point with remarkable consistency to sexism on the part of male workers, women's internalization of stereotyped behaviour, "business unionism," and bureaucratic control as blocks to female participation (Field 1983). Since the current leadership was politically and ideologically formed during the postwar defeat of feminism (and, incidentally, of the left), it owes its position at least in part to male privilege.[12] To put the question sharply, immediately equalizing women's representation in union power structures would require either that some male power brokers lose their positions of financial and sexual privilege or, an unlikely alternative, that the number of such positions be almost doubled to accommodate women. Thus the question of representativeness in general is raised by women's demands for equality. In the rank and file, as well, a pro-woman economic program has sometimes generated conflict between male and female workers.[13] Even if political education tends to homogenize the ideology of trade union *activists*, convention resolutions do not necessarily represent the views of the membership. As recently as 1971, many Quebec unionists still thought that men had a prior right to jobs and that women should, in any case, stay at home, union policy to the contrary (Geoffroy and Sainte-Marie 1971). Even allowing for economically irrational employer resistance, so-called "women's issues" such as daycare, rights and benefits for part-time workers, and maternity leave seem sometimes to have been included in contract demands merely as bargaining points to be traded off.[14]

The resources of unions, never elastic, are particularly stretched by basic defensive tasks in the current recession, whether because of loss of membership from layoffs or intense strike activity. In this situation, continuing pressure from rank-and-file and more particularly women's caucuses is necessary to ensure that social concerns are taken up by the union (Routledge 1981). In this regard, trade union feminism has passed through two stages of development. Having taken the first consciousness-raising and mobilizing step, it has gone on to formulate claims *from the point of view of women* as a special group: the right to work, equal pay, and so on. In agitating for the acceptance of these demands, women have sometimes breached gendered ghetto walls and created a class demand supported equally by, and understood to be in the interests of, women and men—again, equal pay is the classic case in point. Other innovative trade union policies, like a reduced working week without pay cuts or multi-patronal bargaining units, could also be sought in terms that educate female and male workers alike—in these cases, as a way to equalize paid labour and domestic labour in the household or to organize small workplaces of often female office and retail workers.

But at no point has feminism reformed the institutionalized forms of politics — bureaucratic by some accounts, patriarchal by others — which cyclically alienate women and impede their participation (Hartman 1976; Warrian 1981; Frogett 1981). Formal norms of political procedure, for example, can be manipulated to define *what can be heard*, to block rank-and-file initiatives or to reinforce existing ideology. That bureaucratic responses are not limited to male power brokers but ingrained in union functions was shown at the 1980 CLC Women's Conference, where a proposal from the floor for plenary discussions and time to evaluate the conference was blocked by the chair, a president of a national public sector union and a noted feminist; militancy was not stressed; and the discussion of how to acquire power was limited to lobbying (McCune 1981). Thus only a certain range of feminist complaint and militancy can be taken account of, and women who have not yet learned the ropes (or those who go too far) are ruled out of court. Lest this process be thought of as simply one of self-censorship or internalized submissiveness on the part of women, it should be emphasized that "ruling out" not only takes place from the chair of conventions but is often backed up in private by threats or promises about future union careers or outcomes in private life. On balance, trade unions provide organizational continuity, material resources, and an established constituency in contrast with the more ephemeral, poorer, yet creative, self-directed, and consciously holistic structures of the autonomous women's movement. Nevertheless, formal democratic norms have provided a means for trade union feminists to take advantage of the political and ideological space created by general feminist agitation, whether that be as a result of real sensitivity to women's needs or merely to their explosiveness.

Trade union feminists are caught in a contradictory situation. Their position inside the labour movement is vulnerable and their room to manoeuvre depends upon the extent of feminist radicalization and trade union militancy of women in the rank and file—which, in turn, exists in a complex relation with general feminist and class mobilization. In isolation, trade union feminists, especially union staff, are not only subject to the usual pressures of bureaucratic and reformist integration of normalized union practice, but must also bear the brunt of sexism inside the unions. On their other side, feminist peers outside the labour movement often expect that a maximal program for women's liberation can and should be propagated without modification in the trade union arena and that any failure to do so amounts to a sellout of women's interests. The task has been complicated by the existence of real resistance among rank-and-file women (let alone men) to sexual and cultural issues "expressed in feminist jargon" — particularly to abortion and lesbian rights. The resources that have been available to staff women have been far from adequate to carry out general consciousness-raising programs on these questions (or even on basic trade unionism) among the workers whose interests they are supposed to represent. And, although their position allows them to speak with the political weight of the trade unions in the broader women's movement, what they say is restricted by the ideological horizon of the constituency that they represent. Overall, they must mediate between the feminist movement, including its working-class component, and working-class sexism and sexual oppression.

The Check to Feminist Syndicalism

A second grouping of trade union organizers located mainly in British Columbia has adopted a feminist syndicalist approach by attempting to construct exemplary independent unions in female-dominated industries — for example, the Service, Office and Retail Workers Union of Canada (SORWUC) among restaurant, office, and bank workers, and the Association of University and College Employees (AUCE), both formed in 1972. The initial success of their organizing drives demonstrated how lessons derived from sixties women's organizing—small group consciousness raising, a stress on democratic, anti-hierarchical principles, and feminist policies of daycare, equal pay, and promotion — could be applied to the class ends of union solidarity; in the process, they disproved the contention of malestream trade unions that service and clerical workers were too difficult to organize (Ainsworth et al. 1982). Relying on support from women's groups, the social-democratic New Democratic Party, and CLC and Congress of Canadian Unions (CCU) locals and members for long-term leafleting campaigns and essential financial support during strikes, feminist syndicalist organizers urged women workers to unionize (along with men) not just for economic defence but to combat their special exploitation in the labour market as women.

Since 1978, however, the limitations of feminist syndicalism have become clear. First, employer resistance in the banking sector successfully used both threats and co-optation to limit the union drive (The Bank Book Collective 1979). In the face of what turns out to have been a tactical error in deciding to organize on a branch-by-branch basis, coupled with a financial inability to gain first contracts in certified locals and to carry cases through the Canadian Labour Relations Board, most of the bank locals were decertified, the United Bank Workers dissolved, and several hundred women left without union protection. Secondly, SORWUC, unable to mobilize adequate support from outside the CLC and unwilling to "compromise" the democratic constitution as the price of entry for CLC power, eventually split on the question of integration into the central, with those opposed to the move bitter about what they saw as raiding by rival (and johnny-come-lately) CLC affiliates. Faced with similar financial and political weaknesses, AUCE have voted to lobby the CLC for admission as an independent union in order to protect the democratic and feminist aspects of its constitution. In evaluating their tactics in British Columbia, we have to weigh organizing skills, willingness to organize small work units, and a capacity to create union organizers out of women workers against a purist reaction against "big" unionism. Some of SORWUC's financial weaknesses may be offset by its adhesion to the CCU, which is largely based in British Columbia, but it still remains in opposition to the CLC and, thus, isolated from the largest female-dominated public sector unions.

Along with its organizational character, feminist syndicalism encapsulates an ideology and strategy of workplace organizing to create changes necessary for women's social liberation. As a perspective generated by the material conditions of class and sexual oppression, it is to some degree shared by other feminists in trade unions even if they reject the project of building independent women's unions. The conflict between sexism and feminist radicalization within workers' organizations means that women need and want a political base outside the control of the labour movement's male hierarchy to fight for their needs: in short, feminism. On the other hand, divisions also continue to be created between organized women workers and others in the autonomous women's movement by the institutional framework of the labour movement, by the special needs of working-class women for whom the time pressures are extreme, and by class differences. Often impatient with the consensus styles of work and the diffuseness of global "demands" that have tended to characterize the program and tactics of sixties-based feminism, trade union feminists sometimes reject movement attempts to formulate global analyses and strategy: in short, syndicalism. A strategy of building independent women-controlled unions has long had currency among feminists (Tax 1980; Marchak 1974a). Despite the "failure" of its first attempt, SORWUC has already had an ideological impact on women's groups and labour groups and has plans for another bank drive.

Radicalization through Struggle

In addition to these two consciously organized variants, working-class feminism has also arisen in the course of strikes. Two strikes in Ontario—at Fleck in 1978 and at the International Nickel Company in 1979—spectacularly illustrated how feminism among working-class women strengthens economic struggles and how their mobilization can have an important political impact on the women's movement.

At Fleck, an automobile parts plant, a newly certified UAW local composed overwhelmingly of women struck for a first contract and over wages, union security, and working conditions. As the strike dragged on for months it took on an increasingly class-political tone as a battle about the right to unionize. The UAW, the parent union, rallied to its support with plant-gate collections and busloads of mostly male workers for mass picketing. At the same time, it became a test case for feminism, and socialist feminists in particular saw it in these terms. The general potential for radicalization in the interplay of class and feminist forces was manifested in this strike. By its very nature, a strike situation is an intensive consciousness-raising process. With work rhythms disrupted, the opportunity and the necessity to think collectively and strategically break through the fatigue, political passivity, and mystification of normal production. Militant strike action by women is also an objective challenge to their economic exploitation, their individuation into the illusory privacy of the family, and the ideological construction of women as passive dependants protected by men which is at the core of women's place in the contemporary capitalist sexual division of labour. At Fleck, the strikers explicitly articulated this challenge. They attributed management and police harassment to a complacent assumption that they would be easily intimidated because they were women; instead, maintaining that men would not have been able to hold out so long, they saw their own capacity to resist arising from their *solidarity as women*. By mobilizing union women's committees and groups from the autonomous women's movement for picket-line and financial support, trade union feminists brought a feminist perspective to the strike and, more importantly, legitimated "the women's movement" in the eyes of the strikers (and other unionists), at the same time as non-union feminists were given a deeper understanding of class conflict. Finally, the Fleck strike shows the importance in such radicalization of the interplay between "spontaneous" struggle and conscious intervention "from the outside." As well as the crucial role played by trade union and other feminists in this regard, some journalists also brought a feminist concern to their investigation and reporting of the strike, eliciting the strikers' responses to their situation as women and playing back through the media an ideologically more sophisticated version of the strikers' own feminism.

Historically, the Fleck strike helped to popularize a militant feminist ideology. The intensity of the struggle, and the determination and sharpness with which sex and class lines were drawn, gave it the kind of drama that makes news. The strikers' individual and collective courage, conviction and humour caught the imagination of people well beyond the organized labour and women's movements. They became popular working-class heroines with a message that captured the essence of working-class feminist ideology: women have the right to work; wages are a woman's concern; unionization is a basic weapon; women can find strength from one another in struggle. For feminist strategy, the lesson that they confirmed was that, given the right political conditions, self-organization in struggle will radicalize, mobilize and broaden feminist consciousness and action.

If the Fleck strike showed the radicalization of women at the point of production, then the strike in Sudbury against INCO demonstrated a different possibility: the role of class-conscious feminism in promoting solidarity between the union and the community. During a previous strike in 1958, a mass meeting of "wives" had been manipulated to make it appear that they were in favour of immediate and unfavourable settlement. In 1979, however, partly at the initiative of members of a local women's centre, a women's committee, "Wives supporting the strike," was formed to counter the reputation and repetition of '58. Mobilizing the power of women in the community and including aspects of normally private "domestic" work (children's clothing, Christmas parties, layettes, community suppers) in an overall program of strike defence partially and conjuncturally overcame the structural split in the working-class community between wage-work and housework which is expressed as conflict between women and men. But the resolution was not complete. With the mobilization of women, however, new conflicts were generated. From the power base of the wives' committee, some women pressed, against union opposition, for a greater voice in the direction of the whole strike. An important political issue was thus posed: what should the relation of wives' committees be to strike steering committees when both women and men are dependent upon wages and men's working conditions indirectly affect women's household work? Family and marriage relations were affected by the partial sublation of gender conflict. A preliminary study (Radecki 1979) indicates that, despite the added tensions of economic hardship, family relations were considered to be more satisfactory when men spent more time in the household. Some of the readjustments were precarious, with men pressuring their wives back into the kitchen after the strike. After some initial compliance, however, many women have sought part-time work and become reactivated in local women's committees (Luxton 1982).

Problems of Socialist Feminism

A strong socialist component has made an important contribution to the development of a class-conscious current in this second wave of the women's movement. Marxist women's liberationists saw the campaign for reproduction rights which culminated in the 1970 Abortion Caravan as an opportunity for class as well as feminist organizing. When leafleting at factories and offices met with indifference or hostility and, more importantly, failed to catalyze parallel working-class women's organizations, they explored other avenues. In line with the workerism which seemed to offer a solution to militants of the revolutionary youth and student movements, some sought unionized jobs and, later, jobs with unions where they pushed women's issues. Others, on the west coast, initiated SORWUC. In part this entry into the labour movement was made possible by the particular character of the Canadian scene. By comparison with the U.S.A., there are fewer feminist activists in some of the state sector unions, but the trade unions are more open and the labour movement's affiliation to a social-democratic party provides a leftish ideological cover; thus, movement between sectors is possible. Socialist feminists in unions, however fraught their situation, have been able to link feminists of different generations and class backgrounds.

As individuals, socialist feminists have consistently worked for and provided leadership in union, childcare, abortion, lesbian rights, and equal pay campaigns, but socialist feminist organizations in Canada have had, with one exception, a more precarious fate. Operating from a mainly ideological basis of unity, these organizations have lacked the focus of single-issue campaigns and the institutional cohesion of the self-help services that also evolved from the initial phases of the women's liberation movement. Externally, they have generally met with hostility from the mixed Leninist left, suspicion from the labour movement, and opposition from radical and bourgeois feminists. Given the immense theoretical and practical difficulties of working through their commitment to struggle on two fronts — against patriarchy and against capitalism — and the heterogeneity of the membership, socialist feminist groups have time and again run into difficulty. Unable to agree upon a "correct" and effective program of action, they have dwindled into theoreticism, split, or been reduced to passivity. Throughout the seventies, many of the women activists, organizers, and theorists who might have helped pull these groups together were tied up in far left groups. Those in some far left organizations were hostile to and boycotted such efforts; the initiatives of others were widely suspect because of their affiliation to mistrusted "male-dominated" Leninist groups. After the defeats of the seventies, the radicalization of working-class women provided a pole for the reconstitution of the women's movement.

At present, working-class and socialist feminists together form a strategically located, mutually dependent, but functionally differentiated nucleus for a class-conscious current in the autonomous women's movement. Although trade union feminists are the critical links for this nucleus, they have not been an independent leadership for the women's movement as a whole. Socialist feminists have effectively supported working women's struggles and single-issue and national campaigns (most notably the promotion of International Women's Day as a unitary day of protest and celebration),[15] have contributed to the development of theory, strategy, and ideology, and have consistently sought to play a leadership role for both class-conscious and other feminist forces. But they have little permanent organization, no co-ordination at the level of the Canadian state, and no publication. There are also tensions in the current's whole development, and its homogeneity should not be overestimated. Only in British Columbia and Saskatchewan have there been province-wide organizations that included both unionized and non-unionized women.[16] In other centres in Ontario, city-wide socialist feminist organizations exist (Egan this volume). Even on IWD, the day of symbolic unity, political differences have developed over the relative weight to give demands for abortion rights and maternity leave or how to present demands for lesbian rights.[17] As well as contradictory evaluations of the political impact of these issues by organizers, these disagreements reflect real unevenness of political development of the constituencies involved. For, if trade union feminists are caught between the differing expectations of the bureaucracy and the rank and file, socialist feminists, lesbian and straight, are similarly placed in a conflictual relation with labour and other feminist and socialist currents.

The influence of working-class feminism on the women's movement has not all been in the direction of economism. Working-class and déclassé lesbians, for example, have fought to have the labour movement defend the freedom of sexual orientation and to oppose the new right. Links made on the picket line have been maintained and serve to homogenize the politics of the current. Part of the reason that union women initially came to Toronto IWD celebrations was simple reciprocal solidarity. Through such activities, trade unionists have come to a greater awareness of non-economic aspects of feminism and have, in turn, become leaders able and willing to defend these issues to other women. At a recent IWD, two women from Fleck were talking about the Lesbian Organization of Toronto whose presence was signalled by banners, picket signs, and buttons. While one was uneasy about the presence of "all those lesbians," her friend responded, "Well, that's the women's movement, and you'll just have to get used to it."

Sexual Harassment and Cultural Radicalization

The popularization of feminist analyses of sexuality, rape, and violence has set the stage for the class transformation of earlier concerns with sexual objectification. Sexual harassment on the job has come to be considered a major women's issue in the labour movement. Unlike other women's issues, however (such as daycare, maternity leave, and equal pay), sexual harassment focuses directly upon sexuality and upon the antagonism which pits women, individually and collectively, *against men as agents of their oppression.* Since women are harassed not just across class lines by men in supervisory positions but also by fellow workers, this issue is potentially explosive inside the working class.

Although, strictly speaking, sexual harassment is a feminist issue of sexual politics, it has a class dimension as well. "Quid pro quo" harassment by a supervisor tells women that they hold their jobs only at their bosses' pleasure, reinforcing both class and gender subordination.[18] Although supervisors are also implicated, the more prevalent form, "harassment as a condition of work," is in large part carried out by co-workers through unremitting comment on a woman's appearance, sexual activities, and desires — real or fantasied — often in a joking manner which men aver as "harmless" and even flattering to women (Women's Rights Committee 1982; Kadar 1982). Such statements assert that a woman's sexuality is not hers alone but an aspect of her public personality which belongs by right to any man who wishes to appropriate it through comment.

The direct result of sexual harassment is to keep women in line (in culturally specified places and ways) or to keep them out of where they are not supposed to be. In the labour force, sexual harassment strengthens both vertical hierarchy and horizontal divisions to maintain women in their traditionally inferior position. It is the intimate way in which working-class men police their privileged position in the labour force and let women know they are transgressors on male territory, particularly when they enter non-traditional jobs. Culturally sexist attitudes and behaviour also prevent women's full participation in unions: feminist activists in particular are attacked as "lesbians" and their clothing is scrutinized. Even if all men do not harass or support harassment by silence, its pervasiveness cautions women against trusting men. Structurally, sexual harassment pits all men against all women at the same time as it makes working-class women the target of cross-class sexism. The net result is to reinforce male solidarity across class lines, to blur class divisions through working-class sexism, to fragment the solidarity of a working class that has two sexes, and to reinforce class domination.

How this issue is resolved depends in large part on political choices made by working-class feminists. Union officials are likely to try to contain some of its more radical elements on the understandable grounds that unions are, after all, organizations for economic defence and not for liberation struggles. Opening up the full dimensions of this question may indeed initially be "divisive," if not on the convention floor then on the shop floor. But the full exploration of this issue holds the potential to strengthen unions. Even in the short run, active educational campaigns under the control of rank-and-file women would increase their participation and provide them with some of the political experience and clout necessary to occupy other leadership positions.[19] An understanding of the full implications of this issue *at all levels* of the unions would be an important step in carrying out in the medium term the ideological and organizational reforms that are needed to correspond to the increase in female membership.[20]

More than just equalizing the division of mundane tasks, the generalization of feminist consciousness in the working class requires breaking through the psychological barriers of prevailing gender types and adopting liberated norms. All aspects of femininity and masculinity, including sexuality, must be reformed if women, men, and the relations between them are to change. To underestimate the importance of this struggle is to underestimate the depth and complexity of the interpenetration of sexual oppression and class domination and to ignore the strength and persistence of the unconscious psychological forces that sustain them both. To neglect feminism is to run the risk of replicating the experience of postrevolutionary societies where, despite formal legal equality for women, the material bases of their double burden of paid and domestic labour, their secondary public status, and the emotional bases of machismo and sex-negativity make women dependent upon marriages and families that continue to oppress them. To fear feminism is also to neglect the countervailing forces of class solidarity — whether from shared experience of economic struggle or the ties of kinship and community — that bind women and men alike into class. Finally, beyond even its implications for class solidarity, feminist struggle against the deep sexual fears at the root of sexism is necessary for social reconstruction. "Speaking bitterness" provides, on a mass scale, an essentially psychotherapeutic moment where the violence that festers in the repression of sexuality and the cultural denigration of the feminine can be released. Without such a moment, the eroticization of daily life that women's sexual autonomy implies cannot be realized and the possiblity of freely expressed libidinal lives for children scarcely imagined.[21]

Canadian Feminism: A Turning Point

As a result of the radicalization of women workers that I have described here, the women's movement in Canada and Quebec has reached a turning point. The possibility has opened up for a decisive expansion of "second-wave" feminism's social base, and at the same time the opportunity has been uniquely created for a fusion between the two modes of social opposition, "cultural" on the one hand, class-based on the other, which normally traverse the contradictory universe of advanced capitalism in mutual isolation. The turn, however, to a class-conscious feminism has not been made by the movement as a whole; nor, correlatively, has working-class feminism articulated the full range of programmatic concerns that sixties feminism itself placed on the historical agenda.

The price of not completing the turn is the continued dominance of liberal feminism and the exclusion of socialist feminism from mainstream political debate. Actually, the most anodyne forms of state-sponsored feminism, or radical feminist ideology wedded to reformist tactics, have succeeded in presenting themselves as feminism *tout court*. Socialist feminists were uninterested or in disarray at the time of the discussion on the Constitution in 1982, while better-organized liberal feminists successfully lobbied for the inclusion of an equal rights plank in the Bill of Rights. This achievement should not be discounted; it succeeded where the more protracted efforts of the U.S. pro-ERA (Equal Rights Amendment) lobby failed. However, despite its popular resonance, it made only a limited appeal for equality within the juridico-political framework of the capitalist economy and state. An opportunity was missed to campaign for constitutional guarantees for reproductive freedom, the rights to equal work, equal pay, unionization, self-determination for national minorities, freedom of sexual orientation, and basic economic security for children as important prerequisites for women's equality, particularly for oppressed minorities, and to point out the role of the state in reproducing gender-stratified class hierarchies. Even more recently, liberal and radical feminists and politicians at all levels of government have joined together with Christian fundamentalists in an anti-pornography campaign which, because it offers state censorship as a solution, has a practical appeal for many people partially radicalized by feminist critiques of sexual exploitation and harassment. These developments have helped to legitimate the Canadian state as amenable to women's issues and to align the politics of sexuality on the right.[22]

In order to challenge this recuperation of feminism, it is not enough to denounce it; it is necessary to develop an alternative pole of attraction by furthering the unification of the two moments of left feminist radicalization of the sixties and seventies. The project of building a distinct socialist feminism, which the political integration of these groups both requires and facilitates, itself arose in a particular political and economic con- (or dis-) juncture; where, if you like, the last rose of sixties radicalism met Godzilla, the world-wide recession. Today the economic situation in Canada is changing as technological change and deindustrialization put work as such in question. Paradoxically, this shift may contain possibilities for extending the cultural critiques of gender and family within the workers' movement as a whole, thereby expanding the political base for class-conscious feminism. By way of completing this brief strategic *tour d'horizon*, let us take up these points in turn.

Feminist Ideologies: Integration or Impasse

The key strategic objective is to develop an expanded feminism which incorporates the strengths of each of the generations of feminists while overcoming the one-sidedness specific to each. On the one hand this means recuperating the insights of sixties theory, particularly with respect to sexual and cultural issues; conversely, it means giving it a wider social base. In many ways the development of working-class feminism has already confirmed and extended the socialist feminist effort to pose questions and find answers alike in feminist and marxist terms; that is, by demonstrating that capital and "patriarchal" privilege do structure gender asymmetries in the labour force *and* the household and that both economic and sexual structures are manifested in women's oppression. But the political underdevelopment of working-class feminism, combined with the need to root it in the trade unions on the one hand and to carry out economic struggles on the other, created continuing pressures to relegate sexual and cultural issues to secondary importance. Thus, while there seems to be general agreement in current strategic discussions that the insights of sixties feminism should be retained, there seems to be much less clarity about how to do so. Still, the legacy of sixties feminism, in the changed circumstances brought about by the mobilization of working-class women, means correlatively that feminist theory must undergo a process of class transformation, particularly with respect to the family, which nevertheless preserves the irreducible importance of sexual and cultural freedom (cf. Barrett and McIntosh 1982; Segal 1983).

A starting-point for the necessary work of correction is to realize that the women's movement of the sixties was ideologically limited by its restricted social base — specifically the absence of significant numbers of working-class and unionized women. If its analysis of culture and sexuality was strong, its understanding of the state and class politics was not. Formulated as a call to "smash the family," feminist analysis could not explain why working-class *women* as well as men have fought to defend the possibility of family life. Thus, sixties theory, produced by a particular contradictory dynamic of class and sex struggle, was often age- or class-biased and too abstract to serve as a basis for policy formation. All the same, it *did* contain crucial insights not easily available to working-class activists.

Workplace-based struggles do not generate an insistence on the positively liberating aspects of eroticism or on the need to challenge the family as an institution. On the contrary, as contemporary capitalist developments undermine family stability, and as the fallout from the disco-*Goodbar* commodification of sexuality and from rising rates of social violence produces a climate of fear and uncertainty, one reaction is to defend it. But defensive responses to maintain the illusory privacy of individual family life against impersonal economic rationality are not the only reason for protectiveness about families. As Humphries (1977b) and Luxton (1981) have pointed out, kinship networks have also traditionally provided a support base for working-class struggles. Their steady disintegration in late capitalism thus has a mixed import for class-based politics.

Although there has been a tension between feminist and class politics throughout the history of the women's movement, its form of expression has varied radically according to the circumstances. Much of the sixties emphasis on sexuality and the family as a site of conflict between women and men reflected not just the characteristics of feminists as individuals or the specific character of the cultural conjuncture, but the student/youth social composition of the new left where female-male relations revolved intensely in a movement-defined space that was simultaneously political, erotic, and emotional. In contrast, feminists who are in the labour force are placed in another powerful relation with men as fellow workers, union members, and class members. This surely makes their gender situation even more complex — both richer and more confusing. Ehrenreich (1980: 5) has put the dilemma well: "We are all pulled in at least two directions. On the one hand, as feminists, we are drawn to the community of women and to its political idealization as a sisterhood of free women. It is this sisterhood, this collectivity of women, that we believe to be the agent of revolutionary change. On the other hand, we are pulled by . . . 'fleshy, familial ties' to a community of men and women — fathers, lovers, brothers, sons, neighbours, co-workers — out of which comes our sense of class solidarity."

By now, however, an accumulation of common experience has created the conditions to overcome differences between the two generations of feminists that arose out of their different work and sexual histories. While "middle-class" feminists have entered the workforce for a variety of biographical and financial reasons, feminist critique has been diffused through the mass media, co-optative educational reforms, trade union projects, and so on to other working women. In addition, the issue of sexual harassment has been a vehicle for women workers to confront the ways in which their (economic *and* sexual) oppression is reproduced through maintaining and exploiting female sexual vulnerability. Thus, the fusion of initially different emphases on personal and work life has proceeded, without, however, producing an explicit theoretical or political elaboration. Understanding Ehrenreich's double bind is, I would argue, crucial to left feminism's further progresses.

Feminism and Trade Unions in the New Conjuncture

Today the economic conjuncture in Canada is changing in ways that may help to advance these theoretical and strategic issues by moving the questions of work and family to centre stage in the labour movement. Like most of the advanced capitalist world, the Canadian economy is undergoing a process of structural transformation that seems likely permanently to reduce labour requirements, creating rising unemployment and producing enormous social dislocation and suffering. Whether as a result of technological change or deindustrialization resulting from a shift in the global division of labour, high levels of unemployment have already hit workers of all ages, sectors, skill levels, and educational levels. In particular, an "alarmingly high rate of unemployment among female clerical workers" — as high as 26 percent in 1985 and 46 percent in 1990 — has been projected for the main area where women found work in the expansionist 1960s (Menzies 1981). If these labour reductions are introduced simply in the interests of capital, the consequences for women workers and their movements could be disastrous: sharpening gender inequalities in work, wages, and social power, eroding the membership base of unions and undermining the capacity to resist.

Coming to grips with this problem presents an important opportunity for feminists and unionists because it poses the questions of work, gender, and family in one integrated moment. First, simply in order to carry out defensive struggles it is necessary for the labour movement to combat primitive sexism generated by competition over the remaining jobs, a consequence of unregulated but systematic disemployment. Although women experience disproportionately high rates of unemployment that are often disguised by underemployment in part-time, seasonal, or underqualified work or by being swallowed up in family membership (Armstrong and Armstrong 1980), their continuing visibility as workers provokes attacks that they are "responsible" for the loss of male jobs. To deal with job loss in general, Canadian trade unions have already initiated a call for the reduction of the working week in order to redistribute employment more equitably and in order simply to work less. To be effective, such a campaign must take on the question of women's and men's relationships to work and "family." In the short run, demands for the redistribution of work must also find ways to integrate affirmative action and equal pay policies that have only recently become part of the labour movement's *active* policy. To be effective in the long run, however, what is required is a reconsideration of the nature of work in late capitalist society. Gorz has suggested that in conditions of job scarcity the possession of a job becomes a social privilege that serves to fragment sections of the working class—to confer privilege on the traditional organized proletariat which is politically fragmented from the unemployed and the new mass workers.[23] Indeed, possession of a job/salary or "breadwinner power" has long been a material basis of male privilege within the family.

Whatever the success of efforts to redistribute work, the social effects of economic transformation may also affect relationships within families and marriages. For men, a loss of work puts not only economic survival but also personal identity at issue. Deprived of "breadwinner power," men will be willy-nilly "freed" from a hitherto forced reliance on a masculine ethic of work, stripped of a material base of male power, and faced with the prospect of rebuilding individual character structure and relationships with women on something other than these patriarchal bases.[24] Simple resistance is, of course, possible, but so are other outcomes. As part of a complex process, some men will, through an interest in their wife's wages, move to support equal pay while others who find themselves conjuncturally dependent or unemployed over the long term may, like the Sudbury miners, become more responsible for domestic and childcare activities, with positive results for family relations. Given the real need and widespred acceptance of women's right to work, women are likely to resist measures reminiscent of the 1930s which scapegoat them or solve the crisis on their backs. At the same time, since they are well aware of the costs *and* benefits of the double day and the wage, they are also likely to use any opportunities to press for greater equality both in the workplace through unions and in the guerrilla struggles that go on with regard to domestic and emotional life — that is, those who choose to maintain permanent and particularly childraising relationships with men.

While neither the social transformation of masculinity[25] nor the sharing of domestic labour resolves the question of the family, together they promote greater equality. Similarly, while even a highly sophisticated and militant campaign to redistribute work and to gain some benefit from technological change will not cause class structure to melt magically away, it does introduce important debates into the labour movement. And if heightened consciousness of the perniciousness of sexual oppression does not mean liberation, or only makes present situations sometimes seem too much to bear, without this awareness no progress is possible. With these questions on the agenda, whether as a result of feminist agitation or economic transformation, the mixed and labour left must respond to issues in the reconstruction of culture that have been a feminist concern for some time now; indeed, the task of forging an opposition bloc on feminist and socialist bases becomes more pressing.

Notes

1. Originally solicited for a book on the left in Canada in the 1980s (which did not appear), in one sense, this article provoked the decision to set out on the long process of producing the current collection: "One article on women? Impossible, we'd need a whole book!" It was previously printed in *New Left Review* no. 141, and is reprinted here with permission.
2. The effects of this transformation appear everywhere in women's writing: in fiction by Nicole Brossard, in Mary Daly's philosophical poetics, and in Dorothy Dinnerstein's provocative psychology. For a discussion see Catherine Stimpson, "Neither dominant nor submissive," *Dissent* (1980).

   Much of the material for this piece was gathered from interviews with trade union feminists. Since some of them wish to remain anonymous, I have not attributed any statements. I would like to thank Gay Bell, Dierdre Gallagher, Meg Luxton, Gail Scott, Wally Seccombe, and Andrew Wernick, who read and commented on an earlier draft; the women who offered their views on the women's movement; and all those who offered much-needed support as I went through the identity crisis of facing its past and future. An earlier version of this paper was presented at the "Socialism in the 1980s" conference, Vancouver, January 1981.
3. The federated pan-Canadian state is, first of all, riven by the effects of unresolved national questions with regard to Quebec, Acadian, Inuit, Dene,

and the many Indian nations. Secondly, the ten provincial governments, as well as those of the territories, control labour, education, family law, most human rights provisions, and some aspects of cultural policy, while other specific aspects of educational and research funding, human rights, divorce law, and taxation are federal responsibilities. Finally, the population is gathered into dispersed regional economic and political centres across the continent. These political and economic conditions obviously affect the women's movement in all sorts of practical and political ways. For example, the two most consistent campaigns in Quebec and British Columbia for repeal of the *same* federal law on abortion were carried out in isolation from each other. National meetings—on, for example, daycare—almost always require federal funding, which brings with it attempts at political control. Finally, immigrants—particularly women — are often isolated by language and intimidation.

4. The terms of the debate were largely defined by Sheila Rowbotham, Lynne Segal, and Hilary Wainwright in *Beyond the Fragments*.
5. The fact that these forces are also anti-labour is the conjunctural basis for an alliance of unionists, feminists, and lesbian and gay liberationists.
6. Interview, December 1982. For a similar statement from U.S. women, which points to equal pay as a feminist issue, stresses the difficulties of media-distorted "feminist jargon," and points to unions as "the main tool that women have, that workers have," see District 65, "Union Women on Feminism," *Heresies* 9 (1980): 85.
7. Julie White, *Women and Unions* (Ottawa 1980); 27 percent of the female workforce is unionized in comparison with 43 percent of the male labour force, and over 60 percent of the female membership are in public sector unions. In the decade following 1966, female membership increased 160 percent in comparison with 40 percent for men.
8. Public health nurses in Toronto and hospital workers in Winnipeg demanded equal pay for work of equal value, as have hospital and clerical workers, nurses, and teachers in Quebec's Common Front. For historical material, see Judi Coburn, "'I see and am silent': a short history of nursing in Ontario" and Elizabeth Graham, "School marms and early teaching in Ontario," (Acton et al. 1974).
9. For example, with Steelworkers, at Stelco in Hamilton. The list includes a joint campaign by machinists and local women in St. Thomas, a Women into Rail campaign, and the integration of the sawmills in B.C. These situations deserve to be studied in depth.
10. The major reports to conventions of the *centrales* include CSN, "La lutte des femmes: combat de tous les travailleurs" (1976) and "La lutte des femmes: pour le droit au travail social" (1978); CEQ, "Condition féminine" 1974; and Fédération des Travailleurs du Québec, "Femmes et syndiques," 1973.
11. *Resources for Feminist Research/Documentation sur la Recherche Féministe* 10, no. 2. Reissued in Briskin and Yanz (1983).

12. Women's struggles against exclusion from the auto industry in the U.S. met with at least an ambivalent response from their union (Gabin 1982). It is likely that similar exclusions occurred in Canada.
13. Unionization, of course, benefits women and men economically (Gunderson 1975; White 1980: 57). Nevertheless, higher-paid skilled workers have refused to bargain for across-the-board increases which effectively erode their own income, particularly with respect to peers, in an inflationary period.
14. Recently, however, benefits for women have been strike issues in the context of a pro-natalist policy. The Quebec public sector Common Front obtained the best maternity/parental leave provisions in the country—twenty weeks at full pay (instead of fifteen weeks at 60 percent with an obligatory loss of two weeks' salary provided by federal insurance benefits) with up to two years of job security; the Canadian Union of Postal Workers struck unsuccessfully for maternity benefits among other issues; in 1980 CAIMAW (affiliated to the mainly B.C.-based Congress of Canadian Unions—membership about 40,000—which has a good record on women's issues) held out for seven months in a strike for equal pay for work of equal value for seven female data processors; equal pay became an issue in a strike by the Vancouver Municipal Workers later in 1981.
15. In Montreal, IWD celebrations were held by the unions as a "fête populaire" with little political content in 1973 and 1974; in 1975, women from the inter-central *commission féminine* along with those from abortion and health work, daycare, and the far left held a teach-in which led to several co-operative demonstrations. In 1978, drawing on the Montreal example, women in the Revolutionary Marxist Group—now defunct—promoted IWD celebrations/demonstrations to link up with union women across English Canada. Some centres, notably Vancouver, had already begun to mark IWD.
16. B.C. Federation of Women, Saskatchewan Working Women.
17. These were roughly on union/non-union lines. In Montreal in 1976, the union women demonstrated for maternity leave; the *groupes autonomes* for abortion rights. Lesbian rights were an issue in Toronto in 1978 and 1979.
18. The typology of harassment is taken from Catherine A. MacKinnon, *Sexual Harassment of Working Women: A Case of Sex Discrimination* (New Haven 1979).
19. Women are vulnerable here because they are isolated and often because, untrained by unions, they may break shop-floor standards. Sexual insult playing on homophobia can of course be used against men, but, whether it's a woman or a man who is called a "stupid cunt," the insult is misogynistic.
20. Some unions have held sexual harassment workshops, offered assertiveness training, adopted resolutions, and so on. But Kadar (1982: 176) concludes: "Apart from the high profile and very positive influence of the National Union of Provincial Government Employees . . . the unions, despite good intentions, have not held their own in this area." Women are often discouraged from reporting incidents, particularly against fellow workers.

21. Kate Millett (1979) illustrates a negative outcome of this relation in her discussion of the torture and murder of a young girl accused of being sexually promiscuous.
22. It is important to stress the contradictoriness of these developments. On the one hand, the kind of equality "in and under the law" promised by the Bill of Rights is, as Juliet Mitchell (1976) points out, a limited form of equality that cannot challenge class inequalities under capitalism. It also gave Judy Erola, then minister responsible for women in the Liberal government, wide non-partisan support. But victories are more energizing than defeat, and liberal feminists in particular now have a legal basis and an organizing precedent to carry out the legal reforms that have been in their bag for some time now. Its impact on developing feminist consciousness on a wider scale remains to be seen, and the whole question deserves to be studied (Findlay this volume).
23. It is appropriate to discuss André Gorz's *Farewell to the Working Class* (1982), because it was one of the key texts discussed by top union leadership at the CLC winter school in 1983.
24. As the European peasantry was freed from the land by the development of capital.
25. This transformation has been underway since the 1950s as a result of changes in the nature of work, the commodification of male sexuality on a well-defined feminine model, and women's and experts' demands; witness the spate of books like Marc F. Fasteau's *The Male Machine* (New York: McGraw-Hill, 1975) and Ehrenreich 1983.

6 Socialist Feminism: Activism and Alliances[1]

CAROLYN EGAN

Introduction

The development of feminist political economy or socialist feminist theory has always been closely linked to the development of a socialist feminist practice. Theoretical work in an academic context is readily available in books and journals. What is not available is the history of the practice of socialist feminist groups and organizations.

This article presents an analysis of the history of the political development of one of these organizations — the Toronto International Women's Day Committee (IWDC) from 1978 to 1986. IWDC has evolved from a coalition to organize a demonstration and celebration for International Women's Day in 1978 to a permanent multi-issue socialist feminist organization which is unique in Canada and internationally (if only for its longevity). What IWDC illustates is the necessity for and the richness of an analysis which rests on both class and gender, not merely for understanding the situation of women in the abstract, but for the development of an action-oriented political practice which seeks to liberate women.

In 1977 the women's movement in Toronto was for the most part a loose network of services and single-issue organizations. Although many women identified themselves as part of a women's movement, unified political action was very rare. There had not been a multi-issue, activist group since both the Toronto Women's Liberation Movement and the Toronto Women's Caucus ceased to exist in the early seventies. Although they saw service organizations and single-issue campaigns as necessary, feminists were critical of their limitations and attempted on several occasions to develop a basis for broader politics through conferences, setting up a feminist centre (Women's Place), the founding of the Lesbian Organization of Toronto, and a protest march in International Women's Year, which brought together several sectors of a fragmented feminist community, and restated by now fundamental demands for reproductive rights, childcare, and equal pay.

In the fall of 1977 women from the Revolutionary Workers' League proposed organizing an event for International Women's Day 1978 which would pull the movement together publicly in the face of widespread proclamations that the women's movement was dead. In their analysis, an autonomous women's movement, essential to women's liberation and the struggle for socialism, must include working-class women from the trade union movement, black women, native women, and other women of colour, as well as other feminist activists. After several discussions with ten women from different areas of organizing, most agreed that there was potential for such an event, and began to plan a more representative meeting.

When about 200 women responded to the call to organize International Women's Day (IWD), it appeared that the feminist community could unite to mobilize on a multi-issue basis. But political differences focused on whether or not men should be allowed to participate in the IWD demonstration soon surfaced. On the one hand, socialist feminists supported an open march with all those who wanted to support women's struggles. They argued that a display of broad-based unity was needed to show our strength and to challenge the state to respond to our demands. On the other hand, Women Against Violence Against Women, a radical feminist group, argued that men should be excluded and the day reserved for women. Both groups supported the principle of an autonomous women's movement, a women-only celebration/dance, and women taking responsibility for organizing the day. The real issue was deeper than a conflict over a male presence on the march.

The disagreements derived from the difficulties of developing ways to organize on the issues of class, race, and gender in a situation where contradictions arise from the particular manifestations of sex oppression for women with different class backgrounds or perspectives. Although most of the women supported some version of socialism, and certainly all of them supported women's liberation, we disagreed about priorities and how to build a movement.

For socialist feminists, it was a question of whether the coalition would take a broad orientation, move beyond a self-defined feminist community, and reach out to women who had not been involved before, such as trade unionists, immigrants, black women, native women, and other women of colour. We wanted to fight the misconception that the goals of the women's liberation movement were divorced from the lives and realities of working-class women and women of colour, and to begin a process of building long-term alliances.

After an unfortunately acrimonious debate and a vote (2 to 1), WAVAW and its supporters walked out. Those remaining constituted ourselves the Coalition for March 8th and went on to organize a march and rally in which almost 2,000 people participated. The demands at this event were control of our bodies; free quality childcare for all; a stop to cutbacks in social services and education; full employment rights and economic independence for women; the right to express our sexuality as we choose, and not to be harassed and discriminated against for a lesbian orientation; full rights for native, immigrant, and black women; and an end to all violence against women. On the day itself "End The Deportation of Jamaican Mothers" emerged as a major focus.

This march, the largest feminist presence Toronto had seen in years, responded militantly to the media's pronunciation of feminism's death. It also began revitalizing and reshaping the Toronto movement. Its success reaffirmed the potential of broad-based, multi-issue, mass organizing. As a result, a number of women felt the need for an ongoing group which would maintain the solidarity we had developed, provide a vehicle for consistent political practice, and enable us to use newly established links to reach out and build much wider participation in the women's movement. Without any elaborate planning or major ideological struggle about our self-definition or our direction, the International Women's Day Committee was formed.

International Women's Day Committee: The First Year

During its first year the group was very active in the areas, identified as priorities, of abortion and employment rights. We helped to organize a meeting on women and employment and initiated a very successful public meeting on the right to abortion, linking the struggles in Ontario and Quebec. A hoped-for campaign did not develop, for lack of community support at that time.

A number of strikes involving women provided opportunities for trade unionists and feminist activists to work together, for example by organizing a women's picket and benefit to support the mainly women workers at Fleck, with Organized Working Women (see Maroney this volume). Later, in the fall of 1978, after trade union organizers put us in contact with a committee of wives supporting a strike against INCO in Sudbury, we worked very hard to organize a support meeting for the strikers and their families where $15,000 was raised. This work, which involved several months of contact with women in Sudbury, strikers, trade union officials, and local women's groups, showed us the growing feminist militancy of union women and the crucial importance of connecting with their energy and consciousness. At the meeting, speakers from the labour movement stressed the need for cooperation between the labour and women's movements, but, although IWDC had done much of the organizing for the event, it was not represented by a speaker. After evaluation, we felt that it was important to take the opportunity to publicly present our political perspective at such meetings and not to be content with only a service role as organizers.

With our general strategy validated by our first year's experience, we continued on the same lines through a second, even larger, International Women's Day in 1979. In the first two years we did not try to define our politics more explicitly but relied on what we thought were our shared objectives and understandings. But however successful this way of working had been, after IWD 1979 we reached an organizational dilemma. Some felt that we were not providing political initiative and were in danger of becoming a service organization whose primary role was to initiate annual IWD celebrations for the women's movement. After one and a half years, it was time to make our implicit political orientation more explicit.

Developing a New Basis of Unity

Operating on the basis of assumptions that had not been debated gave IWDC an appearance of unity while obscuring differences. Largely depending on individual histories and current affiliations, members had very different levels of political knowledge and of commitment to socialism. As a result, some women with long political backgrounds and more developed verbal skills were able consistently to play leadership roles. Many of those in the RWL (or other organized left-wing groups) argued that IWDC should remain a primarily activist group open to most women and not develop a higher degree of self-clarification. Others, both long-term feminist activists and women whose first experiences in the women's movement were much more recent, wanted to maintain the activist approach so crucial to our early development but nevertheless felt the need to discuss basic political issues such as the relationship of capitalism and patriarchy, socialism, the role of lesbians in the women's movement, the state, etc. A third group of experienced women who wanted to discuss socialist feminism more theoretically were impatient with what discussions there were in IWDC. After a period of some confusion, it was decided to discuss basic political issues more openly in order to develop a formal basis of unity which would make clear what we stood for and how we saw change taking place.

Since activism had brought success to the group, we were aware that introspection could be dangerous. Our original attempt to integrate a process of reflection and dialogue with a full program of activism was too much for the membership and so not very successful. At the end of concentrated discussions which lasted almost six months, our numbers were significantly reduced. While activism gave a sense of dynamism to the group, these discussions were nonetheless a very important step for us.

In developing a basis of unity we wanted to clarify the purpose of IWDC, its political presence, its role in relation to other groups, and the methods for achieving our goals. Although we were committed to building a mass movement of women in the long term, we understood that we were a current, not the movement itself. We agreed that capitalism must be fundamentally altered to achieve the liberation of women, that patriarchy and capitalism are interwoven, that mass action is necessary to win gains from the state, and that we need to make alliances with other progressive forces, particularly within the trade union movement, if we are to achieve our goals. We also wanted the basis of unity not to exclude women currently in the group, to encompass the range of thinking within IWDC at that time, and to allow new members to join on the basis of a clear political statement.

Important lessons were learned from the discussions. They included a renewed sense of the role of practice in the development of our politics, and a new recognition of the necessity of allowing the space for thought, analysis, and evaluation at the same time. We also learned that political assumptions had to be made clear to enable both less and more experienced members to take part in making decisions and choosing priorities, while at the same time to allow breadth and flexibility in our political orientation.

As time went on our membership felt increasingly comfortable in calling ourselves socialist feminist. In our practice we continued to work with trade union women, helping to organize support for striking workers at Fotomat, Puretex, Radio Shack, Blue Cross, Bell, the hospitals, the post office, Irwin Toys, and Mini-Skools. A trade union subcommittee was established to co-ordinate this work. Although we had a number of successful meetings and workshops on the issue of women and microtechnology, we learned that it was difficult for a group like ours to initiate a campaign on this kind of issue on our own and that it was important to work with others. As a group we have also been involved in activities in support of equal pay for work of equal value, daycare, reproductive rights, the lesbian movement, affirmative action, the peace movement, and struggles against racism, imperialism, and violence against women. We have sponsored public forums alone and with others on topics such as the rise of the right (which dealt with abortion, racism, and the oppression of lesbians and gays), lesbians and the women's movement, capitalism and patriarchy, and women in Central America.

Coalition Politics

In the following years, IWDC became one of the most successful and dynamic organizations in the women's movement and the left in Toronto. In our first and subsequent statements of purpose one of the main principles has been building mass actions. Three other principles guide our organizing. First, in particular struggles we attempt to work toward two goals: immediate concrete gains, as well as a much larger process of building alliances for a longer-term struggle for a transformed society.

Secondly, we see building such a movement as a process of organizing coalitions of oppressed groups including women; immigrants, blacks, and people of colour; lesbians and gays; and workers. Coalition politics link and integrate struggles and ideally help each constituency broaden its consciousness of the others' oppression and take seriously a much wider range of issues than they would otherwise. The alliances that we've worked to build have not been just between organized groups, but also between different constituencies that have historically had little to do with one another — the immigrant and the lesbian and gay communities for example. Third, we have attempted to develop socialist feminist process and methods of organizing, which are aimed at empowering people through the struggle for change. We feel that the manner in which we organize and structure ourselves today should reflect the type of society we hope to create.

The way these principles guide our political activities can be illustrated with two examples: our work supporting the postal strike; and the way in which we have helped to bring a multi-issue, broad-based perspective to the most recent campaign for full access to free abortion.

When the Canadian Union of Postal Workers went on strike for paid maternity leave in 1981, CUPW's leaders understood that they needed widespread support to win their fight against the federal government. The union president, Jean Claude Parrot, wrote to women's groups across the country asking for their support. Although there was no formal coalition, most women's groups supported this demand, organizing press conferences and holding rallies and demonstrations. In Toronto IWDC helped to organize weekly solidarity pickets and built support within the women's movement for the strike. For us it was quite important that the issues of working-class women be strongly supported. But there were strong political differences within the wider feminist community. Not all feminist groups supported the larger trade union issues, particularly the right of a public sector union to strike. Because of IWDC's socialist feminist analysis and its previous strike support, we understood that the right to strike is also a feminist issue. We put out a leaflet arguing that working-class women need this right in order to win their demands.

This strike and the strong women's support for its goals paved the way for gaining better parental leave benefits for both organized and unorganized workers, demonstrated the clout of a united trade union and women's movement, and broadened consciousness and understanding within both communities.

Coalitions have since become more common in the women's and trade union movements. The Ontario Coalition for Abortion Clinics (OCAC) came together with a very specific goal, the legalization of free-standing clinics providing medically insured abortions, and repeal of the federal abortion law. Given the failure of hospitals to provide abortions to all who require them, and doctors' extra billing, such clinics, operated on good medical and feminist principles, are one way to provide more equitable access to abortion for all women. Through OCAC the women's movement has initiated a major offensive against state and medical control of women's bodies with the possibility of winning real gains for reproductive rights. In Canada, the strategy of establishing freestanding clinics outside the law was first adopted in Quebec in the early 1970s, largely at the initiative of Dr. Henry Morgentaler in conjunction with the women's movement (see Gavigan this volume). After a long struggle, the Quebec government has allowed abortions in public community clinics and the independent Centre de Santé des Femmes and covered by the provincial medical insurance plan.

While OCAC is not a socialist feminist group, the fact that many of its core activists are and come from IWDC in particular, give it a strategy that I see as socialist feminist. OCAC believes that winning the struggle for the legalization of freestanding clinics requires a broad-based movement willing to be vocal in its support and able to defend the clinics against attacks by the right and the state. Sharing a class analysis, the socialist feminists in OCAC have turned to the labour movement as a potentially powerful ally. As a result of the work of women activists within the unions, it has provided the most consistent support outside the women's movement for the abortion issue.

The legalization of clinics is vital economically for most women. The campaign also stresses that legalized clinics, as important as they are, will not in themselves bring full reproductive freedom for most women. When we use the word "choice" we are addressing something beyond formal, legal freedom: real possibilities for all women. For working-class, native, and black women and other women of colour, full access to free abortion means not just the legal right to choose, but good, free clinics under their control, located in their communities, and staffed by people who speak their language and understand their culture. In fact, in past coalitions, black women, immigrant women, and women on family benefits have insisted that reproductive rights also include the right to have children. OCAC also takes the position that we require economic independence, paid parental leave, free universal childcare, and custody rights for lesbian mothers, if the choice to have a child is to be a real one. In *The Anti-Social Family* Barrett and McIntosh (1982) argue that the demand for freedom of choice leads to only a partial victory and that liberal individualism of this sort wins changes which are limited according to women's ability to pay. But they also insist that we must at the same time continue to demand the legal right to choose, because we cannot leave control of our bodies or our lives to men, the church, the state, or any other power.

OCAC wants to make it crystal clear that we are asking for greater access to abortion not only because the economic crisis makes it more difficult to raise children, but as part of a challenge to conventional views on motherhood and gender roles. Socialist feminists argue that the right to control our reproduction is a fundamental aspect of the struggle for women's liberation, but that it must be seen as one of a whole range of feminist issues that must be won. OCAC attempts to link economic, ideological, and sexual aspects of women's oppression. It stresses the class exploitation of women in the workplace who are denied paid parental leave and childcare, whose inadequate wages leave us the largest percentage of the poor. It also speaks of racism, rape, violence, the forced or coerced sterilization of native and other women, the denial of the right to determine our own sexuality, and the role of the state, as well as the fact that we still bear the major responsibility for domestic work and childraising. By raising the demand for abortion rights within this broader context, OCAC exemplifies a socialist feminist perspective.

Socialist Feminist Process and Vision

I want to say a few words about group structures and the manner in which socialist feminists try to work, keeping in mind that I'm not suggesting that we have developed a model for non-authoritarian political activity. We are all products of a sexist, racist, heterosexist, class society, and have internalized what it teaches us. We often reproduce its patterns unconsciously, and have a tendency to put more value on skills that are prized in a patriarchal, capitalist world.

For us as socialist feminists politics is more than just a question of a united front for socialism. We want to build an understanding that the way we organize today is inseparable from the kind of society we want to create: a society without class, without racism, without sexism, without heterosexism, without oppression. We want to learn not merely how to allude to each other's struggles in our programs through coalition politics, but also to begin, in concrete ways, to more fully include them. In other words, we want to do more than support each other's goals; we want to truly integrate them as part and parcel of the same struggle, so that an analysis of the oppression of women is integral to the trade union movement, and the women's movement takes up strong anti-racist and anti-imperialist perspectives.

The new forms of political life that we are trying to create are attempts to overcome internalized oppression that affects us all. We don't always succeed, but the important point is commitment to the process of transforming our consciousness as an integral part of organizing for economic and structural change, to integrating our future vision with our present practice. Taking the time to build the links between theory and practice allows us to become more effective politically, and to develop greater capacities for collective political analysis and leadership. Because equalizing people's skills is a crucial component, we try to function in a non-authoritarian manner, using non-hierarchical structures and non-intimidating styles, rotating tasks and responsibilities, and making a commitment to develop the talents of all, including newer, members of the group. We often don't succeed, and more skilled and more experienced people continue to play more dominant roles. We are trying to integrate our theory into our daily political functioning, learning from our practice, and attempting to keep in mind our principles when we evaluate our work and develop our future strategies.

The socialist feminist synthesis of marxism and feminism into a working politic has challenged the traditional left in a very profound way. It has sparked a broader consciousness of the oppression and exploitation of women, and demonstrated the strategic importance of the struggle for the liberation of women to the class struggle. Traditional marxist theory has not adequately dealt with the ideology and structure of women's oppression, which is deeply rooted in contemporary capitalism. And while the ulitimate emancipation of women may depend on the struggle for socialism, it cannot be subordinated to it as has traditionally been the case (see Weir this volume). Socialist feminist practice and theory have a constructive role in the socialist movement and a responsibility in the overall process of social change. We have influenced the vision of socialism so that it differs from more orthodox visions in significant ways.

Our experience brings invaluable lessons, but we need to reflect on its broader implications and not neglect developing theory from our practice. We have a tendency to prioritize local experiences and not go beyond them. And obviously, though our goal is a mass movement of women with a class analysis, the greatly increased consciousness of women's issues has not been transformed into a broad-based movement made up of large numbers of poor, working-class, black, and native women and other women of colour.

The model of coalition politics, linking struggles of people of colour, trade union, immigrant, lesbian and gay, and feminist groups, is itself no longer new. But coalition politics is still a valuable experiment which could help in building a broad political movement. The model can help us to gain the sensitivity, knowledge, and experience to overcome the problems of isolation we face in each of our movements and increase our understanding and appreciation of each other's situation and the role we play in each other's oppression. We can learn not only how to reflect each other's struggles in our own, but also, without diminishing the significance of the oppression each is fighting, to begin to develop in practical and concrete ways a strategy of working in common. We can build on the strength of the localized, grassroots mode of organizing with its attention to process and practice, but combine it with the development of an analysis which speaks to the need of building the unity and efficiency that in the long run is necessary.

In 1984 IWDC went through a difficult process, facing the same questions and uncertainties affecting most political movements, unsure how to consolidate the gains that we had made, or how to move forward in the economic crisis. We had become reactive, not taking the political initiatives that we had in the past or integrating discussion fully enough into our practice. Although some women left the group, and the organization's continuing existence was questioned, a strong core of women decided to stay together, hoping to collectively work through the political and organizational problems that we faced.

IWDC's political history allowed us to reexamine our perspectives and priorities and provided the foundations for future directions. We needed to come to grips with a very basic question — What should the role of a socialist feminist group be in the 1980s? — and to rethink our views on political discussions and education and organizational functioning. In setting goals and priorities for 1985, along with our traditional areas of work, we took a higher profile in mainstream organizations such as the National Action Committee on the Status of Women, involved ourselves in mass campaigns such as the end to medicare extra billing, and took on anti-racism as a major focus. We had worked in the past in RACAR (a community anti-Klan group) and the Albert Johnson Committee (named for a black man who had been murdered by the police), and with the Committee Against the Deportation of Jamaican Mothers, but hadn't integrated an anti-racist perspective into our socialist feminism. The work of autonomous black women's and women of colour's groups, the writings by black and women of colour feminists as well as specific individuals heightened our consciousness for the need to deal with both the personal privilege and structures of racism. We helped to initiate the proposal that March 8, 1986 have the single focus of "No to Racism from Toronto to South Africa." As a predominantly white group, we had to recognize that we must take an active role in developing an anti-racist feminism and in building a women's movement with the participation and leadership of black, native, and South Asian women and other women of colour.

As our process of political development continues, there are many questions for which we are still seeking answers. Once again growing in membership, we are clearer in our political direction. We want to continue our activism, but we have learned that we must take the time for dialogue among ourselves and with others which will help us to clarify our political perspectives and allow us to take an active role in the political community.

Note

1. I want to thank many women for their help in developing this article: Linda Gardner, Andrea Knight, Mariana Valverde, Cindy Wright, and other members of IWDC; Meg Luxton and Heather Jon Maroney for their invaluable editing; and, most particularly, Judy Persad and Maria Wallis for helping me to understand the need for a truly integrated and anti-racist socialist feminism.

II Political Economy and Gender: The Division of Labour

7 A Gendered World: Women, Men, and the Political Economy of the Seventeenth-Century Huron

KAREN ANDERSON

Much of feminist writing on the social position and status of women relative to that of men has been theorized from advanced capitalist situations. This focus has shaped certain problematics and understandings. It has been frequently argued, for example, that women's status relative to that of men in capitalist societies is largely the outcome of a series of historical events combined with a specific set of social structures which results in the confinement of women to the "domestic sphere" and the relegation of men to the "economic" one. This division, which gave women the home and "private life" as their special "sphere," rendered them and their children dependent on the wages of working husbands/fathers (see for example Zaretsky 1976).

For many North American feminists the family has been identified as a central locus of women's oppression. However, the very separation between men's and women's work and lives, which appears to be such a liability for women in capitalist societies, has to be viewed in a different light when found in precapitalist ones. Thus the family, which takes on such a special meaning for women's oppression under capitalism, cannot be automatically imbued with the same meaning in other modes of production.

The seventeenth-century Huron are a case in point. Although Huron women's and men's lives were distinctly different from each other and although kinship relations and the family played a central role in Huron society, a reading of the historical record left by explorers and missionaries indicates that Huron women held extensive decision-making power over their own activities and sometimes over those of men as well. The world of the seventeenth-century Huron, divided as it was into male lives and female lives, and dominated by kinship and the family, was also characterized by "non-incursive" relations between the two genders. The central problem of this paper emerges from that observation. How was it that

Huron women and men occupied egalitarian positions even though they had little in common in terms of their economic, political, and even emotional roles in society? Phrased another way, under what conditions do differences between men and women lead to egalitarian relations, rather than to oppression?

Theoretical Issues: Women as Producers or Reproducers?

Although the issue of whether or not women have ever occupied an egalitarian position with men in any society is still being debated,[1] this paper begins with the affirmative assumption. Rather, the issue of concern here is why, under conditions of obvious differentiation, seventeenth-century Huron women were free from male oppression. Two possible directions in answering this question emerge from the writings of anthropologists specifically concerned with precapitalist societies. One set of explanations focuses on the position of women as *producers* of the means of subsistence, the other on the role of women as *reproducers* of society's members.

A certain number of theorists, influenced by Frederick Engels's *The Origin of the Family, Private Property and the State* have argued that the explanation for women's high status in many non-capitalist societies lies in the way in which they are integrated into economic life. In *Origin,* Engels developed the argument that at one point in human history women were free from male domination. Although men engaged in economic activities and women in domestic ones during this era, the division of labour did not result in women's subordination. Everything necessary for the existence of society's members was held in common, with both women and men having equal right of access. It was only with the introduction of both male-owned private property and a state structure to regulate property relations that women and children, as propertyless members of society, were relegated to positions of chattels and excluded from full participation in society.[2]

The work of such modern-day researchers as Eleanor Leacock has been influenced by Engels's theoretical propositions. In her work on the Montagnais-Naskapi, for example, Leacock argues that the women of this hunter/gatherer society were not subordinated to men until colonialism undermined traditional economic arrangements. Colonialism forced women into a position of economic dependence when it introduced commodity exchange exclusively in the hands of men.[3]

Other anthropologists less influenced by Engels also note a "separate but equal" status for women, but attribute that status to women's special position as mothers. Colin Turnbull, writing about Mbuti elders, notes that "as elders both male and female revert to their former, almost asexual state, except that whereas the one has not created life out of his body, the other has, out of hers, and is consequently held in considerable esteem" (1981: 205–19; see also Sacks 1974).

Like Turnbull, Peggy Sanday attributes women's "separate but equal" status in certain precapitalist societies to their role as mothers, but seems to agree with Leacock that male dominance is most likely to occur in societies under stress, especially stress from colonialism (Sanday 1981: 9). Unlike Leacock, however, Sanday does not attribute the appearance of male dominance to changing economic relations between men and women, but situates her explanation in the need for biological survival. "The social body is sometimes entrusted to men," Sanday states, "as a reward for being the expendable sex . . . ; if women willingly embraced mass slaughter [in defense of their dying traditions], there would be no social body to preserve" (cited in Jackson 1983). Thus it would seem that under certain circumstances women's role as mothers allows them egalitarian status with men, while under other circumstances, it relegates them to less powerful positions.

Although understanding women's roles as producers of the means of subsistence and as reproducers of society's members is important to any attempt at theorizing the nature of male/female relations in precapitalist societies, an exclusive focus on either creates more problems than answers. If we focus solely on the role of women in economic production to explain their status in precapitalist societies, we are soon faced with a number of anomalies. Why, for example, do women make important economic contributions in all societies, but only achieve egalitarian status in some? If control over the product of one's labour is really at the bottom of things, why is it that some women, typically those of peasant societies, produce and dispose of a number of products of their own accord, but still suffer from relatively low status in society?

Focusing on women's roles as reproducers has its own set of problems. Although motherhood may confer high status on women in a society like that of the Mbuti, it is no guarantee of such a status in other societies.[4]

Concurrent with developments in theorizing about the status of women in precapitalist societies, but rarely intersecting with them, is the work of marxist economic anthropologists.[5] Writers in this tradition, such as Godelier, Meillassoux, and Terray, have concerned themselves with the relation between kinship as social relations of production and the economic, political, and ideological "instances" of specific precapitalist modes of production. Disagreements are frequent and cannot be dealt with in this paper. What is of importance for us, however, is that in spite of their preoccupation with kinship as social relations of production, few of these writers have paid attention to the relations between the two genders which form the basis of all kinship systems. Where the issue of female/male relations is raised, as in Claude Meillassoux's work on the Guru, it is to argue that women are subordinated to men because of their (economic) importance as bearers of new members of society.[6] Although this argument is most likely valid for the Guru, the work of other writers has made it clear that it is not acceptable as a general theoretical statement.[7]

A Proposed Synthesis

If we compare the more general theories of precapitalist societies on the one hand, and theories dealing specifically with the status and/or position of women in those societies on the other, it appears that there is an unfortunate disjuncture. This disjuncture has retarded the development of theorizing and needs to be surpassed. If we wish to understand the dynamics of precapitalist societies we must first understand the significance of kinship as economic, political, and ideological relations. This task, in turn, requires us to begin with the most fundamental division in precapitalist society: the division between female and male. It is from a perspective that considers the ways in which women and men are both divided from each other and then reunited into functioning economic, political, and emotional structures that a deeper understanding of the general nature of social relations in precapitalist societies can be obtained.

Using the seventeenth-century Huron as a case study, it is argued that the relative statuses of women and men can best be understood in terms of the ways in which the gender-specific division of labour first separates men from women and the ways in which the kinship structure reunites them into economic, political, and familial units. The relations between Huron women and men were largely the outcome of structural arrangements, arrangements which placed kinship and the family at the centre of society and gender at the centre of kinship and the family. In this paper I take a step toward developing a theory of the significance of gender and kinship in precapitalist societies by evaluating the conditions necessary for maintaining "non-incursive" relations between female and male spheres of activities as well as the conditions under which kinship structures either support or undermine such "non-incursive" relations. While I do not suggest that the case of the seventeenth-century Huron can be used as a general model of male/female relations in all precapitalist societies, I do suggest that an understanding of the dynamics of social relations within most precapitalist societies can best be understood in terms of the intersection of gender and kinship.

Kinship and Gender: The Case of the Seventeenth-Century Huron

When French explorers, traders, and missionaries arrived at the turn of the seventeenth century they found the Huron,[8] or 8endat[9] as they called themselves, living on a strip of land about thirty-five miles long and twenty miles wide, bounded on the west by Georgian Bay and on the east by Lake Simcoe (Trigger 1976: 27). The Huron were a confederacy, composed of four tribes — the Attignawantan, the Arendarhonon, the Attigneenongnahac, and the Tahontaenrat (Thwaites 1896–1901, Vol. 6: 227). A fifth group identified by the Jesuits as the Ataronchronon was most likely a division of the Attignawantan.[10]

Modern-day scholars have suggested that the Huron population was between 18,000 and 21,000 persons when they were first contacted by the French in the early seventeenth century. Following a series of European-introduced epidemics, that population was reduced to about 9,000 in the 1630s.[11] During the period between their first contact with the French in 1609 and their destruction by the Iroquois in 1648–49, the Huron were distributed among eighteen to twenty-five villages[12] ranging in size from 300 to possibly 1,600 persons.[13] Villages were "clusters of longhouses" (Heidenreich 1971: 125), in some cases surrounded by a palisade and separated from each other by intervening agricultural land and forests.[14] They were placed in naturally defensible locations, near streams for canoe travel and near well-drained, sandy soil for corn cultivation (Trigger 1976: 52).

The Huron's location on the southern shores of Georgian Bay gave them easy access by water to the hunter/gatherer tribes of the Canadian Shield and placed them between those groups and other horticulturalists settled to the south. It was this strategic location that allowed them to become intermediaries between the French and the fur-producing tribes in the interior. This location, too, marked them as the first settled group of native peoples Jesuit missionaries chose to proselytize.

It is difficult to study the seventeenth-century Huron and remain unimpressed by the extent to which both gender and kin relations affected every aspect of their lives. Each individual Huron was embedded in a series of ever-widening kin-based relations which began with the nuclear family and extended outward to finally embrace other nations. We can distinguish six levels of social, political, and economic organization: the nuclear family, the longhouse (an extended, matrilocal, matrilineal familial grouping), the matrilineal clan, the village, the tribe, and, finally, the confederacy. At each of these levels individual Huron were located in relation to one another in terms of rights and obligations based both on their gender and on the specific kinship relations they held to each other.

The relatively egalitarian status of men and women[15] within Huron society as a whole is best understood, not in terms of a single summary statement (such as their roles as producers or reproducers) but as a series of gendered "locations" within a fairly complex structure based on kinship. We must look, therefore, both to the division *and* to the union of women and men to understand the relative statuses each gender occupied in Huron society. What follows is an examination of the implications of genderic separation and its kin-structured recombination for the relative statuses of women and men in the economic, political, and personal spheres.

The Economic Sphere

The mainstay of the Huron economy was the shifting cultivation of corn, beans, and squash, supplemented with fishing and to a lesser extent with hunting and gathering. The production and distribution of those foodstuffs were carried out on the basis of gender-specific tasks mediated through complementary sets of kin relations. Men's work and women's work together made up that totality necessary to sustain individuals from day to day and to ensure the succession of generations.

Each Huron occupied a gender-specific position within a structured set of kin relations. These kin relations in turn functioned as social relations of production. Each set of kin relations was ascribed with mutually complementary rights and obligations. Broadly speaking, those sets of rights and obligations extended from the nuclear family to the matrilineal, matrilocal longhouse and finally to the members of a clan segment resident in a single village. The longhouse, however, made up the most important unit in which Huron economic and social life was carried out. Each longhouse was typically composed of surviving first-, second-, and third-generation female descendants of a common female ancestor, their husbands (from other clans), and most unmarried male children. The longhouse might also contain some married men of the female members' clan and their wives (from other clans), especially if those men were clan leaders.[16] Generally, three to six matrilineally related nuclear families lived together in one longhouse.

Since most subsistence activities took place in nature, the economic lives of the Huron were regulated by seasonal cycles. In agriculture men and women of the same longhouse[17] engaged in different but complementary tasks, with women taking the larger share of responsibility. In the early spring, both men's and women's work teams set out to prepare the land for planting; men's teams cleared trees, while women's teams burned the land over to rid the fields of felled trees and underbrush.[18] Here labour was organized on the basis of simple co-operation within work teams. Two other economic activities carried out in early spring were hunting (done by the men) and wood gathering (done by the women of each longhouse).

Huron villages were generally abandoned in the summer. Men left during the early months to go fishing, trading, and warring (Thwaites 1896–1901, Vol. 35: 142). Women went to work in their fields, where they lived in small cabins with their children. The women planted their crops in late May, and during the rest of the growing season they and their children hoed and weeded their crops and chased small animals and birds out of the fields. Often women worked in teams, moving from one field to the next in succession. During the late summer they gathered wild berries, fruit, and hemp. They harvested the corn, dried it, and stored it in bins especially designed for that purpose. Although each woman most likely had her own field, all women of the same longhouse kept their grain in common, each taking what she needed for her family's daily meals from the longhouse's common store.[19]

While women tended the fields, men were free to trade, hunt, and engage in warfare. After the first decade of the seventeenth century, with the coming of the French, the fur trade played an ever-increasing role in the Huron economy. Although the Huron produced little or no fur of their own, they rapidly came to be the most important intermediaries in the French fur-trade network. They achieved this position by trading European goods and Huron corn with interior hunter/gatherer tribes for furs which they then transported to trade with the French on the St. Lawrence.

Only a small portion of Huron men were directly involved in the fur trade as actual traders. Since these men traded as representatives of their clans, trade goods were clan, not private, property. One indication that women received their share of trade goods is the number of trade axes found on excavated historic sites. Trade axes were largely women's tools, used for clearing underbrush and collecting firewood.

By the end of harvest time, Huron men returned to their villages from trading and warring expeditions (Thwaites 1896–1901, Vol. 8: 91). They were joined by the women, who, freed from agricultural duties, accompanied their male relatives on hunting and fishing trips to clean and prepare the catch. Like corn, fish was a foodstuff that the Huron dried and stored in common in each longhouse. Hunted game, on the other hand, was either eaten on the spot or taken back to the villages to be shared among the men's clan members. This meant that a married man gave meat to his mother's and not to his wife's longhouse. Meat, both hunted and domesticated dog, was mostly consumed as part of clan feasts. Husbands and wives, being from different clans, did not attend the same feasts. Since children took their clan membership from their mothers, they, too, did not attend feasts given by their father's clan. The production and consumption of food, then, as well as commodity exchange, were two of the most important ways in which kinship served both to separate male and female, and at the same time to unite them into economically viable units.

Winter was a time of socializing and feasting, especially after hunting or ice-fishing expeditions returned to the villages. Winter gave women and men time to engage in household tasks: women wove mats, made pottery, spun twine, and did decorative arts. Men made nets and snares and manufactured implements for war, hunting, fishing, and agriculture.

Even these activities were marked by an interdependence between men and women. Women used the hemp they gathered to spin twine which the men then fashioned into the shields and armour used in warfare.

Every eight to twelve years, when the agricultural land and firewood sources were depleted, the yearly cycle of the Huron would be interrupted by the movement of a village and marked by the great "Feast of the Dead."[20] Historical accounts of this feast left by the Jesuits indicate that as well as being an emotional event in which feelings about all those who died during the tenure of the village were vented, the feast served as a major vehicle for the redistribution of goods.

At each phase of the Huron's yearly production cycle, then, women clearly made important contributions. The French explorers, traders, and missionaries who visited and wrote about them were all impressed with the extent to which women participated in economic life. As the trader and adventurer Samuel de Champlain noted:

> Among these tribes are found powerful women of extraordinary stature; for they till the soil, sow the corn, fetch the wood for the winter, strip the hemp, and spin it, and with the thread make fishing nets for catching the fish and other necessary things they have to do; likewise they have the labour of harvesting the corn, sorting it, preparing of it and attending to the house and besides are required to follow their husbands from place to place, in the fields, where they serve as *mules* to carry the baggage with a thousand other kinds of duties and services that the women fulfil and are required to carry out. As to the men, they do nothing but hunt deer, and other animals, fish, build lodges and go on the war-path.[21]

Champlain's observations were echoed by the Recollect lay brother Gabriel Sagard who lived among the Huron from 1616 to 1620. Sagard noted that women and girls did more work than the men "although they are not forced or compelled to do so."[22] Of the men Sagard noted the following:

> [The] occupations of the savages are fishing, hunting, and war; going off to trade, making lodges and canoes or contriving the proper tools for doing so. The rest of the time they pass in idleness, gambling, sleeping, singing, dancing, smoking or going to feasts, and they are reluctant to undertake any other work that forms part of the women's duty except under strong necessity. (Wrong 1939: 96)

It is clear that seventeenth-century Huron women made economic contributions which, if anything, surpassed those made by the men. Women, for example, provided most of the labour necessary for producing corn (and for turning it into a consumable food), a staple that accounted for about 65 percent of Huron caloric intake.[23] Women, moreover, seemed to control the distribution of this important foodstuff, since corn was stored and used in common by members of each matrilineal longhouse, and since it was women who prepared meals. The hunted foods distributed by men to their clan members, although ritually and symbolically important, accounted for less than 5 percent of caloric intake.[24]

Yet this imbalance between men's and women's contributions to the economy does not in itself explain the relatively egalitarian status of Huron women. While it is true that Huron women exercised control over both their labour processes and the products of their own labour, they did so under specific sets of relations with other women and with men. If we wish to understand why Huron women were undominated by Huron men, we have to uncover the conditions which held the relations between the two genders in place. In economic matters, in matters of day-to-day living, working, and eating, it was clearly the matrilineally structured kin relations which supported women's right of undominated access to the necessities of life. How did those kin relations work to ensure women their fully adult status in Huron society? To answer this question we need to turn to an examination of what can loosely be termed the Huron political structure. It is precisely in the organization of the clan system — which tied tribal politics to domestic structures — that the real strength of the position of women in Huron society is to be found.

The Political Sphere[25]

Maurice Godelier (1981: 10) argues that in the last instance women everywhere are subordinated to men because nowhere do women dominate the political processes of any society. A first reading of the evidence on the Huron leaves the impression that, at least on the political level, men were firmly in control. A closer examination, however, raises a number of important questions, especially when we begin to examine the intricate relation between domestic and political structures.

The most significant unit of political organization for the Huron was the matrilineal, exogamous clan. Eight such clans formed the basis of Huron political organization (Thwaites 1896–1901, Vol. 33: 243, 247; Vol. 38: 283). All political representation, whether at the longhouse, village, tribal, or confederacy level was made on the basis of clan membership.[26] Clan membership, too, was an important factor in the distribution of material goods, social support, and the choice of marriage partner. Each matrilineal clan was represented on village, tribal, and confederacy councils by male civil leaders (Thwaites 1896–1901, Vol. 14: 231). At the village level, these civil leaders[27] dealt with social and political aspects of life that affected all residents, including feasts, ceremonies, games, public projects, and the care of orphans, destitutes, and foreigners (Thwaites 1896–1901, Vol. 14: 229). Separate from the civil leaders were war leaders, who organized both the rituals surrounding warring and the war parties themselves.

The role of any clan leader, however, whether civil or war, was to *exhort* the members of his clan to carry out the decisions made in council meetings. According to Jesuit observers a clan leader "exercised small authority over his subjects" and was unable to govern by command or with absolute power, having "no force at hand to compel [his people] to their duty" (Thwaites 1896–1901, Vol. 10: 233). This is a significant point, for when it came time to enforce decisions made in clan councils, Huron men had to rely on the good will of all their clan members, including women. Without their co-operation, decisions could be made, but not acted upon.

Although little direct information exists on the role of Huron women in relation to the functioning of clan councils, information on the Iroquois, who had similar social, economic, and political structures, points to an important role for them. In her work on Iroquois women, Judith Brown (1970) found that while women never held public office among the Iroquois, they did exercise considerable influence through their ability to elect and depose clan leaders. There is every reason to expect that Huron women also had this capacity. While major decisions such as succession of the clan leader were usually made by "clan mothers," that is, by the older matriarchs, many other Huron women were able to exercise a certain amount of "political clout" by either complying or not complying with the decisions made by male clan leaders.

An indication of the power of some Huron women to override decisions made by clan leaders can be found in the Jesuits' reports on their own attempts to set up a seminary for Huron boys at Quebec. One of the most ardent wishes of the Jesuits was to bring young Huron boys to their seminary at Quebec, instruct them in the ways of French Catholicism, and then return them to their own people as missionaries. The fur trade was used as a lever to obtain these children. Huron clan leaders were persuaded that trade and military relations with the French partly depended on a certain number of boys attending the Jesuit seminary. In response to this demand Huron clan leaders promised to deliver male children into Jesuit hands at Quebec City. The mothers of these promised children, however, refused to comply. As the Jesuits reported, when the children were ready to leave Huronia for Quebec, the mothers "and above all the grandmothers" would not allow it. The fathers then offered a "hundred excuses" and the Jesuits had to content themselves with the grandson of a clan leader (Thwaites 1896–1901, Vol. 9: 283). A similar incident occurred a few years later when, in the Jesuits' words, "the extraordinary tenderness which the savage women have for their children stopped all proceedings and nearly smothered our project in its birth — only one went and he was nearly full grown" (Thwaites 1896–1901, Vol. 12: 29–41).

When we consider the relative locations of men and women in the political sphere it is necessary to keep in mind the underlying structures of Huron society. Certainly men *visibly* dominated the political processes. It was men who were clan leaders; men sat on councils, made decisions, and were charged with realizing them. It was men, too, who had direct relations with foreigners, who traded, went to war, and forged political, military, and economic alliances with other nations. But even the most important arrangements that clan leaders made with their French allies risked undoing if they involved something that women could not, or would not, support.

As with their economic roles, then, we need to evaluate Huron women's political power in terms of the underlying structure of kin-based social relations that supported or undermined them. Although male clan representatives made political decisions in council, those same representatives had to bring their decisions back to the longhouse to be implemented. The Jesuits' observation that clan leaders had no means at hand to force or compel others to follow their decisions applied to women as well as to men. "In the last instance," regardless of what decisions were made in political councils, it was up to individual Hurons, both men and women, to carry them out.

This is not to suggest, however, that anarchy reigned. Very powerful sets of rules and conventions came into play when any individual tried to exercise his or her own will against the general consensus. Those persons who continually manifested anti-social behaviour were unceremoniously dispatched as witches or traitors. If we look at the issue more deeply it is possible to discern that women as well as men exercised *some* personal power and that power varied from individual to individual. One of the most structurally powerful positions within Huron society was that of matriarch or "clan mother." Within each longhouse these older women exercised a certain degree of personal power that was not available to men. If any son-in-law displeased his real or classificatory mother-in-law, he found himself barred from her longhouse. Often this was not such a hardship since the man was usually welcomed back into his own clan's longhouses. But if this man also displeased his own or classificatory mother(s) he found himself without food or shelter.

The particular configuration of male/female relations in Huron society, produced by the intersection of kin arrangements with gender-based economic relations, gave those Huron women who had achieved the role of clan mothers a kind of political power that even clan chiefs had to recognize. As with their position in the economy, women's strength in politics stemmed from the extent to which underlying kin relationships supported them, as well as the men, in different but mutually interdependent roles. While Huron women may not have held formal political office, their position within the kinship structure afforded them a considerable amount of informal political power equal to, if not at times surpassing, that of men.

Marriage, the Family, and Divorce

A final sphere in which Huron men and women were both separated from each other by distinctly different roles and united together through kinship relations was marriage and divorce. Among the Huron, as in most societies where kinship functions as social relations of production, marriage, childbirth, and divorce were important life events — not just on the personal and emotional level, but also in terms of establishing economic and political ties. It was through marriage that two important economic relations — the exchange of labour obligations between women and men and the exchange of the products of labour — were established. Marriage, too, was usually followed by the birth of children, which in turn guaranteed the continuation of the clans that formed the basis of Huron political life.

Marriage ties not only linked single men and women together as economic partners and potential producers of children, they also provided links between clans (as political groupings) and longhouses (as economic groupings). Marriages served to tie extended kin together to ensure the reproduction of Huron society. Since residence was mostly matrilocal, each longhouse contained a core of matrilineally related females whose husbands were drawn from different clans. These men owed labour as well as the products of their labour both to their wife's kin and their mother's kin. Because children of Huron marriages belonged to their mother's clan rather than to their father's, men identified more closely with their sister's children than with their own. Ultimately men's most secure ties were with their mother's and not their wife's longhouse. The self-sufficient tendency of each longhouse, then, was counteracted by the links provided when male children came of age and married outside of their clan. Although marriages were undertaken within the context of emotional and personal considerations, they constituted one of the major bases, along with birth and adoption, on which the genders were united into functioning economic and political units.

In spite of the economic and political importance of marriage alliances, as well as the importance of children to the continuation of each clan, male clan leaders did not exercise absolute authority over the marriage choices of their female kin. The role of the extended family as an economic unit, combined with a political structure based on matrilineal clan representation, allowed both women and men a great deal of freedom in their sexual and marital arrangements. Within the guidelines set by rules of clan exogamy, Huron women and men exercised personal autonomy in choice of sexual partners, marriage partners, and divorce. Although young women were expected to take parental advice when choosing their first husbands (Huron women often divorced these first choices), no young woman was forced to accept a suitor she did not want, and consent of both partners was required before a marriage would be socially recognized (Thwaites 1896–1901, Vol. 27: 31; Vol. 30: 37; Vol. 33: 87; Biggar 1922–1936, Vol. 3: 138; Wrong 1939: 122). The rate of marriage, divorce, and remarriage among the Huron provoked the sarcastic comment from one of their Jesuit observers that it was "the ordinary practice of the savages . . . to change wives at almost every season of the year" (Thwaites 1896–1901, Vol. 15: 77).

Personal autonomy in marriage and divorce extended to the right of young women and men to exercise discretion over choice of premarital sexual partners as well as over frequency of contact. Sagard, Champlain, and the Jesuits all expressed shock that Huron women not only willingly engaged in both premarital and extramarital relations but that they often actually initiated the contact. Young girls, Sagard reported, vied with one another over who could have the greatest number of lovers. Each village, he added, had its "procurers" whose occupation it was to bring men and women together for intercourse (Wrong 1939: 133–34).

An individual Huron's capacity to change marriage partners or to marry a partner of his or her own choice rested on a firm economic and political basis. As we have already seen, the longhouse served as a unit of production, consumption, and residence. As long as there were enough males and females of working age in relation to the number of dependent children and elderly members in any one longhouse, a woman or man of marriageable age but without a spouse was not an economic liability. Although an unmarried adult did not have access to the product of labour of a spouse, he or she did have access to the product of labour of other members of the longhouse. Clan and longhouse membership provided most Hurons with a sufficient number of kin relations to give them economic and social security. Moreover, Huron women were under no pressure to produce large numbers of children to guarantee their own, their husbands', or some elders' economic security. The kinship structure of the Huron, functioning as social relations of production, provided most members of society with enough economic partners and co-workers in the form of either real or adopted kin to adequately ensure their existence through all stages of their lives.

When the Jesuit missionaries arrived in Huronia with the expressed intent of converting the Huron into a loyal, Catholic, Frenchified peasantry, they immediately came face to face with the real strength of the Huron kinship structure. Although the Jesuits' understanding of the need for Christian marriages was often phrased in terms of bringing the "Savages" under the yoke of Christian law, the issue went much deeper than a correct moral attitude to marriage, divorce, and sexual expression. To institute Christian marriages meant to break apart the existing family structure, a structure which gave women an egalitarian status with men. With Christian marriages women's authority in the longhouse was broken. The power that was once wielded by individual matriarchs was moved outside the longhouse and into the hands of the church and the state.

The structural position Huron kin arrangements afforded women had traditionally meant that they were capable of exercising their own wills in matters pertaining to marriage, divorce, and the adoption of new beliefs. It also meant that they could exercise some control over the actions of their husbands, their sons, and more frequently their sons-in-law. As we have seen, while all Huron women were not capable of influencing the behaviour of all Huron men, even clan leaders were at a disadvantage in relation to their own mothers and wives, as well as to their mothers-in-law. Given their structural position women proved to be formidable foes to the instituting of Christian marriages. Although they often excused themselves by saying that they could not agree to stay with the same man for the rest of their lives, or that they could not remain "faithful" to their husbands, their hostility to Christianity can best be seen as resulting from the real threat it levelled at traditional household arrangements and thus at the true basis of women's authority in Huron society.

The Basis of Non-Incursive Gender Relations

Seventeenth-century Huron women and men lived in a gendered[28] world: a world clearly divided into female and male lives and experiences. What was women's work, tools, or responsibilities was not men's. What men lived could not be part of women's experiences. Yet, what was divided was also united; men and women, separated in almost all aspects of their lived experiences, were brought together in nuclear and extended families. It was through the co-operative labour of family members that the political economy of the Huron functioned.

Unlike capitalist societies where economic production and exchange is potentially independent of either gender or kin and potentially dependent only on the sale of labour in an impersonal market, the economy of the Huron depended on the existence of both gender and kin. Gender established what types of work, kinds of tools, and manner of social activities an individual experienced, used, and engaged in. Kin relations, defined in terms of mutually complementary and gender-specific sets of rights and obligations, called the labour process and political life into being. Kin relations, moreover, were set in motion at each individual's birth and altered only in relation to demographic events—birth, death, or adoption.[29] If gender structured what kinds of life experiences a newly born Huron would have, kin structured the persons with whom those experiences would be played out.

Within this gender-specific, kin-centred "order of things" the day-to-day life of a seventeenth-century Huron contained little leeway for blurring male/female distinctions and few if any opportunities for questioning gender roles. In spite of this rigid differentiation, Huron women and men led their dissimilar and non-interchangeable lives in an astonishingly egalitarian manner. An examination of the records documenting seventeenth-century Huron social relations has revealed a society which, within certain limits, granted discretionary power to both women and men as they lived and worked within their own "gendered" spheres of activities. Men's work and women's work, men's lives and women's lives, so very different in their content, rhythms, and meanings, seemed to fit together with minimal interferences.

Although men occupied positions that were closed to women, they could not use those positions to aggrandize themselves at women's expense. As we have seen, women were structurally in a better position than men—due to particular kin-based configurations—to exercise coercive power on an individual basis. Women's power base in the longhouse had extensive political ramifications.

It was this matrilocal, matrilineal kin configuration combined with a gender-specific social division of labour which laid the structural basis for the relative power members of each gender were able to exercise in their own spheres of activities. The very structure of kin relations — which recombined what the gender-based division of labour had first separated into active social, economic, and political units—provided women with a firm position from which they could resist any incursions into their spheres of authority. The power of women included, as we have seen, the right to determine what happened to their children and the right not to have to endure culturally offensive behaviour (as for example when men began to convert to Christianity).

At the beginning of this paper I suggested that the disjuncture between the work of marxist economic anthropologists and feminist theorists concerned with the status of women in precapitalist societies needs to be bridged.[30] A number of economic anthropologists have correctly pointed to kinship as social relations of production but few have recognized the gender content of those relations. Feminist writers, by contrast, while pointing to the significance of women's roles in precapitalist societies, have largely failed to give kinship as social relations of production the attention it requires. The case of the seventeenth-century Huron strongly suggests that gender and kinship need to be analyzed together. Among the Huron gender was the most important aspect of kin relations in establishing rights and obligations related not only to labour and its products but also to shelter, social and political recognition, and political effectiveness.

Because Huron women derived so much of their power from the structure of gender and kin relations, it was these very relations that had to be smashed before any new form of centralized, patriarchal authority could be put in their place. Until the Iroquois invaded Huronia itself, killing or capturing the majority of the population, Jesuit attempts to "civilize" these people fell on barren ground. The gender-based social division of labour combined with domestic and political arrangements provided a formidable obstacle to women's subordination.

Notes

1. For a summary of the arguments see Sacks (1979). Chapter 2, "The Case against Universal Subordination," is especially useful. In the Introduction to *Woman and Colonization: Anthropological Perspectives*, Etienne and Leacock (1980) also present a strong case against women's universal subordination to men. For another perspective, also argued from a feminist viewpoint, see Friedl (1975); Ortner (1974), and Rosaldo (1974).
2. For a summary and commentary on Engels's arguments see Karen Sacks (1974).
3. Eleanor Leacock, "Montagnais Women and the Jesuit Program for Colonization" in Etienne and Leacock (1980). For a more developed critique of this position see Karen Anderson (1985).
4. The fact that women bear children may even be, as Meillassoux suggests is the case among the Guru peasants of the Cote d'lvoire, a major reason for their subordination to men. See Meillassoux (1975).
5. Some of the theorists include Maurice Godelier, Claude Meillassoux, Georges Dure, Pierre Philippe Rey, and Emmanuel Terray. For a discussion of these and other theorists see Copans and Seddon (1978). For a discussion of the term "economic anthropology," see Godelier (1978).
6. A critique of this position can be found in Etienne and Leacock (1980: 3–4); in Jackson (1983: 304–7); and especially in Sacks (1979: 96–123).
7. Both Sacks (1979) and Etienne and Leacock (1980) provide good counter-examples.
8. According to the Jesuit Father Lalemant the name "Huron" was first used by French soldiers and sailors as a nickname, inspired by the resemblance of some Huron men's haircut to the fur on the head of a wild boar (*hure*) (Thwaites 1896–1901, Vol. 16: 231–32). Trigger (1976: 27) suggests that the word *huron* was a slang term signifying a ruffian or rustic. The first written record of the use of the term "Huron" comes from Champlain, who recorded the word in July 1623. See Heidenreich (1971: 20). Gabriel Sagard, the Recollect lay brother who was resident among the Huron for several years, used the term throughout his writing.
9. *8endat* (pronounced "wendat") possibly means "the one island" or "one land apart" (Heidenreich 1971: 21–22; Trigger 1976: 27). 8endat refers not to a tribe but to a confederacy and is analogous to the Iroquois *Hodenosaunee*—people of the longhouse. The term referred collectively to the five nations making up the Iroquois confederacy. See Trigger (1976).
10. The spellings adopted here are those used by Trigger (1976). For a discussion

of various spellings, sources, and possible translations of these names see Heidenreich (1971: 301–2).

11. For a detailed discussion of contemporary population estimates as well as current methods of estimating Huron population size see Heidenreich (1971: 91–103). For another opinion see John Dickinson, "The pre-Contact Huron Population: A reappraisal" in *Ontario History* LXXII, no. 3 (1980): 173–79.
12. As of 1976, 117 sites containing large amounts of European trade goods had been discovered. Assuming these sites date after 1610 and the villages shifted every ten years, Trigger (1976: 237) estimates that 29 sites would have been occupied at any one time.
13. For a discussion estimating the size of the largest Huron village, Teanaostaiae, see Anderson (1982).
14. Archaeologists have been able to accurately delineate Huron villages by the distribution of middens. These garbage dumps were "piled up against or just beyond the palisades; or, if palisades were absent just beyond the longhouses" (Heidenreich 1971: 125).
15. Traditionally, the term "status" has been used to refer to the degree to which a person does or does not possess characteristics valued in a particular society.
16. This is a fairly common occurrence among people with matrilineal descent and matrilocal residence practices.
17. For a full discussion see Heidenreich (1971).
18. The Huron temporarily raised the fertility of the soil by burning to remove undergrowth, weeds, and the previous year's corn stalks. Although the short-term results were increased fertility due to release of plant nutrients, the long-term results were thorough depletion followed by a long period of recovery (Heidenreich 1971: 81).
19. According to Sagard, longhouse corn supplies were stored in "large vats or casks of tree-bark" which were kept in porches at the end of each longhouse (Wrong 1939: 94).
20. For discussion of this important feast, see Trigger (1976).
21. Biggar (1922–36, Vol. 3: 131). Possibly Champlain was trying to play on the sensibilities of the French courtiers to whom his writing was addressed. In any case his characterization of Huron women as "mules" should be compared with Sagard's description of them quoted in this paper.
22. Wrong (1939: 102). Sagard's comment that women do more work than men "although they are not forced or compelled to do so" is interesting. Sagard's statement implies an understanding of male/female relations in which the only reasonable explanation for women undertaking arduous labour is that men force them to do it.
23. For an interesting analysis of the relation between work and caloric return see Lee (1969).
24. For a discussion of Huron diet and caloric intake see Heidenreich (1971).
25. Hindess and Hirst (1975) have identified the political as the existence of classes and a state. They argue that without either there can be no political

level. Here, however, I use the term "political" to refer to a socially legitimate body which co-ordinated relations between longhouses, villages, and tribal groupings. Political in this sense does not depend, as Hindess and Hirst suggest, on the existence of a state to enforce one class's will over that of another.

26. For a fuller discussion of the Huron political system see Heidenreich (1971) and Trigger (1976).
27. The Jesuits called these leaders "captains."
28. On the issue of the differences between "gendered" and "sexist" economics see Ivan Illich's *Gender* (1983). In this work Illich opposes "the regime of scarcity" (capitalism) to the "reign of gender" and argues that "the loss of vernacular gender is the decisive condition for the rise of capitalism and a life-style that depends on industrially produced commodities" (1983: 3). Although Illich's ideas are provocative, his solution to the sexism of contemporary capitalist economies is to call for a return to "gendered" or "vernacular" society. This return to past situations where men and women held distinct but egalitarian roles is only possible if we neglect the fundamental differences in the significance of different roles for men and women in capitalist and non-capitalist societies. As I try to demonstrate in this paper, the very structures that support an egalitarian status for women in precapitalist societies (kinship and the family) undermine them in capitalist ones.
29. For a discussion of the relation between demography and kinship see Howell (1976, 1979).
30. Karen Sacks (1979) has attempted such an integration of marxist economic anthropology and feminist concerns.

8 A World of Difference: The Case of Women Workers in a Canadian Garment Factory

CHARLENE GANNAGÉ

Introduction

Men and women in the garment industry have in common "a world of pain."[1] The majority of workers receive low wages, experience layoffs during the slack season, and suffer the ill effects of piecework, including fatigue, heart conditions, nervous disorders, respiratory problems, hernias, and family tensions. One worker referred to piecework as a "rat race — where workers eat each other alive." Another worker stated that his pacemaker was the medal he earned from working in the needle trade. While the list of common grievances is endless, the evidence presented in this paper suggests another world — a world of difference. Both male and female workers are victims of the vicissitudes of wage labour, but what I demonstrate is that the gender division of labour, both as an integral part of the capitalist labour process, i.e., in the social organization of work, and as an ideological force external to the labour process, shapes the experience of women workers. I argue that it is impossible to understand the situation of women workers without taking into account their position within their families. In addition to understanding how the gender division of labour leads to profoundly different experiences for male and female workers, this paper will examine how an ethnic division of labour makes the situation of women and men in the garment industry more complex, not only in obscuring class differences in the factory, but also by forging alliances between male workers and certain female workers.

Traditionally, gender differences have not been a central problematic in the field of industrial relations. Richard Brown (1976) found that most researchers have adopted either a unisex approach to work in which gender does not hold any particular significance or a view that women's participation in the labour force is a special problem for employers. Especially noteworthy are the classic Hawthorne Studies, which did not draw out possible implications of the gender division of labour in explaining why female workers in the Relay Assembly Test Room exhibited more co-operative attitudes toward management than a cohesive group of men in the Bank Wiring Room. Recent critical developments in the study of the labour process which draw on the tradition of Volume 1 of *Capital* (Marx [1887] 1976) have, like their non-marxist predecessors, tended to ignore gender (Braverman 1974; Burawoy 1979; Edwards 1979). A major focus of Burawoy's book is to understand how the labour process "obscures and secures" surplus value by generating consent at the point of production. Burawoy's case study does not address the significance of gender difference partly because he studied an almost totally male factory. More importantly, however, he claims that consciousness is shaped by the labour process and that the labour process is "relatively autonomous" from external factors such as age, sex, and race.

One of the most significant challenges to the sex-blindness of socialist theory and strategy has been the reemergence of the women's liberation movement. Within this flurry of practical and theoretical activity the socialist feminist and marxist feminist current offers the most cogent possibility of transforming marxism by insisting on the centrality of women's role in production in order to understand women's oppression (Benston 1969; Mitchell 1971; Seccombe 1974; Barrett 1980; Fox 1980; Luxton 1980). Contemporary feminist deelopments within marxism have challenged the sex-blind view of industrial relations by arguing that gender is important to understanding the labour process, the organization of the labour market, and analyses of trade union structures and politics (Pollert 1981; Cavendish 1982; West 1982; Cockburn 1983; Briskin and Yanz 1983; Penney 1983; Maroney this volume). Feminists criticize the reserve army of labour thesis used by Braverman and the labour segmentation theory used by Edwards for their inability to account for the specificity of female labour, i.e., why women *as women* are found in certain low-paying sectors of the economy (Baxandall, Ewen, and Gordon 1976; Beechey 1978, 1982; Barrett 1980; Milkman 1976, 1982).

While major strides are being made in the area of gender and work, some of the literature tends to reinforce a bifurcation between women's work outside the home and domestic labour. Rather than focusing on the double day of labour of women who work outside the home, much of the theoretical literature on reproduction has emphasized the political economy of domestic labour and not the interplay of work and family life. Nevertheless, the importance of transforming the women's liberation movement by focusing on the experiences of working-class women remains the main objective of socialist feminists like Sheila Rowbotham. More than ten years ago, she wrote:

> . . . the fortunes of the new feminism will depend on our capacity to relate to the working class and the action of working class women in

transforming women's liberation according to their needs. (1973: 169)

This paper draws upon in-depth interviews of working women in a Canadian garment factory to examine their experiences in the workplace, in their union, and in their family lives.[2] By focusing on the gender division of labour at all three levels of women's experience, this paper will attempt to provide a critique of existing labour process literature and to demonstrate the absolutely crucial necessity of including gender in social science analysis.

Political Economy of a Small Firm

In 1982, the clothing industry employed 75,000 people in Canada. Together with the textile industry it was the third-largest manufacturing employer and the largest employer of women among the manufacturing industries. The average wage in the clothing industry is low; workers earn 63 percent of the average industrial wage. It takes little capital to open up a business —a few sewing machines, a pressing machine and a cutting table—but, as in all small businesses, the owners of the garment shop must be able to capture a corner of the small Canadian market.[3] The business is highly competitive, and the threat of imports from countries with lower wage economies drives prices down on the home market. Clothing establishments tend to be small factories employing on average less than fifty workers.[4] Despite recent technological improvements, the firms are labour intensive. What is striking is the uneven technological development in which conventional shops exist alongside shops using sectionalized methods or semi-automated systems.[5]

A major feature of employment in the garment trade is a relative lack of job security. One worker that I interviewed called the needle trade "a hit-and-run industry" (Bob Zlinger). Unlike large corporate enterprises, small owner-occupied firms do not usually survive if the owner dies or retires. The workers in the plant are dependent on the good health and financial prosperity of their employers for continued job security. Skilled workers in the cloak industry, usually men, are in short supply and are able to find work more easily. Women, employed as less skilled workers, are particularly vulnerable if shops close. The continued threat of factory closures tends to weaken union militancy.

Seasonal unemployment is a regular feature of the needle trade. Although direct government subsidy of the garment industry is small, employees' low wages are supplemented by unemployment insurance and, in the case of workers over sixty-five years of age, government pensions.

Due to predominantly low levels of technological development and the consequent labour intensiveness of the industry, increased productivity and profits are obtained through speedup rather than through capital investment or improvements. Garment shops are dirty, crowded settings often lacking change-room facilities or lunch rooms. Washrooms are not kept clean, and air conditioning is not a priority. Poorly lit work areas, faulty equipment, and unsafe work materials increase the possibility of accidents on the job.[6]

The subject of this case study is a conventional cloak shop where skilled tailors make the whole garment. Located in one of the major garment centres in Canada, Edna Manufacture was portrayed by its employees as a successful small manufacturing firm. In continuous operation since the late 1930s, it employed at the time of this study less than fifty workers, with one-third of its workforce made up of women. Until recently the workers enjoyed steady work and some reported overtime work during the busy season. But given the present economic crisis and the owner's age and ill health, the shop has recently undergone a slump and subsequent scarcity of work.

The Gender Division of Labour

The division of labour in Edna Manufacture corresponded to a horizontal segregation between crafts and a vertical division between craft workers and non-craft workers. Women were ghettoized in the finishers' craft[7] and in non-craft jobs. Men were cutters, pressers, and operators. Each craft in the union had its own autonomous local, although the operators' and finishers' locals have been amalgamated in recent years. The pressers, operators, and finishers were paid by the piece and each had their own separate price list. The cutters, special machine operators, button sewers, and a busheller were paid "time work"; the cutters were paid by the week and usually made the highest wage in the industry. The special machine operators, button sewers, and a busheller were paid by the hour, with button sewers, the lowest paid, earning less than $4,000 a year at the time of this study.

The Men

Many of the operators in the shop apprenticed as tailors[8] in small custom tailoring shops in Poland, where they learned the entire work process including how to cut, press, and sew the whole garment. For those who lived under fascism and were forced into concentration camps, tailoring offered a lifeline to survival. In Canada, they adapted to making the garment in factories where the work process was subdivided into specialized crafts. They were proud of their European training, their ability to transform cloth into a quality product. One operator explained the importance of his work to the production process:

> Henry Klein: The cutter just cut according to the pattern. That's the whole thing. The operator he's got to know the style, the stitching, the making, and the finishing. . . . Every responsibility he got as an operator.

As a skilled craftsman,[9] Bob Zlinger, former shop chairman and operator, took pride in the quality of his work: "The workmanship that I do is still number one." His work was purposeful and required planning and care:

> Well, if I do work, of course, I enjoy it. I still do. Take a garment, let's say. I don't work the same as the others do. In my case, it has to be just perfect. And if it isn't the way I understand it to be, then I rip it and sew it over. I wouldn't let it go through like the others do. That's what I mean by a good operator. You're a little bit more careful. You understand a little bit. Use a little bit common sense too. When you do something, you plan before. You think about it. How it's going to be, how it's going to come out. You look at it like a painter paints a picture.

At its peak Edna Manufacture made over 150 different styles which changed every season. Innovations in styles made the work interesting. The attention to detail and the complications of the design presented a challenge and involved a certain amount of creativity. Part of the skill of the job involved solving difficult problems:

> Al Steinberg: I have a lot of skill in my job [that] I think I can be proud of . . . any complications arise at work, I solve it with my own mind, with my own hands. . . . It's good results and I am proud of myself. I am cloaks operator for thirty-three years. Some people told me I could be a doctor . . . I could be an engineer because there's a lot of other things . . . [that] I can do. I do really a masterpiece.

It was not uncommon for operators to know each other and the quality of their work. They worked together moving from shop to shop when small factories closed. Al Steinberg had a reputation in the trade as "a good and a fast operator." Making a living was important, but enjoying the work made the job rewarding. He derived satisfaction from sewing difficult patterns and outdoing his fellow workers at speed and initiative:

> When I make something and it's good I really am proud. Just like somebody who designed a rocket . . . and it's a success. When I make something, there are people sitting near me, they always ask me what to do. How to start the style. You get a bundle of work. You have to know what to start first. Some is difficult. And I say, "Why you asking me? There's a sample. You go over, have a look and you'll know how to make it." Why don't I have a look? I never look. I take it I make it. Why? I'm gifted.

The Women

Women were primarily concentrated in the less skilled sectors of the factory as finishers[10] and non-craft workers. There were fewer women in the factory; their work was more repetitive and their jobs were viewed as less important because they performed the adjunct tasks of working on the already made-up garment. The finishers received the garment from the special machine operators. Traditionally, the finishers performed the operations that could not be done with a sewing machine. By hand, they tacked the facings, finished the buttonholes, sleeves, and neckpiece, put in the shoulder pads, sewed the hem of the lining, and tacked the lining to the coat.

Finishers at Edna Manufacture did not work overtime. When they were laid off between seasons they experienced long periods without work. Because machines had been developed to take over work, their craft was diminishing. With fewer factories hiring them, it was more difficult for them to find work when a factory closed. The low piece rate for finishing work meant that they had to work harder and faster to make a decent wage.

One finisher described her work as less important because it was less skilled and easier to learn. For her finishing was not challenging since the work was routinized and more repetitious, varying only in the number of buttonholes on the coat. Asked if operators and cutters were treated better, Ruth Domanski replied:

> Yes, with more respect from everybody. . . . Maybe that's because they are the main skill in the needle trade. Without a cutter and without an operator you can't run a factory. Anybody can be a finisher. They'll take anybody from the street and tell them how to do it and they'll do it. That's the difference. All you need is just a little bit attention, a little bit of time to put into it to see what you're doing and that's it. All the finishing you can learn is speed. Everything is the same. . . . It's a standard. You make the buttonhole. You make the facing. You put on the shoulder pads. An operator has to make a straight line. Have to make the fashion. Have to fit. An operator is a skill but not a finisher and that's why finishers are looked down on.

While finishers did not require years of experience to learn their craft, the "working knowledge" that they learned on the job resulted in greater dexterity, speed, and knowhow, abilities which were not positively valued by their male co-workers, the union, or the employer. In recent years, new specialized machines have been developed to take over some of the tasks of the finishers, resulting in a new category of semi-skilled operators, who were usually women. This work was physically demanding, repetitive, and tedious. A special machine operator described her work as an automatic process involving little conceptualization:

Carol Lenski: I hate it because it's physically hard. Because it's not a great deal of intelligence required. It's not challenging. Usually while I'm working I think about other things . . . all kinds of things. Oh God. My mind wanders because I'm so used to doing my job now. I can do it automatically.

Donna Jakubenaite, the lining maker, compared her work to the operator's job. Her job was to sew straight seams, which did not require much ingenuity compared to the skilled tailors who shaped the cloth to fit the contours of the body:

Well, operator must know better how to put pockets, how to put button holes, and make completely the garment. . . . [The] lining maker . . . just sew the seams, that's it, no pockets, no buttonholes, no nothing.

Women's work was not only less skilled and less prestigious, but it was also devalued in material terms because it paid less:

Carol Lenski: Now this is a hangover from the past when men worked and women didn't. So of course the men got the more responsible type of jobs. And men got better paid. An operator or presser gets far better pay than a special machine operator or a finisher.

Men's work was creative and purposeful and required care and planning. They spent more time making the whole garment and identified with the quality of the product. As craft workers they placed a lot of importance on individual accomplishment and expertise. In short, the men had more control over the labour process. Women's work, on the other hand, was repetitious, more automatic, more routinized. Because of the nature of their work, they spent less labour time on each garment. Compared to the male operators, women had less control over their labour process. Although women workers had developed on-the-job knowledge involving speed, dexterity, and knowhow, these abilities were not recognized as skills, but rather the nature of their work was mediated by an ideology of skill differentiation which defined "women's work" as less prestigious or marginal work which deserved less pay.

Gender Ideologies

The owner was primarily responsible for maintaining the gender division of labour in the factory. Mr. Levine was selective in hiring Polish Jewish men to do the operators' jobs. He explained his hiring policies to one worker who reported:

David Lupinsky: The boss that used to be there he didn't like women operators. He didn't like gentile workers in general. You want to

> know why. He told us "No matter, if I have a dispute with a Jewish worker," he says, "time it goes by, we're the best of friends. But with gentile workers you think that you've settled the thing in a day or two he could leave you. You have to search for other workers." And with women he says, "The worst part of it sometimes they start to cry. The majority start to cry," and he decided he just couldn't take it. In this respect, he wasn't entirely wrong as far as women have a habit of crying. They have a habit of crying right away. Not every person that is alive, but the majority of them do show tears.

Maria Lebella told the story of a Portuguese female operator who was not hired despite first-class work. It was not her skill but her ethnicity and sex which was the basis for a hiring decision:

> Another lady was come for work by machine. And she was work very nice. She finish a coat and I say "Oh, you make very nice coat," I met her in the toilet. She say "I don't think so he likes." I say, "Why?" She say, "Because I am a woman. I'm not Jewish." I say "No. I don't think so what difference?" I do not even know. "Everybody is a man just two woman." I say "What's the difference? If you work he going to look at your coat." Everybody say she . . . make a nice coat. It was lunchtime. After lunch the foreman say "Oh you make a nice coat. You go home. We going to call you," he say. "Now not so busy."

The immediate agent of the ideology of the gender division of labour is often male skilled workers found in the leadership of the trade union who safeguard their privileges by espousing the employer's view of women workers. A former machine operator and retired business agent of the Cloakmakers' Union responded to a question about women's lack of trade union participation in terms of the marginality of womens' work:

> Abe Boksenbaum: They had no ambition to advance themselves and come and say "All right, I'm going to run for election." Because their work was of minor calibre, so they probably felt that they would not make it. . . . It was important to be done, but you didn't have to have that experience that an operator or cutter or even a presser has to have to do the work.

The union leadership through the hiring hall had co-operated with the owner's request to hire male Jewish operators at Edna Manufacture. Even if a small percentage of women were successful in being hired as skilled operators, they were continually reminded that they had entered a male preserve. Theresa Green was one of the few female skilled operators in the cloak industry who could make the whole garment. She described her first job in Canada working at Hosannah Garments with male operators who, she felt, found it difficult to accept her years of experience:

> To begin with I think they objected to me being a woman, having the experience I had. Does that sound crazy? Because many times different men would ask me where did you learn this as if it was something [out of the ordinary]. And I told them it was all women I worked with in my country but I think they resented the fact that I knew my job. I just didn't feel comfortable working there.

She did not like "the atmosphere" at Hosannah Garments. She was one of few women; the shop chairman gave her single coats and "rotten bundles" made up of lower-priced merchandise. She felt isolated because the other operators spoke Yiddish. She often lost money because she didn't understand the prices of certain styles.

She tried to leave Hosannah Garments but the union hiring hall made it difficult for individual operators to change jobs without the agreement of union officials. A friend from Edna Manufacture told her about a job in his factory. Bob Zlinger, the shop chairman, interviewed her. When she approached Mr. Boksenbaum, business agent, for a working card to move from Hosannah Garments to Edna Manufacture she encountered an unforeseen problem:

> Mr. Boksenbaum called a shop meeting. And you know what the meeting was about? About me wanting to quit. And I was sitting there and he ignored me and said, "Now there's this person she could be a grandmother for all I know." Stupid things like this, he was saying. He had been drinking. "I didn't know who she thinks she is—she can come and go as she pleases." I swear. It was ridiculous. Anyway it come to nothing, it was a stupid meeting. I come home and cried my eyes out. Really I was sick.

After working at Hosannah Garments for more than fifteen years, she finally obtained a job at Edna Manufacture. She was one of several women operators. For the first few months she found herself in intimidating situations in which the owner embarrassed her in front of her fellow workers. She vividly recalled one altercation:

> There was this coat with no name on it. So they looked around. Who made this coat? And I looked inside the coat and saw it was mine. Well he got onto me in front of everybody. He said, 'Do you think you're going to make more money if you don't put your name on the tickets?' Things like this — it seems like such a little thing but there were different occasions when these things happen that you feel, "Gee, why would I do this intentionally?"

Similar to the practices at Hosannah Garments, the shop chairman gave her single coats and low-priced styles in an attempt to break her spirit. She felt that she was the victim of humiliating scenes in which the shop chairman played the role of foreman instead of union representative.

A Theory of Wages

In *Manufacturing Consent* Burawoy identified what he called a "theory of profit" which contributed to the consensual nature of the labour process. He argued that workers do not view their own labour as a source of profit, but rather they subscribe to a view that profit is "some form of earned reward for past practices or for the risk of capital investment" (1979: 29). In this way workers' and capitalist theories of profit converge. Some workers at Edna Manufacture strongly subscribed to such a theory of profit:

> Sheila Glaber: The boss has a lot of money. Well, listen, he's lucky. He took chances and he's ambitious. It goes a long ways by the time you make money. You have to be very ambitious, you have to be lucky, you have to take chances. You have to work very hard and you have to fit in with the times. A lot of people got wealthy because they fit in with the times. They took chances. They bought houses. They bought land. They made big businesses. They made big factories.

What makes this theory appear logical in a small firm is that job security clearly depends upon the owners' ability to run profitably.

> Irv Smelser: It's only human. He's in business to make money to make a living . . . maybe more than a living. Well, I [have] been considerate. I wouldn't be in a position not to be able to fulfill my promise. So I have been considerate and I figured I couldn't put too much hardship on him.

The theory of profit on the part of the workers combined with what Edwards (1979) calls "simple control" on the part of the employer, in which personal relationships are used to discipline the workforce.[11] Because of the small size of the shop, the fact that the employer put in long hours and often worked alongside his employees, and because he himself was a former worker, it was easier for him to establish a relationship of paternalism with his employees. One worker referred to the owner as a "friend." Another attended union meetings and at the request of the employer argued for a cut in pay in order to "help out" the owner. Labour discipline involved a one-to-one supervisory relation with the employer.

> Sheila Glaber: So sometimes you have a problem . . . . He said, "It's no good, you have to fix it" . . . . Sometimes even in a harsh way when he gets mad. But you felt that you were guilty, you have to do it. They

> have to sell the garment . . . . It's a business. You have to consider them too. They don't give it away. The garment has to appeal to you. Otherwise they don't buy it, so he has no business, so we have no work. It has to work together.

At Edna Manufacture a "theory of wages" also contributed to the consensual nature of the labour process. It involved gender politics and served to weaken class solidarity at Edna Manufacture by dividing male and female workers against each other. Two strategies were at work, both mediated by women's position in the family. The first was to devalue women's work by arguing that women were economically dependent on men who were earning a "family" wage. Men needed to earn enough to support their wives and children. Women, on the other hand, were wives and mothers first and wage earners second. The second argument concerned the ideology of skill differentiation whereby women's work was associated with less skilled work which deserved less pay. In the latter case, it was precisely because women were working a double shift at home and work that they were seen as temporary workers who lacked the continuity of work experience to become skilled workers, or, as we have seen, as women they were barred from opportunities to become skilled workers.

Family obligations of the male breadwinner were seen to legitimize his claim for higher wages, but women's family obligations were only taken into account when it was argued that women should be excluded from the labour force:

> Sam Gold: Because it's girls, they figure a girl makes a hundred dollars a week, that's enough. But a man wouldn't work for a hundred dollars a week . . . . A girl don't need as much as a man. A man's got a family. You're not sure with the girls. Today they are working. The next day they are not working. They're pregnant. Sometimes they're sick. Before [the employers] didn't have no troubles, I took the garment and had to make everything.

While some male workers subscribed to the view that women were economically dependent and men had to earn a family wage, the experiences of the failing economy often contradicted the gender ideology espoused by employers and trade union leaders. David Lupinsky's short-term gender interest to receive higher wages than women workers contradicted his long-term class interest to increase the wages of all workers:

> You'll say that I'm old-fashioned. I still don't believe that women should work. I think the women's place in the home to bring up children the way supposed to be brought up. Some of them go out just to work for their own purpose just to spend a few dollars more. *Come a time with just two hands you can't make a living nowadays.* (my emphasis)

Implications for Women's Trade Union Participation

Certain feminist studies of women's trade union participation focus on the attitudes of male trade unionists toward women workers and women's issues (Geoffroy and Sainte-Marie 1971; Marchak 1973; Baker and Robeson 1981). Trade unions are viewed as patriarchal institutions without looking at the political economic context of the gender division of labour and its mediation by an ideology which defines women's work on the job and in the home. Attitudinal studies are inadequate, and the situation facing women workers is more complex than these studies would have us believe.

My research shows that the gender division of labour had different implications for the self-organization of male and female workers. For the skilled operators, the union intervened in the daily machinations of the labour process, especially in the settling of piece-rate prices and in the distribution of work. They adopted formal procedures for these practices and elected a shop chairman and shop committee from their ranks to implement these guidelines. Thus, most men had a regular involvement with the union. Because women employed as non-craft workers were paid on a time basis there was no need to settle piece-rate prices or to divide the work. As a result these women had less involvement with union structures at the shop level on a daily basis. The employer or foreman, not the union, directly supervised production.

A different set of conditions were at work for women craft workers. They did not develop permanent structures at the shop level for dividing the work or settling prices. Historically they had been ghettoized into their own autonomous finishers' local which had very little numerical weight and even less political weight in determining union policy favourable to women workers. In addition, perceptions of their work as inferior reflected their conditions of employment.

Because they did not work all the time and because there was a scarcity of finishing work it was very difficult for the finishers to develop a clear consensus about the principles which should govern the division of their piecework. Unlike the operators, the finishers used an informal and ad hoc method of distributing the work supposedly based on trust, but there were varying perceptions about how the system worked. Some finishers claimed that they were supposed to work at their own pace, sharing the work only in the slow period—a practice that was exactly the same as the operators and pressers. Others stated that they were supposed to share the work all the time. In the face of scarcity and impending layoffs, the women were unable to make a decent living wage. Antagonisms were especially sharp when women broke the informal work norms—i.e., when some women tried to "grab the easier work," thus creating a "lateral conflict" among themselves rather than directed at the employer. The lack of formal procedures on the part of the finishers served to reinforce a dependency on the male shop chairperson who was called in to mediate disputes.

Without a clear consensus and formal procedure for dividing the work, one woman played a mediating role in order to resolve tensions that arose from the piecework system. She paced herself so that she completed her work at the exact same time as the other employees in her work group. Compared to the autonomous work pace of the male operators, who received their bundles of work from the shop chairperson at the beginning of the day, the finishers were in constant contact with each other over the division of work.

> Maria Lebella: . . . I'm not supposed to finish before [her] because she's going to die if I finish before her. She's jealous. What's the difference if I finish the minute before her? She's going to finish and she's going to end. I go home if I finish before. I know the girls are jealous for that. I go slow. I finish all the time the last one. I make everyone happy. I'm not arguing. Everyone take before I say nothing. Last one I take it . . . if I sometime want.

The finishers' failure to develop a consensus concerning the distribution of work was a further extension of their position within the gender hierarchy at work, especially their dependency and low status in the factory.

> Ruth Domanski: Finishers are making spending money. The operators are making a living. So everybody looks out for everybody. "You need as much as I do," the operators say, "Look you are a man, you have a family. I want the same work as you." If not they are very much independent of course. If that can't work he goes into another factory where they work differently. The operators all over I would say the whole needle trade is entirely different than what the finishers are . . . . Let's face it, operators, men are more independent. They organize a system and that is the way it goes. Which a finisher in a factory doesn't, I would say, doesn't count. You have no weight or whatever . . . . Somehow on finisher you looking more down than operator.

The gender division of labour in the factory and the ideology which legitimized "women's work" by identifying women as economic dependants made it difficult for women workers to develop strategies to control their working lives.

In addition to how the union operates at the shop level, it is also important to consider the changing political perspective of the union leadership, from one of building the union through militant activity to a perspective of business unionism where bread-and-butter issues are won at the bargaining table.[12] A pivotal point in the union leadership's approach to the employers occurred in the early thirties. After a period of general strikes, "seasonal unionism,"[13] and many defeats to their organizing campaign, the union leadership set out to convince the bosses of the efficacy of a union for regulating the industry. This strategy laid the basis for the employers coming together in a manufacturers' association and provided the groundwork for a policy of class co-operation which was to dominate union policy for a long time thereafter.

The changing structures of the union came to reflect these shifts in policy. Control of the labour process by rank-and-file activity on the shop floor gave way to the business agent servicing individual shops, and the gradual institutionalization of industrial conflict through price settlements twice a year and daily union regulation of the distribution of work. There was more reliance on the impartial chairperson to arbitrate disputes.[14] The union hiring hall curtailed oppositional forces. A rank-and-file committee to oversee piece-rate settlements was dropped from the union structure,[15] another committee which vetoed candidates for union office was maintained,[16] and business agents were no longer elected following a political campaign. The union leadership encouraged favoured candidates to run for office. The gradual bureaucratization of the union leadership resulted in less control for the rank and file, and women were especially disadvantaged.

Women did not have the same access to the social networks which encouraged union participation. Their family responsibilities made it difficult for them to accumulate years of experience working for the union. In addition, they were reluctant to become active because of prevailing ideological constructions of their work as insignificant.

Official trade union practices and policies were often sexist. The trade union leadership was dominated by male skilled workers, and union policies reflected their interest. For example, at the time of this study, pensions were paid only to people holding twenty years' membership in the Cloakmakers' Union, with the last ten years being consecutive. This rule effectively excluded women who left the workforce for family responsibilities and were not able to accumulate the necessary years of continuous membership.[17] The collective agreement governing the Cloakmakers' Union did not provide job security for women on maternity leave. Employers used pregnancy as an excuse for not rehiring women after childbirth. Regulations governing the health and welfare fund only required the payment of sick benefits in the case of "spontaneous abortion or miscarriage,"[18] thereby ruling out payment in the case of therapeutic abortions. Even when there were union rules benefiting women, for example the minimum hourly wages in piecework factories, they were not enforced.

As we have seen, the union hiring hall dominated by male skilled workers made it difficult for women who wished to break through the gender barrier to hold jobs traditionally held by men.

Ethnic Division of Labour

The ethnic division of labour further complicated workers' participation in the union and had implications for their political consciousness. In this firm, an ethnic division corresponded to the gender division and skill differentiation. The skilled craftsmen were mostly Polish Jewish immigrants. Management personnel including the bookkeeper, the shipper, and the foreman were, like the shop owners, also Polish Jews. Among the less skilled and poorly paid employees, especially in the case of the women, there was much greater ethnic variation. The majority of workers were not Canadian born, but were East European. Some Italian women were employed in the shop.

A common Jewish heritage strengthened the solidarity among certain workers and enhanced the relationship between the employer and these workers. They spoke Yiddish together and they also participated in cultural activities. The employer had attended the weddings and the bar mitzvahs of their children. Jewish workers could celebrate Jewish holidays without fear of reprisal; some even attended the same synagogue as the employer. Experiences of anti-Semitism reinforced this bond among Jewish workers and the employer. Ethnicity was thus important in the shaping of class relations in the workplace because cultural identification often obscured the class distinctions between the boss and certain workers.

Ethnic traditions also shaped union policies. In the early days the union membership was primarily made up of Jewish workers. Union meetings were conducted in Yiddish and the minutes were recorded in Yiddish. An English-speaking local was created for the non-Jewish members from all crafts and they continued to meet until the 1970s. Many male skilled tailors were especially indebted to the union for bringing themselves and their families to Canada from Europe after the war. The union minutes indicated a fraternal relationship between the Cloakmakers' Union and the Histadrut, a trade union federation in Israel. Trips of the union leadership to Israel were recorded in the minutes. In addition, a levy on the earnings of union members[19] "for local and communal responsibilities"[20] was used to fund Jewish organizations in Canada. In the early 1950s the minutes recorded purchases of Israeli bonds by the union, as well as campaigns to sell Israeli bonds in the shops. It was reported that "Jewish members were duty bound to purchase" bonds.[21] Workers donated Saturday overtime pay to Labour Palestine. This practice was carried out with the full cross-class co-operation of the manufacturers' association.[22]

Thus, union and work-related activities of the men at Edna Manufacture were synonymous with their ethnic network.[23] A small number of Jewish women were also more fully integrated into the dominant network at work by holding union positions. But ethnic solidarity could not overcome all of their isolation as women. Their union activism followed the family life cycle. One Jewish woman had been active in the 1930s in Winnipeg prior to her marriage, during the time when the union was generally more militant, although she held the traditional female position of secretary. Two other Jewish women were active after their children had grown. They were without husbands at the time of their involvement. Having had a longer experience in this country, they may have had a better command of the English language, but clearly they were encouraged by ethnic networks to hold union office.

Among the non-Jewish women workers, language barriers reinforced their subordination both to the employer and to the trade union leadership while making it difficult for them to develop a common collective appreciation of their working conditions. Here, ethnicity reinforced gender patterning as they retreated into their families and into ethnic-related activities outside of work for meaningful relationships.[24] This was especially the case for women at the very bottom of the pay scale, i.e., the button sewers.[25] Joseph (1981) has argued that cross-gender alliances within ethnically oppressed groups may override common experiences of gender oppression on the part of women. This point is borne out by my research. The female activists saw their alliances with Jewish male co-workers and in some instances with their employer as more important than potential alliances with other women. While their position as trade union activists served as a positive role model for other Jewish women, their sponsorship fostered criticism of younger women of other ethnicities who had immigrated more recently and who were looked down upon for their apparent passivity and ignorance of union matters. In this way, union activism on the part of women from one dominant ethnic group exacerbated divisions between themselves and women of other ethnicities; the employer could use this factor to his advantage in reinforcing the division of the workforce along ethnic lines.[26]

For both men and women, ethnic identification had implications for political consciousness. Because many of the workers at Edna Manufacture were Jewish, their consciousness had been shaped in relation to global debates about political strategies for Jews, particularly communism, Zionism, and the response to the Holocaust.[27] Some workers made links between these global, ideological stances and their position on trade union strategies and militancy.

Sheila Glaber, a one-time union activist, linked her attitude toward strikes with the Second World War and the Holocaust:

> Strike it's a big loss . . . . For the worker that he loses he doesn't work. It's a loss for the manufacturer and they don't gain anything. The strikes don't do anything, just like war. They gain something by war? What did they gain? They killed six million Jews. They ruined people. They don't gain anything by wars.

Bob Zlinger, former shop chairman, continued to be sympathetic to the Communist Party until the events in Czechoslovakia in 1968, and to this day he is critical of the economic situation inside the state of Israel. Lennie Freedman is another Polish Jew who immigrated to Canada prior to the Second World War. In his younger days he was active on the union executive and he was sympathetic to left-wing politics, especially the views of Leon Trotsky. Unlike so many of his fellow workers who became disillusioned with politics, Freedman remains a socialist. In the following statement he offers an alternative view of profits:

> I am against the capitalist system. I was a worker, still a worker. I believe in the working-class system. We have rich and poor. Workers are working in the shop and they're getting just a little bit. And the boss don't work by machine and he gets 90 percent in the profit. We making maybe 10 to 20 percent. People who produce the whole thing. He makes a living from us. The wages are not shared by everybody. I don't want the same wages as the boss but I work for the boss and he gets four times more than I get. That's why I'm against the system. It's not just my boss, the whole government is like that. The whole system, and the Canadian government is the capitalist system.

Ethnicity as it expresses traditions of political and labour struggles that immigrant workers bring with them also affects trade union activity in Canada. A strong trade union consciousness can help to overcome both gender and ethnic barriers to union participation. The intersection of individual biography with global events often marks a turning point in the development of an alternative critical conception of everyday life. Maria Lebella stood out as one of the women workers who demonstrated real leadership potential. Born in southern Italy and married to a northern trade union militant, she moved with him to a northern industrial city where left-wing politics were widespread. In Canada, she not only recognized the importance of organizing but also set out to convince her fellow workers of the benefits of unionization. Higher wages and job security were the two examples she cited:[28]

> I wanted to join . . . . Why we not organize? Why we not pay [union dues]? We get less percentage. The other ones were afraid. Afraid because the boss say, "No not good," and [they] like the boss. Why? He's going to push you out.

She was critical both of the union leadership for collaborating with the manufacturers and of the oppressive working conditions. Although she did not feel comfortable speaking out at union meetings, in less formal settings she encouraged her union sisters to vote for a strike:

> Once we was close. And we went to [make] signs [to] be [a] strike. I convince the girls in there. I say what I think. I don't know about the strike, but I know what the [picket] signs mean. [We would get] more percentage [if we] would strike. I think like that . . . . Just one say "No, I don't want to strike." I say "I [don't] want [to] worse than you [to] strike, but I'm going to vote, because [otherwise] that show . . . how we are a slave" . . . .

Her consciousness as a worker extended beyond her own identity and interests to a recognition of the need for collective solidarity with other members of the working class:

> I am not against people who go [on] strike. If you go to strike because it is necessary to [go] . . . . I think with strike, we can say we are people, we want something too. We not animal.

This solidarity began in her own household, where she supported her husband's right to strike despite any economic hardship that this might bring:

> I was working and we can live. You know, I was not angry to say you should go to work. Nobody wants to go to strike. But if it's necessary. If it come to that. Why I have to be nervous?

Maria recognized that her conception of an alternative society comes from her experience in Italy where her consciousness was first strengthened through her opposition to the rich landowners and to fascism:

> In Italy the rich stay with the rich and the poor stay with the poor. Worker—everybody go together . . . . I am a worker [that's] why I feel different [than] if I was a millionaire. I remember before the war, my God, I want to kill all the rich. Sorry, I say like that. Because at that time they want to kill you . . . . Oh my God, that time I remember the rich people get all the land. Everybody was [living] a terrible life . . . . That's why the South, it's very very [backward]. Even [when] Mussolini was alive . . . . And you ask me why I am with the worker. I remember how it was.

Her political vision has continued to develop in relation to conditions both in Canada and in her home country. Italy is a changing society, albeit a capitalist one which has instituted a number of reforms on behalf of the working class in contrast to its fascist past. Maria's consciousness has changed along with the emergent contradictions of Italian social structure.

> I think . . . everyone [who] came from little town afraid. A lot of people come [to Canada] right away after the war and [they] think they [are] still [in] the same [condition] like in the war . . . . You never

> know was worse than here. Was supposed to be scared. I think those [people still] afraid [from] that time and [fear is] still in the blood of the people . . . . I read a lot of books. What happened before the war, what happened after the war . . . . If you, day by day, know what's going on, you read, your mind change . . . . I read the newspaper. I listen to all the news straight from Italy.

But she was not only aware of class issues; she also boasted about gains the unions have made in Italy on gender questions like childcare, maternity leave, and pension plans for women — the kinds of issues that could begin to transform business unionism in Canada into social unionism.

Women's Double Day of Labour

Women's paid work experience is mediated by both gender ideology and the material conditions of the double day. It is women who are designated as solely responsible for the domestic labour process, and herein lies the basis for their gender oppression. As wives and mothers, women are responsible for making sure that household members are ready and able to work the next day and that children grow up into "properly" socialized and healthy workers, but their family responsibilities also make women vulnerable as workers.

Some women in the garment industry preferred piecework because it gave them the freedom to come and go as they pleased. This freedom was somewhat illusory given the contradictory and mystifying nature of the piecework system, especially when one considers the amount of unpaid time workers spent being available for work. Nevertheless, women felt that under the piecework system they could co-ordinate the demands on their time to meet family obligations like doctors' appointments or being home when children returned from school.

Men and women's responses to layoff were different. Whereas the men came into the factory during slack time to play cards with each other, the women stayed home to "catch up" on their housework. Catching up usually entailed "big jobs" that they were not able to do during the work season, such as cleaning walls, laundering drapes, painting rooms, etc. Many women said that they "looked forward" to layoffs because it gave them the chance to do the domestic labour that they were forced to let slide during the busy season.

Women's family responsibilities affected their ability to hold a job as well as their earning capacity. One woman explained how she lost her job in a factory because the employer insisted that she work overtime and she couldn't because she had to be home when her child arrived from school. The inability to work overtime is one major factor in accounting for the wage gap between male and female wages.

Women's role in the reproduction of the next generation of workers determines at what stage of the family life cycle women will move in and out of the paid labour force. The length of time a woman took off from work for childbirth was partially dependent on both financial and childcare arrangements. Some women remained at home as long as five years and others as little as three months. Often a woman took an extended period of time off because she could not get her old job back.

Women's working day was interrupted for family responsibilities, whether it was to do the shopping during lunch hour, to answer the telephone if an emergency arose at school, or to take care of sick children. The women said that they were always worried about their children while they were working. One woman described tearful goodbyes at the bus stop when she left for work in the morning. Another woman explained how she had to work at two jobs, putting in sixteen-hour days. She was a single mother of two and relied on her young daughter to co-ordinate household responsibilities while she was out working. Another woman recalled the kind of work involved in taking care of her young baby while she held down a job in the factory. She made formula late at night so that she could take her child to the babysitter early in the morning.

While the men had time to go to union meetings after work women had to rush home to their children and to prepare meals.

> Ruth Domanski: The younger ones have families and they're running home. They have no time to be active. They finish their work and they run. I remember the same when I was young, I had to run to my family.

On the weekends women were busy doing the housework that they had little time for during the week. All married women reported that they and not their husbands did the bulk of the housework and childcare. When asked if they had the chance to relax, one woman said when she was sleeping and another said when she was dead.

By contrast, the majority of the men were active not only in their union but also in their ethnic organizations. Most of the men had wives who had worked full-time in the household since marriage. Richard Borowski explained how his reliance on his wife's domestic labour freed him to attend meetings:

> Richard Borowski: My wife she been always home. If I came home the dinner be ready already. But if meeting I go to my wife I say I'm going to be at meeting; I'm going to be late. But I haven't got anything to do in the house because I know my wife does.

Because the small minority of women who were active in the union were over seventy years of age, they were out of touch with the immediate needs of the majority of women workers who had small children. One woman who had to bring her son to the factory on school holidays said that she would like the union to fight for childcare facilities.

Women's double day of labour also prevented them from attending language classes and so built additional barriers to their involvement in the union. Immigrant women's lack of language skills differentiates them from the dominant ethnic group. Their inability to communicate with those outside their ethnic group forces them to experience ethnic oppression just as acutely as class and gender oppression. Maria Lebella was one of the few women who attended union meetings, but I discovered that she had been attending shop meetings for seven years without ever speaking a word.

The men could speak English. They were able to attend language classes in the evening, and most of them were active in the union at some period during their lifetime. Union participation provided an additional avenue for learning English, but speaking at union meetings was seen as a male privilege. As one woman said to me, "I never understand when the men talk." The feeling of solidarity with others who shared a common language was important, as Evelyn Thompson, former staff member of the union, explained:

> I think immediately there's a sense of more intimate feeling because you both come from the same background. The woman can relate to you in the language, particularly on sensitive and personal topics as sexuality or their family life.

Conclusion

Women who work outside the household are beginning to challenge gender ideologies that define them as economic dependants and marginal unskilled workers. At Edna Manufacture, married women's wages contributed to a new relationship of mutual economic dependence between husbands and wives:

> Maria Lebella: My husband say, "You never work before. We can live." I say, "What do you mean?" He make just a little. We going to live OK, yeah for food, but we need other things, clothes and this and that. I say, "I don't want to stay home. I want to go look for job."

Women valued their working lives despite the quality of the work, the ideology of its marginality, and the effort it required to balance the double day.

> Sheila Glaber: I did enjoy my work . . . . I like to go in. And to be busy. And produce. And to make money. And be free with my dollar . . . . I come home and I attend whatever I had. I was well. I was strong. I was younger. I like it. I made a living. I liked the people. I

> liked the place. What would I do at home? It's nice to stay [at home] a day or two then you get restless.

They developed a sense of self-respect and identity from work, based on control of their wage:

> Donna Jakubenaite: I like work. Somehow I feel useful. I enjoy working. You know when you are sick or something I missed work. My husband used to come home and find me crying. He say, "Why you crying?" I say, "I want to go to work." . . . I don't know, maybe miss the people . . . . You know when you start working . . . if you missed your pay or something you feel something is short, is not right. You have your own [money] you enjoy that and you enjoy helping your husband . . . . You feel you belong to the world. You work, you make progress.

Fewer and fewer women live in traditional nuclear families. Ruth Domanski, a single parent, had to take on a second job in a bakery in order to supplement her low wages as a finisher in the garment industry. Despite hard work, long hours, and even painful periods of separation from her children, Ruth opted for a double shift in the workforce rather than staying on welfare.

> Ruth Domanski: This was after I came back from the farm. And I couldn't support two of them. So I left one with my sister, the oldest, and the little one I took to nursery school. And I managed as long as I was with him. Mind you I did odd jobs. I cleaned flats and I cleaned toilets to make an extra fifty cents or a dollar. It was hard on me. Very, very hard on me. But we survived . . . . But when my daughter wanted to come back I had to do something about it. So I had to look for another flat. I couldn't pay my bills. I had to look for another job. And I didn't want to go to the the government for help. The baby was only two years old. I was a citizen already. My daughter was nine years old and everybody used to say "Why don't you go on welfare? They will help you." I said, "No. I'm strong. I have two hands. I'll manage. It's not forever. We'll go down for help." That's why I look for another job. I starting working on two jobs.

This paper has attempted to demonstrate the complexities that shape women's work experience. The failure of the industrial relations literature to recognize how women's wage labour is mediated by the gender division of labour and the double day has led to false assumptions about the conservatism of women workers. At the practical level, the narrow perspective of business unionism must be challenged to develop creative demands and structures so that the majority of women workers can become fully active participants in making decisions that determine their lives.

The workers that I interviewed suggested that the abolition of piecework, the shorter working day, access to non-traditional jobs, equal pay for work of equal value, children, and language training were all issues deserving consideration. The challenge before the women's movement and the labour movement rests on our ability to reach out to immigrant women workers.

Despite problematic policies on the part of the garment unions, and the lack of theoretical insights by non-feminist researchers, in practice women garment workers are on the rise. In August 1983, dressmakers in the Montreal local of the International Ladies' Garment Workers' Union went on a nine-day strike for the first time in forty years. Inspired by a rank-and-file leadership that coalesced around an informal women's committee, these women struggled on three fronts — against the employers who wished to increase their hours and decrease their wages, against a trade union leadership who wished to maintain the status quo, and against patriarchal attitudes which defined women's place as in the home and not on the picket line. As one picket sign read in French, "For forty years we have been slaves, let's struggle for our rights," This was indeed a "strike of pride."[29]

Notes

1. This paper is based on my research for a doctoral dissertation at the University of Toronto titled "Dividing Women and Men: The Role of the Company, the Union and the Family in a Canadian Garment Factory." An earlier version of this paper was presented to the Canadian Sociology and Anthropology Association Meetings in Vancouver, June 1983. I am grateful to the anonymous reviewers of this paper and to editors Heather Jon Maroney and Meg Luxton for their help in improving the manuscript. Thanks to those who gave me encouragement and critical comments: Chris Huxley, Miguel Murmis, Ester Reiter, Janet Salaff, Jim Turk, and the Labour Studies Research Group in Toronto. I am grateful to Richard Lochead of the Public Archives of Canada and the Sociology Research Committee, University of Toronto for providing me with tapes for this study. Special thanks are due to Debbie Field, Shelly Gordon, and Mary Ellen Marus for their supportive discussions and insights. I am especially indebted to Tom Rafferty and to the men and women from the factory for giving me their time and co-operation in this project. Of course, final responsibility for this paper is mine.
2. Field research for this study was conducted from January 1980 to January 1982. I interviewed workers who were currently employed in the shop as well as workers who had retired from the shop. While I was interested in understanding how the double day of labour of women workers had implications for their trade union participation, I also interviewed male workers, who provided me with important additional information about the way the shop

operated and the history of the union. In the majority of cases I interviewed workers in their homes. I also interviewed trade union officials and management personnel. Supplementary information has been gathered from union records. The interviews were tape recorded. In order to assure confidentiality, all names of the respondents have been changed, as has the name of the shop. In presenting the material I have relied on verbatim accounts. The majority of the workers I interviewed were immigrants whose second language was English, but they were able to make themselves understood in English. In order to convey an authentic understanding of their real life experiences I have made only minor editorial corrections of their grammar and I have not attempted to unravel the stated contradictions in their perceptions. Interviews quoted in this paper were conducted on the following dates (in the order in which the names first appear in the paper): Bob Zlinger, June 9, 1981; Henry Klein, July 27, 1981; Al Steinberg, May 26, 1981; Ruth Domanski, October 21, 1981; Abe Boksenbaum, November 14, 1981; Carol Lenski, July 30, 1980 and November 11, 1981; Donna Jakubenaite, August 4, 1980 and November 27, 1981; Maria Lebella, July 20, 1980; Sheila Glaber, November 4, 1980 and October 25, 1981; Irv Smelser, July 2, 1981; Sam Yold, July 17, 1981; David Lupinsky, July 15, 1981; Theresa Green, December 14, 1981; Lennie Freedman, December 2, 1980; Richard Borowski, July 13, 1981; Evelyn Thompson, November 17, 1981.

3. The fact that it takes relatively little capital to open up a small garment shop offers the promise of escape to skilled workers who wish to start their own business, a factor which may contribute to the general lack of militancy.
4. These figures are taken from "A proposed NDP policy for the clothing and textile industry in Canada," April 6, 1983. The report is available from Dan Heap's constituency office in Toronto.
5. In conventional shops, each individual skilled operator makes the whole garment. Jobs in the sectional shops are low-skilled and involve the making of a section of the coat. A skilled craftperson is required to sew the sections together at the end of the labour process, and the entire system requires more supervision and co-ordination than conventional shops. The E-ton system is used in highly sectionalized shops. Developed in Sweden, this system is labour intensive, as it requires one person to run one machine, but it is probably the closest example of a semi-automated system. Pieces of cloth, cut in the cutting room according to the specifications of the pattern, are carried on overhead hangers on an automated conveyer belt which releases the cloth at the press of a button. When the seamstress sews her one operation, usually involving "line sewing," she replaces the sewn material back on the hanger, where it is carried by the conveyor to the next seamstress for another operation. Under this system, the making of a garment is broken down into three hundred separate operations and employs unskilled cheap labour — usually immigrant women. The conventional method for making a coat is in decline in today's industry, whereas forty years ago it was the sole method of making

the garment. The owner at Edna Manufacture claims that as long as there is a demand for quality coats made by single operator the conventional method will continue to be used.

6. Health hazards in the garment and textile industry are well documented in a study prepared by the Centre for Labour Studies, Humber College, "Hazard Inventory for Garment and Textile Workers," Toronto, March 1979.
7. The finishers' craft has not always been a female job ghetto. Men used to do the handsewing, and finishing was seen as the first step in an apprenticeship to becoming a skilled operator. When women began to enter the finishers' craft it ceased to be an avenue to the skilled trades.
8. Very few workers at Edna Manufacture came from working-class backgrounds. Many of the workers had fathers who were members of the petty bourgeoisie, as small businessmen or farmers. A few fathers were wealthy businessmen or rich landowners. Mothers tended to work in the home as housewives.
9. The use of terms such as "chairman" and "foreman" is sexist, but as these are the terms used by people at Edna Manufacture, I have retained that usage.
10. Finishing is seen as a craft. Until recently, the finishers had their own separate craft local, and they still settle their own separate price list for piece rates. Nevertheless, their status as craft workers is not the same as that of the male-dominated crafts, because finishing is seen as adjunct to making the whole garment.
11. Women's experience of "simple control" was different from men's. Women workers reported that the employer often used charm and flattery to persuade them to work on special orders or to work overtime. Although it did not happen at Edna Manufacture, the women recalled previous employers who made sexual advances toward female employees.
12. Daniel Bell (1965) makes the distinction between social unionism and market unionism. He defines social unionism as an ideological perspective "that sees labour as part of a historical trend that challenges the established order" (1965: 211.) Business unionism or market unionism is an economic conception circumscribed by the realities of collective bargaining and usually restricted to wage settlements.
13. Seasonal unionism refers to the practice of organizing workers into a union prior to each season. A strike would be called and some concessions from the employers would be won but after the season's work was completed the union disintegrated.
14. The impartial chairperson was considered an objective outsider agreed upon and paid by both the manufacturers' association and the union to arbitrate disputes that could not be settled on the shop floor in an informal manner. To this day the union has no formal mechanism for filing written grievances.
15. Each craft local in the union elected an Adjustment Committee that was separate from the Executive Committee of the craft local. Every season the Adjustment Committee would prepare a report to the Executive Committee on the price settlements in the shops. If the prices for a particular shop are

not approved by these two committees, the settlement process has to be repeated. This practice has been discontinued. Now each craft local in each shop settles its own prices through a shop committee without any industry-wide co-ordination.

16. This committee was called the Elections and Objections Committee.
17. There are three "industries" in the ladies' clothing industry: cloaks, dresses, and sportswear. Workers who transfer from the cloak industry to another industry cannot transfer their pension from the cloakmakers' union.
18. Toronto Ladies' Coat and Suit Employees Health and Welfare Fund, Rules and Regulations, International Ladies' Garment Workers' Union, December 1, 1978, p. 10.
19. This levy was paid by every member of the union. It usually took the form of a percentage of one week's pay, varying from 12 percent to as high as 33 percent.
20. Joint Board Minutes, Cloakmakers' Union, International Ladies' Garment Workers' Union, December 12, 1947.
21. Joint Board Minutes, September 29, 1953.
22. Joint Board Minutes, December 12, 1947.
23. Conflicts concerning union policies toward Israel were not uncommon. One member was expelled from the operators' local for "his expression of inspired anti-Semitic accusations against the Jewish people, the Zionist movement and the state of Israel" (Joint Board Minutes, April 23, 1953). Another member claimed that he was brought before the grievance board because of his refusal to purchase Israeli bonds, while the union leadership suggested that his action in instigating a work stoppage was the reason for the grievance (Joint Board Minutes, November 5, 1954).
24. To a certain extent the inability of some women to see each other after work was a result of their double day of labour and the vast distances that separated their households. Some women at Edna Manufacture went to lunch together. Others reported that they maintained friendships with workers with whom they worked when they first immigrated to Canada. Although they did not see them as often they were among the guests at family celebrations like weddings, and they usually kept in touch by telephone.
25. Women earning higher wages tended to exhibit less ambivalence about working outside the home.
26. It should be pointed out that common ethnic backgrounds were not necessarily a guarantee of harmonious relationships between workers. The two Jewish women in question were not friends. Antagonisms resulting from piecework, different historical experiences which reinforced divisions between "old-timers" and "newcomers," and competition for the attention of male unionists may be factors in further undermining women's potential solidarity, thereby playing into the hands of the employer, who may exacerbate these divisions by taking sides.

27. Many of the older Jewish workers that I interviewed were sympathetic to the Communist Party prior to the war, but the experiences of fascism and the policies of the Comintern (most notably the Hitler-Stalin Pact) made them more conscious of their identity as Jews. For example, in her youth Sheila Glaber was impressed with the politics of the Communist Party but during the war she turned to Zionism because of the anti-Semitism and repression suffered by Jewish people. Other workers that I interviewed were active in Zionist organizations in their youth in Poland prior to the war and prior to their immigration to Canada. Almost all of the Jewish men that I interviewed were active in Jewish ethnic organizations.
28. In this quote she is comparing the conditions of the unionized male workers in the shop with the non-unionized female workers. It was a common oversight on the part of the union to organize the men and not the women.
29. Carla Lipsig Mumme referred to the strike as "a strike of pride" on a CBC broadcast during the week of the strike, August 1983.

9 Time for Myself: Women's Work and the "Fight for Shorter Hours"

MEG LUXTON

Since the mid-1970s, the Canadian economy, like most advanced capitalist economies, has been undergoing major transformations and reorganizations which have already created massive unemployment and hardship and which threaten to result in long-term reductions in the number of paid jobs available and in serious social dislocation. While it is unclear to what extent this economic restructuring is based on new technological innovations made possible by microchips, or from deindustrialization due to shifts in the global division of labour, it is clear that this restructuring has potentially grave consequences for women (Armstrong and Armstrong 1986). Recently won gains could be lost, resulting in increased gender inequality socially, economically, and politically.

Confronted with increasingly widespread (officially recognized) unemployment, many unions and other economic and social policy analysts have called for a redistribution of work.[1] At the 1984 Canadian Labour Congress convention, for example, a major campaign was launched for a shorter work week (CLC 1984b). To remedy a situation where too many people have no employment while those with jobs work long hours and compulsory overtime, they called for a reduction in hours of work with no cut in pay, so that paid employment could be more equitably distributed among more people. Simultaneously, they reaffirmed the need to fight for "full employment," a principle the Canadian Labour Congress has advocated since its founding (CLC 1984a).

However, such demands for "full employment" and "reduced working hours" have been articulated, for the most part, within a framework which assumes that the problem to be solved is the inequality between those with paid employment and those who are officially recognized as "unemployed." This framework fails to challenge both the prevailing definition of "work" and the more fundamental inequality between women and men. This failure to recognize that the total work necessary for the maintenance of life is not reducible to paid work and that necessary work is distributed unequally between women and men occurs even when "women's issues'' have been identified as important. The CLC's 1984 campaign to promote ''jobs and justice'' followed its demand for ''shorter work time with no loss in pay'' with a call for affirmative action ''to guarantee women their fair share of the economic and social rewards of our society'' (CLC 1984b). Despite their assertion that ''women's issues will be fully integrated into all [CLC] educational and policy materials,'' the CLC campaign, like its counterparts in Great Britain and Europe, did not understand the links between ''women's issues'' and demands for the redistribution of work.[2]

Feminists have pointed out that the failure to take the division of labour between women and men into account has meant that all too often the labour movement has fought for, and won, victories which have benefited certain limited segments of the working class, rather than benefiting the class as a whole and consolidating working-class unity. Too often such struggles have been organized in the interests of men and have either ignored women or have actually been won for men at the expense of women (Briskin 1983). In this paper I argue that the Canadian Labour Congress's campaign for reduced working hours offers the labour movement an opportunity to incorporate into its political strategies for social change the recent acquisitions of feminist theory about the centrality of the sex/gender division of labour. With such an appreciation, campaigns such as the fight for reduced hours are much more likely to succeed.

Women, Men, and the Division of Labour

By the late nineteenth century, typical patterns of work were established which were to become dominant in the advanced capitalist countries of the twentieth century. The most predominant characteristic of these work forms lay in the pronounced differentiation of paid or waged work from all other labour and in the separation of the site of paid work from the newly evolved working-class family household (Luxton 1980: 16; Cameron 1983; Seccombe 1980). This working-class family household, maintained and reinforced by the dynamics of capitalist economics, liberal democratic state policies, and dominant ideologies of familialism, developed as the locus, on the one hand, of working-class subsistence and, on the other hand, of the production of labour power necessary for the operations of capital accumulation. The family household system was predicated on a division of labour between wage work and domestic labour which corresponded to a sexual division of labour. While the historical record is as yet unclear on how widespread this family form of the breadwinner husband/father and the economically dependent housewife/mother has actually been at any particular period, it became the firmly entrenched ideal of the first half of the twentieth century, made possible economically for those male workers able to win a ''family'' or ''living'' wage and for all workers reinforced ideologically and legally (Barrett 1980). The resulting sex/gender division of labour sets up different, unequal, and conflicting experiences for women and men of work and work time and of access to wages.

For working-class men, the resulting patterns of work and family have been, at least analytically, relatively straightforward. The normative pattern requires that men begin wage work shortly after they reach the minimum legal age or finish school. They are expected to work for wages, barring injuries and layoffs, until they reach the maximum legal age, at which point they retire. It is assumed that typically men will marry at some point and have children. The wages they earn are (normatively and legally) supposed to contribute to the maintenance of themselves and the household they live in and the maintenance of those they live with, particularly their wives and children. If they do not marry or have children, they still follow the general pattern of paid employment typical for men, although, with fewer economic dependants, they are often financially somewhat better off.

For working-class women, the patterns of work and family have been consistently more ambiguous and problematic. It is normatively assumed that women, like men, will marry and have children. Women who do not are increasingly able to live alone, though they are unlikely to be as financially well off as their male counterparts. Women with children and without male support are overwhelmingly poor. Married women are almost always at least in part economically dependent on their husbands. Unlike men's, patterns of married women's paid employment have been subject to fluctuations in practice and intense social and political debates in principle. The ambiguity of women's position is rooted in the historical development of class and sex struggle. The character of this class and sex struggle continues to be the subject of intense and contentious debate, with causality attributed variously to a patriarchal cross-class collaboration of men (Hartmann 1979), to a united working-class strategy of mutual survival (Humphries 1977a), or to the logic of capitalist development (Barrett and McIntosh 1980). There is greater consensus regarding the outcome of these struggles for women constrained by the sex/gender division of labour and the family household system (McIntosh 1978).

Wage Labour and the Family Household System

For such a family household to survive, the man must sell his capacity to work in exchange for wages to an employer on as regular a basis as possible. Fundamental to this exchange is the recognition by both the worker and the employer that this transaction exists for a precisely measured period of time. This establishes immediately a dichotomy between work time and non-work time. During work time, employees are unfree in that the employer determines what they must, can, and may not do during the duration of their work time. The employer's aim is to extract as much work as possible from the workers. For the worker, time spent at work is not for the satisfaction of his own needs nor particularly for his own interest or pleasure. Rather, it demands a denial of needs and personal preferences. Work time is spent for, controlled by, and at the service of another; as a result, it is segregated from "real life."

Once workers leave their employer's premises, they are apparently "free," and their non-work time is referred to as "free time." Indeed, one of the implicit promises made when the wage labour contract is entered into is that once workers leave the workplace they are on their own. As far as the employer is concerned, how they live their lives is almost entirely up to them.[3] As a result, the male worker experiences a powerful ideological reinforcement to consider his time off work to be his own, his "real life" to do with as he pleases. He expects to be able to have his time away from wage work free of compulsion and under his own control.

He is able to live because he has acquired a day's pay. In advanced capitalist economies, workers are hired and fired as individuals regardless of their family situations. Wages are payments made to individuals to spend as they will. For the breadwinner husband, this wage is his private property. As long as he fulfills his minimum legal support obligations, he is entitled to dispose of that money as he chooses. This economic power gives a significant material basis to male domination inside the family household. Ideologically the significance of the wage is that it represents and measures his ability to provide not only the legally required minimal support but a socially determined standard of living for himself and his family. By providing the wage which supports the family household, the man maintains his side of the household sex/gender division of labour and discharges his normative obligations to his household. Furthermore, the ideology of the male breadwinner with a dependent wife and children to support has been a major cornerstone in wage negotiations throughout the twentieth century. Male workers and (predominantly male) trade unions have argued that male wage levels must be sufficient to support a man and his family.

While wages are essential for the survival of the family household, they are not, in and of themselves, sufficient. Domestic labour, which transforms the paycheque into goods and services in order to maintain the members of the family household, is the second labour process necessary for the subsistence of the working-class family household. Domestic labour encompasses both the day-to-day survival of working-class people and the generational reproduction of both the human species and of the working class (through the bearing and rearing of children). Overwhelmingly, domestic labour has been women's labour.

Whether the woman also works outside the home for pay or not, her primary responsibility is domestic labour; she discharges her obligations to the family household by caring for the needs of her household's members.

For women who are full-time housewives, there is usually a complete fusion of their domestic-work time and their life. For them, concepts of non-work time, free time, or leisure are basically inappropriate. Women who are employed outside the home must juggle the demands of both waged work and domestic labour. The difficulties in meeting the demands of both spheres have been well documented. The characteristics of domestic labour are completely different from those of wage labour. Because domestic labour is unpaid, the woman doing it is economically dependent on other sources of income. In the wage labour market, women's responsibility for domestic labour has been used as ideological justification for paying women lower wages and for restricting women's access to higher-paying work. In the household, her inability to earn wages equivalent to those of her husband reinforces her economic dependence and her subordination to him.

At its core, domestic labour is about birth, life, and death, and its central time rhythms are shaped by the demands of human subsistence. As a result, domestic labour is primarily task-oriented rather than time-focused. The baby's diapers are changed when they are soiled, not every two hours.[4] When a household member is emotionally distraught, other tasks will be set aside until the person is comforted.

However, it is important to realize that domestic labour is not a natural, ahistoric work process tied inevitably to biological rhythms of human life. All biological functions — sleeping, eating, defecating, conception, and sex — are culturally moulded, and the form that domestic labour takes reflects the patterning specific to a given social formation. Thus domestic labour is not a holdover from earlier feudal work patterns. It is shaped by, and shapes, the dominant socio-economic patterns of subsistence. Thus mealtimes occur, not when people are hungry, but to suit the demands of paid work and school schedules, and people learn to be hungry around typical mealtimes. One of the most common domestic squabbles occurs when a child wants something to eat because she is hungry and her parents tell her to wait until dinner is ready, paradoxically urging the child not to satisfy her hunger immediately "because she will spoil her appetite"!

Where wage labour is precisely bounded, domestic labour is enmeshed in and indistinguishable from the day-to-day activities of living. Its time frame is diffuse and often appears never-ending. The distinction between two measures of work time — production time and labour time — helps to illustrate a critical difference between wage labour and domestic labour. Production time measures the duration of a task from start to finish; labour time measures the specific period during which a worker is actually expending labour (Marx 1967: 127).

From the perspective of individuals engaged in wage work, this distinction is often significant for the amount of effort and energy the worker must actually expend; it rarely has any effect at all on the absolute amount of time spent at work. On an assembly line, for example, the production time measures the time required from when the raw materials first enter the plant until the final product exits. Workers at a particular station may work quickly to get a certain number of items finished so that they can then slack off for a while. While breaking the monotony of the job and giving them a chance to rest, the reduction in their labour time rarely means they can actually leave work before their allotted time. Instead, they may have to engage in a variety of games to convince their supervisors that they are indeed busy.

From the perspective of domestic labour, while the reduction of labour time similarly means an opportunity to rest, production time is continuous — a twenty-four-hours-a-day, seven-days-a-week proposition. While a parent may spend an hour putting a child to bed, and then be free to do other things while the child is sleeping, the parent is nevertheless still responsible for the child throughout the night and for a minimum of fifteen or sixteen years. Because it is the labour of ensuring human subsistence, the production time of domestic labour can never be reduced; it can only be shared or redistributed.

The different experiences and conceptualizations of time engendered by wage and domestic labour are illuminated more vividly when the two labour processes interact with each other. For the majority of married men, the disruption imposed by the interaction of these two discontinuous labour processes with their distinct modes of time appears to be minimal. Because men can assume they have fulfilled their work obligations with wage labour, their involvement in domestic labour is assumed to be discretionary, a voluntary and hence generous offer to lend a hand. In part it is men's lack of responsibility for household work and childcare combined with the services they get from their wives which render them particularly vulnerable to employers' demands that they work longer hours or unexpected overtime, and also enables them to work longer, to travel further to get better jobs, to undertake training programs or be active in union politics. While they benefit materially through higher wages and in a variety of other ways, they are deprived of the possibility of intimacy with young children and alienated from the life-generating activities which tend to be centred in the home.

The extent to which individual men actually take on domestic labour is largely determined by ongoing struggles between individual wives and husbands (Luxton 1983). In general, men tend to appear willing, when pressured, to take on specific tasks. Their resistance intensifies when confronted by demands to take on general responsibility. As a result, women are more likely to win reductions (usually modest) in their labour time. Recent studies suggest that full-time homemakers put in 50 to 60 hours of labour time each week, but that they are rarely able to contract the production time required of them; for most it remains twenty-four hours a day, seven days a week (Szalai 1972; Luxton 1980: 148–58).

The differences, and potential for conflict, experienced by women and men over the allocation of time between paid work, domestic labour, and leisure is exacerbated when, as has been increasingly typical in the last forty years, married women take on paid work. While paid employment begins to alter the dependency relationship for women, it is insufficient to transform the breadwinner husband–dependent wife family form or to significantly challenge the division of labour on which that family form is predicated. Instead, as has been extensively documented, married women's paid employment intensifies their total labour time dramatically, reducing the prospects for regular leisure time to virtually nil. Most studies show that employed married women with children work between 70 and 80 hours each week (Luxton 1980: 148–58).

The struggle which goes on between women and men in the family household over the allocation of wage-work and domestic-labour time, and the consequent relative access to non-work or leisure time, occurs within the private family household and as a result is often experienced by the individual woman and man as a personal disagreement. In fact such apparently private struggles must be understood in the larger context of the overall division of labour, and reallocation of that division, in industrial capitalism. The main publicly recognized struggle over the allocation of work and work time occurs between labour and capital over access to jobs and the required duration of wage working hours.

The Campaign for Reduced Working Hours

For Canadian industrial workers the first organized fight for the reduction of working time was for the nine-hour day; then for the eight-hour day and the six-day week (*Labour Gazette* August, September 1951; July, August, September 1954; August, October 1958). The latter, a forty-eight-hour week, was generally achieved by the late 1930s. In the second round, the labour movement raised demands both for a further reduction in the number of days worked each week to five and for the idea of a paid vacation each year (Woods and Ostry 1962: 333–39). The acquisition of reduced working hours and of the paid vacation was uneven, depending as it did on labour militancy and the state of the labour market in any industry or region. Thus various sectors of the working class achieved reduced hours and vacations at different points. In general, by the late 1940s, most workers had won the right to one week's paid vacation after working full-time for one year. By the late 1950s, the majority had won both the five-day or forty-hour week and a two to three-week paid vacation depending on the number of years worked (*Labour Gazette* 1955: 690–91).

The arguments used by various proponents of the reduction of wage-work time illustrate how women and men were perceived both by the male leadership of the trade unions and by female and male social reformers and political activists. Women, they argued, first of all needed more time off work because they were frail, tired easily, and were more susceptible to illness. Secondly, it was noted, wage-working women, married or not, have responsibility for domestic labour and therefore need more time at home to get that work done. Finally, and with no apparent sense of irony, they also argued that women needed time to be with their families. In contrast, reduced wage-work time was advocated for men first because more time for relaxation would mean workers would be more fit and renewed when they returned to work and hence productivity would increase. Secondly, increased free time would allow those men to "improve" themselves through education and participation in community affairs (Hackett 1920: 627; Pugh 1923: 435–36; Matthews 1902: 3516–20).

These perceptions, rather than providing adequate justification for reducing wage-work time, actually unwittingly described the effects of the inequality of work and free time allocation between women and men. For men, both days off and vacations provide opportunities for rest, relaxation, leisure—opportunities won from capital but maintained at women's expense (Seccombe 1980: 84). For women, especially if they are employed, days off and vacations rarely result in free time.

Gender Inequality and Non-Work Time

When a man comes home with his paycheque, he has finished work. For the man, there is a distinct separation between his workplace and his home, between work time and non-work time. No such separation exists for the woman responsible for domestic labour. Whether she also works outside the home for pay or not, her home is also her workplace; for her, work time and non-work time are often indistinguishable.

The weekend or its equivalent, time free of wage work and school, means that household members are much more likely to be at home, using the facilities and wanting meals, and in so doing increasing the amount of housework to be done and complicating the conditions under which it occurs:

> During the week I clean up before I leave in the morning and of course with no one there it stays nice all day so I come home to a clean house. And when they are all getting ready to go out, it's easy to tidy up. On the weekend when they're all at home, the mess just goes on and on and just when I get something clean, they mess it up and I have to clean up around them too. (Interview #17).[5]

Personal and emotional servicing intensifies when more people are at home. Many women find that on weekends, more interpersonal tensions erupt, requiring tension managing by the wife/mother. Husbands and children often expect the wife/mother to be available during their free time, oblivious to the fact that her domestic work continues.

> My husband and I always get into these fights on the weekend. He really likes to go out and have a good time and he wants me to come with him. When I say I don't want to go, he says I don't care about our marriage. But when the house is a mess or the shopping isn't done, then he says I don't care about our marriage either. But if I go out, I can't get the house tidy or the shopping done . . . . (Interview #12)

As a result of the unequal division of wage and domestic labour, women work longer hours than men and have less time which is unequivocally "free." For some women, especially those with small children who are juggling paid and domestic labour, time free from external obligations is rare or nonexistent:

> Time to myself is when I get to sit down and do my work with my feet up. (Interview #3)

While individual women respond to pressures of their work in different ways, one consequence of the unequal distribution of work is that it generates and perpetuates conflict between women and men (Luxton 1983). Most individuals experience this conflict as a personal one, failing to recognize that structurally determined differences of interest, not personality, are at issue:

> I come home from work at the same time he does. But I go on working, making supper, tidying up, looking after the children and he's off work, he's home. He doesn't think he should work in the evening. . . . I get so mad sometimes I can't see straight. How can he be so selfish? I wish I'd never married him. (Interview #7)

The consequences for women of the unequal distribution of non-work time have direct implications for the labour movement. First of all, the demands on their time make it very difficult for many women, and especially those with small children, to become involved and active in the labour movement (White 1983; Guberman 1983). Their inactivity is often reinforced by their perception (correct or not) that the labour movement is largely indifferent to their concerns. However, as long as people with their concerns are not active in the labour movement, it is difficult for even the most sympathetic leaderships to promote those concerns (Briskin 1983). Secondly, for many women, the pressures created by the double demands of paid and domestic labour make part-time employment look relatively attractive (White 1983; Armstrong and Armstrong 1983). However, the organized labour movement in Canada has been strongly opposed to part-time work, arguing that employers hire (cheaper) part-timers in an effort to weaken the power of organized labour.[6] As a result, the different interests of part-time women workers and of union members often serve to drive the two groups further apart.

A Redistribution of Work through the Fight for Shorter Hours

The campaign for reduced hours of paid work provides the labour movement with an opportunity to open a public debate about the division of labour between formally recognized paid work and socially necessary but unrecognized domestic labour. Drawing on the analyses developed by feminists over the last decade, this campaign presents the possibility for rethinking in new and creative ways how the work that keeps people alive and maintains the society might be organized and distributed.[7] The challenge to those organizations and social policy analysts who are attempting to begin such a discussion lies in developing policies which promote equality, not perpetuate inequality.

In developing policy alternatives, many issues must be considered. Here I want to suggest a few that derive from feminist theory. Formally paid work is not the totality of necessary work, so discussions about the redistribution of work must include domestic labour in their calculations. The "tradition" that women are or should be economically dependent on men is relatively recent. These patterns developed historically, and they can be changed. As a result, all working people, men and women, must be able to earn a "living wage" while still having time and energy available to do the household labour necessary for their own subsistence. The implications of this are difficult. Any major shift in the sexual division will mean sacrifices for men. Taking work as a whole — waged work and domestic labour—men work fewer hours than women and get much more pay. When men have privileges, equality may mean they must give these up. Shorter hours at work can begin to challenge this, but only if the change is informed by feminist theory. First, as long as women receive about half of what men earn, domestic economic rationality will dictate that women, not men, take time off for domestic responsibilities. Therefore a central demand of the women's movement and the labour movement must be to eliminate pay differentials between women and men and to make all jobs available both to women and men. Second, the demand for reduced working hours must be linked to other related policy provisions. If, for example, a shorter working week is won through intensifying work, the gains will be limited. If the man who used to work fifty hours comes home exhausted after thirty, there will be no change on the domestic front. Furthermore, there is the question of how the shorter hours should be distributed. When unions talk of shorter hours they often advocate the three-day weekend, but children and housework cannot be packaged into a three-day-a-week slot. Instead, what is needed is an hours strategy which admits the needs of children. This means not just shorter but more flexible hours and a working pattern which recognizes that childcare is a social responsibility, not a personal hobby. Just as the costs of education are collectively borne, so the time, energy, and financial expenses involved in childcare must be borne socially. Furthermore, childcare responsibilities occur not just when the children are small but continue through the teens at least. As a result, the scheduling of work hours must take into account the needs of parents. For example, in the German Democratic Republic all single parents and one parent of two-parent households are allowed to leave work three-quarters of an hour early with no loss of pay. Parents can take time off without penalty to attend school meetings, take children to doctors' and dentists' appointments, or care for sick children without, as mothers do in Canada, using up their own sick leave.[8]

Finally, the effort to develop new policy alternatives has to acknowledge the fact that previous demands for full employment and reduced hours were formulated within a framework which took for granted the existence of a sex/gender division of labour. The feminist challenge requires that campaigns for social change challenge the existence of this sex/gender division of labour itself.

Notes

1. Most European trade unions are campaigning for a reduction in the "working week" and many have won such reductions. For example, the West German metal workers' union IG Metall, with 170,000 members, struck in 1984 for a 35-hour working week with full pay. They settled for 38.5 hours (from 40) with a pay increase of 3.3 percent. More than one million Dutch workers (19 percent of the workforce) have recently concluded deals to shorten their work week to, typically, 36 hours. A number of European governments, particularly that of France, have also supported this objective. See *European Centre for Work and Society News*, Issue 5 (September 1984): 3–4.
2. A socialist feminist researcher for one of the largest private sector unions in Canada wrote a policy document for her union on reduced work time. In it she argued that a shorter work week will allow a more equal distribution of both paid and domestic labour. A (male) colleague read the document and became extremely irate. He argued that instead of producing the required piece on shorter work week, she had written a "women's document." He had no objection, he insisted, to her writing a women's document, but she should not confuse it with something on the shorter work week.
3. While it is generally the case that employers do not concern themselves with what employees do off the job, there are important exceptions which illustrate how fragile that freedom is. Lesbians and gays are all too familiar with the threat of job loss if they "come out." Civil servants have been told they cannot engage in public political campaigns; teachers with Catholic school boards have occasionally lost their jobs for getting married to non-Catholics or for getting divorced.
4. Various experts have tried to introduce into housework and childrearing the principles of time and motion studies. In the 1940s and 1950s mothers were

urged to feed and cuddle their babies only at set times, and while many mothers tried to do what they were told was "best," their ability to carry out such strictures was always undermined by the imperatives of life.

5. From an interview with a housewife in northwestern Ontario that was part of a study of women in northern mining communities conducted during the summer of 1982. This research was funded by the Arts Research Board of McMaster University. All subsequent quotes are from interviews done as part of this study.
6. Employers' practices in times of economic recession of laying off higher-paid male workers and increasing the proportion of lower-paid part-time women workers exacerbates existing tensions between male and female workers and perpetuates different interests within the working class, which militates against unified labour response. See Pat Armstrong, *Labour Pains* (1984), especially Chapter 6.
7. See André Gorz, *Farewell to the Working Class* (1982) for a discussion of the importance of opening a debate on ways of reorganizing and redistributing work.
8. I am grateful to Heather Jon Maroney for this information on the GDR, which she collected through interviews conducted there.

III The Political Economy of Women's Work

10 Motherwork, Stress, and Depression: The Costs of Privatized Social Reproduction

HARRIET ROSENBERG

Introduction: The Political Economy of Pain[1]

"Mother who killed two sons says she's paid price," announced a front-page headline. In 1970 a woman smothered her six-week-old son; two years later she smothered a second infant. Both deaths were recorded at the time as crib deaths. In 1984, "frayed by more than a decade of struggling for her sanity," she said that she wanted to warn other women about the postpartum depression that led to the killings. "At the first sign of that, don't hesitate to . . . . For God's sake, ask for help," she said. "I just wouldn't want any woman to go through what I went through" (*Toronto Star,* March 3, 1984).

Why did this happen? Such violence is usually explained in individual psychological terms: people go crazy and do violent things. Yet other violent crimes such as rape, murder, and suicide have been linked to underlying social causes. The correlation between increases in suicide rates, for example, and rising levels of unemployment (Brenner 1973, 1977, 1979) establishes a link between crisis in individual lives and crisis in an economic system. But, because childbirth and childrearing are widely considered to be a "natural" female condition, the possibility of social structural origins of "postpartum depression" have rarely been investigated (Friedan 1968; Oakley 1972). Rather, the dominant contemporary explanatory model, constructed and maintained by a powerful medical establishment, is explicitly asocial. It defines the emotional distress of mothers as an exclusively individual problem called "postpartum depression" and has developed a variety of individual therapies including psychoanalysis, drugs, and vitamins to deal with it. To combat the tendencies which constantly push analysis of motherhood and depression in a personalistic direction we must start with a fresh perspective — one that has both feminist and political economy underpinnings.

Producing or not producing human beings is part of the political discourse of most societies. Historically, as nation-states developed, debates about population grew with them. From the mercantilists to Malthus, demography, taxation, and militarization all became intertwined problematics (Seccombe 1983; Davin 1978). Furthermore, the institutions which turned children into soldiers, taxpayers, and workers have always been part of the public debate on how societies organize to reproduce themselves. Public funds are now seen as being legitimately allocated to these tasks, through school systems and the armed forces, for example. It is the proportions which are debated, not the appropriateness of the undertaking.

And yet the daily work of childrearing within the household/family is almost entirely eclipsed from political discussion and considered to be a private matter. The fact that motherwork is integral to social reproduction and not a personal pastime is obscured. In the public domain debates rage about sexuality, abortion, and birth control, but not about the social condition of motherwork.

This radical separation of motherwork from social reproduction has a variety of consequences, including depression, anxiety, and violence. But if we start with the premise that the personal is political and that political economy is a significant component of even the most seemingly personal experience, we can analyze motherwork as an integral part of social reproduction.

Such an approach enables us to view postpartum depression not just as an issue of private medicine but as one of public health, and to explore the consequences of the denial of parenting as a form of social labour under capitalism. Ultimately, a central aim of the socialist feminist project is to stimulate inquiry into the deep structural links between so-called private and public spheres and to locate apparently private pain in its socio-political context.

Emotional Pain after Birth or Adoption

> When they say to me, "Oh, what a wonderful baby. How lucky you are," I look around in a daze to see who they're talking to. I'm in a fog all the time. I'm so tired I can't think straight. I hate it. I want my life back.

In Western societies between 60 percent and 80 percent of mothers have emotional problems after childbirth (Davidson 1972; Dalton 1971; Yalom 1968; Hamilton 1962; Balchin 1975; Kruckman 1980). Depression and anxiety are also experienced by women who adopt[2] and by men (Bucove 1964). About 20 percent of women continue to experience depression for many months after birth or adoption, or even occasionally throughout life (Kruckman 1980; Welburn 1980; Rosenberg 1980).

In the medical and popular literature the terms "postpartum depression," "baby blues," and "postpartum psychosis" are often used interchangeably. "Baby blues" is frequently applied to all forms of postnatal psychological problems. Ideologically dismissive, it is akin to the blame-the-victim connotation of "blue-collar blues." However, more precise medical usage distinguishes different forms of the depressed experience. More carefully defined, the term "blues" is restricted to a depressed mood and transitory tearfulness that is experienced by about 80 percent of mothers on the third or fourth day after birth. This mild postpartum depression lasts for a few hours only. Although some explanations have associated it with hormonal changes at the onset of lactation (Dalton 1971), others have pointed out that there is little cross-cultural evidence for such a claim and have argued that there is a historical link in North America between the medicalization of birth and the appearance of mild postpartum depression (Catano and Catano 1981).

At the other extreme, "postpartum psychosis" is also frequently conflated with postpartum depression, especially in medical literature. This confusion results from the fact that medical studies are frequently based on hospitalized populations. Actual psychosis is relatively rare, occurring in one in a thousand cases. It is treated by psychiatric intervention, hospitalization, and electroconvulsive therapy (ECT).

There is also a "mid-range" depression which may be expressed as slow, tired, hopeless behaviour, eyes filled with unshed tears or constant crying, or by intense anxiety and frantic behaviour. In this form, feelings of anger and conflict with children or mates is common. About 65 percent of the 1,000 women who sought the services of the Post-Partum Counselling Service (see note 1) expressed fears of harming their children, although very few actually did so. Physiological symptoms like constant colds and rashes, as well as frequent accidents and alcohol and drug abuse, are all associated with this form of postpartum depression (PPCS files). It is a terrifying and debilitating experience, made all the more frightening by the fact that it is rarely mentioned. "You never hear about this," said one woman. "No one ever talks about it. Are they all lying?"

It is this mid-range form of postpartum depression which will be discussed in this paper. It is this type of depression which can be clearly seen to have social structural causes amenable to a socialist feminist political economy analysis.

Treatment: Medical Models, Feminist Models

> My doctor is very squelching. He says, "It's just cabin fever, dearie. Don't worry."

> Sometimes I think my volunteer [at Post-Partum Counselling Service] is the only person in the world who puts the mother first.

There are two competing general models for the treatment of postpartum depression. The medical model stems from an analysis of depression as an individual problem; the feminist model identifies it as a problem related to the oppressed social position of women.

Although there have been different explanations of the etiology of postpartum depression and consequently different fashions in its treatment, the medical model has consistently tried to "cure" the individual. Treatment has included the use of drugs, sleep cures, and prolonged hospitalization in the nineteenth century and electroconvulsive, insulin shock, and psychoanalytic therapies in the twentieth century (Kruckman 1980). One practitioner in the 1940s was so fond of shock therapy that he claimed a 75 percent recovery rate and was not at all alarmed by the 5 percent death rate resulting from it (Kruckman 1980). By the mid-1950s, a new psychopharmacological approach had come to dominate in research and treatment. Psychoactive drugs, often coupled with hormonal injections, were widely used by doctors claiming phenomenal success rates.

The psychoanalytic theories of postpartum depression which developed in the 1930s rested upon the normative conception that biological mothering was the essential mark of femininity. A pioneer of this approach, Zilboorg, stated that depression after childbirth was related to "symbolic castration" and was common "in narcissistic, frigid, latent homosexual women" (cited in Kruckman 1980: 8). The psychiatric literature still characterizes women with postpartum depression as infantile, immature, having unresolved conflicts with their mothers, failing to adjust to the feminine role, and having penis envy. And contemporary medical analyses continue to rely heavily on theories of biological causality (Butts 1969; Karacan and Williams 1970; Seltzer 1980).

> Therapy is usually directed at the conflictual areas — helping the patient accept the feminine role or express jealous feelings toward the child, occasioned by thwarted dependency needs. . . . (Seltzer 1980: 2549)

However, the studies of hormonal and genetic causes of depression tend to be poorly designed and yield insufficient and even contradictory results (Weissman and Klerman 1977; Parlee 1980; Livingston 1976). The poor quality of research on the physiological causes of postpartum depression should not cause us to discount this line of inquiry, but should alert us to the inadequacy of relying on the simplistic, unicausal models which medical research tends to favour.

A path-breaking alternative feminist model has been developed by the Vancouver Post-Partum Counselling Service (PPCS) after over a decade of experience in working with more than a thousand women (Robertson 1980; Robertson with Howard 1980). The PPCS model is explicitly woman-centred, and looks to find the causes of depression in the structure of society rather than solely in individual pathology or hormonal imbalance.

This perspective has informed the PPCS definition of depression, the population at risk, and the organization of treatment.

> Basically we redefined the term. We invented a definition separate from blues and psychosis.

A social perspective has enabled them to identify situations likely to generate postpartum depression. Since they do not see the causes of postpartum depression to be either exclusively physiological or a manifestation of failed femininity, the counsellors and volunteers at PPCS are able to respond to symptoms of depression in all new parents, including men and adoptive parents. It has also enabled them to draw a profile of the person who is most likely to get postpartum depression. The most striking feature of the profile is that the woman who is expected to make the most trouble-free transition to motherhood is the one who is most at risk.

The average woman seen by PPCS is twenty-seven, married, middle-class (in terms of occupation and income),[3] and has had at least two years of postsecondary education. She has held responsible paying jobs (e.g., nurse, teller, social worker, hairdresser, secretary, teacher). The pregnancy was planned. Both parents attended prenatal classes. The father was present at the delivery. The woman chose to breast-feed. No significant prior incidents of depression were found among these women. PPCS also found that there was no significant correlation between Caesarean sections and depression, although many of the mothers had negative hospital experiences.[4] Nor have they found that the supposed closeness or bonding said to be inherent in non-medicated childbirth and in breastfeeding has been a mitigating factor (Arney 1980; Robertson 1976).

The societal model used by PPCS has identified loss, isolation, and lack of social support as significant factors contributing to depression. Women who have lost their connection with their paid workplace are particularly vulnerable to depression (cf. Heitlinger this volume). Some women keenly feel the loss of status as a "girl" in this youth-oriented culture, an ironic situation when we consider that many societies count motherhood to be the resolution of a crisis period and the onset of social adulthood for women (Silverman 1975). Other feelings of loss stem from the very real experience of many women who report feeling deserted by their friends and family members after the first few weeks of their child's life (Saulnier, forthcoming). They have few sources of reassurance, advice, or assistance in their work as mothers. They feel their husbands do not understand the pressures of "full-time mothering." And even men who "help" can be undermining because they define the problem solely as the woman's. They do not seem to be able to offer emotional support ("I want a hug and he vacuums the living room"). Past miscarriages, the recent or past death of a parent, or loss of emotional contact with a significant person because of illness or alcoholism can also contribute to feelings of depression.

In an overall sense, postpartum depression is an expression of social isolation accompanied by loss of personal identity, loss of confidence in one's ability to cope. To understand why this should be so, we need to look at how motherhood and motherwork are structured in our society.

Mothering as Social and Personal Work

Defining mothering as work is crucial to the PPCS strategy for postpartum depression.

> It is very important for women to realize that what they are doing is work. When I talk to women, I consciously change the language I use. I talk about the job and the fact that the woman is the manager. That's one of the hardest parts about the job and it usually isn't even recognized as work — even by husbands who are "nice guys" and "help" [with housework and childcare]. They don't seem to realize that helping is not the same thing as carrying the weight of responsibility that mothers carry.

This redefinition is also a prerequisite for a feminist analysis of the political economic determinants of mothering as an aspect of social reproduction under capitalism. The overlapping organization of gender relations and the division between what are called "the public" and "the private" (or the domestic household and the economy) effectively assigns the major responsibility for the social work of reproduction to women without any social recognition or social support. Geographical mobility and segmented households, combined with the ideology of family privacy, mean that women with babies get very little on-the-job training from experienced workers.

For many women, becoming a parent is often devastating and confusing because they suddenly find themselves in unfamiliar work situations. Although they have prepared for childbirth by taking classes and reading books, they suddenly find that they have not just given birth to a birth but to an endlessly demanding human being. The care of that human being is not defined as work: it is seen as a private, natural, and essentialist enterprise. When women complain or despair they are frequently told, "Well, you were the one who wanted this baby. . . ." But raising a baby is not a personal hobby like raising begonias, it is an undertaking which reproduces society as well as expressing the individual need to love and cherish children.

Examples from kin-ordered societies demonstrate that childrearing is usually viewed as being both social and personal, and most cultures have provided very rich systems of social support to new parents (Lewis 1958;

Mead 1962; Oakley 1976; Bettelheim 1954; Metraux 1963; Dawson 1929, Kupferer 1965; Newman 1966). While postpartum customs and rituals may seem obscure or unusual to Western eyes, they serve the very concrete social function of making a public statement that a new birth is significant to the community as a whole and that social attention must be focused on care for the new child. In industrial capitalist societies the spotlight tends to be on the fetus, the doctor, and the technology of hospital births (Arms 1977; Jordan 1978). After a mother leaves the hospital, the thousands and thousands of socially approved dollars and hours and hours of work energy crystallized in the hospital setting evaporate. The woman is on her own: she moves from the public realm of hospital medicine to the private world of her household.

In contrast, in kin-based communities mothers can usually command social support as their right in custom and ritual. Mothers can expect kin to cook, clean, protect, and advise. A new mother may be ritually prohibited from preparing food, thus placing the onus of meal preparation on her kin (Solway 1984). In such settings new mothers are not expected to know or do everything for themselves. They are seen to be at the centre of a social drama and are understood to be entitled to help with caregiving and household tasks. The existence of amulets, special foods, and behavioural taboos constantly reinforce the sensibility that mothering is a public concern and not a private pastime.

In part these social concerns reflect fears for the health of mother and child in societies with high rates of infant and maternal mortality. Postpartum ritual is at one level a communal attempt to deal with a time of real danger for babies and mothers. But such cultural supports can persist and have other effects even when mortality rates are not obviously at issue. By maintaining these rituals communities symbolically testify to their collective responsibility for children and mothers. In one study, Mexican-American women in Chicago who adhered to customary rituals in the postpartum period had no incidence of depression (Kruckman 1980). The confidence these mothers had in the social importance of childrearing was revealed in their attitude toward the evil eye. Mothers felt that if a stranger were to look at a baby he or she must immediately touch the child to ward off the evil eye. One woman recounted how when she spied a man looking at her baby, she crossed a crowded restaurant and insisted that he touch the infant. This belief, which defines uninvolved onlookers as dangerous, presses encorporating claims which prohibit looking without touching. What may look like "superstition" to those outside the culture is actually a cultural safety-net which asserts community responsibility for infant and maternal well-being. The women in this study, unlike those that PPCS found to be vulnerable in their isolation, did not find that they had to solve all problems by themselves.

For most women in North America and western Europe, however, the capacity to override claims of social non-involvement in childcare is quite limited. Unwaged caregiving in the household is rarely recognized as either a contribution to social reproduction or as real work; rather, it is seen in essentialist biological terms for women and as a private and personal reward for waged work for men. Mothers are not supposed to need, nor have the right to need, social services or social funds. Public funding for social services to alleviate the work done by mothers in households is identified as a "frill"—an unnecessary expenditure which is unwarranted, especially in times of economic decline (see Armstrong and Armstrong this volume).

Furthermore, for women who do the work of caregiving there are contradictions between the low status of the work they do and and the seemingly high status of the role.[5] "Mother," "motherhood," and "mothering" are words that bring forth flamboyant, extravagant, romantic images. In contrast, the work itself includes many tasks which are not socially respected. Motherwork involves dealing with infant bodily functions: people who clean up human wastes have low status (Luxton 1983). Few jobs have this contradiction so deeply ingrained.

Equally significant to the stress of mothering tasks is the fact that many women do not really know what motherwork involves until they are faced with doing it. They have only a series of platitudes to go on, about it being "the most important job in the world." It is as if one were hired for a new job with the understanding that the job description would be so vast and so vague as to be undoable, that little assistance would be provided, and that any errors would be the employee's sole responsibility. Motherwork, like any other job, must be learned. Books and courses have become the major means of learning: for most it is an inadequate method, because it is not based on experience. There is no apprenticeship period in our society as there is in small-scale kin-ordered societies where young girls learn the ropes as caregivers to younger children. In industrialized societies, a falling birthrate has resulted in small families in which girls (and boys) grow up playing in peer-oriented, age-segregated groups. Many leave home having experienced little or no contact with newborns and infants. Said one North American mother, "When the baby was born, I knew I wasn't ready. I hadn't got through the reading list."

One should add that the experts, the writers of childrearing guides, are often men who in fact rarely do the daily work of caregiving themselves.[6] ("Provide a stimulating environment for the infant but don't overstimulate him," says one TV advice-giver.) Advice-givers define the job goals, and they judge the outcome. They garner wealth, prestige, and status by explaining three-month colic, thumbsucking, and toilet training, without experiencing the day-to-day working conditions of mothers. This separation between expert and worker can lead to condescending attitudes on the part of the expert. For example, Dr. Frederick W. Rutherford, in *You and*

Your Baby, has some inkling that all may not go well for mothers. He had no index entry under depression but does mention "baby blues." His advice:

> If you are feeling blue, pour out your troubles to someone who will make no moral judgments, someone who will understand that *no matter how little real basis there is for your depression* you nevertheless feel it strongly, but who also knows that with a little help you will manage nicely before very long. Try not to wallow in the blues, but don't be ashamed to express your feelings. You don't have to act like a cheerful cherub when you feel like a Pitiful Pearl. (Rutherford 1971: 167; emphasis added)

To the non-worker, the pain of the worker is not quite real.

Contradictory, guilt-inducing "how-to" books, magazines, and TV talk shows cater to the isolated model of caregiving and miss the social context — people with whom to talk, ask questions, share experiences. Some doctors fill this role, but the medicalization of parenting has been a risky business for mothers. Visits to the doctor can further reinforce the isolated and individuated nature of childrearing. Medical consultations are usually brief and centre on the health of the child, not the work of childrearing or the mental health of the mother. Simple-minded measures like weight gain can become an index for whether the mother is doing a good job. The fact that the child may be gaining and the mother falling apart may not be perceived by the doctor. Furthermore, family doctors may be reluctant to raise the issue of postpartum depression because they feel that women are suggestible and will get the symptoms if the issue is discussed.

Yet women are very dependent on advice from the medical establishment. Mothers may be labelled overinvolved or hysterical, but since they so rarely have alternative methods of assessing health and nutrition matters, they must rely on their doctors. If they go outside the doctor-patient dyad, women risk criticism for listening to "old wives' tales" (i.e., other women) or for negligence (e.g., attacks on home birth). Thus the privatized, asocial model of childrearing is constantly reinforced.

Stress, Depression, Burnout

> This is a very scattered job. I can't think any thoughts more than halfway. At least when my husband goes to work he gets silences.

> I work 24 hours a day. He [her husband] doesn't. At night when the baby cries, he never wakes up first. I have to wake him and he goes to the baby. Then he's so proud because he let me sleep!

> I wish I could remember what it felt like not to have a knot in my stomach.

If we step back from the issue of mothers learning a new job, to the larger context of workplace stress, we gain some useful insights into the predicament in which many women find themselves.

The effects of stress (Selye 1980, 1975, 1956; Holmes and Rahe 1967; Lumsden 1981) on mental health are now being widely studied. Unions representing police, firefighters, public employees, and teachers in Canada and the U.S.A. have become very concerned with psychosocial stress in the workplace. Unions, employers, and courts are increasingly reading symptoms like chronic anxiety, depression, fatigue, and substance abuse (alcohol, drugs, overeating) as signals of strain produced on the job (Ellison and Genz 1978).

Some extreme forms of mental strain and emotional exhaustion have been called "burnout" (Freudenberger and Richelson 1980). It has been argued that ". . . any kind of frontline person — teacher, social worker, therapist, nurse — who is at the beck and call of needy individuals is prone to burn-out" (Murdoch 1981: 6). The literature on burnout among professionals offers some important insights into what unwaged mothers experience in the home. Burned-out front-line workers complain of unrelenting demands, little time away from intense personal interaction with clients or patients, shift work, and constant responsibility for two or more things at once (Maslach and Pines 1977). Burned-out professional childcare workers are reported to experience feelings of "inarticulated personal distress" and fatigue as do lawyers, psychiatrists, nurses, and clinical psychologists when faced with the tense conditions of their jobs (Mattingly 1977; Maslach and Pines 1977; Maslach 1976; Pines and Kafry 1978).

If they are not alerted to burnout as a potential response to these stressors, professionals may respond by blaming themselves and seeking psychiatric help for what they perceive to be personal deficiencies. Those who have studied this process among daycare workers, for example, argue that it is the structure and intensity of the job, and not personal idiosyncracies, that cause some workers to develop feelings of worthlessness. Psychiatric intervention, according to this research, rarely succeeds unless the work situation is taken into account (Maslach and Pines 1977).

These stressful job conditions are also true of motherwork. Most of the psychological and physical symptoms associated with burnout are the same as those reported by mothers diagnosed as having postpartum depression. Thus I would argue that postpartum depression, like burnout, is actually a syndrome in response to the organization of work.

Not all professionals have emotional problems; nor do all mothers. But there are times in any worker's life when job demands deplete, exhaust, and undermine. Motherwork, especially in relation to an infant, is a job of high demands. For many women it is a job of perpetual shift work — of always being on call (see Stellman and Daum 1973 on health and shift work). In that respect it is like policing or nursing, wih the exception that in motherwork there are rarely shifts off. Furthermore, unlike other workers, mothers are not encouraged to separate home and work life. Since mothering is seen as a role, and not as work, mothers are supposed to always remain in character. They rarely get restorative "time outs," let alone extended vacations or sick leave. The disorientation caused by lack of sleep and the disappearance of predictable routines of eating, sleeping, and waking contribute to a "twilight zone" atmosphere. In addition, women who do motherwork also do housework and frequently must combine both jobs in a space like the kitchen that can be unsafe for infants and young children (Rosenberg 1984). Time-budget studies (Meissner et al. 1975; Proulx 1978) and case studies (Luxton 1980, 1983) tell us just how unrelenting these jobs are.

Low Control and High Demands

Those who study industrial workers argue that the most stressful job situations are not caused by high demand levels alone. Multiple demands, under the right circumstances, can create positive work experiences. It is situations of high demand combined with low levels of control in decision making that cause the highest levels of worker stress, measured in terms of exhaustion and depression (Karasek 1979). Daycare workers who feel that they have high levels of participation in their centres, or social workers who feel they participate in agency decision making, express high levels of job satisfaction (Maslach and Pines 1977; Pines and Kafry 1978).

Mental strain from high demands and low control occurs more commonly among assembly-line workers, whose movements are often rigidly contained, than it does among executives, who can set hours and control working conditions (Karasek 1979). Mothering is usually thought to be more similar to an executive job than to assembly-line work. But for many women

> It's a myth that we are our bosses or that we can have a cigarette and a coffee when we want. You can't plan a thing, especially when they are young. You are lucky if you can find time to go to the bathroom. And even then, you don't go alone.

Women as mothers are like women in many other work situations: they have the appearance of wide "decision-making latitude" or control,[7] but in reality they have little power to define their work situations. Typically, women's waged work (nursing, teaching, social work, working as bank tellers, as well as pink-collar jobs) is structured by institutionalized gender hierarchies. Female teachers have responsibilities within classrooms, but major decisions are usually made by predominantly male administrators. Men supervise women in social service agencies, banks, department stores, and beauty shops (Armstrong and Armstrong 1984; Howe 1975; Bank

Book Collective 1979; Tepperman 1976). Women who quit underpaid, undervalued jobs for the "freedom" of domestic work and childrearing may find themselves escaping into more of the same. They may make trivial consumer choices between brands of detergent, but ultimately they can be very dependent. Women who give up waged work become financially dependent on mates; they become dependent on "expert" advice-givers; and they are tied to infant-defined schedules, the schedules of other children, and the schedule of the wage-earner.

In motherwork, one of the most devastating aspects of lack of control is the absence of feedback. The isolation of the job severely limits the feedback which is so essential to decision making. Daycare workers who work with under-two-year-olds argued that isolation from adult company is what they felt most distinguished motherwork from daycare work. As one teacher said,

> Even though the job description is sometimes vague, I know I will get support and feedback from other [teachers] on how I am doing and how a child is doing. That's the big difference between us and mothers.

Some mothers have compared their isolation to being a prisoner of war. Said the nursing mother of a two-month-old whose mate was frequently absent because of job commitments,

> It's pure torture. Your street clothes are taken away and you wear a bathrobe, since all you do all day is [breast-] feed the baby. Just as you fall asleep, you are woken again. You're afraid to fall asleep anyway. What's the point? But God, the worst is that there is no one to talk to.

Strategies for Job Redesign

Occupational health and safety research on stress and social science studies of burnout situate the problems of exhaustion and depression in the workplace. They argue that solutions are social and structural, and lie in redesigning the job to lessen demands and increase control.[8] This is also true for motherwork stress and burnout, and is a solution that was first suggested by nineteenth-century feminists.

Over ninety years ago, feminist economist Charlotte Perkins Gilman wrote a short story called "The Yellow Wallpaper" ([1899] 1973). It is a nightmarish account of postpartum depression based on Gilman's own experience. Gilman's pioneering economic and architectural writings go further. They outline plans for job redesign which take up the whole question of how housework and motherwork should be socially structured, albeit from a somewhat elitist perspective (Hayden 1979). Other thinkers and activists struggled to bring housework and motherwork overtly into the public sphere through daycares and producers' and consumers' cooperatives (Hayden 1981). But by the 1930s these movements were defeated. Housework and motherwork became thoroughly identified as women's individual, private projects, and as "natural" expressions of femininity.

The reawakened women's movement of the 1960s once again introduced housework and mothering as social issues. Such a task is not easy and has led to reassessments of stereotyped patterns of the division of labour. With the exception of breastfeeding, motherwork is not sex-typed labour. Caregiving may be performed by other adults, including men, or by older children, within and outside the nuclear family unit. This work is not "help," which still pins organizational responsibility on a supposedly all-knowing mother, but rather inclines toward the development of strategies for sharing responsibility, which may require women to relinquish some of the pleasures of feeling indispensable. Said one woman,

> When it was his shift with the baby, I had to leave the house. Otherwise, I just hovered over him the whole time. He got anxious and insecure and then I'd take over. It took me a long time to let go and let him be really in charge.

Such a restructuring of jobs and responsibilities forces women and men to face very deep currents of internalized socialization about what mothers and fathers should do and how they should act. It may require constant struggle with previously unacknowledged feelings and fears. At times it may seem that the struggle to assign tasks fairly is just too difficult. But discussions within the household and actions which aim to deliberately involve community members (e.g., drop-in centres, paid maternity/paternity leave or paid leave for a designated caregiver, flexible work hours, choice of workplace or community daycare, babysitting exchanges, co-operative non-profit daycare and political pressure groups that lobby for the maintenance and enhancement of locally controlled social services for parents) all ultimately serve to create dense networks of involvement which can lessen the ambivalences, stresses, and burnout of motherwork.

At the level of political practice, the women's movement has provided the context for this kind of debate. Local self-help groups, such as the Vancouver Post-Partum Counselling Service, have provided immediate crisis support and have helped to reduce women's dependency on experts, enhanced self-perceptions of competence, and enabled women to break down the tendency to personalize domestic problems. Since the 1960s, the lesson of consciousness-raising groups has always been that groups of women who have shared experiences begin to see that their private pain has social roots. This type of collective experience has often served as a prelude to the formation of a variety of helping organizations, from rape crisis centres to shelters for battered wives to groups like PPCS.

However, attempts to socialize childcare outside the household — a project crucial to the redesign of motherwork and parenting — continues to meet with enormous resistance. In North America there is still much popular and official hostility to "institutionalized" daycare. While it may be tolerated for "working mothers," the idea that women who do not work for wages should have access to publicly funded childcare arrangements raises even stronger negative reactions.[9] The intensity of the "fight for good day care," defined as top quality, universally accessible, twenty-four-hour-a-day and community controlled (Ross 1979), illustrates that redesigning the job of parenting is deeply ideological, because it challenges the essentialist ideologies of "the nuclear family" and "motherhood," and the allocation of resources and funds.[10] But such struggles — economic, ideological, and political — are necessary to dismantle the crazy-making structures of privatized motherwork and in its place to create the social job of caregiving.

Notes

1. Data for this paper were collected during visits to the Post-Partum Counselling Service (PPCS), Ministry of Human Resources, Vancouver, British Columbia, in 1980, 1981, and 1982. PPCS was founded in 1971 and has served over 1,000 women. Despite the efforts of hundreds of people, PPCS was closed by the Social Credit government of British Columbia in 1983. This paper is dedicated to Joann, Jim, Penny, Allison, and Fran, former counsellors who truly fought the good fight.

   I would also like to thank the men, women, and children whom I interviewed in New York, Toronto, and Vancouver for their time and the effort they made to share their understanding of parenting with me.

   Thanks, too, to Gloria Gordon, Jeanne Stellman, Lawrence Kruckman, Jan Schneider, Rayna Rapp, Joan Jacobson, Don Hale, Meg Luxton, and Richard Lee for their encouragement and suggestions.
2. Based on interviews with Post-Partum Counselling Service counsellors and interviews with adoptive parents in Toronto.
3. Most of the women who went to PPCS are middle class in terms of income level, lifestyle, and education. The counsellors have assumed that this self-selection was an artifact of a class-based society in which middle-class people have better access to services. However, some poor women do come to PPCS. They tend to be young (late teens or early twenties) single parents on welfare. PPCS counsellors concluded that their depressions were so concretely rooted in economic and social deprivation ("Dealing with the welfare system is automatically depressing") that their situation was not technically post-partum depression.

   Over the years PPCS has received letters from women across Canada in response to various radio and television broadcasts they have done. This admittedly informal and unscientific survey seems to indicate that postnatal depression does cut across geographic, occupational, and ethnic lines.

Since so little research has been done on the question of postpartum depression and class, we cannot make any assumptions about differential rates between working-class, upper-class, and middle-class women. One community study in London on depression and marriage (i.e., not specifically the postnatal period) found that, subject to equivalent levels of stress, working-class women were five times more likely to become depressed than middle-class women. Working-class married women with young children living at home had the highest rate of depression (Brown, Bhrolchain, and Harris 1975; Rice 1937).

This data should caution one against assuming that working-class women are automatically plugged into networks of support that mitigate the effects of stress and depression.

4. J. Croke, *Postpartum Depression* (Master's thesis, School of Social Work, Carleton University, Ottawa, 1982) shows that women who have had home births are less likely to experience depression after birth. However, her sample is small and further research is needed to obtain more significant data.
5. There exists a body of literature (reviewed by Parlee 1980) which links postpartum depression to a woman's difficulty in her *role* as a mother. With the exception of Luxton (1980), however, there has been little discussion of the actual work that women do as mothers on a day-to-day basis.

   Since mothering is constantly defined as a role, women who don't like to do some parts of the job may be considered crazy. See Boszormenyi-Nagy and Spark (1973) for family therapists who criticize women who do not fulfill the female domestic role, and Ehrenreich and English (1979) for criticism of the experts.
6. See L. Bloom (1976) for a short summary of the vagaries of childcare advice from the mid–nineteenth century to the late 1960s, as well as Ehrenreich and English (1979).
7. The terms "control," "decision-making latitude," and "discretion" as used in Karasek's study deserve a closer look. Karasek based his data on male labour force statistics in the U.S.A. and Sweden. "Control" was defined through the questions in the questionnaire that received a yes answer to whether the job was at a high skill level; one learned new things; the job was non-repetitious; creative; allowed freedom; permitted one to make decisions; and to have a say on the job. These were collapsed into the definition of "control" over tasks and conduct during the day. Two measures—"decision authority" and "intellectual discretion"—were selected for the study because of their similarity to other measures in the literature. Karasek argues that the literature shows that "decision authority" and "intellectual discretion" are highly correlated. He argued that highly skilled work rarely combined with low decision-making authority.

   This combination may be rare in male jobs, but it is more common in female jobs, where the contradiction of high skill but low authority is built into a sex-segregated labour force. Thus female nurses, teachers, tellers, and social workers are usually in the position of knowing that male authority can override their decisions. This sexist structure, coupled with the fact that women are more vulnerable to layoffs than men, argues for more sensitive measures in aggregate data studies to pick up the special stressors to which women are subject. Furthermore, in relation to (unwaged) domestic labour like motherwork, we find the contradiction between high skill levels and low authority levels to be important. The popular myth that housewives/mothers are autonomous and have high degrees of decision-making power in their jobs is belied by their economic dependence on a male breadwinner (Smith 1973; Zaretsky 1976; Luxton 1980).

8. Karasek (1979) argues for work teams rather than single-task assembly lines. Maslach and Pines (1977), Pines and Kafry (1978), Freudenberger and Richelson (1980), and Mattingly (1977) all include mention of techniques which can give professionals more control in their workplace, including rotations and times off from the constant face-to-face patient or client contact. Collegial support, awareness sessions, and variation in tasks are considered useful ways of restructuring work situations.

   Other stress-reducing techniques operate on an individual level. They include strenuous exercise (Freudenberger 1977) and biofeedback (Greenspan 1978). These individual solutions are frequently difficult for mothers of new infants, who may be overwhelmed by lack of energy, time, and money, and by the difficulty of finding babysitters to take over while they go out.

   The mother of an infant said in this regard, "I know exactly why I didn't get postpartum depression. I bought my way out. We hired a housekeeper to come in five days a week, make meals, clean, and babysit. I went out and just sat in the library. Eventually, I got a job and felt less guilty about the housekeeper."

9. When I proposed this solution to a group of previously quite sympathetic upper-middle-class women, they balked. Said one woman, "Sure, it sounds like a good idea, but our husbands would never give us the money. It'll never work."

10. In Toronto, it now seems that over $225 million of public funds will be allocated for a domed sports stadium. This money could provide more than 10,000 new daycare spots for five years. A group of anti-dome pro-daycare fathers demonstrated in opposition to the project but met with little success.

11 Rational Capitalism and Women as Labour

PATRICIA MARCHAK

If employers normally seek the least-cost labour supply, and if women are the cheapest source of labour in the capitalist economy, why are men and women channelled into separate labour pools?

The question expresses the contradiction in our assumptions and in much of our theorizing about women as a labour force. On the one hand we assume that capitalists are rational in their profit-maximizing behaviour, meaning that they consistently seek the best available means of achieving the highest possible profits, and that non-economic considerations are not normally involved in the calculations (the term "rational" has nothing to do with morality). To this end capitalists seek to reduce labour costs, and sustain a reserve labour pool as a means of exerting downward pressure on wages. Both marxist and non-marxist theorists assume the rationality of capital, and both theoretical traditions are built on that assumption.

But if this is so, then the splitting of the total labour force by gender, the restriction of women to a limited range of occupations, seems to be irrational behaviour. Assuming men and women are equally capable of performing all or even most tasks, one might reasonably suppose that economic rationality would dictate the use of women as a fully competitive labour pool.

The question is particularly challenging at this moment because writers who defend capitalism argue that lower wages and restricted employment opportunities for women are legacies of history and essentially irrational, therefore removable. Some add that women, though equally capable of performing all tasks, have a superior role in the bearing and raising of children which dictates the social division of labour. The addition is an ideological statement important to our understanding of what is occurring in the 1980s, but in this article I will concentrate on the first argument. The puzzle here is that capitalists are understood to be rational profit-maximizers on other grounds, yet to be subject to irrational prejudices with respect to women.

The term "split labour force" refers to job segregation by gender. In 1980, half of all Canadian women were in the labour force. By occupation, they were concentrated in clerical, sales, and service jobs, making up 78 percent, 40 percent, and 54 percent respectively of all employees in these jobs; and they were employed mainly in the service industries, the public sector, trade, and finance. As the accompanying table (from Armstrong and Armstrong 1983) demonstrates, women were not employed in the major resource industries of Canada, forestry and mining, and a very small proportion were employed in the construction, transportation, and machining industries. In these latter sectors where women were employed, they were more frequently in clerical and service jobs than in production work.

Table 1
Employed by Occupation and Sex, Canada, 1980

Occupation	Women as % of all female workers	Men as % of all male workers	Women as % of occupation
Managerial	4.9	9.5	25.2
Natural science	1.3	5.2	14.0
Social science	1.8	1.3	47.8
Religion	0.1	0.4	14.8
Teaching	5.8	2.9	57.2
Medicine	8.6	1.7	76.9
Artistic	1.4	1.4	38.4
Clerical	34.6	6.3	78.2
Sales	10.4	10.4	39.6
Service	18.1	10.1	54.0
Farming	2.8	6.2	23.1
Fishing		0.5	
Forestry		0.8	
Mining		1.0	
Processing	1.8	5.1	19.2
Machining	0.3	3.9	4.9
Fabrication	5.4	11.6	23.4
Construction	0.2	10.0	1.2
Transportation	0.6	6.4	5.7
Materials handling	1.3	3.5	19.1
Other crafts	0.6	1.8	17.0
All occupations	100.0	100.0	39.7

Source: Calculated from Statistics Canada, unpublished data by Armstrong and Armstrong 1983, Table 5: 252.

Men, by contrast, were employed in a larger range of occupations and were dominant in the resource and heavy manufacturing industries.

In a study conducted in 1977–78 in British Columbia's forestry towns (Marchak 1983), I found general employment patterns similar to those described in Canadian statistics for the labour force as a whole. Of special interest, and spurring on the enquiry of this paper, I discovered that: (1) the public sector was the major employer of women (resource towns having few employment opportunities outside the resource sectors); (2) the public sector employed women in a greater range of occupations than the private sector (in fact the sampled large resource companies employed no women in professional or managerial capacities, and very few in production jobs); (3) the wage rate for specific clerical jobs held by women was higher in the public than in the private sector; (4) the disparity in wage rates between men and women was less great (though still very large) in the public than in the private sector; but (5) average wages in the public sector as a whole were lower than in the private sector. These findings hinted that the division of labour between the private and public sectors, as well as that between occupations and industries within the private sector, required further examination.[1]

Clerical and service jobs in general provide lower wages than production jobs in general, and while women in the public sector may (as the 1977 study suggested) receive wages closer to those of men than in the private sector, the majority of women's jobs in both sectors pay less than the majority of men's jobs. The job segregation must be related to the low wages, but in fact we do not know the precise nature of the relationship. The unequal rewards may be the cause of the segregation, a consequence of it, or similarly caused by a third condition.

It seems to be possible to explain the low wages with reference to history and without violating the assumption of capitalist rationality. In virtually every society known to us from anthropological and historical studies, women have been accorded lower rewards for their work, and this appears to be true even where there is very little division of labour by gender. The feudal mode of production certainly accorded lower status and lesser rewards to women (Middleton 1979), and thus capitalism emerged with that legacy. Since lower wages would be consistent with the objectives of capitalists, there was no incentive to alter women's lesser rewards. But the same is not true for the persistence of the division of labour.

The division also has historical roots, but the advantages to capitalists of a split labour force are not similarly self-evident at this stage of history. During the industrial revolution women (and children) were employed together with men in factory conditions, suggesting that at the time many of the new capitalists did not choose to differentiate labour by gender. The division of labour which subsequently emerged does not offer an *obvious* advantage to capitalists: if they could obtain cheap labour from women, why would they not choose to increase their cheap labour force in all kinds of work?

In this article I propose to examine alternative explanations, critically assessing each in turn. The basic assumption throughout will be that capitalism is rational in the sense of consistently operating on a profit-maximization principle. This implies that neither as a class nor as individuals would capitalists surrender to prejudice unless it could be used to increase profits. If no explanation using this assumption can be found, then we have to question the validity of the assumption. I will argue, after rejecting alternative explanations, that the assumption is, in fact, valid, and that the division of labour continues to be in the interests of capitalists acting rationally. The key to this is the elasticity of domestic labour.

Unequal Physical Capacities

To this point I have assumed that women and men are equally capable of performing all jobs within advanced capitalism. However, since that assumption may be questioned, it should be dealt with immediately. The only difference between men and women likely to be pertinent to industrial work is physical strength. If women are actually less strong than men, it would be rational behaviour for employers to reject them as workers in jobs specifically requiring strength.

Prior to the mechanization of industries, and in some sectors perhaps as late as the 1950s, physical strength may have been an important job requirement. Possibly managerial and many professional jobs in the prewar era could also be explained in terms of physical strength, not because they required it but because workers in production sectors moved up into managerial jobs prior to the professionalization of management. However, several decades have passed since these arguments could be entertained. Production jobs may now require sheer endurance or agility, but with mechanization and automation, the importance of physical strength has declined; and management has become professionalized, requiring now educational credentials rather than production work experience. Women have no physical disadvantages in performing these tasks, and their educational backgrounds are not inferior to those of men (in the resource towns study, I found women to have slightly higher average educational attainments). Why has there not been a steady increase in female employment in these sectors since the 1950s, given the decreasing importance of physical strength and the increasing importance of literacy and education?

A related objection to the equal capacities assumption might be that women's childbearing absences make them less stable workers. However, stability is not a characteristic of many of the jobs in which women are rarely employed (e.g., resource sector employment), and is characteristic of some of the jobs they moved into in such large numbers after 1950 (e.g., teaching, nursing). As well, since the 1960s, with the development of more effective contraceptives, women have had more control over their fertility and the birthrate has declined.

Culture, Perceptions, and Ideology

Notwithstanding the actual facts regarding physical strength and child-bearing absences, it may be argued that employers did not necessarily recognize these changes or their implications, and that the culture and ideological context of the 1950s and even up through the 1970s inhibited their consideration of women as a potential labour supply for production jobs.

This may well be true, but two objections make it a weak defence of hiring practices. The first is that in a few production industries women were hired for jobs that were physically demanding: fish and other food processing, textiles, and some assembly line jobs in manufacturing. In those industries the *apparent* explanation is that women were either a traditional labour force for unique historical reasons or that, in the 1950s, men in the regions of these industries were otherwise employed. Why would employers in these sectors be able to ignore a cultural and ideological context while other employers never considered such behaviour?

The second objection is this: employers were able to overcome ideological predispositions quite rapidly in numerous other instances — e.g., the hiring of racial minorities where racism was widespread — whenever the adaptation provided cheaper labour. One would have to suppose that either the hiring of women was just far beyond the bounds of acceptable behaviour (which clearly it was not), or that for some solid economic reason this would not provide cheaper labour.

Employees' Fear of Job Competition

One line of argument is that male employees, already entrenched in production and managerial jobs when women entered the labour force after 1940, resisted the entry of competitive labour. This resistance was a rational defence of self-interest, though prejudice may also have existed. Certainly unions, dominated by men, did not grasp the opportunity to organize women, much less to promote their interests; very few production unions even considered the inequalities by gender before the 1980s, and then under the leadership pressures of the public sector unions in which women were a much greater component (Marchak 1974b). Geoffroy and Sainte-Marie's study (1971) provided attitude data supporting the argument that male members of unions in general held views inconsistent with active support for women employees in their own fields.

At the same time, the 1950s to early 1970s were years of an expanding economy. There were sufficient employment opportunities that men were not obliged to compete for extremely scarce jobs nor to defend jobs they already held. In fact there was room for recruits, and employers actively sought out new sources of labour power. In Canadian resource industries, for example, they actively recruited immigrants. If employers could seek out immigrants, and if there were sufficient jobs to employ these in addition to already employed labour, and if the unions did not want to oppose these new workers or were unable to prevent their employment, how and why would they have prevented women's employment?

It seems highly unlikely that capital would accede to a bifurcation of labour because male employees feared female competition, unless there were some clear advantage for capital. Capitalists qua men might share interests with male employees, but unless these interests increased their wealth then any explanation resting on general male prejudice abandons the assumption of rationality.

Male Domestic Requirements

A possible rationale is that capitalists qua capitalists as well as qua men required the domestic labour of women and would have lost this had women been fully embedded in wage labour. But this argument lacks cogency in view of the fact that women were even so inducted into wage labour. For the purpose of providing domestic services, it does not matter whether women are employed outside the home in one kind of work or another: the threat of withdrawal of domestic services is the same either way. In fact, of course, women ended up doing both domestic and wage labour.

A further explanation along this line may be advanced: that if women had been paid equally, they would have had the capacity to free themselves from men, the family, and domestic labour. To the extent that the maintenance of involuntary domestic labour was in the interests of capital (as well as of men) this explanation is consistent with a theory of rational economic behaviour for capital. In that case we might have an explanation for low wages paid to women. But we still do not have an explanation for the streaming of women into a restricted range of jobs unless we can argue that only by restricting access to men's jobs could capital keep women in dependent domestic arrangements and low-wage employment.

The Advantages of Flexible Labour Supplies

One possibility is that capital required a flexible labour force which could be employed and laid off according to market fluctuations, and which could be geographically relocated according to economic conditions in companies and in regions. As long as men and women live together in domestic units flexibility is impeded where both have employment, unless the employment of one invariably takes precedence over the employment of the other. This could be arranged if the jobs of one always paid more than the jobs of the other. Since men were already employed, and since prior to 1950 some proportion of the jobs did require physical strength more often possessed by men than women, men received the higher incomes and women were barred from entry to the jobs even when physical barriers ceased to be a reason (or excuse).

While it is doubtful that capitalists got together and decided that the employment of women in equal capacities would impede the development of a flexible labour force, if we look as this possibility for a single industry it is not difficult to imagine the calculations of employers. Forestry and mining companies established townsites to attract labour during an expansionary phase. They needed a stable labour force in some industrial sectors (e.g., pulping) but an elastic labour supply in others (e.g., logging and lumber). If they employed women and men equally and the women and men were married to one another, their flexibility would be impeded. This implies the willingness of the employers to hire men at a family wage since they could not guarantee the employment of women in company towns. It also involves the assumption that over the long run, flexibility was more advantageous to employers than a homogeneous labour force in which sheer numbers competing for jobs plus the low cost of women on entry would reduce overall wage bills. These are very strong assumptions and on their own seem rather far-fetched. However, another argument may be added which questions the assumption that women would have provided lower-cost labour on entry.

Unionized Industries

In unionized industries all entry labour would have received the same wage rates. Forestry and mining, for example, were unionized by the time these company towns were established; thus women would have been no less costly than men in production jobs. To hire women at lower cost, employers would have had to either challenge strong unions or make deals with them. Challenges would have been unwise in a time of buoyant markets. Making deals would have required the labelling of some jobs as "men only." There were precedents for such action, as in fish-processing, but these tended to be in regions or industries where there was a marked shortage of male labour; thus the recruitment of women posed no competitive threat (Muszynski 1984).[2] There is no evidence that a deal was ever contemplated in forestry or mining (and I have not seen any study on other industries which would suggest they are different). Possibly unions already dominated by men would have resisted this particular bifurcation of labour and its potential competitive thrust much more than unions without a large male labour force to defend. However, one does have to ask why employers did not attempt to make such a deal if thereby they could have obtained cheaper labour for at least some jobs. Even if flexibility was a desirable condition, would there not have been advantages in opening up a restricted range of production jobs to women?

The Reserve Labour Force Argument

Connelly (1978) provides one of the most challenging arguments to explain women's low wages. Capitalists have a variable need for labour as well as an incentive to keep wages down for the permanent labour force. It is in their interests on both counts to have a reserve labour pool from which to draw in times of expansion, and which sustains a competitive pressure against rising wages for the employed in times of contraction. The reserve may be latent, as when a potential labour pool exists untapped over long periods of time; stagnant, as when pauperized labour is unused; or floating, as when workers are employed in casual and temporary jobs from time to time. Her argument is that women have, historically, provided reserves of all three kinds. A latent reserve was tapped when women were inducted into the labour pool during World War II, then were expelled as men returned to fill the jobs. A stagnant pool is tapped when welfare recipients are pulled into jobs, and the floating reserve is tapped regularly for domestic and clerical labour.

Connelly argues that women meet the three criteria of a reserve force: they are competitive, available, and cheap. The causes of these attributes are historical, and capitalists have maintained women in this historically derived condition becuse it suits their needs to have a labour pool in reserve. As well, it suits them to have women rather than men as a reserve because their variable employment has less impact on the capacity of the domestic unit to reproduce another generation.

Two of the arguments here pose no problems: (1) that demand for labour is variable, and a reserve labour force is an essential component of the system; and (2) that women are available and cheap and in this respect provide a ready reserve. But a problem arises with the competition argument, and with the differential impacts on the domestic unit.

As long as women are streamed into particular jobs, they are not competitive with men, and thus not a reserve force relative to the jobs men do. They have been paid low wages but their cheapness has not had a direct depressant effect on men's wages in sectors where men are in the majority. What Connelly demonstrates is that there is a surplus supply of female labour for the restricted range of available jobs. True, these jobs vary in number with expansion and contractions, but so do the jobs performed by men. Many jobs are temporary and casual in the clerical and service industries which employ women, but many of the jobs in industry are also temporary. Connelly is no doubt correct in identifying women as a reserve; the problem is that in this respect women, especially in the resource economies, are not unique, and this in itself will not explain why the job market is bifurcated.

With respect to the example of the war, as well, there are objections to this line of argument. Though there was a 6 to 8 percent rise in female employment between 1942 and 1945, followed by a drop to the 1941 levels by 1946, there is otherwise a gradual but fairly steady increase in female employment over the entire twentieth century.[3] The majority of employed women before, during, and since the war have been in the clerical and service sectors. Thus, while it is true that a latent reserve labour pool was tapped during the war, employment trends throughout the century have not otherwise substituted women for men or brought them into competition with one another.

The general approach so far links capital to women's employment, focusing specifically on women. Perhaps we could reconsider the problem from a different angle, linking capital to social services instead. This approach is aided by some of the contributions to the domestic labour debate (Seccombe 1974; Gardiner 1975; Coulson, Magas, and Wainwright 1975).

The Welfare State

Ignoring gender for a moment, let us consider the peculiarities of the postwar period, during which a considerable range of services were socialized. The range included care for the elderly and ill, cushions against unemployment, retraining and extensive public education, some degree of childcare, some subsidized housing, and welfare. What brought about the socialization of these services which formerly were provided, if at all, in the domestic unit?

The welfare state developed first out of the Depression and the Keynesian solution, which required greater consumer power and thus more cushions against unemployment, then in response to pressures both from labour for greater security and from capital for a more secure labour force during the expansionary phase which followed the war. Labour could bargain more effectively at this time because the demand for labour steadily increased and as long as markets expanded there were advantages to capital in the development of the welfare system. The provision of unemployment insurance allowed capital to maintain an elastic labour force in regions where seasonal production or fluctuating markets required labour on less than a steady basis. Basic welfare cushions reduced internal dissent and criticism of capitalist employment methods, and also allied the employed with their employers as both paid taxes to maintain the unemployed. Extended public education provided labour with greater opportunity for upward mobility while providing capital with the bureaucratic, professional, and technical workforce suitable to the changing technological and marketing systems of the era (Gough 1979). In other words, during this particular period, capital was served by the socialization of services formerly performed in the domestic unit.

This expanded state required a labour force. Labour could be obtained if the state competed with private capital for the labour force already employed (primarily men) or by drawing on the reserve pool of women who were, as Connelly argues, available and cheap. Obviously it would not be in the interests of private capital during a period of high labour demand and expansion to allow the state to compete for scarce labour resources at the same wage levels. This would provide one possible reason for the state becoming the major employer of women, and since the majority of jobs in the state sector are service jobs it would also provide an explanation for women being employed primarily in such jobs.

Service versus Surplus-Producing Work

The state may be the major employer of women, but women are also employed in the private sector in similar service jobs. These jobs also increased in number in the postwar period. Is there something about the jobs in both sectors which would induce employers to attempt to restrict entry of men (which is, of course, a reverse way of phrasing the usual question, but which would follow from the argument on the restriction of competition, above?)

What these jobs have in common is that they service capital rather than directly increase its accumulation. They are essential to the training of labour, the maintenance of citizens' docility or at least acceptance of capitalism, the orderly processing of capitalist marketing activities, the smooth organization and sometimes supervision of labour, and the functioning of the legal system which upholds property rights. But their tasks do not result in new products or the direct accumulation of capital. In the marxist literature these jobs are labelled "unproductive" in the sense that they do not produce surplus to capital. The term, however, is widely misunderstood to imply a value judgment and an ideological stance, and because most women are employed in these jobs the term too easily lends itself to a sexist interpretation: women rather than jobs are labelled unproductive (see, e.g., Gough 1972). For this reason the terms "service" versus "surplus-producing" jobs will be used here.

Some service tasks have always been performed by the state, and private capitalists have usually required some labour to perform servicing tasks as well. But historically, the ratio of these tasks to direct surplus-producing tasks has been low. As well, because they are a direct cost against revenues, capitalists have striven to keep them low. There are exceptions, mainly those emerging from the reorganization of management when it ceased to be performed entirely by owners. Such jobs were often necessary for the extraction of surplus value from production workers, and were well paid as a consequence. But the phalanx of new service jobs added with the expansion of capitalism in the postwar period was less directly related to extraction of surplus or marketing of products on a world stage.

As long as the ratio was low, the cost of this service labour within the capitalist enterprise itself could be borne by individual capitalists. As the ratio increased in favour of service labour, the cost became a significant barrier to the growth of capital. Yet at the same time this labour was essential to the process, whether it consisted of keeping files in order, preparing sales documents, communicating information, nursing workers back to health (and to the labour force), managing the welfare system which maintained the reserve labour force, selling products, teaching the next generation of workers, or any of the other tasks that the emerging world economy and welfare state required. Socializing the costs via the welfare state was a means of reducing the burden on individual capitalists, but it developed its own contradictions: as more workers were required by the state, more of the services formerly done in the domestic unit had to be socialized just to maintain that level of total adult employment.

If the wages paid to this burgeoning army of service workers were equal to wages paid to surplus-producing labour, the accumulation process would come to a halt. All of the surplus would be used to service the process of surplus production. The process, then, required some means of obtaining labour for the service sectors at lower cost than the prevailing wages in industry.

If, at the same time as this historical process occurred, the demand for labour in surplus-producing sectors had markedly declined, then, hypothetically, excess supplies would have moved toward the service sectors and overall wages would have been reduced by total competition. The hypothetical condition would not actually have occurred because the growth in the service sector was dependent on industrial expansion. Though the labour component in any one production process declined with the introduction of machinery, the overall demand for labour increased as production itself increased to meet world consumer demand after the war. As long as this was true, the service sectors could not be filled with workers from the other sector. Indeed, the co-existence of the two growths increased the advisability of keeping wages low in the service sectors, since if wages were competitive, workers might migrate by choice to service work. This seems particularly likely in view of the difference in the nature of the jobs in the two sectors. Workers do not rate jobs on a service–surplus continuum; apart from wage differences, they rate them in terms of safety, comfort, security, collegiality, creativity, sense of social worth, and the like. On simple comparisons, it is probable that more jobs in the service than in the surplus-producing spheres provide agreeable, or even tolerable, working conditions in these terms.

The argument, then, is that it was highly advantageous, possibly even necessary, for capital to provide much lower wages to workers in service sectors. It was not male prejudice, union obstinance, or men's fear of competition from women that created this condition.[4]

This brings us back to Connelly's argument and poses the question: have women been maintained as a reserve precisely in order to allow for the expansion and contraction of socialized services? The relationship between the domestic unit, where work can be intensified or dispersed with economic changes, and the socialized services which have the same characteristic is surely not coincidental.

Elasticity of Domestic Labour

If socialized services lose their value to capital, the alternative means of supplying them is through the domestic unit. Traditionally the domestic unit has provided a wide range of these services, and as Connelly observes this is where women are located when they are on reserve. Gardiner (1975: 54) provides an argument which links the domestic unit to changes in markets and technology for capital. In her view, a given standard of living for workers "can be achieved by varying the contributions to it of commodities purchased out of wages on the one hand and domestic labour performed by housewives on the other. Thus at a given level of subsistence and a given level of technology, necessary labour may in fact be a variable."

The surplus value of wage labour may be redivided according to the relative profits under varying market conditions to be obtained by leaving the services necessary for the maintenance of labour to the household or involving more members of the household in the labour force while charging a higher proportion of the services against revenue (i.e., socializing the services). An important characteristic of domestic labour is that it can be intensified or dispersed. It is intensified when the range of alternatives is reduced, e.g., when childcare, homemaker, senior citizen care, aids for care of the handicapped, etc., are unavailable. It can be dispersed when these are socialized, and when some other components of the maintenance of labour are produced as commodities, e.g., fast foods and home janitorial and telephone answering services. In fact, dispersion may also include the construction of houses with features that reduce the need for constant care —vacuumable carpeting rather than hardwood floors that require weekly waxings, automatic washing machines and the like.

This is the argument that, when linked to a recognition of the nature of paid work for women, may explain their reserve status as well as their limited occupational opportunities. This is not to underrate the other functions of domestic labour. Gardiner points out that the domestic unit socializes children into the capitalist society, provides the basic forms of competition (between families for incomes), creates an authoritarian model, and sustains women's passivity. All of these contribute to the maintenance of a relatively docile labour force; quite possibly more so than any other means of maintaining labour.

Is capitalism so rational that individual capitalists can deliberately calculate the long-term advantages of maintaining half the population as a domestic reserve to be used for socialized services as required? This seems to stretch the notion of rationality rather far, and besides would require a remarkable degree of altruism on the part of capitalists in, say, 1949: to forgo a cheap labour supply in their own units so that at some (unspecified) future time socialized labour could be reprivatized. Besides, at that stage not even the best-informed capitalist organization could have predicted that in 1980 a restructuring would dictate the advisability of desocializing many services.

But one need not depend on such an unlikely degree of consciousness among capitalists. Women did perform domestic tasks and were available for employment; they would have provided a cheap labour force for production, but only if employers were prepared to challenge unions or create a bifurcated labour force within each production unit and with the connivance of unions; at the same moment in time both private sector employers and the state sought a cheap labour force with appropriate skills to perform a growing number of service tasks. Women were the obvious source of that labour. The rational calculation for capital need not have gone beyond the quite simple observation that if these jobs were restricted to one labour pool which was then available at cheaper rates than the already employed production workers, their own labour force would not be attracted to the jobs, the necessary but not surplus-producing service work could be performed cheaply, and labour, overall, would be maintained at a sufficient level to facilitate expanded production.

Reversal of Trends

What we have attempted to explain is actually a historical phenomenon occurring between the late 1940s and the mid-1970s. This was the period of expansion for industry, and during the period there was an overall advantage for capital as a class to maintain a high level of socialized services. The technology was not in place which would diminish the need for labour for these services, nor diminish the need for labour in the surplus-producing sectors. However, these needs were temporary. In the surplus-producing sectors both technological change and a vast reorganization of capital began in the late 1960s and reached proportions labelled "crisis" by 1980: capital's demand for labour in the industrialized countries decreased, and with that the advantage of socializing all these services also decreased.

The disparity in incomes between these two sectors seems to have been fairly constant through to the mid-1960s. After that, public service unions became a major bargaining influence, and their wage settlements necessarily affected the wages for service workers in the private sector. Since the majority of public service workers were women, these unions produced two platforms: (1) the argument for equal wages in the public and private sectors irrespective of surplus value differentials; and (2) the argument for equality by gender.

The major problem with the growth in overall cost of the service sector was, of course, that it produced no surplus value of its own. Unless surplus from elsewhere keeps growing at a greater rate, the costs eventually meet and exceed revenue. This is particularly true with respect to the state sector, because virtually all of that (by definition) is service work whereas for capitalists in the private sector, service workers are a smaller segment of the total workforce. The so-called "fiscal crisis of the state" is in substantial part a reflection of the diminished advantage to capital of socialized services.

As wages increased with the unionization of the public service, and, in lesser extent, of clerical and technical workers in the private sector, so did the incentive to automate these service jobs where they could not otherwise be totally eliminated. The technology for eliminating a broad range of clerical and service jobs became widely available in the late 1970s.

The elasticity of the domestic unit becomes the backdrop for the changing structure of capital. Services are desocialized, and women continue to perform them, but now at private rather than public cost. Women were brought into the labour force as a cheap labour supply, were restricted to a particular range of jobs *because* rather than in spite of their cheapness, and are pushed out when that range of jobs is no longer necessary and their cheapness begins to diminish.

It may be noted, though another paper is required for expansion of the note (Marchak 1985), that private capital during the disemployment phase in North America and Europe moved offshore to Southeast Asia and Latin America where it employed women as a new source of the world's cheapest labour for production of silicon chips, garments, and toys.

Summary

I have argued that where production workers were already unionized, there would have been no cost advantage to individual employers in the recruitment of women unless employers struck deals with unions to restrict their employment, but that there was a cost advantage to capital as a whole in their recruitment into the expanding and non-union service jobs in both the public and private sectors.

The state of the postwar period created jobs necessary for an expanding economy but draining on the revenue of capital. For this reason, the state sought the least costly labour and did not compete against private capital for labour with previously established wage levels in industry. As well, the expanding private sector bureaucracies required new labour, and this too was a net drain on revenues; private sector employers likewise sought a labour pool which did not have the same wage demands as already employed labour. The availability and cheapness of women made them the appropriate labour pool for jobs which were unlike the production jobs performed already by men, thus a division of labour by gender was embedded in postwar capitalism which was rational from the point of view of capital as a class.

Women were a reserve pool of labour, and their cheapness and availability are historical conditions which impeded their capacity to bargain for higher wages or mount effective opposition to a disadvantageous division of labour. Undoubtedly there were cultural and ideological impediments both for capital, which shared as well as created versions of the world in which a gendered division of labour was assumed to be natural; and for women themselves, who accepted that version even while seeking paid employment. But the question posed at the beginning involved the seeking of explanations consistent with an assumption of rational employment strategies by capital, and if this explanation has been advanced then the cultural and ideological impediments may be viewed as additional factors rather than primary causes.

Had the economy continued to expand, women might have ceased to be a distinctive reserve pool of labour. Had public sector unions succeeded in arguing a case not simply for equal pay between men and women but for equality in the evaluation of jobs, there would have been no continuing advantage in job restrictions, and men and women should have become fully competitive for all jobs. However, as that possibility came into view, the willingness of private capital to support the expanded state and private bureaucracies in the industrialized countries declined. From 1980 onward, employment in the service sector declined. Women are being pushed back into domestic labour, and as this occurs, the domestic unit reexpands to perform reprivatized roles not because women are women but because women performed the service tasks of the bureaucracies.

The point of arguing this case is to demonstrate that the division of labour under capitalism is not merely a function of leftover prejudice (though the existence of prejudice is not denied). The division has been rationally developed in the interests of profit accumulation, and has been an integral component of advanced capitalism between 1945 and 1980.

Notes

1. Unfortunately, Statistics Canada does not provide breakdowns of employment statistics in terms of public versus private sector employment. The industrial sector "public administration" omits a wide range of jobs, and the omissions

are inconsistent from province to province. The only comparable statistics might be comparisons within sectors largely funded through taxation, such as teaching and medicine. In both cases, a higher proportion of all employed women than of all employed men are in these fields, and the proportion of women to men is greater even though twice as many men as women are in the labour force as a whole.

2. The history of the United Fishermen and Allied Workers Union, in its representation of women in fish processing plants in British Columbia, is more complex than this comment suggests, as analyzed by Muszynski both in the publication cited and in a forthcoming publication.
3. As may be deduced from Appendix Tables 7.1, 7.2a, 7.3 in Connelly.
4. On this point I revise my own argument which put much of the onus on men's fear of competition and unions representing male interests (1974).

12 Looking Ahead: The Future of Women's Work[1]

PAT ARMSTRONG and HUGH ARMSTRONG

Introduction

There are signs of an economic recovery, at least in profit rates. In order to maintain this recovery, we are told, restraint, especially in government expenditures and in employee demands, and investment, especially in microelectronic technology, are necessary. In the meantime, official unemployment rates still hover close to the double-digit level, poverty continues to increase, wages and benefits fail to keep up with prices, and battles between employees and governments are becoming more frequent as well as more intense. The people most aware of the consequences of these trends — the growing depression, stress, violence, family disruption, and the increasing inadequacy of food and housing — are women. Because women in general and those in the caring professions in particular must deal with this reality, their attention is focused on the pressing practical problems of surviving through the day, on the how rather than the why, on the now rather than the when, on the parts rather than the whole. However, precisely because they are in immediate contact with this reality, they know that the bandaids are proving increasingly inadequate to treat the rapidly spreading wounds. They are the ones who are in a position to, and who need to, search for explanations, to look for future trends, to make the connections by asking the larger questions, to relate theoretical explanations to practical issues in a way that can lead to more comprehensive strategies for dealing with the problems exposed and created by the current economic crisis.

At one and the same time, the crisis increases the pressure to provide temporary means for handling immediate problems and offers the opportunity to question the entire structure of our social systems. The crisis has encouraged politicians such as Ronald Reagan and Margaret Thatcher to seize the opportunity to raise fundamental theoretical questions and to implement radical solutions. Australia and Canada, influenced as they are by policies developed in the United States and Britain, are being pushed in similar directions. Women, especially those in the social service sectors, are particularly well placed to evaluate such developments critically, but only if they do so from a sound theoretical base.

The Theoretical Task

Such theory must be integrated and sex-conscious. It must not only fit together parts of the economy to develop a picture of the overall pattern, but also connect the formal economy to the household, in a context of changing state intervention and of new technologies. Such theory must also begin with the understanding that there is a single system in each country, a system dominated by the search for profit and reinvestment and characterized by a sexual division of labour that subordinates women to men and household to formal economy. This sexual division of labour reverberates throughout the entire political economy, with the result that changes in the formal economy, in government programs, in technology, in households, affect women and men differently. All economic and social policies, then, are women's policies.

While such theory must take into account the dominant ideas which primarily support the interests of owners and of men and which play a central role in maintaining things as they are, it must begin by focusing on structures and conditions, because these set the limits, establish the parameters, in any society. Such theory is necessary because, although there are identifiable trends resulting from the search for profit and from sex segregation, the outcome is not predetermined. People can and do make their own history, if not under conditions of their own choosing. And people can do this most effectively if they understand what the trends are, as well as why and how they are supported.

Women's Work

Of course, the development of theory and strategy for coping with the current crisis is an enormous, continuing, and collective project. This paper seeks to demonstrate the need for such a project by examining some aspects of women's work. It focuses on women's work because work not only provides meaning and identity in our lives but also shapes our resources, our social contacts and our opportunities, because the subordinate position of women is located in the work they do, and because the overwhelming majority of clients (Andrew 1984; Owen 1984b: 217) and workers in the social service sector, where the current crisis is most clearly reflected, are women.

Similar political economies, histories, and geographical barriers have led to similar patterns in Australia and Canada. In both countries, women's labour force participation rates have been rising, at the same time as their unemployment, underemployment, and poverty have been increasing. Government "restraint" programs and the introduction of microelectronic technology threaten a further deterioration in women's condition. On the other hand, differences in the degree of unionization, in government strategies, and in geographical location have helped create variations from which we can learn and which clearly indicate that we can be active participants in making history. The examination here of current trends—trends which have developed more quickly in Canada—is designed as a warning as well as a call for more theoretical and strategic work, a warning that if programs based on an integrated, sex-conscious theory are not developed, women will emerge from this crisis in a more secondary position than before.

Two important developments in the political economy have set the context for women's rising labour force participation: the growth of the state and deindustrialization.[2] As a result of these developments, relatively few jobs, if any at all, have been created on farms and in forests, mines, fisheries, and factories—traditionally male areas of employment—and relatively many have been created in stores, offices, restaurants, schools, and hospitals—traditionally more female areas. Women were hired because they were cheap and available, and because they had the appropriate skills, training, and attitudes to do the work.

Some of the new jobs were in technical and professional fields, particularly in teaching and nursing where women had long formed the majority of the workforce. But most of the additional work was in low-level clerical, sales, and service work which offered few rewards in terms of pay, intrinsic satisfaction, or opportunities for advancement. Although over half of Canadian women, and about 45 percent of Australian women, are now counted as active members of the labour force, about a third of them do clerical work, at least one in ten has a sales job, and about one in six does service work. (Armstrong 1984: Table 5:15; Eccles 1984: Table 5:4). In Canada, the concentration of women in clerical, sales, and service occupations, taken together, has been remarkably stable since the 1940s. (Armstrong and Armstrong 1984: 18–63).

So has their concentration in the professional and technical field. Over the last 40 years, there has been an increase of only 1.4 percentage points in the proportion of women employed in this field. Moreover, this slight increase is more than accounted for by the rapid growth in technical, as distinct from professional, jobs. By contrast, the concentration of men has been increasing in the professions themselves (Armstrong and Armstrong 1984: 41). In Australia, women's share of professional, technical, and related jobs actually declined between 1976 and 1982 (Eccles 1984: 86).

In addition, much of the new work is part-time, also in clerical, sales, and service jobs. Although methods of collecting data make comparisons difficult, it is clear that at least a quarter of employed women in both countries have part-time jobs and part-time pay, that part-time employment accounts for much of the growth in female labour force participation (Eccles 1984: 82), that an increasing number work part-time because they cannot find full-time work, and that, in spite of this changing demand, women's hours in part-time work are decreasing (Armstrong 1984: Tables 4.22 and 4.24; Owen 1984a: 9). By 1982, women accounted for only 28 percent of full-time workers in Australia, an increase of less than 3 percentage points since 1966 (Eccles 1984: 82). In Canada, just over a third of the full-time workers by 1984 were female, indicating an increase of 8 percentage points in the female share of full-time employment since 1966. Between 1981 and 1982 the number of full-time, mostly female nurses, for example, declined while the number of full-time, mostly male health care executives grew (calculated from Health and Welfare Canada 1983).

Part-time employment means low pay and an intensification of labour (Armstrong and Armstrong 1986) for women in both countries. Full-time work, however, provides different rewards relative to those of men. In Australia, there has been "a dramatic increase in the income of women who work full-time for a full year from 60 per cent of male earnings in 1968–69 to 78 per cent in 1978–79" (Power et al. 1985: 58). In Canada, on the other hand, the change during a similar period was much smaller, with women in 1970 paid 60 percent of male income and those in 1980 paid 64 percent (Armstrong and Armstrong 1984: Table 8). Equal pay legislation was much more effective in Australia primarily because a significantly higher proportion of workers is unionized and because many wage settlements are nation-wide. However, further gains are unlikely without a desegregation of the labour force, and even this limited victory is in jeopardy with the continuing hard times pushing women's demands to the bottom of the agenda.

The rising labour force participation rates that have created the impression of dramatic moves toward equality hide the rising female unemployment and underemployment in part-time jobs, and hide the fact that the proportion of women with good jobs and good pay has risen only slightly over the last 40 years.

Economic Need

Women have responded to the rising demand for female employees, in spite of their continued responsibility for housework, childcare, and tension management (Luxton 1980; Gowland 1983: 36–53), primarily because they needed the income. With significant increases in energy, housing, and transportation costs and in taxes, women could not compensate for falling wages and rising prices by working harder at their domestic chores. Taxes could not be paid in fresh baked bread, even if it is still cheaper to make your own, a questionable economy at best.[3] Some women earned income by undertaking what the International Labour Organization (1984: 51) calls clandestine work, work that "is carried out on the fringes of the law or outside it altogether." They cleaned other people's houses and did dressmaking, typing, catering, sewing, and babysitting in their own homes, often because they could at the same time fulfill their domestic responsibilities. But many more entered the labour force, often taking part-time jobs in order to accommodate their domestic work. Between 1971 and 1981, the income of Canadian wives "was the significant factor in preventing family income from declining in real dollars" and family economic resources continue to deteriorate. "By 1979–81, increases in wives' income were no longer able to offset the decline in husbands' average income" (Pryor 1984: 102). O'Laughlin and Cass (1984: 4) demonstrate that similar forces are operating in Australia. In both countries, it has been estimated that poverty in husband-wife families would have increased by between 50 and 100 percent if women had not gone out to work for pay (National Council on Welfare 1979: Table 3; Edwards, quoted in Cass 1984: 10).

With women's rising economic need come demands for maternity leave to allow women to have babies and keep their jobs. A partial victory here in turn permits women to stay in the labour force, while the limited provisions often force them to return very quickly to their paid jobs and ensure that women retain responsibility for childcare. Opposition to better maternity and paternity leave rights grows, however, as employers argue that no organization can compete in hard times with part of the labour force away for months on end. Yet Australia's long service leave provision, open to large numbers and varieties of workers who won lengthier vacations in part because trips to North America and Europe make sense only for months at a time, clearly demonstrates that such leave need not disrupt the economy.

The dramatic increase in women's labour force participation cannot then be taken as a simple indication of progress or as a simple matter of choice. The growth has contributed to increasing demands from women for greater equality, which have in turn contributed to the movement of some women into traditional male areas of work, to some narrowing of the pay gap, and to some government programs, policies, and services designed to deal with or prevent women's subordination. Most women have, however, continued to work at women's jobs in and out of the labour force, and to be paid women's wages or no wages at all, despite their economic need. Meanwhile, more and more of those counted as part of the female labour force are unemployed.

Unemployment

Signs of a developing crisis appeared early in the 1970s, as women's economic needs continued to grow while jobs failed to expand at their earlier rate. More women entered the labour market, but an increasing number failed to find jobs there. Official statistics indicate that between 1973 and 1981, female unemployment rates rose much faster, and remained higher, than those of men (International Labour Organization 1984: 43). Combined with the statistics on segregation, these numbers show that women cannot be blamed for male unemployment. Women are not putting men out of work. And such figures significantly underestimate the numbers of women who want and need paid work (Armstrong 1984: 185–87; Power et al. 1985: 63–70). Women constitute the majority of the hidden unemployed, because most still have their domestic work to do when their paid jobs disappear. If all the women who want and need paid work were counted, the female unemployment rate would, by conservative estimate, more than double (Power et al. 1985: 65).

For the most part, the segregated labour market and the growing crisis have meant that women are competing with a large supply of other women for declining work in female job ghettos. When they do compete directly with men, the women usually lose (Armstrong 1984: 67–98). Although the recession in the early 1980s hit first, hardest, and most obviously the sectors where men work, reducing differences in official male and female unemployment rates and for a short period pushing male rates above the comparable ones for women, some recovery has reduced male rates, while female rates have failed to decline. In 1985, the unemployment rate for Canadian women over twenty-five years of age was a full percentage point higher than that of their male counterparts (Statistics Canada 1985b: Table 88).

High unemployment rates and the shift in jobs away from the primary and secondary sectors have encouraged men to search for work in traditional female areas, especially in part-time work (Armstrong 1984: 67–98). At the same time, high unemployment means that women, as the last hired in traditional male areas, are the first to go. And unemployed women often find it more difficult than men to find other paid work. An Australian study of workers laid off from an electrical goods manufacturer found that the men were much more successful than women in finding new jobs (Curtain 1985: 20). And when their husbands are unemployed, women also bear the burden of stretching a significantly smaller food dollar. Unemployment, too, is a women's issue.

The Feminization of Poverty

It is within this context of increasing female unemployment and underemployment, of continuing segregation and low wages (Bryson 1977), that what even *Business Week* (Cahan 1985: 58) calls the feminization of poverty must be understood. When growing family disruption — itself related to worsening economic conditions and rising female labour force participation—and women's increasing longevity, although not good health (Wilkins and Adams 1983), are added to these processes, the explanation for women's increasing deprivation is almost complete. More women are poor and more of the poor are women. This is not surprising, given the groups most susceptible to poverty. Being young or old places people at high risk, and women constitute over 40 percent of the unemployed young, while at the other end of the age spectrum, they make up the majority of the elderly, and a large majority of the elderly without private pensions, superannuation, or spouses. Lone parents are also a high-risk group,[4] particularly in societies such as ours with only limited childcare facilities (see Status of Women Canada 1986) and with few means of enforcing child support orders; and women are the overwhelming majority of lone parents. Low-wage earners frequently face poverty, and it is women who make up the majority of those paid minimum or part-time wages.[5] Unemployed and disabled people are often forced to live on very low incomes, and while women do not form the majority of this group, their numbers are large, and, as is the case with other high-risk groups, growing.

Statistics Canada (1985a: 2) concludes that

> Poverty is a major concern of Canadian women. One in 10 Canadian families is headed by a lone parent woman, and 50% of these women are supporting their families on incomes that are below Statistics Canada low-income cut-off lines. One in three Canadian women over 65 years of age lives alone, and 60% of those who live alone are supporting themselves on an income that is below the low-income cut-off lines.

Marriage does not necessarily protect women either. "Families with children have experienced a substantial increase in poverty in recent years" (National Council on Welfare 1985: 18).

In her study of poverty in Australia, Bettina Cass (1984: 21) found that

> As a result of the marked deterioration in the labour market in the recession since 1974 resulting in increased rates and duration of unemployment; as a result of the increased proportion of single parents excluded from paid employment; as a result of the increased costs of forming a household for families with children; as a result of the decreased value of income support for children through the tax/transfer system in comparison with the slightly increased real values of income support for pensioners without children — the impact of poverty has shifted to the younger stages of the life cycle. The groups most vulnerable to insufficient income, economic and social marginality in the current period are women-headed single parent families and other low income families without at least one parent in full-year, full-time work; the long-term unemployed; non-aged single women.

The economic crisis, combined with continued sex segregation of domestic and wage work, means the increasing feminization of poverty (Bryson 1983).

State Responses

As women's poverty, unemployment, and underemployment continue to rise, signs of a recovery continue to be weak, and governments respond with what Graycar (1983) calls a retreat from the welfare state. When governments introduce "restraint" programs, as they have in Canada and as they promise to do again in Australia, women bear the brunt of the belt-tightening because they constitute such a high proportion of those receiving and delivering benefits and services.

In the past, government expansion has not only meant more jobs for women, it has also meant more good jobs for women. A large proportion of the women with technical, professional, managerial, and administrative jobs work directly or indirectly for the government (Armstrong 1984: 78–81) in education, health, and public administration. Women have also found their best opportunities for promotion and their best pay, absolutely and relative to men, in the state sector (Denton and Hunter 1982: 40). These better conditions are, in turn, related to the high rate of unionization in the public sector. With fewer jobs, with increases in part-time employment, and with government attempts in Canada at least to limit the power of these unions (Armstrong 1984: 127–30), women's strength is being, and will be, significantly reduced. The privatization of state services also threatens women's jobs and their collective strength. In the Canadian case at least, so would the current prospects for freer trade with the United States, which if implemented would reduce employment in female-dominated industries in particular (Cohen 1985).

"Restraint" programs also mean reductions in benefits and services for women. The growth rate in expenditures on social security has slowed considerably in Australia (Graycar 1983: 4), while the numbers requiring assistance have increased significantly. Moreover, the allocations within social security expenditures have shifted away from assistance to families toward help for the unemployed (Graycar 1983: 4). Most of those receiving family support payments are women; the majority of those deemed eligible for unemployment benefits are men. In Canada, family allowances have been partially deindexed and pensions attacked. Unemployment insurance is under review, and social welfare payments are threatened.

When public expenditures on items such as childcare facilities, services for the elderly, housing and transportation subsidies, and rape crisis and other women's centres are either reduced or frozen in times of increased need, the impact is much greater on women. Their dependence on these services, which are mainly services for women delivered by women, reflects their subordinate position in the home and in the labour force. When the state fails to provide these services, pressure is placed on women to provide them without pay. Yet as fewer and fewer women can rely on male financial support, and as more and more of them seek paid employment, they have less time, fewer resources, and often little desire to provide at home or in the volunteer sector what the state fails to provide in the public sector. Indeed, many of the services the state is threatening to "deinstitutionalize" and place in unpaid women's hands have never been in the home.

At the same time as governments are introducing "restraint" programs in areas which primarily affect women, they are developing job creation programs in areas which primarily affect men. As Borowski (1984: 42) points out, higher Canadian unemployment rates over the last decade have meant that "Canada has a much larger number of employment-related programs in place than Australia." But rising unemployment rates are encouraging Australia to follow suit, so the time is ripe for a brief examination of Canadian programs and their impact. Although all these programs contain clear statements about equal access, sex segregation means that the impact has been different for women and men. In 1983, three of the four largest programs were directed toward creating employment in the primary and secondary sectors dominated by men, implying that here, at least, the problem was jobs, not people (Armstrong 1984: 123–27). Another strategy has involved what could be termed the financing of bankruptcy through the provision of small sums of seed money for investment in private enterprise. This money too is much more likely to go to males.

A third strategy involves spreading the work around. A government Commission (Labour Canada 1983) established to investigate part-time work recommended expansion of part-time jobs for women as well as for the young and the elderly, and recommended some increased protection for workers in these part-time jobs. The Commission also suggested the active encouragement of job-sharing, of two people doing one job. This scheme is most applicable to a limited number of women working in technical and professional jobs, where half a salary is often equivalent to one woman's full pay in other sectors. Adoption of these proposals would not only mean that more women would receive part-time pay and part-time benefits in jobs lacking opportunities for promotion, but that they would retain the primary responsibility for domestic work as well.

Another strategy for spreading employment is work-sharing, a program which in Canada permits employees in certain hard-hit areas to work four days a week and be paid for the fifth out of unemployment insurance funds. Largely directed toward the primary and secondary sectors, this scheme too has mostly served to maintain male jobs (Armstrong 1984: 124). It is worth noting that the major advantages listed for part-time work, job-sharing, and work-sharing—higher productivity, more time for family responsibilities, higher employment, and the maintenance of skills—are equally applicable to a shorter work week and to men as well as to women.

Women and young men have been the targets of a fourth strategy, skills upgrading and on-the-job training schemes. Such schemes imply, however, that for women and young men the problem is people, not jobs. They often involve narrowly training people for specific jobs or specific skills, yet if there is one thing we know about the future, it is that many of the skills and jobs of today will not be in demand tomorrow. Moreover, an emphasis on skills and training, as opposed to broader educational development, also redirects education funds away from areas in which women have traditionally taught toward those where men predominate. And finally, employment schemes which offer subsidies to employers to hire and train young people may also lead to labour substitution, especially to the substitution of young men for older women, rather than to the creation of new jobs. Job creation schemes in Canada, then, have done little to create or even maintain employment, but when they have been successful, more of the benefits have gone to men.

The New Technology

While few would pin their hopes for the future on state job creation schemes, many would place their bets on the new technology. Employers are understandably enthusiastic about the possibilities of microelectronics. The invention of the microchip—a tiny, cheap, relatively sturdy piece of silicon that contains complete electronic circuits and that can do what a large, expensive, fragile, and therefore limited mainframe computer did in the past—allows the dispersion and application of computer processes to an incredible range of tasks, at a price and in a form that many can afford and understand. Primarily designed to increase productivity and managerial control, the new technology is particularly applicable to information processing, an area long resistant to these processes. While employers generally acknowledge that there may be some short-term reduction in employment as a result of technological change, they argue that, although much of the equipment is already in use, it has had little employment impact and that, in the long run, the new technology will create more jobs than it destroys.

Precisely because this technology is designed to increase productivity and managerial control, employees—especially female employees—are more pessimistic about its consequences. With one-third of employed women doing clerical work, work which is in the process of being radically altered by microelectronics, and with a large proportion employed in labour-intensive sectors of the trade and manufacturing industries which can now be technologically transformed, women's pessimism is not surprising. And it can only be reinforced by the impact the new technology is having on promotion ladders, as the lower administrative positions disappear from offices (Menzies 1981; Windsor 1984).

The new technology is, at one and the same time, a cause, a reflection and a resolution of the current crisis. Its introduction is both justified and hidden by the crisis. Its current impact is difficult to measure because the high unemployment rates are blamed on the crisis in general, rather than on technological change in particular. Moreover, the impact is hidden by silent firings, by jobless growth, and by the failure of most governments to record turnover rates. And the impact is delayed by technological change clauses in union contracts, by the need to train customers to do the work, by the sometimes increased employment during changeover to the new technology, and by the staged development of the technology, which often prevents employment from declining significantly until the fully automated office or plant is in place.

While this microelectronic technology is creating some new jobs, it is likely to destroy many more jobs than it creates for women (Armstrong 1984; Power et al. 1985). As Benston (1983) points out, there are basically five areas in which jobs will be created. First, there are jobs operating the new equipment. Many of these new jobs are in word processing, and these jobs are going mainly to women, although the use of technology is encouraging some men to move into the field. However, there will be fewer and worse jobs in information processing. Female word processors are merely replacing female typists, and doing the work at a much faster rate, primarily because the machines require fewer skills and allow the organization of work in such a way that women do nothing but type. It is this kind of work which gives rise to repetitive strain injury and which leads researchers like Wilkins (1983) to argue that half of the health hazards related to the new equipment are the result not of machines, but of the organization of the work that such machines permit. Australia's higher unionization rate has led to more investigation of health consequences and greater restraint on the introduction of new technologies, but neither country has yet worked out an overall strategy on the health hazards of the work. Furthermore, because these new machines can automatically time and record the errors of the operator as well as communicate through telephone lines to a main office, they also make it possible to have much of the work done at home by women. Women could be forced to purchase their own equipment, pay overhead costs, do the typing, and babysit the children all at the same time, away from the distractions of union organizers or chats with other workers.

The second area of microelectronic job creation is the production of the hardware. Jobs are expanding for women here too, but they are low-paid jobs which involve detailed, monotonous factory work which is mainly done by women in Third World countries, until their health is ruined.

The third area for job expansion is the production of software. Developing programs can be interesting work, although tasks are being automated in this area as well. Men's skills, education, training, and socialization mean they have the advantage here. Some women have been developing skills in this field, but automation may mean both that job expansion will be limited and that women, as the later arrivals, will get the more automated work.

A fourth field often listed as growing with the technology is maintenance and repair. Most of these jobs have already been captured by men. Moreover, this is unlikely to be a significant growth area because much of the equipment takes new components rather than requiring repairs, because the small machines are so inexpensive and changing so rapidly that people are more likely to replace than to repair them, and because the larger machines are increasingly being built with self-diagnostic capacities which can either correct problems or tell people how to do so.

Finally, there will be some expansion of jobs in teaching and research, but these too are likely to go to men rather than to women, given that for a variety of reasons, computer science has already been established as a male field. Moreover, as educational institutions shift their emphasis toward microelectronic technology, they are reducing their staffs in other, traditionally more female, areas.

Technology, then, will likely mean fewer, and worse, jobs for women.

Conclusion

If present trends in Canada and Australia are allowed to continue, the future does not look bright for women. Their economic need will increase, while their support from men and governments will decrease, as will their opportunities for full-time, meaningful paid employment. At the same time, their unpaid employment, both domestic and volunteer, will grow.

But this future is not inevitable. The new technology is not determining. Policies can affect outcomes, as the current differences between Australia and Canada indicate. The new technology could be redirected and redesigned to eliminate rather than expand monotonous, repetitive work. Increased productivity could mean shorter work weeks for everyone rather than no paid employment for some and forty or more hours for others. Work of both the domestic and wage variety could be redistributed and redefined rather than sex-segregated and only sometimes rewarded with pay. Policies could expand and redirect human services rather than weaken them. Poverty could be reduced rather than extended and intensified. But such alternatives are possible only if those in a position to ask fundamental questions, to connect the daily reality to explanations, to relate the parts to the whole, do so. Only an integrated and sex-conscious analysis can be the basis for the development of strategies for a future that will work for women and for men.

Notes

1. This is a revised and updated version of the Phillip Law Lecture, presented in May 1985 at the Phillip Institute of Technology, Bundoora (Vic.), Australia. With slight revisions, the lecture was published in *Australian-Canadian Studies* 3 (1985). Hugh Armstrong acknowledges the support provided, through a Post-Doctoral Fellowship, by the Social Sciences and Humanities Research Council of Canada.
2. At least in Canada, these developments have been consecutive rather than concurrent, as the state share of jobs ceased to grow in the early 1970s (Armstrong 1977), just as deindustrialization started to take hold, notably in the textiles and clothing industries (Mahon 1984).
3. In Canada, the prices of prepared foods (e.g., bakery products) have in recent years been rising less quickly than have the prices of basic ingredients (e.g., flour). Unlike the prices of such food, whether prepared or not, those of restaurant meals and ready-made clothes have been rising more slowly than has the Consumer Price Index in general (Armstrong 1984: 104). To cope with inflation by making meals and clothes from scratch is thus a more costly and less viable strategy. Intensifying domestic labour increasingly means shopping more carefully.
4. According to one study (Boulet and Lavallée 1984: 39), 44 percent of Canadian single-parent families are below the poverty line, while the Australian figure may be as high as 60 percent (Edwards, Harper, and Harrison 1985: 18).
5. Among full-year, mainly full-time labour force workers in Canada, women now earn 64 percent of what men earn (Armstrong and Armstrong 1984: 43), while in Australia the full-year, full-time figure is 78 percent (Power et al. 1985: 58). Yet as Power and her associates go on to argue, this full-year (mainly) full-time focus is misleading, reflecting as it does the non-participation of men in household work and childcare. Both in Australia (Jones 1984) and in Canada, "By far the largest factor in explaining women's low wages is their concentration in low-wage occupations" (Ornstein 1983: 46).

IV The State

13 The Hidden Curriculum of School: Reproducing Gender and Class Hierarchies

SUSAN RUSSELL

The school is a pivotal social institution mediating between ascriptive factors given at birth, namely social class and gender, and ultimate position in society. It is through schooling, mainstream functionalist sociologists posit, that all members of society are offered equal life chances, based on their own ability and achievement. This "rosy" view of an egalitarian and just society cannot be taken seriously by feminist and marxist sociologists, keenly aware of gender and class inequalities in the labour force and the gender hierarchy in the family. For them, the task of a sociology of education is to reveal both the ways in which students in schools are encouraged to consent to these social inequalities, and signs of their resistance to them.

Girls in school, it is revealed through an analysis of the education process, are the focus of pressures to encourage them to accept subordinate positions in both the labour force and the family. They are encouraged to believe that their exclusive role is or ought to be childbearing and rearing, and that work that they take on in the labour force is secondary to their role in the family. School personnel exert these pressures through job counselling and through undermining the academic ability of girls while focusing on their domestic futures. It is under these pressures that the vast majority of girls sail through school and assume their subordinate roles in the domestic sphere and in the labour force.

It is not that schools "invent" these social hierarchies. They exist in male-dominated, capitalist society. Students, because of prior pressures from the home and media, enter school with a predisposition to accept these class and gender hierarchies and their place in them. Studies in the sociology of education reveal the ways in which these categories are also accepted in schools and students are encouraged to consent to them and not to consider alternatives. Thus schools contribute to the social reproduction of class and gender inequalities. The signs of resistance on the part of girls to these pressures can also be seen, but these are little, if at all, recognized as valid in schools.

In this chapter a brief discussion of the functionalist perspective in the sociology of education will be presented first, in Section I, since this is the analysis to which all subsequent ones respond. The contradictions inherent in that analysis led to other, more sophisticated, research questions and methods. The issues which generated debate are the impact of social class and gender in the school and classroom. Thus Section II concerns findings of research by marxist and feminist sociologists of education. It will be divided into three sections, each representing deeper levels of analysis of education: (1) the social organization of schools and how these are established formally to channel students to reproduce class and gender hierarchies; (2) the culture of working- and middle-class girls, both the elements which they share due to gender and those on which they diverge largely because of class differences; and (3) phenomenological research in the school, divided into three sections: (a) the advice of guidance personnel, (b) teacher-student interaction in the classroom, and (c) the content of classroom interaction, including "lessons" in the gender hierarchy and signs of resistance to them.

Although section 2, noted above, is not strictly speaking part of the sociology of education, since uncovering the world views and aspirations of students does not necessarily implicate schools, it is included here as an important transition to the subsequent section. What is revealed by this research is that school personnel accept and reinforce the "motherhood," "marriage," and "anti-school" aspects of girls' culture, while ignoring any others.

The primary data presented in this paper were collected in an academically oriented high school in Ottawa, Ontario, and offer insights into the process of schooling (Russell 1978, 1979–80). The research was in-depth, employing several modes of data collection: classroom observation in twenty-seven classes in the senior grade; interviews with a random sample of forty senior students, twenty-five of whom were girls; twenty-five teachers of the senior grade; and the five guidance counsellors in the school. Grades achieved by the entire Grade 12 class in Grades 8 and 11 were also analyzed. The initial purpose of the research was to study gender socialization in the school, but this was quickly seen to be impossible without also considering issues of social class. This realization that gender and class are intricately interrelated and must both be explored in analyzing students' behaviour and aspirations and school personnel's channelling of students highlights the importance of using both feminist and marxist perspectives. The experience of students in school varies enormously by both gender and class, and it is the goal of this chapter to explore some of the ways in which this is true.

I. The Functionalist Perspective: Mainstream Sociology of Education

According to functionalist theory, which provides an ideological snapshot of how liberal democratic society is supposed to achieve its goals (O'Brien calls it "high-class daydreaming" (1981: 2)), schooling exists to provide equal opportunity for all children, regardless of ascriptive factors of birth (Parsons 1959). As long as schools are open, and access to them is available, indeed required, at least to a certain age, schools are seen to be providing equality of opportunity. So-called "critical functionalists" such as Bourdieu, who writes about the social reproduction of social class in society (Murphy 1979), and Porter, who shows through large-scale survey research in Ontario that girls and working-class students have lower aspirations to attend university than their middle-class and male peers (Porter, Porter, and Blishen 1982), question whether education is in fact offering equal educational opportunity. This they do without doubting that schools should and might offer equal opportunity, regardless of a society built on class and gender inequalities.

What draws together these three functionalists, who are on the surface very different, is their insistence that inequalities which do exist among students stem exclusively from the home and peer background, which either prepares a student successfully to take advantage of what school offers, or leaves him/her inadequately prepared to cope and compete in that milieu. Thus underpinning the work of Parsons and Porter is the "culture of poverty," while central to Bourdieu's work is the concept of "cultural capital," which bourgeois children possess in abundance from family ("correct" language, knowledge of the "arts," and information about and familiarity with the education system), and which working-class children lack. These related theories undervalue working-class culture and methods of negotiating in capitalist society, and by extension help to maintain and justify social class boundaries. As critical functionalists, both Bourdieu and Porter argue for compensatory education classes or financial assistance for further education. Thus the process of schooling itself is not criticized by functionalist researchers. They just want more of it.

II. Marxist and Feminist Analyses of Schools

In opposition to the functionalist approach, marxist and feminist researchers of education turn their attention to the ways in which schools contribute independently to the perpetuation of male-dominated, capitalist society. Having rejected the dominant ideology that schools, by their simple existence, offer equal opportunity, or potentially might do so, educational researchers with a marxist or feminist perspective are free to examine the ways in which schools actively process student behaviour and activity to perpetuate social class and gender divisions.

1. Social Organization of Schools

The main contribution of schooling, as seen by marxist sociologists, is to legitimate the existing social hierarchy of jobs and rewards in capitalist society. The work by Bowles and Gintis (1976) develops a theory of "correspondence" between social class, classroom relationships, and work in the labour force. They argue that "ability" tests (IQ tests) used to separate children into the categories of "fast" or "slow" learners do not test the children's own potential as students, but, rather, their family backgrounds. Children, streamed by social class, are exposed to different types of education, both in terms of content (academic or vocational), and social relations with teachers and peers in the classroom. These different forms prepare them for different academic futures and, in turn, feed into different types of jobs — working-class, bourgeois, or petty bourgeois. A sensitive and personalized account of the marxist theoretical framework is to be found in "Downtown Kids Aren't Dumb," a brief presented by Toronto parents concerned with their children's welfare (Park School Community Council 1974). It shows how ability testing and high school programs in Canadian schools process working-class children to maintain them in vocational streams which lead into poorly rewarded jobs. On the basis of this evidence, the marxist argument that schools reproduce the social class division of labour is well established.

Using a similar perspective, some feminist researchers focus on the ways in which schools are formally organized to ensure that girls and boys receive different educational experiences. Gaskell (1981) studied girls in Vancouver high school programs, showing how they moved directly into the sex-segregated labour force. She demonstrates that there are short-term advantages to both the girls and their employers, but that there are long-term detrimental effects for the girls with limited skill training and jobs without opportunities for advancement.

This type of analysis has prompted some feminist researchers to reexamine the contentious issue of the effects of single-sex versus co-educational schools. In many ways this remains a British and Australian issue. Canadians have tended to follow the American lead into comprehensive and co-educational schools as the ones which, it is argued, offer greater equality (by class, race, and sex). Arnot (1983) contends that both options should remain open for parents choosing a school for daughters and sons, and urges feminists to continue to study this issue. Shaw (1980) argues that although they may provide better facilities for science labs, co-educational schools may in fact contribute to greater sex role typing. Even if the move to single-sex schools is perceived as a retrogressive step, perhaps students — especially girls in the thirteen-to-fifteen-year-old group, whose academic achievement typically falls — might benefit from the segregation. However, as Arnot has pointed out, in a society marked strongly by a sex-segregated labour force, a minimal separation in school would make little difference. Similarly, Canadian data substantiates Wolpe's (1978) point that even when girls achieve appropriate credentials in school, they are not likely to obtain positions in the labour force commensurate with their qualifications.

Thus, despite strategic differences, feminist researchers concur that the school system, from sex-typed courses through to its larger organizational structure, reproduces gender, like class, hierarchies.

2. Student Culture

The work by McRobbie, Llewellyn, Sharp, and Willis on the culture of working-class girls and boys, as this is played out in schools, indicates the futility of the functionalist theory of equality of opportunity offered through education, and expands a marxist structural paradigm. McRobbie (1978) finds that working-class girls enter school with a predisposition to marry and have children, and so to ignore other kinds of work which they might also do. The anti-school culture of femininity and the short-term goal of romance take priority, in McRobbie's research, for working-class girls. Llewellyn's participant observation study of the culture of girls and girls' friendship groups offers interesting comparative findings to McRobbie's study, while at the same time adding to the underlying finding that school merely provides a setting for the playing out of an anti-school female culture deemed legitimate for young women in a male-dominated social environment (Llewellyn 1980). The research by Sharp and her colleagues on the transition of working-class girls from school to work offers added insight into this process which depends on girls' perceiving family and motherhood as their central goals (Sharp and Roberts 1983). Similarly, it is found that working-class boys develop an anti-school culture based on a disparagement of academic work, combined with an overvaluation of heavy labour and masculine superiority (Willis 1977).

Anyon's recent work on the accommodation and resistance by working-class and upper-middle-class girls to the contradictory expectations of future work and motherhood provides valuable insight into forms of female culture (1983). After exploring both public and private forms of resistance and accommodation to the contradictory expectations of the female sex role, Anyon concludes that overall "their accommodation and resistance does not seek to remove the structural causes of the contradiction" (1983). Their resistance and accommodation represent creative and individually liberating forms of managing, but ultimately only assist women to survive in a male-dominated milieu where roles which are actually open to them are circumscribed.

The Ottawa study provides support for several of the ideas put forth by Anyon. Of the twenty-five girls interviewed, sixteen were middle or upper middle class from professional or managerial families, while nine were working class from unskilled or semi-skilled families. For the middle-class group, going to university was an accepted course of action, taken for granted. However, only three of them integrated plans for postsecondary education with a commitment to subsequent careers. For the majority university was seen as a time "to get my head together" or to fulfill parental dreams. For one it was something to do in case she was "late" in getting married. As she said, "when you get to be twenty-five or twenty-six everyone starts looking at you and wondering when you are going to get married."

For these girls, going to university or art college (a popular choice among the highest status) is mainly a route to motherhood. This, they were quite clear, would put an end to other activities:

> I wouldn't want to work, after I had kids.
>
> If I had kids I'd definitely stop working.
>
> If I had kids I'd want to stay home and help them.
>
> My career would be working with children and having my own kids would be my career.

Thus these middle-class girls for the most part foresaw a truncated future. Their way of solving the contradictions of being a middle-class woman was a two-stage program: some further education followed by full-time motherhood. The three who seemed committed to pursuing a career were clearly aware that this might prove problematic. One said she would be expected to do all the housework *and* have a job, while another said "anyone I had an interest in would just have to realize that my career was important to me."

All but one of the working-class girls were bemused by questions about education after high school. Some mentioned it as an ideal but one quickly dismissed it:

> Sometimes my mother asks me if I'm thinking of going to college, and I say "I don't know, I think I might get a job first." And she says, "Oh, that's okay." She's pretty reasonable.

Another said, "I want to do something, but if I don't I won't be upset . . . . I always wanted to be a housewife." Another said that she didn't think she could do university work even though she wanted to be a teacher and had high grades. For the most part they anticipated getting a job at the end of high school. That was what parents wanted: "they just don't want me to be a slob. They want me to earn a decent living, like being a secretary." For others the motivation was to be financially independent: "My boyfriend always said he'd support me, but I don't want that. I can't stand that." Although university is not in the minds of working-class girls, they share the motherhood ideology with their middle-class sisters: "If you're going to go on with work and be married at the same time, I don't think you should have children."

The range of desires and expectations reveals how class differences arise within the structurally prescribed limits of femininity. While middle-class girls may be able to live out both of their typical future plans — full-time motherhood and a cyclical career — this is likely to be at some cost both to their work lives and earning capacities, and to their experience in childcare (cf. Rosenberg this volume). Given the levels of female and male working-class wages, it is highly unlikely that the working-class girls will be able to be financially independent or to not work to help support a household.

This research on the future plans of female high school students adds further support to the critique of functionalist theory and moves beyond organizational analyses where sex and class are all too often rigidly separated. Because functionalism assumes a high degree of consensus on middle-class values of achievement, it cannot see student cultures which develop partly in retaliation to socially imposed gender and class constraints. Given student resistance to what middle-class schooling has to offer in a capitalist, male-dominated society, there is little wonder that the functionalist aspiration that schools provide equal opportunity has failed. Functionalist and critical organizational analyses share a methodological assumption: they separate the formal organizational aspects of the school from the culture of the student population. Phenomenological research which focuses on what happens in schools in a largely informal way shows how the relationship between school personnel and students in the school and classroom contribute to the persistence of the status quo.

3. Phenomenological Research on Interaction between Students and School Personnel

Overall, it becomes evident in this research that at least two processes are operating in the classroom and school to lead students to accept and reproduce society based on class and gender hierarchical divisions. First, it becomes clear that sex and class are recognized by school personnel usually implicitly, as social categories to consider in guiding students in making "appropriate" future occupational and educational plans. They do not consider it to be appropriate for individuals to cross the gender division of labour or part ways with their own social class background, despite academic achievement which would allow them to do so. Middle-class girls are encouraged to go to university to achieve some professional or semi-professional skills *before* settling down to childbearing and domesticity, while working-class girls are expected to work, at least part-time, while investing their main attentions in family. Both are actively encouraged to put family first. These decisions are made with little or no consideration of actual school achievement or for individual interests.

The second factor which becomes apparent concerns the implicit devaluation of subordinate (non–middle-class male) cultures. This is most usually expressed by refusing to recognize or deriding resistant or opposing cultures. Girls' interests—or what Rosenberg calls feminine culture—are particularly subject to derision in the school. In writing about the successful hegemony of bourgeois culture in the school, Dale states

> . . . what seems to be involved is the prevention of rejection, opposition or alternatives to the status quo through denying the use of the school for such purposes. (Dale 1982)

Although Dale rejects seeing the school as "active" in the maintenance of this hegemony, choosing rather to see the status quo as being maintained by the "normal process" of the relatively autonomous school, it is a matter for research to investigate how much the "prevention of rejection, opposition or alternatives" is the passive stance of the school, and how much it is actively accomplished. Delamont (1983) argues that the school is active in promoting the preservation of the hierarchical gender status quo and in fact is regressive in ignoring social change which has taken place.

Research presented here supports Delamont's view of the school, while at the same time showing how, simply by avoiding issues, the school takes stands supporting existing gender and class hierarchies. The following is broken down into three components for in-depth analysis: (a) the advice of guidance personnel, (b) teacher-student interaction in the classroom, and (c) the content of classroom interaction.

a) The Advice of Guidance Personnel

The evidence from this research indicates that students are not led to consider future work which would be inconsistent with their social class background or gender, regardless of personal academic achievement. Although survey research has found that scores on mental ability do not correlate very highly with educational aspirations, particularly for working-class students (Porter, Porter, and Blishen 1982), it is useful to examine how this is accomplished in the school. The statement holds true for girls and boys, but with the added twist that girls, no matter what their social class or academic achievement, are rarely urged to think of work as anything but secondary, with family responsibilities as primary. Thus the surplus labour force of largely unskilled or semi-skilled women who can be pulled into the labour force as required and pushed out again, back to the family, during times of economic recession, is also reproduced (Connelly 1978, 1983).

The names of the forty students interviewed were given to the guidance counsellors, who were asked what they knew of these students' future plans. The counsellors knew nineteen of the students well enough to discuss their plans, and, in a few cases, students were discussed by more than one counsellor. The counsellors assumed that none of the students aspired to break with their social class backgrounds. They were unaware of the one working-class girl who did aspire to go to university and study science. Instead, two counsellors claimed that this student was planning to be a legal secretary; and both thought that this was a good choice. On the other hand, the student herself stressed several times in her interview that she did not want to be a secretary. She realized that the counsellors knew of this "plan" because her mother had spoken with them about it. This was the only student interviewed who was consciously trying to overcome both social class background and stereotyped gender roles, and she obviously received no support from counsellors.

In some cases, counsellors discussed students whose academic achievement was inconsistent with what might be anticipated for their future work — that is, where it was "too high" for a working-class job, or "too low" for a middle-class or professional job. The working-class girl with the highest achievement of all forty in the sample had wanted to be a doctor but now planned to become a hospital technician. Her lowered goal met with approval from a counsellor:

> She's always been an A student . . . . She is someone who is independent and doesn't have any financial backing behind her, so it's a case of economic necessity that she take on a job.

Another counsellor positively accepted a high-achieving working-class boy's decision to go directly into the army:

> [A]s a counsellor I'm not going to say to someone who is unfamiliar, let us say, with the university career situation, perhaps not monetarily too well off, they have no aspirations in that line for that sort of thing, it's no use *my* saying "you should go to university". . . . My idea of guidance is to present to the student what opportunities there are for them to take that suits them, what they feel comfortable with. And a lot of that comfort and advice and discussion goes on in the family.

These examples of working-class experience show that not only do most students seem predisposed to train for jobs that will maintain their social class background, but also that there is little positive encouragement and sometimes active discouragement from the school to alter these patterns.

Upper-middle-class students also seemed likely to maintain their class position, regardless of low academic achievement. Of the two boys in this situation, one intended to go to an American college and eventually to enter the marine business owned by his uncle. Doing this, he would probably be able to maintain his social class position. The second would also go to college, much as he preferred not to. In the meantime one had football, the other a jazz group to deflect attention from poor achievement. In both cases, family resources and direction, not advice from school, were instrumental in assuring their futures. In fact, the counsellors chose not to offer any comment or information on these two students, thereby showing the school's passivity in allowing the reproduction of class relations.

One upper-middle-class girl who was managing the academic program with great difficulty wished to move into the technical stream of another high school. Her parents forbade such a move and thus forestalled her chance of acquiring a skilled manual job. The guidance counsellors were unaware of her desire to go to the technical school and merely viewed her as a problem student.

Gender was a category used more explicitly than class in advising students, particularly girls. Several middle-class girls also had aspirations for working-class jobs. However, this was not seen as problematic, as long as the jobs were in the female segregated segment of the labour force. In four of five interviews, counsellors explicitly stated that girls had to realize that being future wives and mothers was of primary importance to their future plans. As one said:

> I have certain feelings about home, etc. . . . Can a surrogate or substitute mother . . . replace the mother? There's no way. The bond is simply not there.

Another felt that a woman could do neither properly if she tried to have both a family and a job. A third said:

> I think that the girl who is interested in marriage and children . . . might look for a career that she can leave for a few years and then go back to . . . where the knowledge of the job takes second place to the personality of the job.

He then proceeded to list several jobs in the predominantly women's branch of the labour force: social worker, teacher, saleswoman, secretary.

Overall, maintaining social class background was seen as appropriate by the counsellors. For the most part this implied also maintaining the sexual division of labour, but in several cases gender took precedence over social class. This meant that some of the sixteen girls from the middle class were heading for working-class jobs which were conspicuously open to women and would be compatible with their jobs as mothers, since they could be dropped and perhaps resumed. It would be incumbent upon these girls to maintain their social class position through marriage.[1]

An important way in which counsellors sidestep issues of class is by "converting social hierarchies into academic hierarchies" (P. Bourdieu, quoted in Wexler 1982: 278): upper middle class translates perniciously into "bright," working class into "dull." According to Keddie (1971), teachers talk about the "dull" students in the lower stream (mostly working-class students) and the "bright" students in the higher stream (mostly middle-class students). It is through doing this that school personnel are able to maintain the myth of being "class-blind." Thus the words themselves may be neatly avoided, and a great step may be made in the social reproduction of class.

Student class origins affect the interpretation of falling grades by school personnel. Low-achieving middle-class children were labelled by guidance counsellors as "bright" but not well enough motivated. One middle-class girl whose grades had declined was "probably very bright. Her father's in the diplomatic corps." Another was "extremely bright, as are her brothers, . . . but there's no effort there whatever." On the other hand, working-class students whose grades declined were not seen as presenting problems. They were achieving according to what was expected of them. A girl from a divided family was a "very, very average student." A working-class boy whose grades dropped was a "solid 60 percenter. . . . It may be that there isn't the drive, the motivation in the family."

Social class and gender played closely connected roles in the advice of the high school counsellors. A content analysis of comments made about students indicated that counsellors knew as much about student family background as they did about academic achievement. Thus, school personnel actively contributed to homeostasis in the class and sex divisions of labour.

b) Teacher-Student Interaction

The observation of classroom activity confirmed previous findings that boys dominate in the classroom and that teachers contribute to this male dominance by focusing greater attention on the boys (Sarah 1980; Spender 1980; Sears and Feldman 1974). Furthermore, teachers' interviews clearly revealed that they evaluated female and male academic abilities differently. Together, these teacher practices devalued girls and rendered them invisible in the classroom.

In the observation sessions in twenty-seven Grade 12 classes (eleven English literature, twelve math, two chemistry, two world religion), girls were found to dominate verbal interaction with the teacher in only 7 percent of the classes, while boys dominated in 63 percent. There were only minor discrepancies by sex in the remainder. On the one hand, in the English and math classes it was found that teachers directed between one and a half to five times as many questions to boys as to girls. On the other, in two exceptional classes (the woman teacher in the chemistry class and the man teacher in the numerically female-dominated world religion class), teachers directed equal numbers of questions to girls and boys. In all class periods boys independently asked more questions and made more comments than girls. Thus it was clear that both teachers and students were responsible for the dominance of boys in the classroom. Why teachers directed more attention to boys in their classes is illustrated by their comments on the behaviour of girls and boys in class. Although the typically non-disruptive behaviour of girls and their relative silence is often a relief to teachers, this does not lead teachers to appreciate them as students (Scott 1980). Girls do not fit the "ideal client" image which Becker (1952) found was the student who responded to and appeared to learn as a result of the teacher's efforts. Several comments made by the women in their interviews revealed that they preferred boys as students; the men indicated that they thought boys were brighter. Teachers responded to girls' quietness in class and their decline in achievement over the years in school in ways which turned quietness into invisibility.[2] Ultimately teachers' attitudes fostered girls' further rejection of the school.

Eight of the ten women in the school who taught academic courses at the Grade 12 level confirmed that they preferred the classroom behaviour of boys. As one said:

> The boys are very pointed in their questions. They want very specific information. The girls have a tendency to be vague, whereas the boys will be very specific. And I appreciate that, because then I can help more.

Boys were also seen as more fun than girls, as evident from this statement from another teacher, which opens with a clearly stated preference for male students:

> The fellows I prefer to teach, more than the girls, because they don't get as up-tight about little things. Like I find in my Grade 10s they don't hold grudges and they're fun, while the girls are taking themselves far more seriously.

The issue of holding grudges and the duplicity of the girls was taken up by two other teachers. One talked with great admiration about how easy the boys made it for her, a petite young woman, to discipline them:

> You know I even scold some of them, those tall guys. But the next day it's "good morning miss" and "good-bye miss" and that's it.

Girls, she said, were less forgiving. Another said:

> I think in general that the boys are a bit more forthright. You're not as inclined to see somebody and say "now I wonder what he's thinking" as "I wonder what she's thinking." You feel that the boys are pretty much more open about things.

The women teachers spent much more time during the interview discussing the behaviour of the boys than that of the girls. One spoke extensively about the boys, comparing the dedicated student with the "he-men" whom she "tamed" in her classes. When prompted to discuss the girls, she said briefly:

> Girls haven't caused me any trouble in years and years. They tend to talk a bit much, but it's never been any problem for me for years to stop the girls.

Boys were the subject of other "plugs" from the women, but the girls never were. A chemistry teacher noted that boys liked to put on airs about doing well even though they did no work. "But mind you," she said, "whenever you look at their homework it's done, and you only assigned three questions but they've got twenty-three done."

The sexual dynamic is a clear underpinning to the attraction between women teachers and the young adult males in their classes. It is only half perceived and unspoken, but it clearly led to admiration and respect. The mirror attraction, on the other hand, which must have existed (and had led to one marriage in the recent history of the school), did not generate a parallel respect of men teachers for female students. On the contrary, twelve of the fifteen men clearly denigrated the academic abilities of the girls. They were more aware than the women that the early high achievement of girls declined in the later years of high school. They called the girls in the junior grades "overachievers"; they did not see them as "underachievers" in later years. Rather, girls' decline in achievement over the years was felt to be due to the fact that in the upper grades "ability starts to take over." Another, who said that most overachievers were girls, defined the term:

> By an overachiever I mean somebody who's getting marks above and beyond their innate ability level. Which can be done very easily at the 9 and 10 level by doing two hours of homework a night.

Implicit in this statement is a judgment that achievement is more a sign of ability in the upper grades since it is impossible to exceed ability at this level. The same teacher remarked that as he looked back, more boys stood out in his mind as "really bright students."

The "overachievement" of girls in the lower grades is, according to several teachers, a result of their docility and conscientiousness. Girls gave the "party line," as one teacher said, and as a result were more successful than boys. They noted that girls passed through puberty and "settled down" before boys, and so they were initially able to do better. It took boys a bit longer to settle down and achieve according to their ability. One teacher said that girls did well in the early grades because at that stage they were still keen to learn things "by rote," and that "they could cope with this."

Girls did continue to excel in senior English classes. The male English teachers recognized this but attempted to explain away the success. Girls did well because "their work habits were so good" and "they read more." One painted a scenario of a girl spending the evening babysitting, since she had to wait for an invitation out, and this would provide a lot of quiet time to read. One noted that the pattern of girls excelling in English ended at the university level.

Two corollaries followed from the overachievement thesis. First, girls who declined in achievement and were doing relatively poorly by the end of high school were seen as achieving according to their ability. Boys, on the other hand, who did *not* do well by the end of high school were underachieving. The teacher of the "slow" senior math class said:

> Girls are there pretty well because they should be there. I don't find too many underachievers amongst the females. You're going to get the boys in there who are capable of doing well but don't do well. They have *decided* not to achieve the way they should. (my emphasis)

Thus for boys there was seen to be an aspect of low achievement not strictly related to ability; but this possibility was not suggested for girls.

As a second corollary, girls who did manage to achieve high grades in the upper years were seen not as clever, but as plodders. In other words, they merely continued in the pattern of overachievement. As a teacher of chemistry said about the girls in his class:

> . . . they tend to be very good workers. Maybe not the brightest, maybe not the cleverest, but they have plugged and done all their work to get there. . . . Some of the boys have gotten there completely on their cleverness. But the girls who are there tend to be the ones who have worked.

Although it is not a disparaging comment to say that the girls worked hard, it was unnecessary to say that they were not really bright. The message was clear that these male teachers felt that the low achievement of the girls but not the high achievement was related to ability.

Thus there is an important, although largely hidden, way in which teachers in school undervalue female students and encourage their withdrawal from the educational field. Certainly the emphasis in the wider society on marriage and children is a source of their limited future aspirations, but the undervaluation of their behaviour and achievement in school is an important contribution to this outcome. It is probable that teachers themselves are also influenced by what they "know" about the future expectations of girls. It is not a finding particular to this research that teachers perceive boys as the better students (Clarricoate 1980; Stanworth 1983). However, this merely serves to add support to the thesis that this is one way in which girls are rendered invisible in the school and are undervalued as students.

These assessments of the unequal relation of achievement to ability in boys and girls echoes those made about class and achievement. In both cases the dominant group — male and middle-class students — were assumed to be capable but unmotivated, whereas the subordinate group — female and working-class students — were judged to be simply intellectually unable. The conversion of preexisting social hierarchies of class and gender external to the school into achievement hierarchies in and by the school serves to reproduce them in the educational system and for the whole society.

c) The Content of Classroom Interaction

Ideology of male-superior, female-subordinate arises frequently in classroom conversation and discussion, and is accepted uncritically as natural. Previous research has shown that the acceptance of a gendered status quo has profound implications for girls' classroom experience and ability to learn. Spender cites the example of a male history teacher who encountered problems in getting girls to participate in a class discussion on war. When one girl did speak, she was ridiculed by boys in the class. Since most topics covered in classes do traditionally have a male orientation and since girls are discouraged from speaking to these topics, they withdraw and learn silence and passivity — a lesson well learned, judging from the classroom observation sessions.

One example from classroom observations in the Ottawa study shows how patriarchal culture is reproduced. In the world religions class, the teacher asked who in the Christian religion might be a good role model. When no-one answered, he suggested St. Paul, but then added that Paul would not be a good model for a woman, because he did not like women. Then he went on to note that few religious leaders had liked women. He also stated that woman had been created from a rib from Adam's side, to help and please him. At this stage I heard a girl in the class whispering that women and men had the same number of ribs. The misogyny inherent in the great religions of the world is an important topic, but it was never critically discussed or presented as in any way problematic. Instead misogyny was presented as "objective" classroom knowledge.

In another class, an English teacher criticized a play written by a student because in it the daughter did not cry or show enough emotion in pleading for the family car. A mathematics teacher merely smiled and nodded when a girl in his class said she wouldn't have to learn how to complete an income tax form because her "husband" would do it.

In each of these classroom episodes, the status quo is accepted as normal and natural. In the first, gender stereotypes are actively offered as legitimated knowledge; in the second they are used to judge student work; while in the third, the student is silently rewarded for conforming to gender stereotypes. None of them led to any critical discussions. Nor did any of the teachers challenge gender typing. Consequently, gender hierarchies are removed from the purview of education and given a status as fact of life.

In contrast is the example provided by a discussion in an English literature class which was remarkable because of the overwhelming participation of the girls. The content of this discussion is worth exploring. In this class, the teacher raised questions for discussion on Hardy's novel *Tess of the d'Urbervilles*. Did Tess know she was being seduced (it is often difficult to tell in Victorian novels!)? Did she love her baby as she said, or was she secretly relieved when the baby died? The girls participated fully in this class, not because the teacher altered his usual pattern of calling more often on the boys, but because the girls were eager to discuss these questions and independently raised issues elaborating on them. In fact, the teacher was overwhelmed by the flood of discussion he had started, and actually appeared withdrawn and even embarrassed by it.

The fact that the teacher and the boys withdrew from the discussion suggests that the cultures of the girls and boys are kept very separate in the school. Male culture dominates in the school, as elsewhere, and the alternate culture, the feminine voice, is silenced, by being either ignored or undervalued when it does surface. The discussion about *Tess* obviously did strike a very responsive note among the girls. Since they are not even encouraged to discuss the issues which are of immediate concern to them, they learn to be silent generally in class, and the process of learning, of pursuing important questions, is stunted. Teachers encourage passivity on the part of girls and then criticize them for being silent and not participating in class. Conforming to female standards of passivity in patriarchal culture undermines the intellectual growth of girls, and teachers judge them as being less capable students.

The class discussion which I heard on *Tess* was in all probability rare, given that most topics covered in classes are from a masculine orientation. If the girls had been encouraged and respected for their participation in that discussion, they would feel more free to pursue their own orientation to issues in others.

Conclusion

A great deal transpires within the school and classroom to encourage students to accept the sex and class divisions of labour, at both a societal and a personal level. In part, alternatives are seen as unacceptable, in part the status quo is assumed to be just and appropriate.

As a result the school is characterized by these two related patterns which contribute to the social reproduction of society marked by economic and sex inequality. One way of accomplishing this is by ignoring the fact that inequalities do exist in male-dominated, capitalist society.

The dominant culture is accepted as the only reality. The experience of students whose background or sex indicates that they are living another face of this reality is not recognized in the school. Consequently, students from subordinate cultures tend to reject schooling and all it represents.

A related way in which the school contributes to the hegemony of the dominant culture is by accepting that students' choices concerning their educational and occupational futures be consistent with the sex-segregated labour force and their social class background. Very often students who have not rejected schooling (usually because of parental pressure, or because they are very bright and curious) are encouraged because of their own financial limitations, or because of their future "plans," to become wives, mothers, and low-status workers; in other words, to make sex- and class-appropriate future choices. In these cases, actual academic achievement is placed second to factors of sex and class.

Thus these two components of schooling interact to contribute to the persistence of the dominant culture: at one level subordinate cultures are undervalued and most students make their own choices to reject schooling; at another, students are not encouraged to make "inappropriate" choices, given their sex and social class. They are, on the other hand, lauded for making "appropriate" choices. In this way, schools do in fact contribute to the inequalities inherent in male-dominated, capitalist society.

The enthusiasm that the girls showed in their discussion of *Tess* indicates that schools might be forced to change if girls generally assert themselves and do not rest with whispering, "Women and men have the same number of ribs." However, the subordinate position of women in society is clearly reflected and promoted in schools as they exist now.

Notes

1. This research on the gender bias of guidance counsellors is strongly supported by previous research. See, for example, Bingham and House (1977); Thomas and Stewart (1971); and Pietrofessa and Schlossberg (1972).
2. For similar findings from research, see K. Clarricoate, "The importance of being Ernest . . . Emma . . . Tom . . . Jane: The perception and categorization of gender conformity and gender deviation in primary schools." In *Schooling for Women's Work*, ed. R. Deem (London: Routledge and Kegan Paul, 1980); M. Stanworth, *Gender and Schooling: A Study of Sexual Divisions in the Classroom* (London: Hutchinson, 1983).

14 Maternity Leaves, Protective Legislation, and Sex Equality: Eastern European and Canadian Perspectives

ALENA HEITLINGER

In North America, at the levels of both feminist theory and feminist practice, there is a concern about the connection between reproductive rights, protective legislation, sex equality, and the optimal social organization of motherhood. Thus feminists confront a major strategic problem of how to develop social structures that encourage the equality of women without ignoring the fact that they bear children. In Canada, there has been a renewed interest in these issues in recent years. For example, the Women's Bureau of Labour Canada published a new booklet in 1983 entitled *Maternity and Child Care Leave in Canada* which critically reviews current provisions including paternity and adoption leave. The Canadian Advisory Council on the Status of Women, in its 1981 publication *Women and the Constitution*, laments (on p. 211) the lack of special rights for mothers in the new constitution.

More recently, the Canadian Advisory Council on the Status of Women has turned its attention to the issue of reproductive health by sponsoring the publication of Nancy Miller Chenier's (1982) excellent study of reproductive hazards at work. Among other things, Chenier (1982: 65, 73) urges Canadians not to rely so heavily on the United States and the United Kingdom for information on reproductive hazards, because

> a great deal of relevant research has been carried out by countries in Eastern Europe . . . . Information initiated in these countries [the Scandinavian countries and the U.S.S.R.] on the health aspects of anaesthetic gases, on hormones, on vibration, on non-ionizing radiation has alerted others to carry out complementary research. Unfortunately, much of their work dealing with reproductive hazards is inaccessible to researchers until translated.

Thus one goal of this article is to present material which is hard for English-speaking researchers in Canada to obtain. Another analytically more important objective is to look at the problem of the optimal social organization of childbearing and sex equality from a comparative perspective, by examining existing social policies in Eastern Europe, which have already attempted for many years to resolve the question of the dual role of women as mothers and workers.[1] However, it should be noted right at the outset that the definition of the term "socialism" (or "state socialism") is by no means clear. As Molyneux (1981: 169) points out, "there is a large and contentious literature on how to define socialism and how far any one definition can be applied to existing post-revolutionary societies." While all East European societies have a state-owned, more or less centrally controlled and planned economy and a politically dominant communist party, they do not constitute a monolithic entity. Considerable differences exist in their sizes, social and economic development, urbanization, living standards, social habits, religion, political traditions, and other characteristics. All of the East European countries, therefore, have unique features as well as common ones. All face somewhat similar population situations due to a common set of tensions among (1) the socialist state concern over fertility rates at or below levels of population replacement—hence a desire by the socialist elites to increase birthrates, (2) a chronic shortage of labour—hence a commitment to maximizing employment of married women, (3) the realities of women's daily lives, for whom the current situation (e.g., low wages, inadequate socialization of domestic labour) does not encourage having many children, and (4) an official ideological commitment to sex equality. As we shall see below, one outcome of these tensions has been a policy that assigns a privileged position to women's childbearing roles. This contrasts with the contemporary socialist and liberal feminist emphasis on non-differentiation and an end to the sexual division of labour and gender coding.

Protective Legislation and Sex Equality

Socialist protective legislation has been based on the ideological principle of equality based on sex differences. For example, a Czech trade union pamphlet, *Working Women in Czechoslovakia* (1975: 9–10), published as a contribution to International Women's Year, defines sex equality in the following terms:

> Equality, i.e., generally equal position for women, requires taking into account certain differences in comparison with men. Woman's psychological and physical peculiarities and the demanding situations resulting from the many roles she fulfills at certain times, call for a special adjustment of her working and living conditions. The socialist society does not consider them as advantages or even benevolences but as measures required for the development of the entire society.

This fairly typical socialist definition of sex equality goes only part way toward solving a major feminist dilemma: how to take into account women's reproductive biology without falling into the trap of defining women *primarily* in terms of their procreative capacity. As we shall see below, socialist theory and practice have a tendency to overemphasize the extent and the importance of the "natural" differences between men and women by stressing women's reproductive roles at the expense of their productive roles. In other words, the dominant model is that of a wife/mother with a job rather than a woman in a responsible position with a family. Moreover, arguments about "woman's psychological and physical peculiarities" tend to imply that male biology is the norm while female biology is in some sense "deviant."

The 1960 Constitution of the Czechoslovak Socialist Republic (Article 27), defines the basic principles for the realization of female equality and specifies means necessary for its achievement:

> The equal status of women in the family, at work and in public life shall be secured by special adjustment of working conditions and special health care during pregnancy and maternity, as well as by the development of facilities and services which will enable women to fully participate in the life of society.

These general constitutional provisions, which exist in all the East European countries, have been supplemented by a succession of more specific family and labour laws.

As far as employment is concerned, the Czech labour code prohibits women to be given work which is physically unsuited to them or which is detrimental to their organism, especially work endangering their mission as mothers. A Bulgarian author, Fina Kaloyanova (1976: 32) writing for *World Health*, a WHO monthly publication, spells out the socialist rationale for the protection of women from the hazards of the work environment as follows:

> Protection of the health of all employees is considered extremely important in our country. Particular attention is paid to women workers, taking into account three basic considerations. The first of these is the anatomic and physiological particularity of the female body (in comparison to men, women are on average smaller and shorter and their normal lung capacity and blood haemoglobin content are lower; overall, it has been estimated that they have 15–20 percent less physical strength, in terms of physical effort, than men); the second is the reproductive function (a woman menstruates, she becomes pregnant, she gives birth and she breastfeeds her children, and in the course of these processes many regulatory mechanisms in the body are altered); and the third is the woman's social status (that is, her role in bringing up and educating children and caring for the family).

A.P. Biryukova (1980: 56), a secretary of the U.S.S.R. All Union Central Council of Trade Unions, adds "the fact that with the increase in its production potential society can afford to do more to safeguard the health of working women" as an additional reason for the socialist commitment to protective legislation for women.

The ideological content is evident: women are to be protected both on account of their "scientifically" alleged "nature" as well as "place" in the family and society as a whole. However, among these considerations, safeguarding women's "special function of reproduction" is clearly the most important one.

Protecting Women as Potential Mothers

In all the socialist countries, there are extensive lists of jobs forbidden to women in general and pregnant and nursing mothers in particular. However, job categories which are closed to women vary from country to country. For example, Romania, but not the U.S.S.R., forbids women to drive tractors on the grounds "that it has been scientifically proven that the vibrations of the tractor seriously shake up a woman's uterus and thereby raise the risk of damaging her ability to bear children" (Jancar: 1978: 138). Although Czechoslovakia does not explicitly prohibit women from driving tractors, in practice the situation is not that much different from Romania because of sexist interpretations of the legislative term "perilous to woman's health." Male authorities in agriculture have tended to define all tasks connected with higher-paid mechanized work as "perilous" for women, while unskilled, backbreaking manual work, often more tiring and more arduous and always worse paid, was deemed suitable.[2]

Once protective laws restrict the types of jobs women (but not men) may do, they inevitably discriminate against women. While protective legislation may protect women's health (and that of their future children), this is by no means certain, given our uneven state of knowledge of what causes reproductive damage and of what kind. What is certain, however, is that protective legislation has contributed significantly to the feminization of certain job categories and the persistence of wage differentials between the sexes. In socialist countries, equal pay is given only for equal work, and in a sexually segregated labour market, women rarely perform similar work to men. Feminization of certain sectors of the economy also virtually ensures that protective legislation is often not observed in practice, because there are no male workers around who could perform a particular "forbidden" task. For example, the Czech protective labour code forbids all women from manually lifting weights greater than 15 kg, but this restriction is widely ignored, especially in the feminized labour-intensive retail trade, nursing, and some branches of consumer industry (Křížťová 1977: 6; Hrabětová et al. 1975: 17).[3]

The issue of prohibition of night work for pregnant women is also problematic. For example, many pregnant nurses would like to work during the night on the grounds that the work is generally less arduous than during the day, when patients are awake and make many demands, but they are unable to do so. The remaining nurses, all women, are then forced to work more night shifts than they would really like to undertake (Gronský, 1972). Some trade unionists claimed at the nineteenth national meeting of women trade union officials that many more women would like to undertake night work, because of both the higher pay and the opportunity to spend days with their children (*Celostátní aktiv* . . . 1977: 47). Similar preferences were found among women night cleaners in New Zealand (ILO 1982: 213–14). While night work often meant more money, less supervision, more autonomy, a quieter workplace, and a feeling of comradeship with fellow workers, it also had some significant costs in lack of sleep caused not by daylight but by the unending demands of husbands and children. Thus, it appears nightwork facilitates an adherence to traditional family roles, which prescribe total responsibility for childcare and domestic work to the woman, regardless of the nature of her work outside the home.

Overall, it seems that disadvantages greatly outweigh any possible advantages of protective legislation for women workers. Rather than learning from the Eastern Bloc countries or from the International Labour Organization (ILO), which all support protective legislation for women, Canadian feminists would be better advised to follow the Scandinavian countries, which are characterized by virtual absence of such legislation. Their governments believe that measures to ensure health (including reproductive health) in the workplace should be equally applicable to men and women. In fact, the non-discrimination clause in the Canadian constitution may well preclude the adoption of protective legislation which is applicable to women only.

Rights of Childbearing Women Workers

The right to be transferred to easier work during pregnancy has to be seen as an important socialist achievement. It is important to realize that in state socialism the cost of transferring women to lighter work during pregnancy is not borne by the enterprise, but by the socialist system of social security. However, the enterprise often incurs an indirect, short-term cost in the disruption of its productivity — especially if too many women become pregnant at the same time, not an infrequent occurrence in heavily feminized sectors of the economy. In Czechoslovakia, the pay differential between the permanent and the temporary job is made up from health insurance funds. If no suitable work can be found, the employing institution is required to lay the woman off and still pay her regular wage or salary. However, this legislative provision is not always implemented in practice.

A Slovak sociologist, Maria Schvarcová (1978: 93, 97) claims that almost 10 percent of pregnant women workers perform "forbidden" work during pregnancy and within nine months of giving birth. This non-observance of the law occurs most frequently in agriculture (22 percent of cases), engineering (11 percent of cases) and education, culture, and health care (22 percent of cases). Nine percent of employers (out of a sample of 152 enterprises) claim that the forbidden work was requested by the women themselves. Thus women's resistance to paternalistic protective legislation has had some effect. In 1971 in the huge shoe factory *Svit* in Gottwaldov (originally founded by Bata), there were 1,120 new pregnancies among the 12,975 women employees (almost 9 percent), but only 332 women had their work changed (Pokorný 1972: 20–21).

In addition, many expectant mothers who are relocated to what Dr. Michlíček (1978: 397–98), a factory gynecologist, calls "pseudowork," work so poorly that management prefers them not to be around. Many leading factory officials then often put pressure on company physicians to declare "lazy" childbearing women as "disabled for work." Physicians who resent being put into conflict with the law argue that this form of resistance is an abuse of women's rights under the labour code, but Western feminists would see it as an aspect of workers' struggle.

Among all the provinces in Canada, only Quebec provides similar guarantees. A 1979 occupational health and safety act gives a pregnant woman the right to request reassignment to safe work she can reasonably perform. If this request is not immediately met she may stop working until she is reassigned or, if this is not possible, until the date of delivery. An employee exercising the right to job reassignment retains the rights and benefits of her regular employment and must be returned to it after her maternity leave. Under this Act, a female may also request job reassignment on medically certified grounds that there is a danger to the child she is breastfeeding. If this reassignment is delayed she may stop working until she receives such reassignment or until the child is weaned (Labour Canada 1981: 33). The compensation, based on 90 percent of the woman's net earnings, is to be paid by La Commission de la santé et de la securité du travail (Chenier 1982: 70). While one may take issue with the requirement for a medical certificate, one has to applaud the Quebec government's support for pregnant women.

In contrast, a recent case before the Ontario Labour Relations Board involved a pregnant video display terminal (VDT) operator who requested and was refused a job transfer. Murray Hardie, executive director of a federal task force on microtechnology, said in an interview (*Globe and Mail*, October 20, 1982) that some employers have already implemented policies which allow pregnant women to move to alternative jobs, but this is not the case for most companies. His task force recommends that pregnant women who use VDTs should have the right to be reassigned to alternative work without the loss of benefits or seniority, but this has not yet been made into a law. Recent estimates suggest that about a quarter of a million VDTs are in use across the country, with anywhere between 100,000 and 700,000 Canadians, mainly women, spending up to eight hours a day in front of them. As the use of these systems continues to grow, the possibility of any form of ill health, reproductive or otherwise, needs to be fully explored (Chenier 1982: 27).

The situation in the U.S. is much worse, at least partly because the state there is relatively weak and the regulation of "reproductive protection" is left up to individual corporations. The latter are more concerned with avoiding legal liability than with ensuring women's equality at work. According to Felker (1982: 3), "beginning in the mid-1970's certain American industrial firms, including General Motors, Exxon, St. Joe Minerals and Allied Chemical, began to transfer or fire women employees who were of childbearing age. When transferred, these women often lost seniority and were forced to accept lower paying jobs, such as janitorial work, in order to remain employed. Management explained that these steps were taken to protect them from job exposure to chemicals deemed harmful to their reproductive systems. Many were also told their jobs could be retained upon proof of their inability to become pregnant. Needing their jobs more than their fertility, many of these employees were sterilized and many complained subsequently to their unions." Felker (1982: 11) also reminds us that "there is considerable confusion about the actual reproductive risk to employees" and that "there have been no instances reported of male employees given a 'choice' of job loss vs. sterilization, though it is known that some chemicals men work with mutate sperm. Instead, when it was discovered that the pesticide DBCP *caused* male sterility, an uproar ensued brought on by male workers themselves, not by company physicians, ending with a recommendation by the Environmental Protection Agency that the product be banned." Incidents of selective hiring practices on the grounds of potential liability for a damaged fetus have been also reported in various parts of Canada (Chenier 1982: 41–47).

Kaloyanova (1976: 34) implies that such sexist double standards do not exist in the socialist countries and that "if a substance has definitive teratogenic properties, of course, we prohibit its use in industry or agriculture completely." However, a highly placed Bulgarian woman doctor told Jancar (1978: 104–5) that, while it was dangerous for everyone to work with polyvinyl chloride, someone had to work with it. "It was worse that women should be the victims, because they were the bearers of the future generation, so the lot fell to men." Interestingly in this light, Kaloyanova's coverage of Bulgarian research and legislation pertaining to reproductive hazards concentrates entirely on women. We are told that research on the higher incidence of miscarriages and disturbances in the menstrual cycle of workers engaged in growing plants in greenhouses found that these problems were related to the effect of different pesticides at high temperatures, but we are not told anything about male workers.

The same applies to much of Czech research. For example, an investigation of the relatively high incidence of pregnancy complications among airline stewardesses, even two to seven years after such work, deals exclusively with women. Among forty-two Czech airline stewardesses who gave birth to fifty-three children, 68 percent had complicated deliveries and 19 percent gave birth prematurely. In addition, 31 percent of previous pregnancies had ended in a miscarriage among some women repeatedly (Hinšt and Bruchāč 1981). Yet the work of flight attendants (as well as such high-risk categories as nurses or laundry workers) is not included on the long list of jobs from which women are protected. Once more, no information is given about male flight attendants or pilots who might be exposed to similar reproductive hazards during the course of their work. More recently, however, there are some indications that this exclusive emphasis on women might be shifting in the light of the emergence of genetic toxicology, a new discipline that combines methods of genetic analysis and traditional toxicological approaches. In one small case study of miscarriages in North Bohemia—which has the highest concentration of chemical industries in the country — data was collected about the workplace, drinking and smoking habits, health status, contact with infectious diseases, and health status of both parents. For the first time, the potential for male reproductive damage was given equal weight (Šram 1978).

Thus, one set of dilemmas with respect to protective legislation for women stems from the fact that its scope is not sufficiently broad—as well as a whole range of potentially hazardous jobs, men are excluded. Indeed, the recent negative experiences in Canada with the impact of video display terminals indicate that rapid technological development makes existing catalogues of "unsuitable" jobs for women quickly obsolete and irrelevant.

Another set of dilemmas arises from the fact that protective legislation is too broad and too detailed. Feminist critics of these tendencies also exist in the socialist countries. In reviewing some of the responses to the revision of Czech protective legislation in 1965, Hilda Scott (1974: 21) quotes a particularly angry comment from a woman crane operator, voiced at a protest meeting at the Klement Gottwald Iron and Steel Works:

> All of a sudden there's talk about the Geneva Convention . . . but it's nothing new. Why wasn't it observed ten or fifteen years ago? . . . I went to work then, the children on my neck, the youngest only a few months old, and no one asked me whether I minded being in a steel mill or whether I could work at night. . . . It's an injustice, a great

> injustice. As long as you needed us, we were good enough for you. And health conditions were much worse than they are now, when the cranes have airconditioned cabins . . . Now you offer us employment in quiet surroundings, when our hands are used to rough work and our eyes have lost their keenness.

Similar sentiments were also voiced elsewhere. When women were transferred to lighter work at lower pay in the Třinec Iron Works, a woman trade union official publicly pointed out that the transfer was happening over women's objections and at a time when mechanization and air conditioning were actually installed, making the work easier, but only for men.

Overall, all the benefits notwithstanding, protective legislation tends to have a strong controlling and coercive effect on people whom it is supposed to benefit — women workers. The contradictory impact of policies designed to benefit women is also evident when we consider pregnancy and maternity leave.

Short-Term and Long-Term Pregnancy and Maternity Leaves

The "generosity" of maternity leave provisions varies from country to country, both in Eastern Europe and in the West. Among the socialist countries, Czechoslovakia provides the best benefits, while Romanian and Soviet provisions are very similar to those existing in Canada. Every employed woman in the U.S.S.R. receives sixteen weeks of paid maternity leave on full pay, half of it before the child is born, though if there are birth complications the postnatal leave can be extended to 70 days. Romanian paid maternity leave is 112 days, with 52 days before expected childbrith and 60 days after. New mothers receive 85 percent of their regular daily earnings during their leave and 94 percent if the new baby is the third or subsequent child in the family. However, leaves of absence for pregnancy, maternity, or caring for a sick child under the age of two are counted against the yearly vacation (Muresan and Copil 1974: 370), a restriction which does not exist in the other socialist countries.

All childbearing women in Czechoslovakia are guaranteed twenty-six weeks of paid maternity leave (thirty-five weeks for single mothers and women giving multiple births), eight of which can, and four of which must, be taken prior to the expected date of delivery. Postpartum leave cannot exceed twenty-two weeks, with the exception of premature births, for which mothers are not penalized by the loss of four weeks of maternity leave, as they can be in Canada.[4] Many of the strongly pro-natalist socialist countries also provide lump sum childbirth (or "layette") grants, though in the case of Romania the entitlement begins only with the third child.

Among the Western countries, only Scandinavia (especially Sweden) provides better benefits. Swedish paid maternity leave, which used to cover mothers staying at home with their newborns for six months, has been extended to allow either parent to do this. Admittedly, so far only a small, though rising, proportion of fathers has taken advantage of this provision, and then mostly in the case of baby boys.[5]

Pregnancy Leave

The major criticism of short-term paid maternity leave concerns the inflexibility of leave regulations. While many women would prefer to work until the birth to be able to spend more time with their newborn before returning to work, doctors tend to favour extensions of pregnancy leaves. For example, Dr. Gronský (1972), claiming that 60 to 80 percent of all neonatal deaths are caused by premature births, would like to see pregnancy leave extended to at least eight weeks prior to the expected date of birth. He is also a strong advocate of tying maternity payments to early (by sixteen weeks) and regular medical prenatal visits (six to eight times) as is apparently done in the G.D.R. Dr. Štembera (1979: 26), the author of a Czech textbook on high-risk pregnancies, sensibly argues that

> the care for premature newborns (annually 2800, one percent of all newborns) weighing less than 1500g in special intensive care units costs 15–20,000 Czech crowns. If all women with "risk pregnancies" (approximately six percent of all pregnant women) were to go on sick leave from work for two months, the money loss would be similar. Five percent of these women will take the leave unnecessarily, so that economically the situation is even, but healthwise far superior.

In this context, the issue of pregnancy leave overlaps with that of protective legislation, since risk pregnancies seem to be correlated with specific jobs and to some extent also with previous miscarriages and abortions.[6] P. Baran (1980) found a high correlation between employment in sales and the risk of premature delivery, as did the authors of the above-quoted study on airline stewardesses, but this risk appears to be minimal among housewives. Neither author (nor Western feminist demands for that matter) seems to advocate granting of pregnancy leave during the first trimester, when the experience of fatigue and nausea tends to be particularly severe and when some work flexibility might be particularly welcome by pregnant women.

Postnatal Leaves

Unlike many of their Western counterparts, women in socialist countries have a *statutory* right to unpaid maternity leave, ranging from one to three years, without losing their jobs or seniority. This is especially important for safeguarding length-of-service bonuses, pension qualifications, and the like. However, there are also some definite disadvantages to these provisions, which Canadian feminists and policy makers should take quite seriously.

The most obvious disadvantage of any unpaid leave is the economic hardship involved. To maintain what is considered an adequate standard of living nowadays, two incomes in a family are essential; this is one of the major reasons why so many women have entered paid employment in the first place. Childbirth grants, family allowances, and the so-called maternity allowances (more on these below) do not constitute an adequate material compensation for the loss of income of one spouse, invariably the wife. While the Czech government was spending by the early 1970s 10 percent of its annual budget on direct cash payments and subsidies in kind (e.g., daycare, kindergartens, school meals, rent deductions), my own observations of couples with young children indicate that they find it hard to make ends meet. Indeed, many would find it difficult to survive without some form of aid from their own parents. Legal guarantees of jobs tend to ignore the simple facts that these provisions do not bring in any money in the short run and that where the woman is on unpaid maternity leave, couples are forced to make significant financial sacrifices. Single mothers obviously face even worse financial difficulties.

Another problem with maternity leaves, both paid and unpaid, concerns the exclusive way in which they are currently conceived. New mothers are virtually left to their own devices to cope with the feelings of exhaustion, anxiety, depression, and insecurity which so often accompany the postpartum experience. Mothers of newborns tend to work under conditions of fatigue, inexperience, uncertainty, and isolation, and employers do not seem to care. Schvarcová (1978), the Slovak sociologist cited earlier, reports that, among a nationwide sample of 2,621 married women with dependent children, only 10 percent were satisfied with their employer's understanding of, and support for, motherhood. A Czech trade union official went even further and accused enterprises of sexist double standards:

> When we compare the care of women on maternity leave with that of men currently performing military service [lasting up to two years—A.H.], the approaches are radically different, though in both cases we're talking about the fulfilment of important social missions. A male worker without completed military service is hired without too many difficulties, and after his return, his job is given back to him. During his leave of absence, the enterprise is in continuous contact with him, sending him regularly the company magazine. However, pregnant women are hired only reluctantly and, when the woman worker begins her maternity leave, she virtually ceases to exist for the employer. And yet, there is nothing easier to arrange than to inform her regularly about what is happening at her place of work, or to

> invite her for the occasional work meeting (she would easily find somebody who would take care of her child for the two or three hours). It is then hardly surprising that women often do not return to their former employment after the expiry of maternity leave, because during their leave they lost all the connections to their place of work, not to mention that their qualifications have also suffered, a fact which employers almost enjoy pointing out. (*Celostátni aktiv* . . . 1977: 10)

Thus, another major disadvantage of maternity leaves, as currently conceived, is the removal of women from institutional power and politics. The longer the maternity leave, the greater is the loss for the woman. Emphasis on formal guarantees of job security and various accrued benefits tend to ignore the extent to which promotion is due to informal institutional politics. However, it is also important to point out that men on military leave, which can be as long or even longer than maternity leave, do not seem to be affected by their absence from the workplace as much as women. As another speaker at the national meeting of women trade union officials pointed out,

> the majority of our [i.e., trade union — A.H.] functionaries and leading economic officials continue to see in the care of working women only "extra" tasks, which are best left to be sorted out only by women themselves. (*Celostátní aktiv* . . . 1977: 10)

Compare this practice to the official ideology which considers the "special adjustment of women's working and living conditions" not "as advantages or even benevolences but as measures required for the development of the entire society"!

Other negative consequences of long-term paid and unpaid maternity leaves, probably unintended but nonetheless real, are revealed by the Hungarian experience. In order to enhance fertility, Hungary introduced in 1967 the so-called maternity (or childcare) allowance, paying mothers a flat rate (amounting to substantially less than their annual monthly income) to stay at home with any child until it is three. Czechoslovakia introduced a similar measure in 1970, with eligibility starting with the second or subsequent child. After more than a decade of experience with maternity allowances, several Hungarian sociologists have noted a "backlash" in the forms of less aid given by husbands in the home, reluctance on the part of employers to hire women because they will eventually not return to work, subjective feelings of isolation and frustration, and a shift among younger women from the "emancipation" model of the family (generally accepted by their mothers) toward goals based on consumerism (cited in Scott 1978). The East German provision, which gives women, but not men, one day's paid holiday per month to catch up on household chores, must have a similarly inegalitarian effect. However, these provisions are increasingly popular among *all* women, not just those with lower education. In early 1970, 73 percent of Hungarian women with an elementary education applied for maternity allowance, compared to 61 percent of mothers with secondary education and only 30 percent with higher education (Heer 1981: 134). However, in Czechoslovakia in the late 1970s, 77 percent of eligible mothers with university education applied for maternity allowance for the full two years, compared to 88 percent of those with elementary education—a difference of only 11 percent, and the percentages were rather high to start with. Furthermore, the most frequently stated reason for utilizing maternity allowance, given by 78 percent of respondents in a nationwide sample survey, was preference for full-time motherhood as opposed to employment. Lack of available daycare (only 22 percent of children aged 0–3 can be accommodated in Czech daycare centres) came as the second most frequently stated reason, but only 29 percent of respondents answered in this way (Schvarcová 1978). Hence, the strong ideology of motherhood, projected in current pronatalist population policies, is evident among women themselves.

Among the socialist countries, only Hungary has extended (in May 1982) some maternity benefits to fathers. The new provision entitles the father—instead of the mother—to opt for the childcare leave and allowance after the child has reached one year of age. Another new provision enables the parent who is drawing a childcare allowance to enter part-time employment, defined as four hours a day counted on a monthly average, after the child has reached the age of eighteen months, without losing entitlement to the childcare allowance (ILO 1982: 357). Among the Western countries, various versions of parental leaves were in recent years introduced in Finland, Norway, Italy, Spain, France, and Portugal (see Paoli 1982: 12–13, for more details).

Childcare allowances, extended maternity leaves (up to five years), and part-time work are subjects of an ongoing debate in the U.S.S.R. as well, but none of these provisions is being considered for fathers. Moreover, it remains to be seen whether any of these proposals will be translated into practice. As I have argued elsewhere (Heitlinger 1979: 120–21), Soviet law has for several years allowed enterprises to take on women part-time, but as such labour is comparatively more expensive (holiday and pension rights are retained in full), managers of larger enterprises have been reluctant to introduce part-time work for women. Thus the interests of managers, central planners, and women often do not coincide. Moreover, various surveys conducted in the late 1960s and the 1970s have indicated that while a majority of women think it is right to stay at home for the first three years or so after the birth of a child, they personally do not want to sacrifice those years.

Thus maternity leaves and childcare allowances are closely related to economic issues. As we noted earlier, extended maternity leaves entail substantial financial sacrifice, have a negative impact on women's careers, and tend to reinforce the traditional sexual division of labour within the home. While parental leave legislation is an important step forward toward sex equality, its full implementation can be expected only with the equalization of male and female wages. As long as childcare allowance is set at a flat rate, at or lower than the minimum wage, fathers are unlikely to take advantage of parental leaves, because the financial costs of withdrawing from the labour force are so much greater for them (and their families) than is the case for mothers. Thus, for the foreseeable future, it will be mothers who will remain solely responsible for the care of young children.

Conclusion

There are obviously many issues one could discuss in an assessment of the broader implications of state socialist policies relating to motherhood, protective legislation for women, and sex equality. I shall restrict myself to one question which I think has particular relevance for Western feminist ideology and practice: the controlling effect of state policies. As I have argued elsewhere (Heitlinger 1980: 14), "the question of the state has long been one dividing feminists in the West. The liberal and socialist women's movements have been concerned almost uniquely with demands upon the state to organise and administer a variety of services based on women's special needs. As radical feminists have pointed out, one of the implications of demands for more jobs, equal pay, and day-care-centres is that they solicit an increase in state power over women's lives." We now have to add protective legislation for women.

While safeguarding women's—as well as men's—"special function of reproduction" is socially necessary, protective legislation for women as well as long-term unpaid maternity leaves have some definite disadvantages for sex equality. Once protective laws restrict the types of jobs women (but not men) may do, they inevitably discriminate against women. East European protective laws are especially broad and detailed, with the result that women are often unnecessarily excluded from areas where they would like to work. Moreover, protective legislation has contributed to the feminization of certain job categories and the persistence of wage differentials between the sexes. Thus reproductive ideologies and their embodiment in legislation have certain material effects in legitimizing the existing social division of labour. Long-term unpaid maternity leaves have a similarly inegalitarian effect, despite the fact that such measures tend to be popular among women workers themselves.

Finally, it is important not to confuse protective legislation with special rights for childbearing workers and mothers. As I have argued above, the right to be transferred to easier work during pregnancy, six-month fully paid maternity leave, and the statutory right (though not an obligation) to long-term postnatal leave (which in the case of Hungary can be combined with part-time work), have to be seen as important socialist achievements. In contrast, parental (as opposed to maternity) leave legislation has emerged as a policy out of the Scandinavian rather than the East European countries. Ultimately, it is this practice, along with equalization of wages and an end to gender coding, which Canadian feminists should follow.

Notes

1. The material presented in this article is a revised version of Chapter Four in my recently published book *Reproduction, Medicine and the Socialist State*. See Heitlinger (1987).
2. This practice was criticized by the Central Committee of the Czechoslovak Union of Women in an open letter to the government, which was published in the mass circulation women's magazine *Vlasta* on April 24, 1968, during the "Prague Spring." See also Hilda Scott (1974: 22), who quotes a study of women in agriculture published in a Czech farmers' daily in 1969.
3. A complete bibliography of Czech publications cited in this article is available from the author.
4. If early delivery means that the woman has not fulfilled the qualification period for leave, she may not be eligible for leave, let alone pay, and may even be in danger of losing her job. Only British Columbia does not have a qualification period in its labour legislation. See Labour Canada Women's Bureau (1983: 17).
5. According to Paoli (1982), the proportion of eligible fathers taking paternity leave has increased from 2 percent in 1974 to 11 percent in 1977. I was told about the preference for baby boys by Drude Dahlerup from the University of Aarhus.
6. In recent years the problem of long-term outcome of induced abortion has been extensively investigated and discussed in several countries. According to the results of studies involving nine cities in eight countries, designed by the World Health Organisation Task Force on the Sequelae of Induced Abortion, abortion is *not* an important factor in the adverse outcome of subsequent pregnancies, provided that the procedure is performed by the vacuum suction method. In contrast, the dilation and curettage (D & C) abortion technique was found to be a significant factor in accounting for subsequent pregnancy complications. While the D & C abortion technique is still commonly used in Eastern Europe, the more modern method of vacuum suction or aspiration is currently the most widely used technique in North America. For more details on long-term sequelae of induced abortion see Maine (1979) and Belsey (1979).

15 Women and Abortion in Canada: What's Law Got to Do with It?[1]

SHELLEY GAVIGAN

Introduction

The resurgence of the "new" right and the electoral successes of conservative parties in Canada, the United States, and Great Britain in the 1980s pose major political and theoretical challenges to feminism and to the left. We have seen a relentless attack on issues and demands central to the feminist movement, including women's rights to reproductive freedom, particularly legal abortion. The tenuousness of legal victories has been demonstrated in the United States by the legislative and judicial erosion of the historic *Roe v. Wade*[2] decision. In Canada, former Manitoba NDP cabinet minister Joe Borowski has been dogged but as yet unsuccessful in his efforts to have declared unconstitutional the 1969 amendments to the Criminal Code permitting therapeutic abortions in limited circumstances.[3]

More generally, the reforms of the 1960s and 1970s have become the site of political agitation and legal challenge by a self-proclaimed "pro-life" movement. For example, in December 1985 the Saskatchewan Court of Appeal[4] ruled that the province did not have jurisdiction to enact a private member's bill that would have required a therapeutic abortion committee to secure the "informed consent" of the patient (following provision of "a detailed description of the probable physiological age and anatomical characteristics of the unborn child at the time the abortion is to be performed") and spousal or parental consent; the bill also specified a forty-eight-hour waiting period *after* granting of the "informed consent" before the procedure could have been performed.[5]

Indeed, the significance of legislative gains by women is implicitly acknowledged by the right through such actions to restrict women's access to contraception, abortion, childcare, equal employment — the list is almost endless. Not burdened by an economism that has traditionally plagued the left, the contemporary right is centrally concerned with sexual and social issues which much of the left has ignored, and not only challenges feminist activists, but also directly undermines working-class politics. While the women's movement has been criticized for raising issues thought to "split the working class," it is in fact the ideology of the right which tends to divide the working class by providing a rationale for pitting non-unionized against unionized workers, attempting to scapegoat, among others, unemployed youth, single mothers, lesbians, and gay men (Gordon and Hunter 1977–78: 16; Greenwood and Young 1976; Oliker 1981: 96).

Analyzing the law and the state as sites of political struggle is necessary not only to defend women's gains, but also to advance strategies for a radical restructuring of society and gender relations. This article explores the relationship of feminism, the state, and the law with specific reference to abortion legislation in Canada. It is inspired in part by a kindling of marxist interest in law (Hay et al. 1975; Thompson 1977; Hall et al. 1978; Pashukanis 1978; Cain and Hunt 1979; Fine et al. 1979; Sumner 1979; Fine 1984) and in part by the work of British feminists such as Mary McIntosh, Michèle Barrett, Carol Smart, and Elizabeth Wilson.

Feminists are by definition interested in understanding women's oppression and committed to our liberation. How then ought we to define our task? I share the view that what needs to be understood is not simply "patriarchy," but the different forms of women's oppression in different historical contexts and, for our purposes here, the nature of the contribution of the state and the law thereto. Michèle Barrett puts this point succinctly: "What we need to analyse are precisely the mechanisms by which women's oppression is secured in different contexts since only then can we confront the problem of how to change it" (1980: 250). This is no small task given the apparently transhistorical nature of women's oppression and our limited knowledge of the past lived experience of women. However, working with a concept of patriarchy as a universal system determinative and definitive of women's lives leaves no room for an analysis of different "patriarchal" forms or for an appreciation of the forms of women's resistance.

Any analysis of the relationship between women and the criminal law of abortion must acknowledge the specific changes and history of the legal prohibition. At the same time, to examine only the "letter of the law" and the handful of reported cases offers us little in the way of real understanding of the social significance of the law for the people most affected by it: women.

A persistent conundrum confronts those of us who work in and around the criminal law whenever we attempt to unravel and identify the contribution of the state and the criminal law to the subordination of women: women seeking abortions have only rarely been the subject of criminal prosecution (Williams 1958: 145–46; Backhouse 1983: 83). The invisibility of women in the enforcement of a law which affects them no less than it does medical practitioners or lay abortionists has been explained in a facile way as the chivalry of the criminal law and criminal justice toward women (Pollak 1961; Walker 1981); at the same time a contrasting feminist perspective has developed which explicitly identifies the state and the law as directly and ideologically oppressive of women (e.g., DeCrow 1975; Rifkin 1980; MacKinnon 1982, 1983a, 1983b). However, I would agree with Mary McIntosh's observation that "we do not live in a society of individuals who are equal before the law in the sense that the state is equally concerned about their behaviour" (1977: 396), and would argue that it is particularly appropriate in the context of the abortion law: while women seeking abortions outside the law have in the past tended not to be prosecuted, this does not mean that they have been either protected or victimized by it. Nor does this suggest that the criminal sanction is or has been of little consequence to women: the legal "recognition" of the therapeutic abortion has medicalized the issue and legitimized the "moral arbitration of doctors" (Greenwood and Young 1976; see also C. Clement 1983; Cole 1983).

Despite both the extension of the criminal sanction over the entire period of pregnancy and an increasingly interventionist medical profession, women have continued to attempt to control their own fertility. Historical work has shown that it is incorrect to perceive women as passive victims of legal and medical control (Gordon 1977; Knight 1977; McLaren 1977, 1978a, 1978b; Petchesky 1980, 1984). Clearly, the history of restrictive abortion legislation is also the history of women's resistance to it (see Gavigan forthcoming).

To pierce the myth of state benevolence in the non-prosecution of women we need a theoretical perspective which identifies the state as neither a neutral, courteous arbiter nor simply a wicked stepfather, but rather one which examines the nature of state intervention and non-intervention (McIntosh 1978). Recent work exploring the various forms of social control of women has pointed to the significance of informal methods of control in apparently "private" areas, such as the family and sexual and reproductive relations (Smart and Smart 1978; Hutter and Williams 1981). Norwegian feminist criminologists Tove Stang Dahl and Annika Snare (1978) have emphasized the significance of "the coercion of privacy" to the oppression of women.

With respect to abortion, much of the state control of women is mediated by the medical profession. An English court has expressly identified the medical profession as the repository of the "great social responsibility" in ensuring that the letter of the law is followed.[6] As Barrett (1980: 228ff, esp. 236ff) notes, the medical profession is among the most closely regulated by the state. It is at the intersection of state legislation and medical determination that we find the issue of abortion squarely placed.

Women and the Law: The Issue of Formal Equality

> [A]t any given point in time considerable numbers (and classes) of people—lunatics, criminals, blacks, Roman Catholics, women, those who do not own real property, and their ilk — have always been excluded in law from the full rights of (sane, law-abiding, white, Anglo-Saxon, protestant, male and propertied) 'Man'. But these are, precisely, exclusions, and there is—in more than a figurative sense—a world of difference between this and, say, the feudal state of affairs. (Corrigan and Sayer 1979: 32)

Feminism has a long history of engagement with the law, yet the extent to which law ought to be a site of feminist struggle is today a hot issue within feminist scholarship, and here the analytic issues—the question of state neutrality (see, e.g., Picciotto 1979: 166), the limits of formal equality and legal reform, and the role of the state and the law in mediating class and gender relations — are complex. As well, the law within capitalist society needs to be examined from a perspective sensitive to the shifting position and role of law in capitalist society (see, e.g., Hall 1980; Smart 1984).

Inasmuch as Anglo-Canadian law has in the past directly embraced patriarchal principles by, for instance, enshrining a spousal immunity in rape, disentitling a woman "guilty" of adultery to maintenance and limiting her right to custody of her children, the law for women has often scarcely even appeared to embody its self-proclaimed neutrality. And yet — even within the context of the patriarchal family — the twentieth century has witnessed the achievement of a measure of formal equality for women.

Unimpressed with the formal equality gained by women in capitalist societies, Stang Dahl and Snare argue that it renders invisible women's *real* conditions. Indeed, they maintain:

> The principle of formal equality and the principle of protecting privacy both function to uphold unequal social relations. Both are coercive ideological forms which in Scandinavia . . . hinder women's liberation struggles. . . . Law reforms have to be accompanied by a "delivery system" which in essence means a political and economic reorganization of society. (1978: 14)

Similarly, in the American context, Janet Rifkin has begun to explore the relationship between law and "patriarchy" from a perspective which emphasizes the role played by law and legal ideology in perpetuating male domination of women. She defines patriarchy as "any kind of group or organization in which males hold dominant power and determine what parts females shall and shall not play" (1980: 83); in her analysis law is a powerful symbol and vehicle of male authority: "This power is based both on an ideology of law and ideology of women which is supported by law. One function of ideology is to mystify social reality and block social change'' (1980: 84).

Rifkin's assessment is that earlier feminists, for example the suffragists, failed to challenge the ideology of law; rather they ''perpetuated mystifications of law which supported the status quo'' (1980: 87). Full citizenship rights for women today may be considered part of the ''status quo,'' but it is difficult to understand how in the context of the late nineteenth and early twentieth centuries the struggle for women's suffrage may be so characterized. It is a tremendous contradiction for feminist scholarship to dismiss the historical significance and contribution of this century's first wave of feminists: the formal equality and other legal reforms achieved by women were not concessions granted voluntarily by the state; nor were they achieved through a process of gradual evolution — they are the product of determined feminist struggle.[7]

To observe that women have not achieved real equality despite the success of the struggle for the vote does not mean that formal equality need be regarded as only a mystification or a sham, much less a ''coercive ideological'' form. For instance, from a marxist perspective, Branka Magas has discussed the significance of the form and the content of equality:

> Just as the specific character of the economic oppression of the proletariat stands out more sharply after juridical equality of classes has been established (this equality in no way abolishing the antagonism between them) so too the particular character of man's domination of women is brought out more clearly once the two are equal before the law. (1970–71: 87)

Juliet Mitchell, while recognizing that formal equality is ''itself a certain progress which can make possible further advances'' (1971: 113), also points to the need to explore and understand the limitations of the concept of equality:

> Equality always denies the inequality inherent in its own birth as a concept. The notions of equality, freedom or liberty do not drop from the skies; their meaning will be defined by the particular circumstances that give rise to them in any given epoch. (1976: 385)

But what, then, of the elusive nature of ''real'' equality? Although the development of the capitalist mode of production created the precondition of formal equality, women remain substantively unequal. For many feminists the explanation for this continuing inequality is to be found in what they identify as the patriarchal nature of our society. To what extent is the law implicated? While not claiming to set out a fully developed theory of law and patriarchy, Lorenne Clark and Debra Lewis offer a feminist critique of the social causes of rape and the social significance of rape and rape law as it existed prior to the introduction of Canada's sexual assault legislation.[8]

They argue that understanding the contemporary problem of rape requires relating it to the position of women historically and to the development of rape as a criminal offence (1977: 113). Marriage, a key institution in gender relations, traditionally accorded a husband an absolute right of sexual access to his wife, control of her social intercourse and that of their children, and exclusive power to bequeath and divest of family property to *his* heirs. Clark and Lewis see rape law as an expression of this system of private ownership:

> Rape is simply theft of sexual property under the ownership of someone other than the rapist. When women are forms of private property, owned by fathers or husbands, with a value determined by their sexual and reproductive capacities, rape is an act of theft and trespass against the legal owner of the sexual property (that is, the woman) in question. (1977: 116)

This linkage, they maintain, explains why a woman living at home with parents or a husband has been the victim to whom the law has offered its greatest support, while a woman living on her own has been viewed as not having a right to complain: rape is an offence against private property and a woman cannot own herself (1977: 119). They advance a thesis of "women as property," arguing that women are forms of private property whose value is determined by their sexual and reproductive capacities, and that sexual coercion by men is both inevitable and necessary, being deeply rooted in (and presumably important to) "our basic social, political, economic, and legal system" (1977: 131–32).

While in agreement that women have been in a subordinate position to men throughout most of what we know to be our history, I would argue that despite its powerful resonance, the "women as property" metaphor is of limited assistance. If the object is to transform relations between women and men, an approach which stresses the paramountcy of transhistorical male domination to explain both the form and the content of law over the ages offers us very little to work with.

The concern with form and formal equality must always acknowledge the limits and contradictions of the concept of equality. The substantive inequality of women in feudal society, developing capitalist society and contemporary capitalist society cannot be denied. There is indeed a "transhistoricity" to women's oppression, but the *forms* of that oppression have changed as have the forms through which it can be challenged. We are not chattels but full citizens, with the right to vote, to hold public office, to own property: women are no longer objects of exchange, but legal subjects.

Any attempt to develop a historically specific critique in no way denies the longevity of women's subordination. However, the questions such a critique might seek to resolve differ in their emphasis from an approach stressing the transhistorical "fact" of sexism or patriarchy. In the words of Maureen Mackintosh:

> The characteristic of human reproduction is patriarchy, that is, the control of women, especially of their sexuality and fertility, by men. *The first necessity is to separate the fact of this control from the question of the form in which it is exercised.* . . . This then specifies clearly the theoretical problem: . . . [how] do changing modes of production change the forms of patriarchy without changing its existence? (1977: 122; emphasis added)

For our purposes here, the task is one of examining the existence and operation of different forms of law from a perspective that abandons the notion that women are simply objects of a male estate. Such a position makes it difficult to explain why the state regulates — and the medical profession determines — accessibility of abortion in this society. Why, if a married woman is essentially her husband's private property, is his consent to her abortion not formally required by law? How are we to view the Canadian and English cases[9] which hold that a husband is entitled neither to notice nor to consultation, let alone a veto, in the matter of his wife's legal abortion? The contemporary relationship of women and law is more complex and contradictory than the "woman as property" thesis allows.

Women and the State

One cannot examine the contribution of the state to the oppression of women without considering the relationship of the state (and its social policy) to the family. Elizabeth Wilson (1977) has argued that understanding the position of women is *central* to an understanding of the state within capitalist society. Directly implicated, then, is the way the state supports the ideology of the family. As Ann Oakley has noted, "one of the guiding illusions of this world is that the family is a private place, a haven of protected positive emotions safe from the stresses of public labour, commercialism and power" (1981: 79).

The concept of "family privacy" has been seen as key by feminists interested in explaining the nature of the relationship of women to the state. For Mary McIntosh the question is not simply, "how does the state oppress women?" but rather "what part does the state play in establishing and sustaining systems in which women are oppressed and subordinated to men?" (1978: 259). She identifies the family household and the system of wage labour, along with state support thereof, as important sites of women's oppression within capitalism, noting that the relation of women to state agents tends to be indirect, as the state "frequently defines a space, the family, in which its agents will not interfere but in which control is left to the man" (1978: 257). In other words, family privacy ensures men's power and control. Stang Dahl and Snare (1978) speak of the home not as a private haven but as a "private prison" for women, with marriage ensuring house arrest through the "coercion of privacy." They argue that the formal equality of women is undermined by the subordination and control of women by informal means. Thus support for the sacred ground of family privacy is directly implicated in the subordination of women in the current context.

"Not the Church and Not the State: Women Must Control Their Fate"

Women's right to reproductive freedom, including safe, legal, and accessible contraception and abortion, is a fundamental demand of the contemporary women's movement internationally, shifting at times from "Free Abortion on Demand" to "Every Mother a Willing Mother, Every Child a Wanted Child" to (inevitably, it seems) "Drop the Charges!" In 1970, the year following a much-heralded liberalization of Canadian abortion law, the National Abortion Caravan brought women together from across the country to demand the repeal of the abortion law, culminating in a large demonstration on Parliament Hill. The same day inside the House of Commons, women chained themselves to their seats in the Parliamentary Gallery to symbolize the situation of women without access to legal abortion (Pelrine 1972: 14; see also Women's Liberation Movement 1972). Their target was the "therapeutic abortion" amendments to the *Criminal Code* which provided that the only legal abortions in Canada were those performed in an "accredited or approved hospital" by a "qualified medical practitioner" with the approval of the hospital's therapeutic abortion committee (see Appendix).

The limitations of this reform were identified by the Royal Commission on the Status of Women in Canada in its *Report* to the federal government in 1970. The Commission found that the legislation was applied unevenly throughout the country, discriminating against women without the financial resources to arrange for a legal abortion elsewhere (1970: 286). Drawing back from recommending repeal of the abortion law, the Commission did recommend that abortions be allowed by a qualified medical practitioner on the sole request of any woman less than twelve weeks pregnant. In the Commission's view, "A law that has more bad effects than good ones is a bad law" (1970: 286).

While the Commission took what might be characterized as a measured and moral approach to the matter of abortion, it is significant that its recommendation was made on the heels of the proclamation of the legislation and in the dust of the Canadian women's movement "on-to-Ottawa" trek. Canadian women, the people most directly affected by the legislation, had responded very quickly, calling on the government to repeal the law denying them the right to safe, legal abortion.

For feminists, the demand for legalized abortion is part of the demand for full sexual and reproductive freedom, an essential precondition to full and equal participation in society. The criminal prohibition of abortion, and before 1969 of contraceptive literature, immediately brings into question the role and operation of the law and its sanctions. The demand for decriminalization is an issue around which women are able to organize campaigns which challenge the state and its role in the subordination of women.

The control of fertility and reproduction (including abortion) has been an issue not just for capitalist states, but for postcapitalist states as well. For instance, in 1918 the abortion prohibition in the Soviet Union was removed, women obtaining access to legal and safe abortions. However, a vigorous campaign and struggle around issues of morality and women's place in the Soviet family ensued, culminating (in 1936) in changes criminalizing abortion and making divorce more difficult (Farnsworth 1977). The continued regulation of women's reproductive capacity in socialist countries has been the subject of feminist criticism and the source in part of feminist scepticism about the extent of women's emancipation in those states.

Historical developments in abortion legislation in both capitalist and socialist contexts may, for some, call into question the validity of a marxist approach to law and the state. Feminist legal scholarship has begun to examine the theoretical issues involved in marxist positions (see, e.g., Polan 1982; MacKinnon 1983a, 1983b). It is my view that, in fact, a discussion of recent marxist scholarship, including marxist theorizing on law, will help to elucidate the issues.

The concept of mode of production is central to marxist analysis. However, as others have argued, a great deal hinges on how we define the mode of production and whether it includes social and familial relations (Sayer 1975; Picciotto 1979). If every aspect of life is determined solely by the economic base, the physical and technological means of production, then presumably a radical transformation in the control of that base should result in the withering away of the oppression of women. Indeed, when Frederick Engels argued for the importance of achieving legal equality for women, he did so with the following assurance:

> It will then be evident that the first premise for the emancipation of women is the reintroduction of the entire female sex into public

> industry; and that this again demands that the quality possessed by the individual family of being the economic unit of society be abolished. (1972: 82)

Thus did he envisage the solution to the "woman question." In fact, as suggested elsewhere (Lapidus 1977), the question of women's oppression is viewed by some as having been solved in postcapitalist states such as the Soviet Union. However, as indicated above, a critical feminist analysis of the socialist revolutions of this century demonstrates that the oppression of women does not lend itself to so simple a resolution.

There has been a shift away from simple economic determinism in recent marxist work, and instrumentalism in marxist theorizing on law (see, e.g., Hay et al. 1975; Thompson 1977, 1980; Pashukanis 1978; Cain and Hunt 1979; Corrigan and Sayer 1979; Fine et al. 1979; Sumner 1979; Williams 1980; Hunt 1981b). For example, Raymond Williams has urged a reevaluation of the economic base through a broader conceptualization of productive forces; looking at the base differently, we are less inclined to "dismiss as superstructural [or] secondary, certain vital productive forces, which are in the broad sense, from the beginning, basic" (1980: 204). This type of approach, then, allows a radical reassessment of the role and nature of law, politics, the state, and indeed familial relationships within capitalist society.

But is it a kitchen sink approach to theory? Are we left without a determinative or structural framework? Derek Sayer, for one, argues that a reassessment of, *inter alia*, the base/superstructure relationship is wholly consistent with Marx's materialism and his insistence that "production is a precondition of all social life and a materialist approach to history is one which studies the way in which men [sic] produce their means of subsistence — their mode of production" (1975: 781). However, Sayer rejects the interpretation that all aspects of social life are *determined* by the mode of production. He suggests that the "base/superstructure" metaphor with its narrow definition of class and class struggle rests on a fundamental misunderstanding of Marx's view of production:

> Property relations . . . clearly have a legal component and, within the base/superstructure theory, legal relations are supposed to be superstructural. But in that case, the economic must presuppose its superstructure, which makes nonsense of both the distinction and the claim of infrastructural primacy. (1975: 792)

Within this more "open" marxism, modes of production (material conditions and social relations) are examined in their historical specificity, and history "becomes explicable in terms of the *mutual interaction of bases and superstructures*, the former being decisive 'in the last instance' " (emphasis added) (1975: 793; see also Thompson 1977, 1978).

The rediscovery of the work of Evgeny Pashukanis, the late Soviet jurist, has contributed much to the development of a reinvigorated marxist scholarship concerned with law within capitalism (see, e.g., Corrigan and Sayer 1979; Young 1979; Hunt 1981a; Fine 1979, 1984). Pashukanis argued that there can be no theory of law which is transhistorical; only with the advent of bourgeois capitalist society are "all the conditions created for the juridical factor to attain complete distinctness in social relations" (1978: 58). With the creation of free labour as a commodity to exchange like other commodities, law becomes a distinct category existing within capitalist economic relations, not abstract theory existing only in people's heads:

> It has a parallel real history which unfolds not as a set of ideas, but as a specific set of relations which men enter into not by conscious choice but because the relations of production impel them to do so. Man becomes a legal subject by virtue of the same necessity which transforms the subject of nature into a commodity complete with the enigmatic property of value. (1978: 68)

For Pashukanis, bourgeois law is more than the sum of its content. The assertion that "Historical development is accompanied not only by a transformation of the content of legal norms and legal institutions, but also by the development in the legal form as such" (1978: 71) is, I would argue, the quintessence of Pashukanis's insight into the significance of law in the present historical context.

His attempt to develop a materialist theory of law has been criticized by Paul Q. Hirst, who has argued that in the work of Pashukanis law is a simple "read-off" of the economic subject (1979). The suspicion that Hirst places law in a *wholly* autonomous realm tends to be confirmed by later work in which he specifically attacks those who "seek to problematize the form of law" (1980: 101) and in particular the abortion law and its implications for women's reproductive freedom.

Hirst has a long-standing critique of marxist theorizing in the area of law and crime. Reacting to the "marxist turn" of radical criminology in the 1970s (see, e.g., Taylor, Walton, and Young 1975),[10] he argues against the possibility of developing a marxist theory of law, specifically criminal law: "Crime and deviance are no more a scientific field for Marxism than education, the family or sport. The objects of Marxist theory are specified by its own concepts: the mode of production, the class struggle, the state, ideology, etc." (1975: 204).

The problematic nature of Hirst's position emerges most clearly for my present purpose in his 1980 critique of Victoria Greenwood and Jock Young's 1976 work on English abortion law reform. He characterizes their support for women's right to "abortion on demand" and their criticisms of the 1967 English abortion legislation as implying that there will be "no problems of 'social policy' in socialist states, that they will not be faced with the regulation of health, questions of population policy and so on" (1980: 101). His view that legal regulation has little to do with the material or economic base in society leads him to argue that socialist states have the same *need* to regulate access to abortion as do capitalist states. With respect to the issue of a woman's "right to choose," he argues that as abortion involves consumption of medical resources, it cannot be a "private" act (cf. Petchesky 1980; Riley 1981). He views as deeply problematic the (horror of horrors!) demonopolization of medical competence implicit in the demand for "unconditional abortion," showing no appreciation for the problematic and contradictory nature of the therapeutic exception in abortion law, an exception which has less to do with "medical competence" than it does with professional control (see Collins 1982) and moral arbitration by the medical profession (Greenwood and Young 1976). In sum, his (postmarxist, postfeminist) position is a blend of arrogance, paternalism, and unreconstructed sexism:

> The notion that abortion is a matter of "private" choice is characterized by rationalism. It denies the realities of mental illness, neuroses, distress and just plain confusion that surround *our* competence to perform many common place acts, let alone decide whether to have a child or not. (1980: 102; emphasis added)

Hirst, then, views the content as well as the form of law in capitalist societies (not to mention the form and content of women's lives!) as unproblematic. He claims that the British legislation "serves the objective of decriminalizing [abortion] under certain circumstances" (1980: 99), that those same "circumstances" will prevail in a socialist society and that abortion will similarly have to be regulated. If what Hirst's socialism offers women is more regulation, more government control over our lives, small wonder that feminists are sceptical about the results of socialist revolutions and wary of "marxist" theory, even its "non-orthodox" variants (see also Bennett, Campbell, and Coward 1981). Legal notions of freedom, equality, autonomy, and privacy legitimize women's right to demand control of their bodies and to reject state interference (cf. MacKinnon 1983b): women (and other oppressed groups) must "attempt to push bourgeois law to its limit and demand their rights, without necessarily accepting that as the final goal" (Gregory 1979: 144).

Moreover, women have not challenged bourgeois law and demanded equal rights and the recognition of our subjectivity to ultimately become the property of the state in the transition to socialism. The continued restriction by the state of women's right to safe, legal abortion is a reminder of Juliet Mitchell's warning that "Equal rights will always only be rights before the law but these have by no means been won yet nor their possible extent envisaged" (1976: 399).

Women's *right* to reproductive freedom, including safe, accessible, and legal abortion, remains an essential site of feminist struggle within and without socialism.

Abortion Law Reform: Formal and Informal Levels

The liberalization of abortion legislation is consistent with the pattern of the legislation of the welfare state. Britain's 1967 abortion law explicitly located women within the family, and considered the effect a pregnancy would have on a woman's family an important enough factor to enable her to obtain an abortion. The legislation provides that abortions performed by a medical practitioner are legal if two medical practitioners are of the opinion formed in good faith that (a) continuing the pregnancy would involve risk to the life of the woman, or injury to her mental or physical health or that of any existing children in her family, and (b) there is a substantial risk that the child if born would suffer from a serious physical or mental handicap.[11]

Greenwood and Young have argued that this legislation was designed to remove the "burden" of motherhood from "marginal" women, women who were physically, mentally, or emotionally unable to care for a child, or whose families would be threatened or seriously strained by the birth of another child. Simply put, they suggest that this legislation was framed to act as "one means of ironing out the problems which society confronts" (1976: 74). That women might have a right to abortion was denied consistently by those who favoured reform; that women might desire access to safe legal abortion seems to have been beyond the realm of possibility:

> It is because of their belief that the economic system and the family are fundamentally sane institutions in this best of all possible worlds that the reformers deem women seeking abortions — outside of those in the most grim and marginal circumstances — to be not rational and acting frivolously. (1976: 77)

Despite the liberal perceptions that the need for abortion was limited, thousands of "normal" women sought and obtained legal abortions after the change in the law (Greenwood and Young 1976: 78).

Similarly, not many years after the Canadian law was amended, the *Report of the Committee on the Operation of the Abortion Law (Badgley Report)* noted that:

> The total number of induced abortions obtained by Canadian women in 1974 consisted of: (1) therapeutic abortions done in Canadian hospitals (48,136); (2) illegal abortions obtained in Canada (1,441); (3) induced abortions obtained in the United States (9,627); and (4) "assisted" abortions classified under other listings (10,635). (1977: 82)

However, the indictment of the Canadian law contained in these figures emerges when we consider the number of Canadian women who travelled to the United States to obtain legal abortions. Restricting women's access to abortion does not prevent them from obtaining abortions elsewhere, but the hardship, cost, and risk involved in travelling to another country clearly precludes all but those with the stamina and financial resources to afford such a trip. The availability of legal abortion in neighbouring American states seems to lessen the demand for legal abortion in this country, at the same time exacerbating inequality of access.

The particular form of the Canadian state, a federal system in which a degree of state power is vested in the provinces,[12] has had considerable impact on the operation of the abortion section of the *Criminal Code*. Through their ministers of health, the provinces are given the power to *approve* hospitals specifically for the purpose of s. 251, the abortion section. The jurisdiction of the provinces in matters relating to health care and hospitals is explicitly acknowledged in s. 251(5) and (6) (see Appendix). Section 251(5) allows a provincial minister of health to demand from a therapeutic abortion committee or a medical practitioner a copy of the certificate issued by the committee. This power vested in the provincial ministers of health to "order particulars" has serious implications not only for medical and hospital practice, but also for any hope a woman might have for the confidentiality of her medical file. In addition, the role of the provincial governments is important in determining whether hospitals other than accredited (read: large, urban) hospitals will be approved for the provision of therapeutic abortions.

The sharp regional disparities in accessibility documented by the Badgley Committee derive in no small part from the fact that several eligible hospitals chose not to establish therapeutic abortion committees. Compared with those in other provinces, far fewer hospitals in Quebec had therapeutic abortion committees, and far more had residency and patient quota requirements for abortions (*Badgley Report* 1977: 139–40). Since the Committee reported, the number of Quebec hospitals with committees inched up (from twenty-three in 1972 to thirty-two in 1982), although it must be noted that there were some "ups and downs" within this period.[13] However, as a result of the first round of Morgentaler cases in the 1970s, the then Parti Québécois government decided in 1977 that the federal law was unenforceable and "in fact guaranteed immunity from prosecution in Quebec for doctors performing medically safe procedures" (Morgentaler 1982: 117–18). Thus it became possible to obtain a medically safe abortion in Quebec without having to resort to a therapeutic abortion committee as required by the *Code*.

Access to therapeutic abortion committees has not improved since the Badgley Committee reported. In 1976, only 58.5 percent of Canadian hospitals were ineligible to set up therapeutic abortion committees; of the remaining 41.5 percent, 271 had committees and 288 did not (*Badgley Report* 1977: 105). The situation since 1979 is that hospitals with therapeutic abortion committees have become fewer in number, many eligible hospitals have inactive abortion committees (in 1982, for example, forty-seven hospitals *with committees* reported that no abortions were performed; a further forty-nine reported only one to twenty abortions for the year[14]), and hospitals with committees are under constant, concerted pressure from anti-abortion groups to dismantle their committees (see, e.g., Collins 1985: 53–54). From 1979 to 1982, ten hospitals in Ontario eliminated their therapeutic abortion committees.[15]

An additional factor affecting accessibility is the role of medical practitioners:

> Almost half of the doctors [surveyed by the Badgley Committee] (47.7%) felt that abortion lowered the value of human life. Physicians holding this view worked in virtually every hospital in Canada. When they constituted a majority of the medical staff at eligible hospitals without committees, their views significantly determined a hospital's position on the abortion procedure. (*Badgley Report* 1977: 127)

While the nature of the relationship between medical practitioners and hospitals is beyond the scope of this article, it is worth pointing out that, paradoxically, a hospital's decision to dismantle a therapeutic abortion committee (often after a struggle for control of the composition of the hospital board) is often a source of tension between boards and doctors, who are able to force the reinstatement of abortion committees by refusing to sit on other hospital committees.[16] The outcome in at least one such case, however, was the appointment by a hospital board of a new committee with "conservative" views on abortion.[17]

The Therapeutic Exception

The denotation of legal abortion as a therapeutic procedure is common to both British and Canadian legislation. In England, an abortion may be performed if two doctors determine in good faith that the requirements of the legislation are met in an individual woman's case; the Canadian *Criminal Code* provisions result in a much more complex arrangement.

The determination, then, as to whether a woman is "entitled" to an abortion is left to medical professionals. However, the challenge women pose to medical professional control in this area is a fundamental one, for women seeking abortions essentially "diagnose" themselves (Greenwood and Young 1976: 30, Barrett and Roberts 1978: 51). Yet the legislation in both countries ensures that the final decision rests neither with an individual woman, nor even with a woman in consultation with her doctor, but with at least two doctors in England and at least four doctors in Canada.

The state has tended to place great trust in the ability of members of the medical profession to act as final arbiters in this area, provided their opinions are formed in good faith. The first formal acknowledgment in law of the therapeutic exception came about as a result of the case of Aleck Bourne,[18] a preeminent British gynecologist who invited the Crown to prosecute him for performing an abortion upon a fourteen-year-old girl pregnant as a result of multiple rape by a group of soldiers. Bourne performed the abortion only after determining that continuation of her pregnancy would have made his patient a "mental wreck." He made it clear in his evidence that he would not have proceeded with the abortion had she been "feeble-minded" or "of a prostitute mind."[19]

The *Bourne* decision has had considerable significance for Canadian law, having fuelled the defence position in *Morgentaler v. The Queen*.[20] Morgentaler had performed an abortion without complying with the requirements of the *Code*: he had not obtained a certificate from a committee, and had performed the abortion in his own clinic. Although the Supreme Court of Canada rejected the applicability of the general "medical necessity" section to the abortion section of the *Criminal Code*, it neither rejected nor endorsed the common law defence of necessity; the court held that the evidence the doctor led at his trial did not support this defence. In a subsequent trial at which Dr. Morgentaler led evidence of this sort he was acquitted; the Crown appeal from the acquittal was not successful.[21] However, in 1985 the Ontario Court of Appeal overturned a jury acquittal of Morgentaler and his colleagues Dr. Smoling and Dr. Scott, raising doubts about the applicability of the exceptional *Bourne* defence to "routine" medical practice at their freestanding abortion clinic.[22]

Morgentaler is not an ordinary doctor and his prosecutions are not routine matters. His long-time advocacy of repeal of the abortion law and his support of women's right to choose is a matter of public record. With the assistance and support of the Canadian women's movement he has publicly defied and challenged the letter of the abortion provisions of the *Criminal Code*. That the state responded with near-religious zeal in the first round of prosecutions is amply documented elsewhere (Dickens 1976); police raids in 1984 on the freestanding abortion clinics in Winnipeg and Toronto with which he is associated, and the ensuing criminal prosecutions (see Collins 1985), marked a new chapter in a continuing battle.

Within the limited confines of the law, the significance of the Morgentaler challenge is considerable. If a doctor such as Morgentaler, carrying on a practice in a large urban setting with hospitals that do have therapeutic abortion committees, is able to convince properly instructed juries that he acted out of necessity, it seems that this defence should be available whenever a doctor is charged under the abortion section. Clearly, the procedure enunciated in the *Code* is not exhaustive of the availability of legal abortion in Canada. But as the situation now stands, a jury must accept in *each* case that *in the doctor's professional opinion* the abortion was a matter of necessity *and* that it was impossible to comply with the *Code* provisions. Thus the freestanding clinic "strategy" does not fundamentally challenge the concept of abortion as a therapeutic procedure of last resort, but rather the bureaucratic therapeutic abortion committee requirements of the *Criminal Code.*

Conclusion

The experience of the Canadian abortion legislation illustrates both the very real limitations of formal equality and the very real need to continue to defend and extend women's legal rights. Canadian feminists do not need to expose or demystify the abortion law: both the 1970 *Status of Women Report* and the 1977 *Badgley Report* have apprised the federal government of the inequity of this legislation. The women's movement must continue to challenge the intransigence of the state through the establishment of abortion and family-planning clinics controlled and operated by women.

This examination of Canadian abortion law illustrates the need to examine both the form and the content of bourgeois law. The shifts and upheavals in abortion law cannot be understood if we regard the law and the state as simply instruments of the ruling class which might be wielded more equitably by a different class in different circumstances. The continued legal regulation of abortion by socialist states attests to the incomplete nature of those socialist revolutions rather than the inherent and legitimate right of all states to regulate women's lives.

The abortion law is an excellent example of direct state control. Equally central if less visible is the role played by medical practitioners in the day-to-day operation and interpretation of the abortion law and in accessibility to the abortion procedure. The criminal sanction is mediated in practice by the conduct of a relatively autonomous medical profession; it is imperative that the feminist assault on the abortion law be waged on both these levels — formal and informal.

Finally, the Canadian women's movement must continue to wage simultaneous offensive and defensive campaigns. Against the right-to-life challenge represented by the *Borowski* case, the women's movement must struggle to ensure that therapeutic abortion is not removed from the *Criminal Code,* leaving only the criminal prohibition; the law must not be rolled back fifty years. At the same time, without accepting the legitimacy of therapeutic necessity as the sole criterion for legal abortion, the women's movement must mount an offensive campaign against the criminal sanction to decriminalize all safe abortions.

The successful campaigns of feminists in other countries indicate that even in periods of crisis, it is possible to assert and defend women's right to abortion (see, e.g., Caldwell 1981). The pressure must be exerted through vigorous feminist campaigns for freestanding abortion clinics and for repeal of the abortion law — campaigns which, as well, confront the role of the medical profession and challenge medical determination in abortion. Canadian women must be prepared to unburden the medical profession of the "great social responsibility" vested in it by the state.

The Canadian state reinforces the subordination of women through this legal sanction, through the bureaucracy of hospital administrations and therapeutic abortion committees, and through regulation by its designated arbiters, the members of the medical profession. For women to even begin to explore the concept of equality, the right to self-determination and reproductive freedom must first be won. The state and the law are thus an important site of struggle, one which feminists avoid at our peril.

Notes

1. I wish to thank Gordon West, Judy Deverell, Katherine Arnup, Susan Genge, and the editors, Meg Luxton and Heather Jon Maroney, for their comments and assistance in the preparation of this article.
2. 419 U.S. 113; 93 S.Ct. 705 (1973) (U.S.S.Ct.) The U.S. Supreme Court held that the constitutionally protected right to privacy extended to freedom in decisions regarding abortion, and that any state legislation which interferes with a woman's right to decide has to be based upon compelling state interest. Almost immediately, American state legislatures began to enact legislation designed to override a woman's right to privacy: waiting periods, medicaid funding cuts, "informed consent," parental/spousal consent or (when this failed) spousal notification and consultation requirements. For discussion of the political significance of the legislative attempts and judicial responses, see Petchesky (1984); MacKinnon (1983b). See Gavigan (1986) for an examination of the issue of spousal consent in Canadian abortion law.
3. *Borowski v. Attorney General of Canada and Minister of Finance of Canada* (1984), 8 C.C.C. (3d) 392 (Sask. Q.B.).
4. *In re The Constitutional Questions Act: and in re a Reference to the Court of Appeal of Sask. by Order in Council no. 765/75 respecting Bill 53 of 1984–85 entitled The Freedom of Informed Choice (Abortions) Act,* not yet reported, 20 Dec. 1985 (Sask. C.A.).
5. *The Freedom of Informed Choice (Abortions) Act,* Bill 53, 1984–85 (20th Leg. Sask., 4th sess.); the bill, sponsored by "pro-life" Conservative backbencher Gay Caswell, received neither the unqualified support of the province's anti-abortion forces (see "Anti-abortion group rejects 'pro-life bill'," *Star-Phoenix* (Saskatoon), May 29, 1985, p. B1) nor that of the caucus of the governing Conservatives (see "Abortion bill 'to be passed'," *Star-Phoenix,* June 10, 1985, p. A7; "Caswell, colleagues differ on abortion bill chances," *Star-Phoenix,* June 11, 1985, p. A11; "Court referral kills abortion bill," *Star-Phoenix,*

June 12, 1985, p. A1; "Caswell vows to keep fighting," *Star-Phoenix*, June 12, 1985, p. A20); the NDP opposition was muted in its criticism, apparently abstaining from the debate ("NDP stays out of abortion bill debate," *Star-Phoenix*, June 5, 1985, p. B13).

6. *R.v. (John) Smith*, [1974] 1 All E.R. 376 at 378.
7. See also Beechey (1978); Smart (1981); for the historical and political significance of women's suffrage in Canada, see Mahood (1972).
8. *An Act to amend the Criminal Code in relation to sexual offences and other offences against the person and to amend certain other Acts in relation thereto or in consequence thereof*, S.C. 1980–81–82–83, c. 125, s. 6, abolished the gender-specific offence of rape and replaced it with gender-neutral "sexual assault" offences. See Taylor (1981) for an interesting discussion of the significance of feminist demands for law reform in the shaping of the new legislation.
9. *Paton v. Trustees of British Pregnancy Advisory Service*, [1978] 2 All E.R. 987; 3 W.L.R. 687 (Q.B.); *Whalley v. Whalley* (1981) 122 D.L.R. (3d) 717 (B.C.Co.Ct.); *Medhurst v. Medhurst* (1984), 9 D.L.R. (4th) 252 (Ont. H. Ct.).
10. For an analysis of the development of various forms of "marxist" criminology, see Young (1979).
11. *Abortion Act*, 1967, c. 87 (U.K.).
12. See Panitch (1977) and West (1981) for analyses of "neo-marxist" theories of the capitalist state and their significance in the Canadian context.
13. In 1970, according to Statistics Canada (*Therapeutic Abortions 1982*, Catalogue 82-211 Annual, table 13, p. 51), the province of Quebec had sixteen hospitals with therapeutic abortion committees. The peak year was 1975 (thirty-five hospitals); the number dropped in 1977 to twenty-four and remained there until 1979, when it reached thirty and began to rise toward its 1982 level.
14. Statistics Canada, *ibid.*, table 16, p. 52.
15. Statistics Canada, *ibid.*, table 13, p. 51; see also Statistics Canada, *Basic facts on therapeutic abortions, Canada — 1982*, Catalogue 82-215 Annual, table 5, p. 16.
16. In 1984 the area hospital board in the northwestern British Columbia community of Smithers (pop. 4,600) decided "for moral reasons" that the hospital would stop performing abortions, consistent with a reported national trend to disband abortion committees. Doctors in the community threatened to quit all other hospital committees in protest of the hospital's decision ("Smithers hospital to stop abortions," *Sun* (Vancouver), October 12, 1984, p. A3). A few days later, the hospital, "facing pressure from a medical staff that was threatening mutiny," had reconsidered its decision. However, a new committee comprising three doctors who were "conservative with respect to their opinions regarding abortion" had been appointed ("Hospital board eases stand on abortion," *Sun*, October 17, 1984, p. A17). The reports bring to mind earlier events in Surrey, B.C. when a "pro-life" hospital board was elected ("Surrey women must go elsewhere for abortions," *Sun*, September 26, 1980, p. A3). A few months later, the hospital medical staff (supported by

the B.C. Medical Association) had threatened to resign from hospital committees if the board did not rescind its decision ("Surrey doctors backed," *Province* (Vancouver), November 14, 1980, p. A7). Finally, the hospital board acceded to the demands of the medical staff ("Abortions return as hospital bows," *Province*, November 21, 1980, p. A1). The controversy at Surrey Memorial Hospital was still the subject of press comment the next year, and according to one report ("Hospital's decision to ban all abortions angers staff doctors," *Globe and Mail* (Toronto) July 27, 1981, p. N4), had spread to other B.C. hospitals.

17. In Smithers, following the appointment of a "conservative" therapeutic abortion committee, the number of therapeutic abortions "dropped dramatically"; however, it was also reported that one of the three new committee members had recently been replaced by a female physician ("Abortions drop in Smithers," *Sun* (Vancouver), March 1, 1985, p. A2).
18. *R.v. Bourne*, [1938] 3 All E.R. 615 (K.B.).
19. *Ibid.*, see also Dickens (1966), p. 47.
20. (1975), 30 C.R.N.S. 209 (S.C.C.).
21. *R. v. Morgentaler* (1976), 33 C.R.N.S. 244 (Que. C.A.); leave to appeal to Supreme Court of Canada refused, [1976] 1 S.C.R. x.
22. *R. v. Morgentaler, Smoling and Scott* (1986), 52 O.R. (2d) 353 (Ont. C.A.).

APPENDIX

Criminal Code, R.S.C. 1970, c. C-34, s. 251, ss. (1)–(5)

s. 251(1) Every one who, with intent to procure the miscarriage of a female person, whether or not she is pregnant, uses any means for the purpose of carrying out his intention is guilty of an indictable offence and is liable to punishment for life.

(2) Every female person who, being pregnant, with intent to procure her own miscarriage, uses any means or permits any means to be used for the purpose of carrying out her intention is guilty of an indictable offence and is liable to imprisonment for two years.

(3) In this section, "means" includes

(a) the administration of a drug or other noxious thing,

(b) the use of any instrument, and

(c) manipulation of any kind.

(4) Subsections (1) and (2) do not apply to

(a) a qualified medical practitioner, other than a member of a therapeutic abortion committee for any hospital, who in good faith uses in an accredited or approved hospital any means for the purpose of carrying out his intention to procure the miscarriage of a female person, or

(b) a female who, being, pregnant, permits a qualified medical practitioner to use in an accredited or approved hospital any means described in paragraph (a) for the purpose of carrying out her intention to procure her own miscarriage, if, before the use of those means, the therapeutic abortion committee for that accredited or approved hospital, by a majority of the members of the committee and at a meeting of the committee at which the case of such female person has been reviewed,

(c) has by certificate in writing stated that in its opinion the continuation of the pregnancy of such female person would or would be likely to endanger her life or health, and

(d) has caused a copy of such certificate to be given to the qualified medical practitioner.

(5) The Minister of Health of a province may by order

(a) require a therapeutic abortion committee for any hospital in that province, or any member thereof, to furnish to him a copy of any certificate described in paragraph (4)(c) issued by that committee, together with such other information relating to the circumstances surrounding the issue of that certificate as he may require, or

(b) require a medical practitioner who, in that province, has procured the miscarriage of any female person named in a certificate described in paragraph (4)(c), to furnish to him a copy of that certificate, together with such other information relating to the procuring of the miscarriage as he may require.

References

Ainsworth, Jackie, et al. 1982. "Getting Organized: In the Feminist Unions." In *Still Ain't Satisfied*, ed. Maureen FitzGerald, Connie Guberman, and Margie Wolfe. Toronto: Women's Press.

Allen, H. 1982. "Political Lesbianism and Feminism — Space for Sexual Politics?" M/F 7.

Alpert, Jane. 1975. "MotherRight: A New Feminist Theory." Ms., August.

Ambert, Anne-Marie. 1976. *Sex Structure*, 2nd ed. Don Mills, Ont.: Longman.

Amsden, Alice H. 1980. *The Economics of Women and Work*. Harmondsworth: Penguin.

Anderson, Karen. 1985. "Commodity Production and Subordination: Montagnais-Naskapi and Huron Women, 1600–1650." *Signs* 11, no. 1.

——. 1982. "Huron Women and Huron Men: The Effects of Demography, Kinship and the Social Division of Labour on Male/Female Relations among the 17th Century Huron." Ph.D. thesis, University of Toronto.

Andrew, Carolyn. 1984. "Women and the Welfare State." *Canadian Journal of Political Science* 27, no. 4 (December).

Anyon, J. 1983. "Intersections of Gender and Class: Accommodation and Resistance by Working-Class and Affluent Females to Contradictory Sex-Role Ideologies." In *Gender, Class and Education*, ed. S. Walker and L. Barton. London: Falmer Press.

——. 1982. "Ideology and United States History Textbooks." In *Cultural and Economic Reproduction in Education*, ed. M. Apple. London: Routledge & Kegan Paul.

——. 1980. "Social Class and the Hidden Curriculum of Work." *Journal of Education* 162.

Apple, Nixon. 1980. "The Rise and Fall of Full Employment Capitalism." *Studies in Political Economy* no. 4 (Autumn).

Archibald, Kathleen. 1970. *Sex and the Public Service*. Ottawa: Queen's Printer for Canada.

Arms, Suzanne. 1977. *Immaculate Deception*. New York: Bantam.

Armstrong, Hugh. 1977. "The Labour Force and State Workers in Canada." In *The Canadian State: Political Economy and Political Power*, ed. Leo Panitch. Toronto: University of Toronto Press.

Armstrong, Pat. 1984. *Labour Pains: Women's Work in Crisis*. Toronto: Women's Press.

Armstrong, Pat, and Hugh Armstrong. 1980. "Job Creation and Unemployment for Canadian Women." Paper presented at the NATO Symposium "Women and the World of Work," Portugal.

——. 1983. *A Working Majority: What Women Must Do for Pay*. Ottawa: Canadian Advisory Council on the Status of Women.

——. 1984. *The Double Ghetto: Canadian Women and Their Segregated Work*, rev. ed. Toronto: McClelland & Stewart.

——. 1986. "More For the Money: Redefining and Intensifying Work in Canada." Paper prepared for a Conference on Women and Politics: The Feminization of the Labour Force. Harvard University Center for European Studies, March 14–16.

Armstrong, Pat, Hugh Armstrong, Patricia Connelly, and Angela Miles. 1985. *Feminist Marxism or Marxist Feminism: A Debate*. Toronto: Garamond Press.

Arney, W.R. 1980. "Maternal Infant Bonding: The Politics of Falling in Love with Your Child." *Feminist Studies* 6, no. 3.

Arnopoulos, Sheila McLeod. 1979. *Problems of Immigrant Women in the Canadian Labour Force*. Ottawa: Canadian Advisory Council on the Status of Women.

Arnot, M. 1983. "A Cloud over Co-education: An Analysis of the Forms of Transmission of Class and Gender Relations." In *Gender, Class and Education*, ed. S. Walker and L. Barton. London: Falmer Press.

Atkinson, Ti-Grace. 1984. "Le nationalisme féminin." *Nouvelles questions féministe* 6–7.

——. 1974. *Amazon Odyssey*. New York: Links.

Atlantis 7. 1981. "Domestic Labour and Wage Labour." Fall.

Bacchi, Carol. 1983. *Liberation Deferred? The Ideas of the English-Canadian Suffragists, 1877–1918*. Toronto: University of Toronto Press.

Backhouse, C.B. 1983. "Involuntary Motherhood: Abortion, Birth Control, and the Law in Nineteenth Century Canada." *Windsor Yearbook Access to Justice* 3.

Badgley Report. 1977. (Report of the Committee on the Operation of the Abortion Law.) Ottawa: Supply and Services Canada.

Baker, Maureen, and Mary Anne Robeson. 1981. "Trade Union Reactions to Women Workers and Their Concerns." *Canadian Journal of Sociology* 6, no. 1 (Winter), ed. Katherina L.P. Lundy and Barbara D. Warme.

Balchin, P. 1975. "The Midwife and Puerperal Psychosis." *Midwife Health Visitor* 11, no. 2.

Bamberger, Joan. 1974. "The Myth of Matriarchy: Why Men Rule in Primitive Society." In *Woman, Culture and Society*, ed. Michelle Zimbalist Rosaldo and Louise Lamphere. Stanford, CA: Stanford University Press.

Bank Book Collective. 1979. *An Account to Settle: The Story of the United Bank Workers (SORWUC)*. Vancouver: Press Gang.

Barrett, Michèle. 1980. *Women's Oppression Today: Problems in Marxist Feminist Analysis*. London: Verso and New Left Books.
Barrett, Michèle, and Roberta Hamilton, eds. 1987. *The Politics of Diversity: Feminism, Marxism and Canadian Society*. London: Verso.
Barrett, Michèle, and Mary McIntosh. 1980. "The 'Family Wage': Some Problems for Socialist Feminists." *Capital and Class* 2.
———. 1982. *The Anti-social Family*. London: Verso and New Left Books.
Barrett, Michèle, and Helen Roberts. 1978. "Doctors and Their Patients: The Social Control of Women in General Practice." In *Women, Sexuality and Social Control*, ed. Carol Smart and Barry Smart. London: Routledge & Kegan Paul.
Barry, Francine. 1977. *Le Travail de la Femme aux Québec: L'évolution de 1940–1970*. Quebec: Les Presses de L'Université du Québec.
Barry, Kathleen. 1979. *Female Sexual Slavery*. Englewood Cliffs, NJ: Prentice-Hall.
Baxandall, Rosalyn, Elizabeth Ewen, and Linda Gordon. 1976. "The Working Class Has Two Sexes." *Monthly Review*, July/August.
Bebel, August. [1883] 1971. *Women under Socialism*. New York: Schocken.
Becker, Gary. 1965. "A Theory of the Allocation of Time." *The Economic Journal* 80, no. 200.
Becker, H. 1952. "Social Class Variations in the Teacher-Pupil Relationship." *Journal of Educational Sociology* 25, no. 4.
Beechey, V. 1978. "Women and Production: A Critical Analysis of Some Sociological Theories of Women's Work." In *Feminism and Materialism*, ed. A. Kuhn and A. Wolpe. London: Routledge & Kegan Paul.
———. 1982. "The Sexual Division of Labour and the Labour Process: A Critical Assessment of Braverman." In *The Degradation of Work?*, ed. Stephen Wood. London: Hutchinson.
Bell, Daniel. 1965. *The End of Ideology*. New York: Free Press.
Belsey, Mark A. 1979. "Long Term Sequelae of Induced Abortion: Considerations in Interpretation of Research." In *Pregnancy Termination: Procedures, Safety and New Developments*, ed. Gerald I. Zatuchni et al. Hagerstown: Harper & Row.
Bennett, Fran, Beatrix Campbell, and Rosalind Coward. 1981. "Feminists—The Degenerates of the Social?" *Politics and Power* 3.
Benston, Margaret. 1969. "Political Economy of Women's Liberation." *Monthly Review* 21, no. 4 (September).
———. 1983. "For Women, the Chips Are Down." In *The Technological Woman: Interfacing with Tomorrow*, ed. J. Zimmerman. New York: Praeger.
Berger, Thomas. 1977. *Northern Frontier, Northern Homeland: The Report of the Mackenzie Valley Pipeline Enquiry*. Ottawa: Supply and Services Canada.
Berk, Sarah F., ed. 1980. *Women and Household Labor*. Beverly Hills, CA: Sage.
Bernstein, Judy, Peggy Morton, Linda Seese, and Myrna Wood. 1972. "Sisters, Brothers, Lovers . . . Listen . . ." In *Women Unite!*, ed. Discussion Collective No. 6. Toronto: Canadian Women's Educational Press.

Besemeres, J.F. 1980. *Socialist Population Politics*. White Plains, NY: M.E. Sharpe.

Bettelheim, Bruno. 1954. *Symbolic Wounds: Puberty Rites and the Envious Male*. New York: Free Press.

Biggar, H.P., ed. 1922–1936. *The Works of Samuel de Champlain*. Toronto: Champlain Society. 6 Volumes.

Bingham, W.G., and E.W. House. 1977. "Counselors' Attitudes Towards Women and Work." In *Sex Bias in the Schools*, ed. Janice Pottker and Andrew Fishel. East Brunswick, NJ: Associated University Presses.

Binnie-Clark, Georgina. 1979. *Wheat and Women*. Toronto: University of Toronto Press.

Biryukova, A.P. 1980. "Special Protective Legislation and Equality of Opportunity of Women Workers in the U.S.S.R." *International Labour Review* 119, no. 1 (January–February).

Bissonnette, Lise. 1980. "L'appel aux femmes." *Le Devoir*, April 9.

Blaise, Suzanne. 1981. *Des femmes de nulle part*. Paris: Tierce.

Bloom, L.Z. 1976. "It's All for Your Own Good: Parent-Child Relationships in Popular American Child Rearing Literature, 1820–1970." *Journal of Popular Culture* 10.

Blumberg, Rae Lesser. 1978. *Stratification: Socioeconomic and Sexual Inequality*. Dubuque, IA: Wm. C. Brown & Co.

Borowski, Allan. 1984. "Youth Unemployment in Australia and Canada in Comparative Perspective." *Australian-Canadian Studies* 2 (January).

Boszormenyi-Nagy, I., and G.M. Spark. 1973. *Invisible Loyalties: Intergenerational Family Therapy*. New York: Harper & Row.

Boucher, Denise. 1979. *Les Fées ont soif*. Montreal: Intermède.

Boulet, Jac-André, and Laval Lavallée. 1984. *The Changing Economic Status of Women*. A study prepared for the Economic Council of Canada. Ottawa: Supply and Services Canada.

Bourgeault, Ron G. 1983. "The Indian, the Métis and the Fur Trade: Class, Sexism and Racism in the Transition from 'Communism' to Capitalism." *Studies in Political Economy* 12 (Fall).

Bourque, Gilles, and Nicole Laurin-Frenette. 1972. "Social Classes and Nationalist Ideologies in Quebec 1960–1970." In *Capitalism and the National Question in Canada*, ed. Gary Teeple. Toronto: University of Toronto Press.

Bourque, Gilles, and Anne Légaré. 1979. *Le Québec: la question nationale*. Paris: Maspéro.

Bowles, Samuel, and Herbert Gintis. 1976. *Schooling in Capitalist America*. London: Routledge & Kegan Paul.

Boyd, Monica. 1977. "The Forgotten Minority: The Socio-Economic Status of Divorced and Separated Women." In *The Working Sexes*, ed. Patricia Marchak. Vancouver: University of British Columbia, Institute of Industrial Relations.

Bradbury, Bettina. 1984. "Pigs, Cows and Borders: Non-Wage Forms of Survival among Montreal Families, 1861–91." *Labour/Le Travail* 14 (Fall).

Brandt, Gail Cuthbert. 1981. " 'Weaving It Together': Life Cycle and the Industrial Experience of Female Cotton Workers in Quebec, 1910–1950." *Labour/Le Travail* 7 (Spring).

Braverman, Harry. 1974. *Labour and Monopoly Capital*. New York: Monthly Review Press.

Brenner, Johanna, and Maria Ramas. 1984. "Rethinking Women's Oppression." *New Left Review* no. 146, July–August.

Brenner, M. H. 1979. "Unemployment and Economic Growth and Mortality." *Lancet*, March 24.

——. 1977. "Health Costs and Benefits of Economic Policy." *International Journal of Health Services* 7, no. 4.

——. 1973. Mental Illness and the Economy. Cambridge, MA: Harvard University Press.

Bridenthal, Renate, and Claudia Koonz, eds. 1977. *Becoming Visible: Women in European History*. Boston: Houghton Mifflin.

Briskin, Linda. 1983. "Women's Challenge to Organized Labour." In *Union Sisters: Women in the Labour Movement*, ed. Linda Briskin and Lynda Yanz. Toronto: Women's Press.

Briskin, Linda, and Lynda Yanz, eds. 1983. *Union Sisters: Women in the Labour Movement*. Toronto: Women's Press.

Brodeur, Violette, et al. 1981. *Le mouvement des femmes au Québec*. Montreal: S.F.P.

Brossard, Nicole. 1981. "*Notes et fragments d'ignorance*." In *Femmes et politique*, ed. Yolande Cohen. Montreal: Le Jour, Editeur.

Brown, G., M. Bhrolchain, and T. Harris. 1975. "Social Class and Psychiatric Disturbances among Women in an Urban Population." *Sociology* 9.

Brown, Jennifer. 1980. *Strangers in Blood: Fur Trade Company Families in Indian Country*. Vancouver: University of British Columbia Press.

——. 1982. "Children of the Early Fur Trade." In *Childhood and Family in Canadian History*, ed. Joy Parr. Toronto: McClelland & Stewart.

Brown, Judith K. 1970. "Economic Organization and the Position of Women among the Iroquois." *Ethnohistory* 7.

——. 1975. "Iroquois Women: An Ethnohistoric Note." In *Toward an Anthropology of Women*, ed. Rayna Reiter. New York: Monthly Review Press.

Brown, Richard. 1976. "Women as Employees: Some Comments on Research in Industrial Sociology." In *Dependence and Exploitation in Work and Marriage*, ed. D. Barker and S.L. Allen. London: Longman.

Brown, W.A. 1979. *Psychological Care During Pregnancy and the Post-Partum Period*. New York: Raven Press.

Brownmiller, Susan. 1975. *Against Our Will: Men, Women and Rape*. New York: Bantam.

——. 1984. *Femininity*. New York: Fawcett.

Brym, Robert, ed. 1985. *The Structure of the Canadian Capitalist Class*. Toronto: Garamond Press.

Brym, Robert, and James Sacouman, eds. 1979. *Underdevelopment and Social Movements in Atlantic Canada*. Toronto: New Hogtown Press.
Bryne, E. 1978. *Women and Education*. London: Tavistock.
Bryson, Lois. 1977. "Poverty." *Current Affairs Bulletin* 54, no. 5 (October).
——. 1983. "Women as Welfare Recipients: Women, Poverty and the State." In *Women, Social Welfare and the State*, ed. Cora Baldock and Bettina Cass. Sydney: George Allen & Unwin.
Bucove, A. 1964. "Postpartum Psychosis in the Male." *Bulletin of the New York Academy of Medicine* 40.
Bunch, Charlotte. 1981. "Introduction." In *Building Feminist Theory: Best of Quest*, ed. Quest Staff. New York: Longman.
Burawoy, Michael. 1979. *Manufacturing Consent*. Chicago: University of Chicago Press.
Burstyn, Varda, ed. 1985. *Women Against Censorship*. Toronto: Douglas & MacIntyre.
——. 1983. "Masculine Dominance and the State." In *Socialist Register, 1983*, ed. John Saville and Ralph Miliband.
Burstyn, Varda, Dorothy Smith, and Roxanna Ng. 1985. *Women, Class, Family and the State*. Toronto: Garamond Press.
Burton, Clare. 1985. *Subordination: Feminism and Social Theory*. London: George Allen & Unwin.
Cahan, Vicki. 1985. "The Feminization of Poverty: More Women Are Getting Poor." *Business Week*, January 28.
Cain, Maureen, and Alan Hunt. 1979. *Marx and Engels on Law*. London: Academic Press.
Caldwell, Lesley. 1981. "Abortion in Italy." *Feminist Review* 7.
Cameron, Barbara. 1983. "The Sexual Division of Labour and Class Struggle." *Socialist Studies 83 Etudes Socialistes: A Canadian Annual*. Winnipeg: Society for Socialist Studies/Société des études socialistes.
Campbell, Beatrix. 1980. "A Feminist Sexual Politics: Now You See It, Now You Don't." *Feminist Review* 5.
Canada. 1970. Report of the Royal Commission on the Status of Women in Canada. Ottawa: Information Canada.
Canadian Advisory Council on the Status of Women. 1983. *As Things Stand*. Ottawa: Canadian Advisory Council on the Status of Women.
——. 1979. *10 Years Later*. Ottawa: Canadian Advisory Council on the Status of Women.
——. 1981. *Women and the Constitution*. Ottawa: Canadian Advisory Council on the Status of Women.
Canadian Labour Congress. 1984a. "Workers' Rights in the Silicon Age." 15th Constitutional Convention Document no. 19 (May).
——. 1984b. "An Action Plan to Promote Jobs and Justice." 15th Constitutional Convention Document no. 29 (May).

Canadian Radio-television and Telecommunications Commission (CRTC). 1982. *Images of Women: Report of the Task Force on Sex-Role Stereotyping in the Broadcast Media*. Ottawa: Minister of Supply and Services Canada.

Cass, Bettina. 1984. "The Changing Face of Poverty in Australia 1972–1982." Paper delivered at Continuing Education Seminar in the Department of Social Work, University of Sydney.

Catano, J., and V. Catano. 1981. "Mild Post-partum Depression: Learned Helplessness and the Medicalization of Obstetrics." Unpublished ms., St. Mary's University, Halifax.

Cavendish, Ruth. 1982. *Women on the Line*. London: Routledge & Kegan Paul.

Centre for Labour Studies, Humber College. 1979. "Hazard Inventory of Garment and Textile Workers." Toronto: Centre for Labour Studies. March.

Chavkin, Wendy, ed. 1981. *Double Exposure: Women's Health Hazards on the Job and at Home*. New York: Monthly Review Press.

Cheda, Sherrill. 1972. "See Dick Run, See Jane Sit." *Chatelaine*. December.

———. 1971. "Sex Roles in Children's Books." *The New Feminist* 2, no. 4 (October).

Chenier, Nancy Miller. 1982. *Reproductive Hazards: Men, Women and the Fertility Gamble*. Ottawa: Canadian Advisory Council on the Status of Women.

Chodorow, Nancy. 1978. *The Reproduction of Mothering: Psychoanalysis and the Sociology of Gender*. Berkeley: University of California Press.

Cicourel, A., and J. Kitsuse. 1977. "The School as a Mechanism of Social Differentiation." In *Power and Ideology in Education*, ed. J. Karabel and A. Halsey. New York: Oxford University Press.

Clark, Alice. [1919] 1982. *Working Life of Women in the 17th Century*. London: Routledge & Kegan Paul.

Clark, Lorenne, and Lynda Lange, eds. 1979. *The Sexism of Social and Political Theory: Women and Reproduction from Plato to Nietzsche*. Toronto: University of Toronto Press.

Clark, Lorenne, and Deborah Lewis. 1977. *Rape: The Price of Coercive Sexuality*. Toronto: Women's Press.

Clarricoate, K. 1980. "The Importance of Being Ernest . . . Emma . . . Tom . . . Jane: The Perception and Categorization of Gender Conformity and Gender Deviation in Primary Schools." In *Schooling for Women's Work*, ed. R. Deem. London: Routledge & Kegan Paul.

Cleaverdon, Catherine. 1974. *The Woman Suffrage Movement in Canada*. Toronto: University of Toronto Press.

Clement, Connie. 1983. "The Case for Lay Abortion: Learning from Midwifery." *Healthsharing* 5, no. 1.

Clement, Wallace. 1975. *The Canadian Corporate Elite: An Analysis of Economic Power*. Toronto: McClelland & Stewart, The Carleton Library, No. 89.

———. 1983. *Class, Power and Property: Essays on Canadian Society*. Toronto: Methuen.

Cockburn, Cynthia. 1983. *Brothers: Male Dominance and Technological Change*. London: Pluto Press.

Cohen, Marjorie. 1985. "The Macdonald Report and Its Implications." *Feminist Action Féministe* 1, no. 3 (December): 13–15.

Cohen, Yolande. 1981. *Femmes et politique*. Montreal: Le Jour, Editeur.

——. 1982. "Thoughts on Women and Power." In *Feminism in Canada*, ed. Geraldine Finn and Angela Miles. Montreal: Black Rose.

Cole, Susan G. 1983. "The Real Abortion Issue." *This Magazine* 17, no. 2.

Coleman, William D. 1984. The Independence Movement in Quebec 1945–1980. Toronto: University of Toronto Press.

Collectif. 1971. *Manifeste des femmes québécoises*. Montreal: L'Etincelle.

Collectif CLIO. 1982. *L'histoire des femmes au Québec*. Montreal: Les Quinze, Editeur.

Collins, Anne. 1985. *The Big Evasion: Abortion, the Issue that Won't Go Away*. Toronto: Lester & Orpen Dennys.

Collins, L.D. 1982. "The Politics of Abortion: Trends in Canadian Fertility Policy." *Atlantis* 7, no. 2.

Connelly, Patricia. 1978. *Last Hired, First Fired: Women and the Canadian Work Force*. Toronto: Women's Press.

——. 1983. "On Marxism and Feminism." *Studies in Political Economy* 12: 153–61.

Connelly, M. Patricia, and Martha MacDonald. 1983. "Women's Work: Domestic and Wage Labour in a Nova Scotia Community." *Studies in Political Economy* 10.

Conseil du Statut de la Femme. 1978. *Egalité et indépendance*. Quebec: Editeur Officiel.

Cook, Gail C.A., ed. 1976. *Opportunity for Choice: A Goal for Women in Canada*. Ottawa: Information Canada.

Cook, Ramsey, and Wendy Mitchinson, eds., 1976. *The Proper Sphere*. Toronto: Oxford University Press.

Copans, Jean, and David Seddon. 1978. "Marxism and Anthropology: A Preliminary Survey." In *Relations of Production*, ed. David Seddon. London: Frank Cass.

Corrective Collective. 1972. *She Named It Canada*. Toronto: Women's Press.

——. 1974. *Never Done: Three Centuries of Women's Work in Canada*. Toronto: Women's Press.

Corrigan, P., and D. Sayer. 1979. "How the Law Rules: Variations on Some Themes in Karl Marx." In *Law, State and Society*, ed. B. Fryer et al. London: Croom Helm.

Coulson, Margaret, Branka Magas, and Hilary Wainwright. 1975. "The Housewife and Her Labour under Capitalism." *New Left Review* 89 (Jan.–Feb.).

Coward, Rosalind. 1983. *Patriarchal Precedents: Sexuality and Social Relations*. London: Routledge & Kegan Paul.

Cross, D. Suzanne. 1973. "The Neglected Majority: The Changing Role of Women in 19th Century Montreal." *Social History*, Fall. Reprinted in *The*

Neglected Majority, ed. Susan Mann Trofimenkoff and Allison Prentice. Toronto: McClelland & Stewart, 1977.

Cuneo, Carl. 1979. "State, Class and Reserve Labour: The Case of the 1941 Unemployment Insurance Act." *Canadian Review of Sociology and Anthropology* 16, no. 2: 147–70.

Curtain, Richard. 1985. "Lessons from a Closure's Aftermath." *Australian Society* 4, no. 3 (March).

Dale, R. 1982. "Education and the Capitalist State: Contributions and Contradictions." In *Culture and Economic Reproduction in Education*, ed. M. Apple. London: Routledge & Kegan Paul.

Dale, Roger, et al., eds. 1981. *Education and the State, Vol. 2: Politics, Patriarchy and Practice*. London: Falmer Press.

Dalla Costa, Mariarosa, and Selma James. 1972. *The Power of Women and the Subversion of the Community*. Bristol: Falling Wall Press.

Dalton, Katharina. 1971. "Puerperal and Premenstrual Depression." Proceedings of the Royal Society of Medicine 64, no. 12: 1249–52.

Daly, Mary, 1978. *Gyn-Ecology: The Meta-Ethics of Radical Feminism*. Boston: Beacon Press.

David, H.P., and R.J. McIntyre. 1981. *Reproductive Behavior: Central and Eastern European Experience*. New York: Springer.

Davidson, J.R. 1972. "Postpartum Mood Change in Jamaican Women: A Description and Discussion of Its Significance." *British Journal of Psychiatry* 121: 659–63.

Davin, A. 1978. "Imperialism and Motherhood." *History Workshop* 5 (Spring): 9–65.

Dawson, W.R. 1929. "*The Custom of Couvade*. Manchester: Manchester University Press.

de Beauvoir, Simone. 1965. *Force of Circumstance*. London: Penguin.

——. [1949] 1968. *Le deuxième sexe*. 2 tomes. Paris: Gallimard.

——. 1977. *All Said and Done*. Harmondsworth: Penguin.

DeCrow, K. 1975. *Sexist Justice*. New York: Vintage.

Delamont, S. 1983. "The Conservative School? Sex Roles at Home, at Work and at School." In *Gender, Class and Education*, ed. S. Walker and L. Barton. London: Falmer Press.

Delphy, Christine. 1976. "Continuities and Discontinuities in Marriage and Divorce." In *Sexual Divisions and Society: Process and Change*, ed. D.L. Barker and S. Allen. London: Tavistock.

——. 1977. "Nos amis et nous." *Questions féministes* 1.

——. 1984. *Close to Home: A Materialist Analysis of Women's Oppression*. Amherst: University of Massachusetts Press.

d'Emilio, John. 1983a. *Sexual Politics, Sexual Communities: The Making of a Homosexual Minority in the United States, 1940–1970*. Chicago: University of Chicago Press.

——. 1983b. "Capitalism and Gay Identity." In *Powers of Desire*, ed. Ann B. Snitow, Christine Stansell, and Sharon Thompson. New York: Monthly Review Press.

Denton, Margaret A., and Alfred Hunter. 1982. "Economic Sectors and Gender Discrimination in Canada: A Critique and Test of Bloch and Walker . . . and Some New Evidence." Women's Bureau Series A (Equality in the Workplace), No. 6. Ottawa: Labour Canada.

Dhavernas, Odile. 1981. "Féminisme et institutions." *Les temps modernes* no. 418 (May).

Diary of a Conference on Sexuality. 1982. New York: Faculty Press.

Dickens, B.M. 1966. *Abortion and the Law*. Bristol: MacGibbon & Kee.

——. 1976. The Morgentaler Case: Criminal Process and Abortion Law." *Osgoode Hall Law Journal* 14.

Dickinson, John A. 1980. "The Pre-contact Huron Population: A Reappraisal." *Ontario History* 72, no. 3.

Diner, Helen, 1965. *Mothers and Amazons: The First Feminine History of Culture*. New York: Julien.

Dinnerstein, Dorothy. 1976. *The Mermaid and the Minotaur: Sexual Arrangements and Human Malaise*. New York: Harper & Row.

Discussion Collective No. 6. 1972. *Women Unite!* Toronto: Canadian Women's Educational Press.

District 65. 1980. "Union Women on Feminism." *Heresies* 9.

Doerr, Audrey. 1984. "Women's Rights in Canada: Social and Economic Realities." *Atlantis* 9, no. 2 (Spring).

Donovan, Josephine. 1985. *Feminist Theory: The Intellectual Traditions of American Feminism*. New York: F. Ungar.

Drache, Daniel. 1978. Introduction to *The Practical Guide to Canadian Political Economy*, ed. Daniel Drache and Wallace Clement. Toronto: Lorimer.

Drache, Daniel, and Wallace Clement, eds. 1985. *The New Practical Guide to Canadian Political Economy*. Toronto: Lorimer.

Dubois, E., and Linda Gordon. 1984. Seeking Ecstasy on the Battlefield: The Politics of Danger and Pleasure in Nineteenth-century Feminist Sexual Thought." In *Pleasure and Danger: Exploring Female Sexuality*, ed. Carole S. Vance. Boston and London: Routledge & Kegan Paul.

Dumont-Johnson, Micheline. 1968. *Histoire de la condition de la femme dans la province de Québec*. (Etude pour la Commission Royal d'enquête sur le statut de la femme au Canada.) Ottawa: Imprimeur de la reine.

——. 1980. "Des garderies au XIXe siècle: les salles d'asile des soeurs Grises à Montréal." *Revue d'Histoire de l'Amérique française* 34, no. 1 (June): 27–55.

Dworkin, Andrea. 1979. *Pornography: Men Possessing Women*. New York: Perigee.

Eccles, Sandra. 1984. "Women in the Australian Labour Force." In *Unfinished Business: Social Justice for Women in Australia*, ed. Dorothy H. Broom. Sydney: George Allen & Unwin.

Echols, Alice. 1984. "The Taming of the Id: Feminist Sexual Politics, 1968–83." In *Pleasure and Danger: Exploring Female Sexuality*, ed. Carol Vance. London: Routledge & Kegan Paul.

Edholm, Felicity, Olivia Harris, and Kate Young. 1977. "Conceptualizing Women." *Critique of Anthropology* 3, nos. 9 and 10.

Edwards, Meredith, T. Harper, and Margaret Harrison. 1985. "Child Support: Public or Private Duty?" *Australian Society* 4, no. 4 (April).

Edwards, Richard. 1979. *Contested Terrain: The Transformation of the Workplace in the Twentieth Century*. New York: Basic Books.

Ehrenreich, Barbara. 1980. "A Funny Thing Happened on the Way to Socialist Feminism." *Heresies* 9.

———. 1983. *The Hearts of Men: American Dreams and the Flight from Commitment*. London: Pluto.

Ehrenreich, Barbara, and John Ehrenreich. 1978. "The Professional-Managerial Class." In *Between Labour and Capital*, ed. P. Walker. Montreal: Black Rose.

Ehrenreich, Barbara, and Deirdre English. 1979. *For Her Own Good: 150 Years of Experts' Advice to Women*. Garden City, NY: Anchor/Doubleday.

Eichler, Margrit. 1975. "Sociological Research on Women in Canada." *Canadian Review of Sociology and Anthropology* 12, no. 4 (November).

———. 1983. *Families in Canada Today: Recent Changes and Their Policy Consequences*. Toronto: Gage.

———. 1985. "And the Work Never Ends: Feminist Contributions." *Canadian Review of Sociology and Anthropology* 22, no. 5 (December).

Eisenstein, Zillah R., ed. 1979. *Capitalist Patriarchy and the Case for Socialist Feminism*. New York: Monthly Review Press.

———. 1981. *The Radical Future of Liberal Feminism*. New York: Longman.

Ellison, K., and J.L. Genz. 1978. "The Police Officer as Burned Out Samaritan." *FBI Law Enforcement Bulletin* 47, no. 3 (March).

Engels, Frederick. [1884] 1972. *The Origin of the Family, Private Property and the State*. New York: Pathfinder.

Etienne, Mona, and Eleanor Leacock. 1980. Introduction to *Woman and Colonization: Anthropological Perspectives*, ed. Mona Etienne and Eleanor Leacock. New York: Praeger.

European Centre for Work and Society. 1984. *European Centre for Work and Society News*, Issue 5 (September). P.O. Box 3073, 6202 NB Maastricht, Netherlands.

Evans, Sara. 1980. *Personal Politics: The Roots of Women's Liberation in the Civil Rights Movement and the New Left*. New York: Vintage.

Faderman, Lillian. 1981. *Surpassing the Love of Men: Romantic Friendship and Love between Women from the Renaissance to the Present*. New York: William Morrow & Co.

Fahmy-Eid, Nadia, and Micheline Dumont, eds. 1983. *Maîtresses de maison, maîtresses d'école: femmes, famille et éducation dans l'histoire du Québec*. Montreal: Boréal Express.

Fahmy-Eid, Nadia, and Nicole Laurin-Frenette. 1980. "Théories de la famille et rapports familles-pouvoirs dans le secteur éducatif au Québec et en France 1850–1960." *Revue d'Histoire de l'Amérique française* 34, no. 2 (September): 197–223.

Fanon, Franz. 1961. *Les damnés de la terre*. Paris: Maspéro.

Farnsworth, B.B. 1977. "Bolshevik Alternatives and the Soviet Family: The 1929 Marriage Law Debate." In *Women in Russia*, ed. D. Atkinson, A. Dallin, and G.W. Lapidus. Stanford, CA: Stanford University Press.

Fee, Elizabeth. 1981. "Is Feminism a Threat to Scientific Objectivity?" *International Journal of Women's Studies* 4. (September–October).

Feinstein, Karen, ed. 1979. *Working Women and Families*. Beverly Hills, CA: Sage.

Felker, Marcia. 1982. "The Political Economy of Sexism in Industrial Health." *Social Science and Medicine* 18.

Field, Debbie. 1983. "Women's Committees in Unions." In *Union Sisters*, ed. Linda Briskin and Lynda Yanz. Toronto: Women's Press.

Fine, B. 1979. "Law and Class." In *Capitalism and the Rule of Law*, ed. B. Fine et al. London: Hutchinson.

——. 1984. *Democracy and the Rule of Law: Liberal Ideals and Marxist Critiques*. London: Pluto Press.

Fine, B., R. Kinsey, J. Lea, S. Picciotto, and J. Young, eds. 1979. *Capitalism and the Rule of Law*. London: Hutchinson.

Finn, Geraldine, and Angela Miles, eds. 1982. *Feminism in Canada: From Pressure to Politics*. Montreal: Black Rose.

Firestone, Shulamith. 1970. *The Dialectic of Sex: The Case for Feminist Revolution*. New York: William Morrow.

FitzGerald, Maureen, Connie Guberman, and Margie Wolfe. 1982. *Still Ain't Satisfied: Canadian Feminism Today*. Toronto: Women's Press.

Flax, Jane. 1981. "Do Feminists Need Marxism?" In *Building Feminist Theory: Best of Quest*, ed. Quest Staff. New York: Longman.

Folbré, Nancy. 1983. "Of Patriarchy Born: The Political Economy of Fertility Decisions." *Feminist Studies* 9, no. 2 (Summer).

Folché-Delbosc, Isabel. 1977. "Women of Three-Rivers, 1651–63." In *The Neglected Majority*, ed. Susan Mann Trofimenkoff and Allison Prentice. Toronto: McClelland & Stewart.

Foucault, Michel. 1978. *The History of Sexuality: Volume I, An Introduction*. New York: Random House.

Fournier, Pierre. 1976. *The Quebec Establishment: The Ruling Class and the State*. Montreal: Black Rose.

Fox, Bonnie, ed. 1980. *Hidden in the Household*. Toronto: Women's Press.

Fox, Bonnie J., and John Fox. 1983. "Effects of Women's Employment on Wages." *Canadian Journal of Sociology* 8, no. 3 (Summer).

Fox Keller, Evelyn, and Christine Grontkowski. 1983. "The Mind's Eye." In *Discovering Reality*, ed. S. Harding and M.B. Hintikka. Dordrecht, Holland: D. Reidal.

Frechette, Louis-Albert. 1943. "Hommage à la mère canadienne." *L'action nationale* 21, no. 2.

Freudenberger, H.J. 1977. "Burn-Out: Occupational Hazard of Child Care Workers." *Child Care Quarterly* 6, no. 2.

Freudenberger, H.J., and G. Richelson. 1980. *Burn-Out*. New York: Doubleday.

Friedan, Betty. 1963. *The Feminine Mystique*. New York: Dell.

Friedl, Ernestine. 1975. *Women and Men: An Anthropologist's View*. New York: Holt, Rinehart & Winston.

Frogett, Lynn. 1981. "Feminism and the Italian Trade Unions." *Feminist Review* 8.

Gabin, Nancy. 1982. "They Have Placed a Penalty on Womanhood: The Protest Actions of Women Auto Workers in Detroit Area UAW Locals." *Feminist Studies* 8, no. 2.

Gagnon, Mona-Josée. 1974a. *Les femmes vues par le Québec des hommes*. Montreal: Le Jour, Editeur.

———. 1974b. "Les femmes dans le mouvement syndical québécois." *Sociologie et Sociétés* 7, no. 2

Gallop, Jane. 1982. *The Daughter's Seduction: Feminism and Psychoanalysis*. Ithaca, NY: Cornell University Press.

Gardiner, Jean. 1975. "Women's Domestic Labour." *New Left Review* 89 (January–February).

Garner, Shirley Nelson, Claire Kahane, and Madelon Sprengnether. 1985. *The (M)other Tongue: Essays in Feminist Psychoanalytic Interpretation*. Ithaca and London: Cornell University Press.

Gaskell, J. 1981. "Sex Inequalities in Education for Work: The Case of Business Education." *Canadian Journal of Education* 6, no. 2.

Gaucher, Dominique. 1981. "*L'égalité salariale des femmes: Ebauche d'une problématique de la discrimination sexuelle et quelques données*." In *Travailler au Québec*, under the direction of Collette Bernier, Roche Bibeau, Jacques Dofny, and Pierre Doray. Laval, Quebec: Les Editions coopératives Albert Saint-Martin.

Gavigan, Shelley. Forthcoming. "The Development of the Therapeutic Exception in Abortion: Medical Insistence and Women's Resistance." *Canadian Journal of Women and the Law*.

———. 1986. "Women, Law and Patriarchal Relations: Perspectives in the Sociology of Law." In *Social Dimensions of Legal Control*, ed. N. Boyd. Scarborough, Ont.: Prentice-Hall.

Genge, Sue. 1986. "Women, Work and Unions." Public Lecture, Champlain Feminist Issues Series, Trent University, Peterborough.

Geoffroy, Renée, and Paule Sainte-Marie. 1971. *Attitude of Union Workers to Women in Industry*. Studies of the Royal Commission on the Status of Women in Canada, No. 9. Ottawa: Supply and Services Canada.

Gilligan, Carol. 1982. *In a Different Voice: Psychological Theory and Women's Development*. Cambridge: Harvard University Press.

Gillmeister, Dorothy. 1980. "The Equal Opportunity Fantasy: A Hard Look at Voluntary Affirmative Action." *Status of Women* 6, no. 2.
Gilman, Charlotte Perkins. [1898] 1966. *Women and Economics*. Edited by Carl Degler. New York: Harper Torchbooks.
——. [1903] 1972. *The Home: Its Work and Influence*. Urbana: University of Illinois Press.
——. [1899] 1973. *The Yellow Wallpaper*. Old Westbury, NY: Feminist Press.
Gittens, Diana. 1982. *Fair Sex: Family Size and Structure 1900–39*. London: Hutchinson.
Godelier, Maurice. 1981. "The Origins of Male Dominance." *New Left Review* no. 127.
——. 1978. "The Object and Method of Marxist Economic Anthropology." In *Relations of Production*, ed. David Seddon. London: Frank Cass.
Gordon, Linda. 1977. *Woman's Body, Woman's Right: A Social History of Birth Control in America*. Harmondsworth: Penguin.
Gordon, Linda, and Allen Hunter. 1977–78. "Sex, Family, and the New Right: Anti-Feminism as a Political Force." *Radical America* 11, no. 6.
Gorz, André. 1982. *Farewell to the Working Class: An Essay on Post-Industrial Socialism*. Boston: South End Press.
Gough, Ian. 1979. *The Political Economy of the Welfare State*. London: MacMillan.
——. 1972. "Marx's Theory of Productive and Unproductive Labour." *New Left Review* no. 76 (November–December).
Gowland, Patricia. 1983. *Women in Families: The Sexual Division of Labour and Australian Family Policy*. Melbourne: Knox Community Relations Centre.
Gramsci, Antonio. 1971. "State and Civil Society." In *Selections from the Prison Notebooks of Antonio Gramsci*, ed. and trans. Quentin Hoare and Geoffrey Howell Smith. New York: International.
Grand'maison, Jacques. 1970. *Nationalisme et religion*, Vol. 2. Montreal: Beauchemin.
Graycar, Adam, ed. *Retreat from the Welfare State*. Sydney: George Allen & Unwin.
Green, Cecelia. 1985. "Marxist-feminism and Third World Liberation." *Fireweed* 20.
Greenspan, Kenneth. 1978. "Biologic Feedback and Cardiovascular Disease." *Psychosomatics* 19, no. 11.
Greenwood, Victoria, and Jock Young. 1976. *Abortion in Demand*. London: Pluto Press.
Gregory, J. 1979. "Sex Discrimination, Work and the Law." In *Capitalism and the Rule of Law*, ed. B. Fine et al. London: Hutchinson.
Grossman, Atina. 1978. "Abortion and Economic Crises: The 1931 Campaign Against S218 in Germany." *New German Critique* 14 (Spring).
——. 1983. "The New Woman and the Rationalization of Sexuality in Weimar Germany." In *Powers of Desire*, ed. Ann B. Snitow, Christine Stansell, and Sharon Thompson. New York: Monthly Review Press.

Groulx, Lionel. 1919. *La naissance d'une race*. Montreal: Bibliothèque de l'action française.

——. 1924. *Notre maître le passé*. Montreal: Bibliothèque de l'action française.

Guberman, Connie, and Margie Wolfe, eds. 1985. *No Safe Place: Violence Against Women and Children*. Toronto: Women's Press.

Guberman, Nancy. 1983. "Working, Mothering and Militancy: Women in the CNTU." In *Union Sisters: Women in the Labour Movement*, ed. Linda Briskin and Lynda Yanz. Toronto: Women's Press.

Gunderson, Morley. 1975. "Male-Female Wage Differentials and the Impact of Equal Pay Legislation." *Review of Economics and Statistics* 57, no. 4 (November).

Haber, Barbara. 1980. "Is the Personal Still Political?" *Feminist Studies* 5, no. 3.

Hackett, J.D. 1920. "Vacation with Pay for Factory Workers." *Survey* 44 (August 16).

Hall, S. 1980. "Reformism and the Legislation of Consent." In *Permissiveness and Control: The Fate of the Sixties Legislation*, ed. National Deviancy Conference. London: MacMillan, 1980.

Hall, S., C. Crichter, T. Jefferson, J. Clarke, and B. Roberts. 1978. *Policing the Crisis: Mugging the State and Law and Order*. London: MacMillan.

Hamilton, J.A. 1962. *Postpartum Psychiatric Problems*. St. Louis, MO: C.V. Mosby.

Hamilton, Roberta. 1978. *The Liberation of Women*. London: George Allen & Unwin.

——. 1986. "The Collusion with Patriarchy: A Psychoanalytic Account." In *The Politics of Diversity: Feminism, Marxism and Canadian Society*, ed. Michèle Barrett and Roberta Hamilton. London: Verso.

Hansen, Bert. 1982. "The Historical Construction of Homosexuality." Paper presented to the Department of Anthropology, University of Toronto.

Harding, Sandra, and Merrill B. Hintikka, eds. 1983. *Discovering Reality: Feminist Perspectives on Epistemology, Metaphysics, Methodology, and Philosophy of Science*. Dordrecht, Holland: D. Reidal.

Harrison, R., and F. Mort. 1980. "Patriarchal Aspects of Nineteenth Century State Formation: Property Relations, Marriage and Divorce, and Sexuality." In *Capitalism, State Formation and Marxist Theory*, ed. P. Corrigan. London: Quartet.

Hartman, Grace. 1976. "Women and the Unions." In *Women in the Canadian Mosaic*, ed. Gwen Matheson. Toronto: Peter Martin.

Hartmann, Heidi. 1979. "Capitalism, Patriarchy, and Job Segregation by Sex." In *Capitalist Patriarchy and the Case for Socialist Feminism*, ed. Zillah R. Eisenstein. New York: Monthly Review Press.

Hartsock, Nancy. 1983. "The Feminist Standpoint: Developing the Ground for a Specifically Feminist Historical Materialism." In *Discovering Reality*, ed. Sandra Harding and Merrill B. Hintikka. Dordrecht, Holland: D. Reidal.

Hawrylyshyn, Oli. 1978. *Estimating the Value of Household Work in Canada*. Ottawa: Ministry of Industry, Trade and Commerce.

Hay, D., P. Linebaugh, J.G. Rule, E.P. Thompson, and C. Winslow. 1975. *Albion's Fatal Tree*. New York: Pantheon.

Hayden, D. 1979. "Charlotte Perkins Gilman and the Kitchenless House." *Radical History Review* 21:225–47.

——. 1981. *The Grand Domestic Revolution: A History of Feminist Designs for American Homes, Neighbourhoods and Cities*. Cambridge: MIT Press.

Health and Welfare Canada. 1983. *Canada Health Manpower Inventory*. Ottawa: Health and Information Division.

Heap, Dan. 1983. "A Proposed NDP Policy for the Clothing and Textile Industry in Canada." A report prepared by Dan Heap's Office (MP Spadina). Toronto (March).

Heer, David. 1981. "Soviet Population Policy: Four Model Futures." In *Soviet Population Policy: Conflicts and Constraints*, ed. Helen Desfosses. New York: Pergamon Press.

Heidenreich, Conrad. 1971. *Huronia: A History and Geography of the Huron Indians 1600–1650*. Toronto: McClelland & Stewart.

Heitlinger, Alena. 1979. *Women and State Socialism: Sex Inequality in the Soviet Union and Czechoslovakia*. Montreal: McGill-Queen's University Press.

——. 1980. "Marxism, Feminism, and Sex Equality." In *Women in Eastern Europe and the Soviet Union*, ed. Tova Yedlin. New York: Praeger.

——. 1986. *Reproduction, Medicine and the Socialist State*. London: MacMillan.

Henripin, Jacques, et al. 1981. *Les Enfants qu'on n'a plus au Québec*. Montreal: Presses de l'Université de Montréal.

Henripin, Jacques, and Evelyne Lapierre. 1979. *La fin de la revanche des berceaux: Qu'en pensent les Québécoises?* Montreal: Presses de l'Université de Montréal.

Hill, Christina Maria. 1973. "Women in the Canadian Economy." In *Canada Ltd.: The Political Economy of Dependency*, ed. R. Laxer. Toronto: McClelland & Stewart.

Hindess, Barry, and Paul Q. Hirst. 1975. *Pre-Capitalist Modes of Production*. London: Routledge & Kegan Paul.

Hirst, Paul Q. 1975. "Marx and Engels on Law, Crime and Morality." In *Critical Criminology*, ed. I. Taylor, P. Walton, and J. Young. London: Routledge & Kegan Paul.

——. 1979. *On Law and Ideology*. London: MacMillan.

——. 1980. "Law, Socialism and Rights." In *Radical Issues in Criminology*, ed. P. Carlen and M. Collison. Oxford: Martin Robertson.

Hochschild, Arlie Russell. 1983. *The Managed Heart: The Commercialism of Human Feelings*. Berkeley: University of California.

Holmes, T., and R. Rahe. 1967. "The Social Adjustment Rating Scale." *Journal of Psychosomatic Research* 1, no. 2.

Horowitz, Gad. 1968. *Canadian Labour in Politics*. Toronto: University of Toronto Press.

——. 1977. *Repression*. Toronto: University of Toronto Press.

Houle, Danielle. 1972. *Critique de l'orientation du FLF*. Montreal: polycopié, s.m.d.

Howe, Louise Kapp. 1975. *Pink Collar Workers*. New York: Avon Books.
Howell, Nancy. 1976. "Toward a Uniformitarian Theory of Human Paleodemography." *Journal of Human Evolution* 5.
——. 1979. *Demography of the Do be !Kung*. New York: Academic Press.
Humphries, Jane. 1977a. "Class Struggle and the Persistence of the Working Class Family." *Cambridge Journal of Economics* 1, no. 3.
——. 1977b. "The Working-Class Family, Women's Liberation and the Class Struggle: The Case of Nineteenth-century British History." *Review of Radical Political Economics* 9, no. 3.
Hunt, A. 1981a. "The Politics of Law and Justice." *Politics and Power* 4: 3–26.
——. 1981b. "Dichotomy and Contradiction in the Sociology of Law." *British Journal of Law and Society* 8, no. 1: 47–77.
Hutter, Bridget, and Gillian Williams. 1981. *Controlling Women: The Normal and the Deviant*. London: Croom Helm.
Illich, Ivan. 1983. *Gender*. London: Marion Boyars.
Innis, Harold Adams. 1936. *Settlement and the Mining Frontier. Canadian Frontiers of Settlement* Vol. 9, part 2. Edited by W.A. Mackintosh and W.L.G. Joerg. Toronto: Macmillan.
——. [1940] 1954. *The Cod Fisheries: The History of an International Economy*, rev. ed. Toronto: University of Toronto Press.
——. 1956. *Essays in Canadian Economic History*. Edited by Mary Q. Innis. Toronto: University of Toronto Press.
——. 1964. *The Bias of Communication*. Toronto: University of Toronto Press.
——. [1930] 1970. *The Fur Trade in Canada: An Introduction to Canadian Economic History*, rev. ed. Toronto: University of Toronto Press.
——. 1980. *The Idea File of Harold Adams Innis*, ed. William Christian. Toronto: University of Toronto Press.
International Labour Organization. 1984. *World Labour Report* 1. Geneva: ILO.
——. 1982. *Social and Labour Bulletin*. Geneva: ILO.
International Ladies' Garment Workers' Union. 1978. "Toronto Ladies' Coat and Suit Employees Health and Welfare Fund, Rules and Regulations." Toronto: ILGWU, December 1.
Jackson, Jean E. 1983. "Book Review." *Signs*, Winter: 306.
Jacobowitz, Florence. 1986. "Feminist Film Theory and Social Reality." *Cine Action!* Nos. 3/4 (January).
Jaggar, Alison. 1983. *Feminist Politics and Human Nature*. Sussex: Harvester Press.
Jaggar, Alison, and Paula Rothenberg, eds. 1984. *Feminist Frameworks: Alternative Theoretical Accounts of the Relations between Women and Men*, 2nd ed. New York: McGraw-Hill.
Jameson, Fredric. 1983. "Postmodernism and Consumer Society." In *The Anti-Aesthetic*, ed. Hal Foster. Port Townsend, WA: Bay Press.
Jancar, Barbara Wolfe. 1978. *Women under Communism*. Baltimore: Johns Hopkins University Press.
Jean, Michèle, ed. 1977. *Québécoises du 20e siècle*. Montreal: Quinze.

Jessop, Bob. 1980. "The Political Interdeterminacy of Democracy." In *Marxism and Democracy*, ed. A. Hunt. London: Lawrence & Wishart.

Johnson, Leo. 1975. "The Political Economy of Ontario Women in the Nineteenth Century." In *Women at Work: Ontario 1850–1930*, ed. Janice Acton et al. Toronto: Women's Press.

Jones, Frank. 1984. "Income Inequality." In *Unfinished Business: Social Justice for Women in Australia*, ed. Dorothy H. Broom. Sydney: George Allen & Unwin.

Jordan, Brigitte. 1978. *Birth in Four Cultures: A Cross-cultural Investigation of Childbirth in Holland, Sweden and the United States*. Montreal: Eden Press.

Joseph, Gloria. 1981. "The Incompatible Menage à Trois: Marxism, Feminism, and Racism." In *Women and Revolution*, ed. Lydia Sargent. Boston: South End Press.

Kadar, Marlene. 1982. "Sexual Harassment as a Form of Social Control." In *Still Ain't Satisfied*, ed. Maureen FitzGerald, Connie Guberman, and Margie Wolfe. Toronto: Women's Press.

Kaloyanova, Fina. 1976. "Women at Work." *World Health* (August–September).

Karacan, I., and R.L. Williams. 1970. "Current Advances in Theory and Practice Relating to Postpartum Syndromes." *Psychiatry in Medicine* 1: 307–28.

Karasek, R.A. 1979. "Job Demands, Job Decision Latitude, and Mental Strain: Implication for Job Redesign." *Administrative Science Quarterly* 24: 285–308.

Kealey, Linda, ed. 1979. *A Not Unreasonable Claim: Women and Reform in Canada, 1880s–1920s*. Toronto: Women's Press.

——. 1984. "Canadian Socialism and the Woman Question, 1900–1914." *Labour/Le Travail* 13 (Spring).

Keddie, N. 1971. "Classroom Knowledge." In *Knowledge and Control*, ed. Michael Young. London: Collier-Macmillan.

Kelly, G., and A. Nihlen. 1982. "Schooling and the Reproduction of Patriarchy: Unequal Workloads, Unequal Rewards." In *Cultural and Economic Reproduction in Education*, ed. M. Apple. London: Routledge & Kegan Paul.

Kelly-Gagol, Joan. 1977. "Did Women Have a Renaissance?" In *Becoming Visible: Women in European History*, ed. Renate Bridenthal and Claudia Koonz. Boston: Houghton Mifflin.

Knight, P. 1977. "Women and Abortion in Victorian and Edwardian England." *History Workshop Journal* 4: 57–68.

Kome, Penney. 1983. *The Taking of Twenty-eight*. Toronto: Women's Press.

Kostash, Myrna. 1980. *Long Way From Home: The Story of the Sixties Generation in Canada*. Toronto: Lorimer.

Kowaluk, Lucia. 1972. "The Status of Women in Canada." In *Mother Was Not a Person*, ed. Margaret Andersen. Montreal: Our Generation Press.

Kruckman, L. 1980. "From Institutionalization to Self-Help: A Review of Postpartum Depression Treatment." Chicago: School of Public Health, University of Illinois Medical Center. Photocopy.

Kupferer, H.J.K. 1965. "Couvade: Ritual or Illness?" *American Anthropologist* 67: 99–102.

Labour Canada. 1981. *Canadian Women and Job Related Laws*. Ottawa: Labour Canada.

——. 1983. *Part-Time Work in Canada*. Report of the Commission of Inquiry into Part-Time Work. Ottawa: Supply and Services Canada.

Labour Canada Women's Bureau. 1983. *Maternity and Child Care Leave in Canada*. Ottawa: Supply and Services Canada.

Labour Gazette. August 1951, September 1951, July, August and September 1954, September 1955, September 1957, August and October 1958.

Lacelle, Nicole. 1980. "Les Yvettes nous conduiront au oui." *Le Devoir*, April 25, p. 5.

Laclau, Ernesto, and Chantal Mouffe. 1982. "Recasting Marxism: Hegemony and New Political Movements." *Socialist Review* 12, no. 6 (November–December).

Lanctôt, Louise. 1980. La genèse et l'évolution du mouvement de la libération des femmes à Montréal, 1969–1979." M.A. thesis, Université du Québec à Montréal.

Lapidus, Gail. 1977. "Sexual Equality and Soviet Policy." In *Women in Russia*, ed. D. Atkinson, A. Dallin and G.W. Lapidus. Stanford, CA: Stanford University Press.

Latham, Barbara, and Cathy Kess, eds. 1980. *In Her Own Right: Selected Essays on Women's History in B.C.* Victoria, B.C.: Camosun College.

Laurin-Frenette, Nicole. 1979. *Production de l'Etat et forme de la nation*. Montreal: Nouvelle Optique.

——. 1982. "On the Women's Movement, Anarchism and the State." *Our Generation* 15, no. 2.

Lavigne, Marie, and Yolande Pinard, eds. 1977. *Les femmes dans la société québécoise*. Montreal: Boréal Express.

Lavigne, Marie, Yolande Pinard, and Jennifer Stoddart. 1979. "The Féderation nationale St-Jean Baptiste and the Women's Movement in Quebec." In *A Not Unreasonable Claim*, ed. Linda Kealey. Toronto: Women's Press.

Leacock, Eleanor. 1978. "Women's Status in Egalitarian Society: Implications for Social Evolution." *Current Anthropology* 19, no. 2.

——. 1980. "Montagnais Women and the Jesuit Program for Colonization." In *Woman and Colonization: Anthropological Perspectives*, ed. M. Etienne and E. Leacock. New York: Praeger.

——. 1981. *Myths of Male Dominance: Collected Articles on Women Cross-Culturally*. New York: Monthly Review Press.

Lebowitz, M. 1982. "The General and the Specific in Marn's Theory of Crisis." *Studies in Political Economy* (Winter).

Lee, Richard. 1969. "!Kung Bushmen Subsistence: An Input-Output Analysis." In *Environment and Cultural Behaviour*, ed. A.P. Vayda. New York: Natural History Press.

——. 1979. The !Kung San: Men, Women, and Work in a Foraging Society. Cambridge: Cambridge University Press.

Légaré, Anne. 1982. "Towards a Marxian Theory of Canadian Federalism." *Studies in Political Economy* 8.

Leiss, William, Stephen Kline, and Sut Jhally. 1986. *Social Communication in Advertising*. Toronto: Methuen.

Levine, David. 1977. *Family Formation in an Age of Nascent Capitalism*. London: Academic Press.

Lewis, O. 1958. *Village Life in North India*. Urbana: University of Illinois Press.

Lipset, Seymour Martin. 1971. *Agrarian Socialism: The Co-operative Commonwealth Federation in Saskatchewan: A Study in Political Sociology*, rev. ed. Berkeley: University of California Press.

Livingston, J.E. 1976. *An Assessment of Vitamin B_6 Status in Women with Post-Partum Depression*. M.Sc. Thesis, Department of Medical Genetics, University of British Columbia.

Llewellyn, M. 1980. "Studying Girls at School: The Implication of Confusion." In *Schooling for Women's Work*, ed. R. Deem. London: Routledge & Kegan Paul.

League ouvrière révolutionnaire. 1978. *Lutte des femmes et lutte de classe*. Montreal: Editions d'avant-garde.

Lorber, Judith. 1981. "On *The Reproduction of Mothering* Debate." *Signs* 6, no. 3.

Love, Barbara, and Elizabeth Shanklin. 1978. "The Answer Is Matriarchy." In *Our Right to Love*, ed. Ginny Vida. Englewood Cliffs, NJ: Prentice Hall.

Lovenduski, Joni, and Jill Hills, eds. 1981. *The Politics of the Second Electorate*. London: Routledge & Kegan Paul.

Lowe, Graham. 1980. "Women, Work and the Office: The Feminization of Clerical Occupations in Canada, 1901–1931." *Canadian Journal of Sociology* 5.

Lower, A.R.M. 1938. *The North American Assault on the Canadian Forest: A History of the Lumber Trade between Canada and the United States*. Toronto: Ryerson.

Lumsden, D.P. 1981. "Is the Concept of 'Stress' of Any Use, Anymore?" In *Contributions to Primary Prevention in Mental Health*, ed. D. Randall. Toronto: Canadian Mental Health Association.

Luxton, Meg. 1980. *More Than a Labour of Love: Three Generations of Women's Work in the Home*. Toronto: Women's Press.

——. 1981. "Taking on the Double Day." *Atlantis* 7, no. 2.

——. 1982. "The Home: A Contested Terrain." In *Still Ain't Satisfied*, ed. Maureen FitzGerald, Connie Guberman, and Margie Wolfe. Toronto: Women's Press.

——. 1983. "Two Hands for the Clock: Changing Patterns in the Domestic Division of Labour." *Studies in Political Economy* 12.

Luxton, Meg, and Harriet Rosenberg. 1986. *Through the Kitchen Window: The Politics of Home and Family*. Toronto: Garamond Press.

McCaskell, Tim. 1983. "The Left and Gay Liberation." *Canadian Dimension* 17, no. 4.

McCune, Micki. 1981. "Fighting for Our Rights: The CLC Women's Conference." *Resources for Feminist Research* 10, no. 2.

MacDonald, M. 1981. "Schooling and the Reproduction of Class and Gender Relations." In *Education and the State*, Vol. 2, ed. R. Dale. London: Falmer Press.

McFarland, Joan. 1980. "Social Control in a Company Town." *Studies in Political Economy*, no. 4.

McIntosh, Mary. 1977. "Women, Crime and Criminology." Review Symposium, *British Journal of Criminology* 17, no. 4: 395–97.

———. 1978. "The State and the Oppression of Women." In *Feminism and Materialism*, ed. A. Kuhn and A. Wolpe. London: Routledge & Kegan Paul.

MacKinnon, Catherine A. 1979. *Sexual Harassment of Working Women: A Case of Sex Discrimination*. New Haven: Yale University Press.

———. 1982. "Feminism, Marxism, Method and the State: An Agenda for Theory." *Signs* 7, no. 3.

———. 1983a. "Feminism, Marxism, Method and the State: Toward Feminist Jurisprudence." *Signs* 8, no. 4.

———. 1983b. "The Male Ideology of Privacy: A Feminist Perspective on the Right to Abortion." *Radical America*.

Mackintosh, Maureen. 1977. "Reproduction and Patriarchy: A Critique of Claude Meillassoux, 'Femmes, greniers et capitaux.'" *Capital and Class*, no. 2 (Summer).

Mackintosh, W.A. 1938. *The Economic Background of Dominion-Provincial Relations*. Royal Commission Report on Dominion-Provincial Relations, Appendix III. Ottawa: King's Printer.

McLaren, A. 1977. "Women's Work and Regulation of Family Size: The Question of Abortion in the Nineteenth Century." *History Workshop Journal* 4, no. 7.

———. 1978a. "Birth Control and Abortion in Canada 1870–1920." *Canadian Historical Review* 59, no. 3.

———. 1978b. *Birth Control in Nineteenth Century England*. London: Croom Helm.

McRobbie, A. 1978. "Working Class Girls and the Culture of Feminity." In *Women Take Issue*, ed. Women's Studies Group. London: Hutchinson.

Magas, Branka. 1971. "Sex Politics: Class Politics." *New Left Review*, no. 66 (March–April).

Mahon, Rianne. 1977. "Canadian Public Policy: The Unequal Structure of Representation." In *The Canadian State*, ed. Leo Panitch. Toronto: University of Toronto Press.

———. 1979. "Regulatory Agencies: Captive Agents or Hegemonic Apparatuses?" *Studies in Political Economy* 1.

———. 1984. *The Politics of Industrial Restructuring: Canadian Textiles*. Toronto: University of Toronto Press.

Mahood, S. 1972. "The Women's Suffrage Movement in Canada and Saskatchewan." In *Women Unite!*, ed. Discussion Collective No. 6. Toronto: Canadian Women's Educational Press.

Maine, Deborah. 1979. "Does Abortion Affect Later Pregnancies?" *International Family Planning Perspectives* 5, no. 1.

Marchak, Patricia. 1973. "Women Workers and White Collar Unions." *The Canadian Review of Sociology and Anthropology* 10, no. 2.

——. 1974a. "The Canadian Labour Farce: Jobs for Women." In *Women in Canada*, ed. Marylee Stephenson. Don Mills, Ont.: General Publishing.

——. 1974b. "Les femmes, le travail et le syndicalisme au Canada." *Sociologie et Sociétés* 6, no. 1 (May). Reproduced in English in *International Journal of Sociology* 4 (Winter 1975–76).

——. 1977. *The Working Sexes*. Vancouver: University of British Columbia, Institute of Industrial Relations.

——. 1983. *Green Gold: The Forest Industry in British Columbia*, Chapter 8. Vancouver: University of British Columbia Press.

——. 1985. "The International Division of Women's Labour." Paper given at conference on "Women and Technology," Dubrovnik, Yugoslavia (August).

Marcuse, Herbert. 1955. *Eros and Civilization*. Boston: Beacon Press.

Maroney, Heather Jon. 1978. "Sexual Politics in Quebec: The Structures and Dynamics of Class, National and Sex Oppression." M.A. thesis, McMaster University, Hamilton, Ontario.

Marx, Karl. [1893] 1967. *Capital*, Vol. 2. Moscow: Progress Publishers.

——. [1887] 1976. *Capital: A Critique of Political Economy*, Vol. 1. Harmondsworth: Penguin.

Maslach, C. 1976. "Burned-Out." *Human Behaviour* (September).

Maslach, C., and A. Pines. 1977. "The Burn-out Syndrome in the Day Care Setting." *Child Care Quarterly* 6, no. 2 (Summer): 100–113.

——. 1979. "Burnout: The Loss of Human Caring." In *Experiencing Social Psychology*, ed. C. Maslach and A. Pines. New York: Knopf.

Matheson, Gwen, ed. 1976. *Women in the Canadian Mosaic*. Toronto: Peter Martin.

Matthews, F. 1902. "Vacations for the Workers." *The World's Week*. IV August.

Matthews, Ralph. 1983. *The Creation of Regional Dependency*. Toronto: University of Toronto Press.

Mattingly, M.A. 1977. "Sources of Stress and Burnout in Professional Child Care Work." *Child Care Quarterly* 6, no. 2.

Mead, Margaret. 1962. "A Cultural Anthropological Approach to Maternal Deprivation." In *Deprivation of Maternal Health Care: A Reassessment of its Effects*, ed. World Health Organization. Geneva: WHO.

Meillassoux, Claude. 1975. *Femmes, greniers, et capitaux*. Paris: Maspéro.

Meissner, M., et al. 1975. "No Exit for Wives: Sexual Division of Labour and the Cumulation of Household Demands." University of British Columbia. Photocopy. *Canadian Review of Sociology and Anthropology* 125, no. 4, part I (November).

Memmi, Albert. [1960] 1972. *Portrait du colonisé*. Montreal: L'Etincelle.

Menzies, Heather. 1981. *Women and the Chip: Case Studies of the Effects of Informatics on Employment in Canada*. Montreal: Institute for Research in Public Policy.
Metraux, A. 1963. "The Couvade." In *Handbook of South American Indians*, Vol. 5, ed. J.H. Stewart. New York: Cooper Square.
Middleton, Christopher. 1979. "The Sexual Division of Labour in Feudal England." *New Left Review*, nos. 113–114.
Miles, Angela. 1985. "Feminist Radicalism in the 1980's (1)." *Canadian Journal of Political and Social Theory* 9, nos. 1–2.
Milkman, Ruth. 1976. "Women's Work and Economic Crisis: Some Lessons of the Great Depression." *Review of Radical Political Economics* 8, no. 1: 73–97.
——. 1982. "Redefining 'Women's Work': The Sexual Division of Labour in the Auto Industry During World War II." *Feminist Studies* 8, no. 2.
Mill, John Stuart. [1869] 1970. "On the Subjection of Women." In *John Stuart Mill and Harriet Taylor Mill: Essays on Sex Equality*, ed. Alice S. Rossi. Chicago: University of Chicago Press.
Millett, Kate. 1969. *Sexual Politics*. New York: Doubleday.
——. 1979. *The Basement*. New York: Simon & Schuster.
Millman, Marcia, and Rosabeth Moss Kanter, eds. 1975. *Another Voice: Feminist Perspectives on Social Life and Social Science*. New York: Anchor/Doubleday.
Mitchell, Juliet. 1971. *Woman's Estate*. Harmondsworth: Penguin.
——. 1974. *Psychoanalysis and Feminism*. London: Pantheon.
——. 1976. "Women and Equality." In *The Rights and Wrongs of Women*, ed. Juliet Mitchell and Ann Oakley. Harmondsworth: Penguin.
——. 1984. *Women: The Longest Revolution*. New York: Pantheon.
Molyneux, Maxine. 1979. "Beyond the Domestic Labour Debate." *New Left Review* 116 (July–August).
——. 1981. "Women in Socialist Societies: Problems of Theory and Practice." In *Of Marriage and the Market: Women's Subordination in International Perspective*, ed. Kate Young et. al. London: CSE Books.
Monière, Denis. 1977. *Le Développement des idéologies au Québec: des origines à nos jours*. Montreal: Québec-Amérique.
Morgentaler, Henry. 1982. *Abortion and Contraception*. Don Mills: General Publishing.
Morris, Cerise. 1980. " 'Determination and Thoroughness': The Movement for a Royal Commission on the Status of Women in Canada." *Atlantis* 5, no. 2.
Morton, Peggy. 1972. "Women's Work Is Never Done." In *Women Unite!*, ed. Discussion Collective No. 6. Toronto: Canadian Women's Educational Press.
Mouffe, Chantal. 1981. "Hegemony and the Integral State in Gramsci." In *Silver Linings: Some Strategies for the Eighties*, ed. G. Bridges and R. Brunt. London: Lawrence & Wishart.
Muresan, Petre, and Ioan Copil. 1974. "Romania." In *Population Policy in Developed Countries*, ed. Bernard Berelson. New York: McGraw-Hill.
Murphy, R. 1979. *Sociological Theories of Education*. Toronto: McGraw-Hill Ryerson.

Muszynski, Alicja. 1984. "The Organization of Women and Ethnic Minorities in a Resource Industry: A Case Study of the Unionization of Shoreworkers in the B.C. Fishing Industry 1937–1949." *Journal of Canadian Studies* 19, no. 1 (special edition on fisheries).

Nash, June, and Maria Patricia Fernandez-Kelly. 1983. *Women, Men and the International Division of Labour*. Albany: State University of New York Press.

National Council on Welfare. 1979. *Women and Poverty*. Ottawa: National Council on Welfare.

——. 1985. *Poverty Profile 1985*. Ottawa: National Council on Welfare.

Newman, Lucille. 1966. "The Couvade: A Replay to Kupferer." *American Anthropologist* 68.

Ng, Roxana, and Judith Ramirez. 1981. *Immigrant Housewives in Canada*. Toronto: Immigrant Women's Centre.

Niosi, Jorge. 1981. *Canadian Capitalism: A Study of Power in the Canadian Business Establishment*. Toronto: Lorimer.

Noble, Joey. 1979. "Class-ifying the Poor: Toronto Charities 1850–1880." *Studies in Political Economy* 2.

Oakley, Ann. 1972. *Sex, Gender and Society*. London: Temple-Smith.

——. 1976. *Housewife*. Harmondsworth: Penguin.

——. 1981. "Normal Motherhood: An Exercise in Self-Control?" In *Controlling Women: The Normal and the Deviant*, ed. Bridget Hutter and Gillian Williams. London: Croom Helm.

O'Brien, Mary. 1981. *The Politics of Reproduction*. London: Routledge & Kegan Paul.

——. 1984. "Hegemony and Superstructure: A Critique of Neo-Marxism." In *Taking Sex Into Account: The Policy Consequences of Sexist Research*, ed. Jill McCalla Vickers. Ottawa: Carleton University Press.

O'Laughlin, Bridget. 1974. "Mediation of Contradiction: Why Mbum Women Do Not Eat Chicken." In *Woman, Culture and Society*, ed. Michelle Zimbalist Rosaldo and Louise Lamphere. Stanford, CA: Stanford University Press.

O'Laughlin, Mary Ann, and Bettina Cass. 1984. "Married Women's Employment Status and Family Income Distribution." Paper presented to the 54th ANZAAS Congress, Canberra.

O'Leary, Véronique, and Louise Toupin. 1981. *Québécoises deboutte!* Vol. 1. Montreal: Editions de Remue Ménage.

——. 1983. *Québécoises deboutte!* Vol. 2. Montreal: Editions de Remue Ménage.

Oliker, S. 1981. "Abortion and the Left: The Limits of Pro-Family Politics." *Socialist Review* 56.

Ornstein, Michael D. 1983. "Accounting for Gender Differentials in Job/Income in Canada: Results from a 1981 Survey." Women's Bureau Series A (Equality in the Workplace), No. 2. Ottawa: Labour Canada.

Ortner, Sherry B. 1974. "Is Female to Male as Nature Is to Culture?" In *Woman, Culture and Society*, ed. Michelle Zimbalist Rosaldo and Louise Lamphere. Stanford, CA: Stanford University Press.

Owen, Mary R. 1984a. "Changes in Labour Force Participation by Various Sectors of the Australian Population Since 1966." Melbourne: ACTU Working Women's Information Service Bulletin No. 84/3.

——. 1984b. "Women — A Wastefully Exploited Resource." *Search* 15, nos. 9–10 (October–November); 271–75.

Panitch, L. 1977. "The Role and Nature of the Canadian State." In *The Canadian State: Political Economy and Political Power*, ed. Leo Panitch. Toronto: University of Toronto Press.

Paoli, Chantal. 1982. "Women Workers and Maternity: Some Examples from Western Europe." *International Labour Review* 121, no. 1.

Park School Community Council. 1974. "Downtown Kids Aren't Dumb: They Need a Better Program." Brief to the Management Committee of the Toronto Board of Education. In *The Politics of the Canadian Public School*, ed. George Martell. Toronto: Lorimer.

Parker, Kathy, and Lisa Leghorn. 1981. *Women's Worth: Sexual Economics and the World of Women*. London: Routledge & Kegan Paul.

Parlee, M.B. 1980. "Psychological Aspects of Menstruation, Childbirth, and Menopause." In *Psychology of Women: Future Directions Research*, eds. J.A. Sherman and F.L. Denmark. New York: Psychological Dimensions.

Parr, Joy, ed. 1982. *Childhood and Family in Canadian History*. Toronto: McClelland & Stewart.

Parsons, T. 1959. "The School as a Social System. *Harvard Educational Review* 29, no. 4.

Pashukanis, Evgeny B. 1978. *Law and Marxism*. London: Ink Links.

Payette, Lise. 1982. *Le pouvoir? connais pas!* Montreal: Québec-Amérique.

Pedestal Collective. 1972. "Pie in the Sky . . . Royal Commission Recipe." In *Women Unite!*, ed. Discussion Collective No. 6. Toronto: Canadian Women's Educational Press.

Pelrine, Eleanor Wright. 1972. *Abortion in Canada*. Toronto: New Press.

Penner, Norman. 1977. *The Canadian Left: A Critical Analysis*. Scarborough, Ont.: Prentice-Hall.

Penney, Jennifer. 1983. *Hard Earned Wages: Women Fighting for Better Work*. Toronto: Women's Press.

Pentland, H. Clare, and Paul Phillips, eds. 1981. *Labour and Capital in Canada 1650–1860*. Toronto: Lorimer.

Petchesky, R.P. 1980. "Reproductive Freedom: Beyond 'A Woman's Right to Choose.' " In *Women: Sex and Sexuality*, ed. C.R. Stimpson and R.S. Person. Chicago: University of Chicago Press.

——. 1984. *Abortion and Woman's Choice: The State, Sexuality and Reproductive Freedom*. New York: Longman.

Phelps, Linda. 1981. "Patriarchy and Capitalism." In *Building Feminist Theory: Best of Quest*, ed. Quest staff. New York: Longman.

Phillips, Paul, and Erin Phillips. 1983. *Women and Work: Inequality in the Labour Market*. Toronto: Lorimer.

Picciotto, S. 1979. "The Theory of the State, Class Struggle and the Rule of Law." In *Capitalism and the Rule of Law*, ed. B. Fine et al. London: Hutchinson.

Pierson, Ruth Roach. 1977. "Women's Emancipation and the Recruitment of Women into the Labour Force in World War II." In *The Neglected Majority*, ed. Susan Mann Trofimenkoff and Allison Prentice. Toronto: McClelland & Stewart.

——. 1986. *"They're Still Women after All": The Second World War and Womanhood.* Toronto: McClelland & Stewart.

Pietrofessa, J., and N. Schlossberg. 1972. "Counsellor Bias and the Female Occupational Role." In *Woman in a Man-Made World*, 1st ed., ed. N. Glazer-Malbin. Chicago: Rand McNally.

Pinard, Yolande. 1977. "Les débutes du mouvement des femmes." In *Les femmes dans la société québécoise*, ed. Marie Lavigne and Yolande Pinard. Montreal: Boréal Express.

Pinchbeck, Ivy. [1930] 1981. *Women Workers and the Industrial Revolution, 1750–1850*. London: Virago.

Pines, A., and B. Kafry. 1978. "Occupational Tedium in the Social Services." *Social Work* (November) 499–508.

Polan, D. 1982. "Toward a Theory of Law and Patriarchy." In *The Politics of Law*, ed. D. Kairys. New York: Pantheon.

Pollak, O. 1961. *The Criminality of Women*. New York: A.S. Barnes.

Pollert, Anna. 1981. *Girls, Wives, Factory Lives*. London: MacMillan.

Porter, John. 1965. *The Vertical Mosaic: An Analysis of Social Class and Power in Canada*. Toronto: University of Toronto Press.

Porter, John, Marion Porter, and Bernard Blishen. 1982. *Stations and Callings: Making It Through Ontario's Schools*. Toronto: Methuen.

Porter, Marilyn. 1985. " 'She Was Skipper of the Shore-Crew': Notes on the History of the Sexual Division of Labour in Newfoundland." *Labour/Le Travail* 15 (Spring).

Poulantzas, Nicos. 1978. *Political Power and Social Classes*. London: Verso.

Power, M., with C. Wallace, S. Outhwaite, and S. Rosewarne. 1985. *Women, Work and Labour Market Programs*. Commissioned paper for the Kirby Committee of Inquiry into Labour Market Programs. Australia. Photocopy.

Prentice, Allison. 1977a. *The School Promoters: Education and Social Class in Mid 19th Century Upper Canada*. Toronto: McClelland & Stewart.

——. 1977b. "The Feminisation of Teaching." In *The Neglected Majority*, ed. Susan Mann Trofimenkoff and Allison Prentice. Toronto: McClelland & Stewart.

Proulx, M. 1978. *Five Million Women: A Study of the Canadian Housewife*. Ottawa: Advisory Council on the Status of Women.

Proulx, Serge, and Pierre Vallières, eds. 1983. *Changer de société*. Montreal: Québec-Amérique.

Pryor, Edward T. 1984. "Canadian Husband-Wife Families: Labour Force Participation and Income Trends 1971–1981." In *The Labour Force*, May 1984. Ottawa: Supply and Services Canada. Statistics Canada Cat. No. 71-001: 93-109.

Pugh, G. 1923. "Vacations with Pay." *Survey* 50: 435–36.

Les Québécois. 1977. Montreal: Parti Pris.

Radecki, Henry. 1979. One Year Later: The 1976–79 Strike at INCO: The Effect on Families. Sudbury: ISI.

Radicalesbians. 1973. "The Woman-Identified Woman." In *Radical Feminism*, ed. A. Koedt, E. Levine, and A. Rapone. New York: Quadrangle.

Raymer, Elizabeth, and Shaazka Beyerie. 1981. "Sheila Rowbotham — Exclusive Interview." *University of Toronto Women's Newsmagazine* 2, no. 3 (November–December): 3, 9.

Reich, Wilhelm. [1931] 1971. *The Invasion of Compulsory Sexual Morality*. New York: Farrar Straus & Giroux.

——. [1945] 1969. *The Sexual Revolution*. London: Usan Press.

Reiter, Ester. 1985. "Out of the Frying Pan and into the Fryer: The Organization of Work in a Fast Food Outlet." Ph.D. thesis, University of Toronto.

Reiter, Rayna, ed. 1975. *Toward an Anthropology of Women*. New York: Monthly Review Press.

Rice, M.S. 1937. *Working Class Wives: Their Health and Conditions*. Harmondsworth: Penguin.

Rich, Adrienne. 1980. "Compulsory Heterosexuality and Lesbian Existence." *Signs* 5, no. 4.

Rifkin, J. 1980. "Toward a Theory of Law and Patriarchy." *Harvard Women's Law Journal* 3.

Riley, Denise. 1981. Feminist Thought and Reproductive Control: The State and 'The Right to Choose.' " In *Women in Society: Interdisciplinary Essays*, ed. Cambridge Women's Studies Group. London: Virago.

——. 1983. *War in the Nursery: Theories of the Child and the Mother*. London: Virago.

Rioux, Marcel. 1968. "Sur l'évolution des idéologies au Québec." *Revue de l'Institute de sociologie, Université libre de Bruxelles* 1: 95–124.

Ritchie, Laurel, and Majorie Cohen. 1981. "Pierre Trudeau on Women." *Canadian Forum*. March.

Roberts, Barbara. 1979. " 'A Work of Empire': Canadian Reformers and British Female Immigration." In *A Not Unreasonable Claim*, ed. Linda Kealey. Toronto: Women's Press.

Robertson, J. 1976. "The Abusive Parent: A Different Perspective." *Canada's Mental Health* 24, no. 4 (December): 18–19.

——. 1980. "A Treatment Model for Post-Partum Depression." *Canada's Mental Health* (Summer).

Robertson, J., with A. Howard. 1980. *The Post-Partum Counselling Service Manual*. British Columbia: Ministry of Human Resources.

Rosaldo, Michelle Zimbalist. 1974. "Woman, Culture and Society." In *Woman, Culture, and Society*, ed. Michelle Zimbalist Rosaldo and Louise Lamphere. Stanford, CA: Stanford University Press.

Rosaldo, Michelle Zimbalist, and Louise Lamphere, eds. 1974. *Woman, Culture and Society*. Stanford, CA: Stanford University Press.

Rosenberg, Harriet. 1980. "After Birth Blues." *Healthsharing* (Winter): 18–20.

——. 1984. "The Home Is the Workplace." In *Double Exposure: Women's Health Hazards on the Job and at Home*, ed. Wendy Chavkin. New York: Monthly Review Press.

Ross, Kathleen Gallagher. 1979. *Good Day Care: Fighting for It, Getting It, Keeping It*. Toronto: Women's Press.

Routledge, Janet. 1981. "Women and Social Unionism." *Resources for Feminist Research* 10, no. 2.

Rowbotham, Sheila. 1973. *Hidden From History*. London: Pluto.

——. 1981. "The Trouble With 'Patriarchy.' " In *No Turning Back: Writings from the Women's Liberation Movement*, ed. Feminist Anthology Collective. London: Women's Press.

Rowbotham, Sheila, Lynne Segal, and Hilary Wainwright. 1979. *Beyond the Fragments*. London: Merlin Press.

Royal Commission on the Status of Women. 1970. *Report*. Ottawa: Information Canada.

Rubin, Gayle. 1975. "The Traffic in Women: Notes on the 'Political Economy' of Sex." In *Toward an Anthropology of Women*, ed. Rayna Reiter. New York: Monthly Review Press.

Russell, Susan. 1978. "Sex Role Socialization in the High School." Ph.D. thesis, University of Toronto.

——. 1979–80. "Learning Sex Roles in the High School." *Interchange* 10, no. 2.

Rutherford, F.W. 1971. *You and Your Baby: From Conception Through to the First Year*. New York: Signet.

Ryerson, Stanley. 1968. *Unequal Union: Confederation and the Roots of Conflict in the Canadas, 1815–1873*. Toronto: Progress Books.

Sacks, Karen. 1974. "Engels Revisited: Women, the Organization of Production and Private Property." In *Woman, Culture and Society*, ed. Michelle Zimbalist Rosaldo and Louise Lamphere. Stanford, CA: Stanford University Press.

——. 1979. *Sisters and Wives: The Past and Future of Sexual Equality*. Westport, CT: Greenwood Press.

Sahli, Nancy. 1979. "Smashing: Women's Relationships Before the Fall." *Chrysalis* 8:17–27.

Salter, Liora, Melody William, and Paul Heyer, eds. 1981. *Culture, Communications and Dependency: The Tradition of H.A. Innis*. New Jersey: Alex Publishers.

Sand, Cy-Thea. 1985. "Up From Under: Class Notes on Women's Writing." *Fireweed* 20: 6–13.

Sanday, Peggy Reeves. 1981. *Female Power and Male Dominance: On the Origins of Sexual Inequality*. Cambridge: Cambridge University Press.

Sangster, Joan. 1985. "The Communist Pary and the Woman Question, 1922–1929." *Labour/Le Travail* 15.

Sarah, E. 1980. "Teachers and Students in the Classroom: An Examination of Classroom Interaction. In *Learning to Lose: Sexism and Education*, ed. D. Spender and E. Sarah. London: Women's Press.

Sargent, Lydia, ed. 1981. *Women and Revolution: A Discussion of the Unhappy Marriage of Marxism and Feminism*. Boston: South End Press.

Saulnier, K.M. Forthcoming. "Social Networks and the Transition to Motherhood." In *Families and Social Networks*, ed. R. Milardo.

Sawer, Marian, ed. 1982. *Australia and the New Right*. Sydney: George Allen & Unwin.

Sayer, D. 1975. "Method of Dogma in Historical Materialism." *Sociological Review* 23.

Schirmer, Jennifer. 1982. *The Limits of Reform*. Cambridge, MA: Schenkman.

Schultz, Pat. 1979. "Day Care in Canada: 1850–1962." In *Good Day Care*, ed. Kathleen Gallagher Ross. Toronto: Women's Press.

——. 1982. "Minding the Children." In *Still Ain't Satisfied*, ed. Maureen FitzGerald, Connie Guberman, and Margie Wolfe. Toronto: Women's Press.

Scott, Hilda. 1974. *Does Socialism Liberate Women?* Boston: Beacon Press.

——. 1978. "Eastern European Women in Theory and Practice." *Women's Studies International Quarterly* 1.

Scott, M. 1980. "Teach Her a Lesson: Sexist Curriculum in Patriarchal Education." In *Learning to Lose: Sexism and Education*, ed. D. Spender and E. Sarah. London: Women's Press.

Sears, P., and D. Feldman. 1974. "Teacher Interaction with Boys and Girls." In *And Jill Came Tumbling After: Sexism in American Education*, ed. J. Stacey et al.

Seccombe, Wally. 1974. "The Housewife and Her Labour under Capitalism." *New Left Review* 83.

——. 1975. "Domestic Labour — Reply to Critics." *New Left Review* 94.

——. 1980a. "Domestic Labour and the Working Class Household." In *Hidden in the Household*, ed. Bonnie Fox. Toronto: Women's Press. pp. 25–100.

——. 1980b. "The Expanded Reproduction Cycle of Labour Power in Twentieth Century Capitalism." In *Hidden in the Household*, ed. Bonnie Fox. Toronto: Women's Press.

——. 1983. "Marxism and Demography." *New Left Review* no. 137.

——. Forthcoming. *Family Forms in Modes of Production*. London: New Left Review Books.

Segal, Lynne, ed. 1983. *What Is to Be Done about the Family?* Harmondsworth: Penguin.

Seltzer, A. 1980. "Postpartum Mental Syndrome." *Canadian Family Physician* 26 (November): 1546–50.

Selye, Hans. 1956. *The Stress of Life*. New York: McGraw-Hill.

——. 1974. *Stress Without Distress*. Toronto: McClelland & Stewart.

——. 1975. "Confusion and Controversy in the Stress Field." *Journal of Human Stress* 1, no. 2.
——. 1976. *The Stress of Life*, 2nd ed. New York: McGraw-Hill.
——. 1980. Preface to *Selye's Guide to Stress Research*, Vol. 1. New York: Van Nostrand Reinhold.
Sharp, M., and H. Roberts. 1983. "Boys Will Be Boys—but What Happens to the Girls?" *Educational Research* 25, no. 2.
Shaw, J. 1980. "Education and the Individual: Schooling for Girls, or Mixed Schooling — A Mixed Blessing?" In *Schooling for Women's Work*, ed. R. Deem. London: Routledge & Kegan Paul.
Siltanen, Janet, and Michelle Stanworth, eds. 1984. *Women and the Public Sphere*. London: Hutchinson.
Silvera, Makeda. 1983. *Silenced*. Toronto: Ann Wallace Co.
Silverman, S. 1975. "The Life Crisis as a Social Function." In *Toward an Anthropology of Women*, ed. Rayna Reiter. New York: Monthly Review Press.
Smart, Carol. 1981. "Law and the Control of Women's Sexuality: The Case of the 1950s." In *Controlling Women: The Normal and the Deviant*, ed. Bridget Hutter and Gillian Williams. London: Croom Helm.
——. 1984. *The Ties that Bind: Law, Marriage and the Reproduction of Patriarchal Relations*. London: Routledge & Kegan Paul.
Smart, Carol, and Barry Smart. 1978. "Women and Social Control: An Introduction." In *Women, Sexuality and Social Control*, ed. Carol Smart and Barry Smart. London: Routledge & Kegan Paul.
Smith, Dorothy E. 1973. "Women, the Family and Corporate Capitalism." In *Women in Canada*, ed. Marylee Stephenson. Toronto: New Press.
——. 1974. "Women's Perspective as a Radical Critique of Sociology." *Sociological Inquiry* 44.
——. 1977. *Feminism and Marxism*. Vancouver: New Star Books.
——. 1979. "A Sociology for Women." In *The Prism of Sex*, ed. J. Sherman and T. Peck. Madison: University of Wisconsin Press.
Smythe, Dallas. 1981. *Dependency Road: Communication, Capitalism, Consciousness and Canada*. Norwood, NJ: Ablex Publishing Corp.
Snitow, Ann B., Christine Stansell, and Sharon Thompson, eds. 1983. *Powers of Desire*. New York: Monthly Review Press.
Solway, J. 1984. "Women and Work among the Bakgalagadi of Botswana." Paper presented at the Canadian Ethnology Society, Montreal.
——. 1982. *Social and Labour Bulletin*. Geneva: International Labour Organization.
Spender, Dale. 1980. "Talking in Class." In *Learning to Lose: Sexism and Education*, ed. D. Spender and E. Sarah. London: Women's Press.
Šram, R.J. 1978. "Current State and Future Trends in the Estimation of Human Genetic Risk from Environmental Chemicals in the Czech Socialist Republic." *Czechoslovak Medicine* 1.
Stang Dahl, Tove S., and Annika Snare. 1978. "The Coercion of Privacy: A

Feminist Perspective." In *Women, Sexuality and Social Control*, ed. C. Smart and B. Smart. London: Routledge & Kegan Paul.

Stanworth, M. 1983. *Gender and Schooling: A Study of Sexual Division in the Classroom*. London: Hutchinson.

Statistics Canada. 1985. *The Labour Force*. Ottawa: Supply and Services Canada. Statistics Canada Cat. No. 71-001.

Status of Women Canada. 1983. *Towards Equality for Women*. Ottawa: Minister of Supply and Services Canada.

———. 1985. *Informat* (March 2).

———. 1986. *Report of the Task Force on Child Care*. Ottawa: Supply and Services Canada.

Steele, Lisa. 1982. "Varda Burstyn on Sexuality and Pornography." *Fuse* 6, nos. 1, 2.

Stellman, Jeanne M., and S. Daum. 1973. *Work Is Dangerous to Your Health*. New York: Vintage.

Stephenson, Marylee, ed. 1973. *Women in Canada*. Don Mills, Ont.: General Publishing.

Studies in Political Economy. 1979. no. 1.

———. 1981. "Rethinking Canadian Political Economy," no. 6.

———. 1983. no. 10.

Suffrin, E.T. 1982. *The Eaton Drive*. Toronto: Fitzhenry & Whiteside.

Sumner, C. 1979. *Reading Ideologies: An Investigation into the Marxist Theory of Law and Ideology of Law*. London: Academic Press.

Sutherland, M. 1981. *Sex Bias in Education*. Oxford: Basil Blackwell.

Sutherland, N. 1976. *Children in English Canadian Society: Framing the Twentieth Century Consensus*. Toronto: University of Toronto Press.

Synge, Jane. 1979. "Growing Up Working Class in Hamilton in the Early 20th Century." In *Adolescence in Canada*, ed. K. Ishwaran. Toronto: McGraw-Hill Ryerson.

Szalai, Alexander, ed. 1972. *The Use of Time: Daily Activities of Urban and Suburban Populations in Twelve Countries*. The Hague: Mouton.

Talbot, Carol. 1984. *Growing Up Black in Canada*. Toronto: Williams–Wallace.

Tanner, Nancy, and Adrianne Zihlman. 1981. "Women in Evolution, Part I: Innovation and Selection in Human Origins." *Signs* 1, no. 3.

Taylor, Ian. 1981. *Law and Order: Arguments for Socialism*. London: MacMillan.

Taylor, Ian, Paul Walton, and Jock Young, eds. 1975. *Critical Criminology*. London: Routledge & Kegan Paul.

Tax, Meredith. 1980. *The Rising of the Women*. New York: Monthly Review Press.

Tepperman, J. 1976. *Not Servants, Not Machines*. Boston: Beacon Press.

Les Têtes de pioche (édition complète). 1980. Montreal: Remue-ménage.

Thomas, A., and W. Stewart. 1971. "Counsellor Response to Female Clients with Deviate and Conforming Career Goals." *Journal of Counselling Psychology* 18.

Thompson, Eva P. 1977. *Whigs and Hunters*. Middlesex: Peregrine.
——. 1978. *Folklore, Anthropology and Social History*. A Studies in Labour pamphlet. Brighton: John L. Noyce.
——. 1980. *The Secret State: In His Writing by Candlelight*. London: Merlin.
Thönnessen, Werner. 1973. *The Emancipation of Women: The Rise and Decline of the Women's Movement in German Social Democracy 1863–1933*. London: Pluto Press.
Thwaites, Ruben G. 1896–1901. *The Jesuit Relations and Allied Documents*. 73 vols. Cleveland: Burrows Bros.
Tilly, Louise, and Joan Scott. 1978. *Women, Work and Family*. New York: Holt, Rinehart & Winston.
Tomic-Trumper, Patricia. 1986. "The Care of Unwed Mothers and Illegitimate Children in Toronto, 1867–1920: A Study in Social Administration." Ph.D. thesis, Department of Education, University of Toronto.
Tremblay, Louis-Marie. 1970. *Le syndicalisme québécois: idéologies de la C.S.N. et de la F.T.Q. 1940–1970*. Montreal: Les Presses de l'Université de Montréal.
Trigger, Bruce. 1976. *The Children of Aataentsic*. 2 vols. Montreal: McGill-Queen's University Press.
Trofimenkoff, Susan Mann and Allison Prentice. 1977. *The Neglected Majority*. Toronto: McClelland & Stewart.
Turnbull, Colin M. 1981. "Mbuti Womanhood." In *Woman the Gatherer*, ed. Frances Dahlberg. New Haven: Yale University Press.
Vaillancourt, Jean Guy. 1982. "New Socialist Movement in Quebec." *Studies in Political Economy* 8.
Valverde, Mariana. 1983a. "Beyond Guilt: Lesbian Feminism and Coming Out." *Resources for Feminist Research* 12, no. 1 (March): 65–67.
——. 1983b. "Heterosexism — A Challenge to the Left." *Canadian Dimension* 17, no. 1.
——. 1985. *Sex, Power and Pleasure*. Toronto: Women's Press.
Valverde, Mariana, and Lorna Weir. 1985. "Heterosexism and State Regulation: A Problem Not For Lesbians Only." In *Women Against Censorship*, ed. Varda Burstyn. Vancouver: Douglas & McIntyre.
Vance, Carole S., ed. 1984. *Pleasure and Danger: Exploring Female Sexuality*. Boston and London: Routledge & Kegan Paul.
Van Kirk, Sylvia. 1980. " 'Many Tender Ties': Women in Fur Trade Society in Western Canada 1670–1870." Winnipeg: Watson & Dwyer.
Vicinius, Martha. 1982. "Sexuality and Power: A Review of Current Work in the History of Sexuality." *Feminist Studies* 8: 147–51.
——. 1984. "Distance and Desire: English Boarding-School Friendships." *Signs* 9, no. 4: 600–622.
Vickers, Jill McCalla, ed. 1984. *Taking Sex into Account*. Ottawa: Carleton University Press.
Vogel, Lise. 1983. *Marxism and the Oppression of Women: Toward a Unitary Theory*. New Brunswick, NJ: Rutgers University Press; London: Pluto.

Walker, N. 1981. "Feminists' Extravaganzas." *Criminal Law Review*: 379–86.

Warrian, Peter. 1981. "Patriarchy and the Trade Unions." Paper presented at the Committee on Socialist Studies, Ottawa. June.

Watkins, Mel, ed. 1977a. *Dene Nation—The Colony Within*. Toronto: University of Toronto Press.

——. 1977b. "The Staple Theory Revisited." *Journal of Canadian Studies* 12 (Winter).

Webster, Paula. 1975. "Matriarchy: A Vision of Power." In *Toward an Anthropology of Women*, ed. Rayna Reiter. New York: Monthly Review Press.

Weinbaum, Batya. 1978. *The Curious Courtship of Women's Liberation and Socialism*. Boston: South End Press.

Weinbaum, Batya, and Amy Badges. 1976. "The Other Side of the Paycheck: Monopoly Capital and the Structure of Consumption." *Monthly Review* 28.

Weir, Lorna, and Leo Casey. 1984. "Subverting Power in Sexuality." *Socialist Review* 75/76 (May–August).

Weir, Lorna, and Eve Zaremba. 1982. "Feminism and Gay Liberation." *Broadside* (October).

Weissman, M.M., and G. Klerman. 1977. "Sex Differences and the Epidemiology of Depression." *Archives of General Psychiatry* 34 (January): 98–111.

Weisstein, Naomi. 1971. "Psychology Constructs the Female, or the Fantasy Life of the Male Psychologist." In *From Feminism to Liberation*, ed. Edith Altbach. Cambridge, MA: Schenkman.

Welburn, V. 1980. *Postnatal Depresson*. Glasgow: Fontana.

Wernick, Andrew. 1983. "Advertising and Ideology: An Interpretive Framework." *Theory, Culture and Society* 2, no. 1: 16–33.

——. 1987. "From Voyeur to Narcissist." In *Beyond Patriarchy: Writings by Men*. Toronto: Oxford University Press.

West, Jackie, ed. 1982. *Work, Women and the Labour Market*. London: Routledge & Kegan Paul.

West, W.G. 1981. "Education, Moral Reproduction and the State: Some Implications of Activist Interpretations of Recent European State Theories for Canadian Education Policy Analysis." *Interchange* 12, no. 2–3.

Wexler, P. 1982. "Structure, Text and Subject: A Critical Sociology of School Knowledge." In *Cultural and Economic Reproduction in Education*, ed. M. Apple. London: Routledge & Kegan Paul.

White, Julie. 1980. *Women and Unions*. Ottawa: Minister of Supply and Services Canada.

——. 1983. *Women and Part-Time Work*. Ottawa: Supply and Services Canada.

Wilkins, Russell. 1983. "Health and Safety Aspects Associated with the Use of Micro-Electronics Technology in the Workplace: An Overview of the Current Debate Concerning Visual Display Terminals." Report prepared for the Labour Canada Task Force on Micro-Electronics and Employment. Montreal: Photocopy.

Wilkins, Russell, and Owen Adams. 1983. *Healthfulness of Life*. Montreal: Institute for Research on Public Policy.

Williams, Glanville L. 1958. *The Sanctity of Life and the Criminal Law*. London: Faber & Faber.

Williams, Raymond. 1980. "Base and Superstructure in Marxist Cultural Theory." In *Problems in Materialism and Culture: Selected Essays*, ed. R. Williams. London: Verso and New Left Books.

Willis, P. 1977. *Learning to Labour: How Working Class Kids Get Working Class Jobs*. Westmead, England: Saxon House.

Wilson, Elizabeth. 1977. *Women and the Welfare State*. London: Tavistock.

——. 1983. "I'll Climb the Stairway to Heaven: Lesbianism in the Seventies." In *Sex & Love*, ed. Sue Cartledge and Joanna Ryan. London: Women's Press.

Wilson, Sue. 1986. "*Women, the Family and the Economy*," 2nd ed. Toronto: McGraw-Hill Ryerson.

Windsor, Kim. 1984. "Behind the Figures: A Picture of Women in the Specific Industries." Paper presented to "From Margin to Mainstream: A Natural Conference about Women and Employment." Melbourne: Photocopy.

Wolpe, Annmarie. 1978. "Education and the Sexual Division of Labour." In *Feminism and Materialism*, ed. Annette Kuhn and Annmarie Wolpe. London: Routledge & Kegan Paul.

Women's Liberation Movement. 1972. "Brief to the House of Commons." In *Women Unite!*, ed. Discussion Collective No. 6. Toronto: Canadian Women's Educational Press.

Women's Rights Committee. 1982. "Sexual Harassment in the Workplace." Vancouver: British Columbia Federation of Labour.

Woods, H.D., and Sylvia Ostry. 1962. *Labour Policy and Labour Economics in Canada*. Toronto: Macmillan.

Working Women in Czechoslovakia. 1975. Prague: Prace.

Wrong, G.M., ed. 1939. *The Long Journey to the Country of the Huron*. Toronto: Champlain Society.

Yalom, D.I. 1968. " 'Postpartum Blues' Syndrome." *Archives of General Psychiatry* 18: 16–27.

Yanacopoulo, Andrée. 1981. "Sous le signe de l'ambiguité." In *Femmes et politique*, ed. Yolande Cohen. Montreal: Le Jour, Editeur.

Young, Iris. 1980. "Socialist Feminism and the Limits of Dual Systems Theory." *Socialist Review* 50–51: 169–88.

Young, Jock. 1979. "Beyond Left Idealism and Reformism: From Radical Deviancy Theory to Marxism." In *Capitalism and the Rule of Law*, ed. B. Fine et al. London: Hutchinson.

Zaremba, Eve, ed. 1974. *Privilege of Sex: A Century of Canadian Women*. Toronto: Anansi.

Zaretsky, Eli. 1976. *Capitalism, the Family and Personal Life*. New York: Harper & Row.

Zetkin, Clara. 1984. *Selected Writings*, ed. Phillip Foner. New York: International Publishers.

Index of Authors Cited

Index of Subjects